VOLUME 621

THE ANNALS

of The American Academy of Political
and Social Science

PHYLLIS KANISS, *Executive Editor*

The Moynihan Report Revisited: Lessons and Reflections after Four Decades

Special Editors of this Volume

DOUGLAS S. MASSEY
Princeton University
ROBERT J. SAMPSON
Harvard University

The American Academy of Political and Social Science

3814 Walnut Street, Fels Institute of Government, University of Pennsylvania,
Philadelphia, PA 19104-6197; (215) 746-6500; (215) 573-3003 (fax); www.aapss.org

Origin and Purpose. The Academy was organized December 14, 1889, to promote the progress of political and social science, especially through publications and meetings. The Academy does not take sides in controverted questions, but seeks to gather and present reliable information to assist the public in forming an intelligent and accurate judgment.

Meetings. The Academy occasionally holds a meeting in the spring extending over two days.

Publications. THE ANNALS of The American Academy of Political and Social Science is the bimonthly publication of the Academy. Each issue contains articles on some prominent social or political problem, written at the invitation of the editors. These volumes constitute important reference works on the topics with which they deal, and they are extensively cited by authorities throughout the United States and abroad.

Membership. Each member of the Academy receives THE ANNALS and may attend the meetings of the Academy. Membership is open only to individuals. Annual dues: $94.00 for the regular paperbound edition (clothbound, $134.00). Members may also purchase single issues of THE ANNALS for $18.00 each (clothbound, $27.00). Student memberships are available for $52.00.

Subscriptions. THE ANNALS of The American Academy of Political and Social Science (ISSN 0002-7162) (J295) is published six times annually—in January, March, May, July, September, and November—by SAGE Publications, 2455 Teller Road, Thousand Oaks, CA 91320. Telephone: (800) 818-SAGE (7243) and (805) 499-0721; Fax/Order line: (805) 375-1700; e-mail: journals@sagepub.com. Copyright © 2009 by The American Academy of Political and Social Science. Institutions may subscribe to THE ANNALS at the annual rate: $714.00 (clothbound, $807.00). Single issues of THE ANNALS may be obtained by individuals who are not members of the Academy for $97.00 each (clothbound, $142.00). Single issues of THE ANNALS have proven to be excellent supplementary texts for classroom use. Direct inquiries regarding adoptions to THE ANNALS c/o SAGE Publications (address below). Periodicals postage paid at Thousand Oaks, California, and at additional mailing offices. POSTMASTER: Send address changes to The Annals of The American Academy of Political and Social Science, c/o SAGE Publications, 2455 Teller Road, Thousand Oaks, CA 91320.

All correspondence concerning membership in the Academy, dues renewals, inquiries about membership status, and/or purchase of single issues of THE ANNALS should be sent to THE ANNALS c/o SAGE Publications, 2455 Teller Road, Thousand Oaks, CA 91320.Telephone: (800) 818-SAGE (7243) and (805) 499-0721; Fax/Order line: (805) 375-1700; e-mail: journals@ sagepub.com. *Please note that orders under $30 must be prepaid.* SAGE affiliates in London and India will assist institutional subscribers abroad with regard to orders, claims, and inquiries for both subscriptions and single issues.

Printed on acid-free paper

THE ANNALS

Editorial Office: 3814 Walnut Street, Fels Institute for Government, University of Pennsylvania, Philadelphia, PA 19104-6197.
For information about membership* (individuals only) and subscriptions (institutions), address:
SAGE Publications
2455 Teller Road
Thousand Oaks, CA 91320

For SAGE Publications: Allison Leung (Production) and Sandra Hopps (Marketing)

From India and South Asia, write to:		From Europe, the Middle East, and Africa, write to:
SAGE PUBLICATIONS INDIA Pvt Ltd		SAGE PUBLICATIONS LTD
B-42 Panchsheel Enclave, P.O. Box 4109		1 Oliver's Yard, 55 City Road
New Delhi 110 017		London EC1Y 1SP
INDIA		UNITED KINGDOM

*Please note that members of the Academy receive THE ANNALS with their membership.
International Standard Serial Number ISSN 0002-7162
International Standard Book Number ISBN 978-1-4129-7401-1 (Vol. 621, 2009) paper
International Standard Book Number ISBN 978-1-4129-7402-8 (Vol. 621, 2009) cloth
Manufactured in the United States of America. First printing, January 2009.

The articles appearing in *The Annals* are abstracted or indexed in Academic Abstracts, Academic Search, America: History and Life, Asia Pacific Database, Book Review Index,CABAbstracts Database, Central Asia: Abstracts &Index, Communication Abstracts, Corporate ResourceNET, Criminal Justice Abstracts, Current Citations Express, Current Contents: Social & Behavioral Sciences, Documentation in Public Administration, e-JEL, EconLit, Expanded Academic Index, Guide to Social Science & Religion in Periodical Literature, Health Business FullTEXT, HealthSTAR FullTEXT, Historical Abstracts, International Bibliography of the Social Sciences, International Political Science Abstracts, ISI Basic Social Sciences Index, Journal of Economic Literature on CD, LEXIS-NEXIS, MasterFILE FullTEXT, Middle East: Abstracts&Index, NISC, North Africa: Abstracts&Index, PAIS International, Periodical Abstracts, Political Science Abstracts, Psychological Abstracts, PsycINFO, SAGE Public Administration Abstracts, Scopus, Social Science Source, Social Sciences Citation Index, Social Sciences Index Full Text, Social Services Abstracts, SocialWork Abstracts, Sociological Abstracts, Southeast Asia: Abstracts& Index, Standard Periodical Directory (SPD), TOPICsearch, Wilson OmniFileV, and Wilson Social Sciences Index/Abstracts, and are available on microfilm from ProQuest, Ann Arbor, Michigan.

Information about membership rates, institutional subscriptions, and back issue prices may be found on the facing page.

Advertising. Current rates and specifications may be obtained by writing to The Annals Advertising and Promotion Manager at the Thousand Oaks office (address above).

Claims. Claims for undelivered copies must be made no later than six months following month of publication. The publisher will supply replacement issues when losses have been sustained in transit and when the reserve stock will permit.

Change of Address. Six weeks' advance notice must be given when notifying of change of address. Please send the old address label along with the new address to the SAGE office address above to ensure proper identification. Please specify name of journal.

OF THE AMERICAN ACADEMY OF POLITICAL AND SOCIAL SCIENCE

Volume 621   January 2009

IN THIS ISSUE:

The Moynihan Report Revisited: Lessons and Reflections after Four Decades

Special Editors: DOUGLAS S. MASSEY
ROBERT J. SAMPSON

FORTHCOMING

The Globalization of Class Actions
Special Editors: DEBORAH HENSLER, CHRISTOPHER HODGES,
and MAGDALENA TULIBACKA

Race, Crime and Justice: Contexts and Complexities
Special Editors: LAUREN KRIVO and RUTH PETERSON

*Fathering across Diversity and Adversity: International
Perspectives and Policy Interventions*
Special Editor: FRANK FURSTENBERG

Keywords: Daniel Patrick Moynihan; *The Negro Family*; poverty; race; employment; incarceration; family structure

Moynihan Redux: Legacies and Lessons

BY
DOUGLAS S. MASSEY
and
ROBERT J. SAMPSON

The Moynihan Report is probably the most famous piece of social scientific analysis never published. Completed in March 1965 as an internal document by a young assistant secretary of labor, it was written as input into an ongoing debate within the administration of President Lyndon Baines Johnson about how to move forward in grappling with "the Negro problem" in the wake of the landmark passage of the 1964 Civil Rights Act. The report argued that ending legal segregation in the South was not enough and that black poverty was more intractable than white poverty owing to the legacy of slavery and the persistence of discrimination and segregation throughout the country. These factors combined to put unique pressure on the black family, which was buckling under the strain in ways that amplified the effects of other social problems and led to a "tangle of pathology" that perpetuated black poverty over time and across the generations.

The purpose of the report was to make an impassioned moral case for a massive federal intervention to break the cycle of black poverty and put African Americans on the road to socioeconomic achievement and integration into American society. Moynihan was never shy about using vivid prose to make his points, especially in private, and in his report, he was in full flower, by remarking that race relations were in a state of "crisis" and referring to the rising share of

NOTE: The articles in this volume are based on presentations given at a conference held at Harvard University in September 2007, sponsored by the American Academy of Political and Social Science; the Department of Sociology, Harvard University; and the W. E. B. Du Bois Institute for African and African American Research, Harvard University. Podcasts from the conference are available at conference.aapss.org.

DOI: 10.1177/0002716208325122

female-headed households as "pathological." He even argued that the black family as a "matriarchy" prevented black males from fulfilling "the very essence of the male animal from the bantam rooster to the four star general . . . to strut" (Moynihan 1965).

The key to arresting the alarming rise in family instability, he felt, was a dedicated federal effort to provide jobs for black men. He was, after all, assistant secretary in the Department of Labor, not in the Department Health, Education, and Welfare; his purview was the workforce and not the family. The crisis in the black family was his justification for a federal jobs program. Along with education, training, and apprenticeship programs that would enhance the employability of black men, he favored a major public works effort that would guarantee jobs to all able-bodied workers. If full employment for black males—especially young black males—could be achieved, he thought, then family stability could be restored and government would be in a better position to attack more entrenched problems such as discrimination and segregation.

Although references to matriarchy, pathological families, and strutting roosters are jarring to the contemporary ear, we must remember the times and context.

Although references to matriarchy, pathological families, and strutting roosters are jarring to the contemporary ear, we must remember the times and context.

Douglas S. Massey is the Henry G. Bryant Professor of Sociology and Public Affairs at Princeton University. His most recent books are Strangers in a Strange Land: Humans in an Urbanizing World *(Norton 2005) and* Return of the L-Word: A Liberal Vision for the New Century *(Princeton University Press 2005). He is also coauthor of the award-winning books* American Apartheid: Segregation and the Making of the Underclass *(Harvard University Press 1993) and* Beyond Smoke and Mirrors: Mexican Immigration in an Age of Economic Integration *(Russell Sage Foundation 2002).*

Robert J. Sampson is the Henry Ford II Professor of the Social Sciences and chairman of the Department of Sociology at Harvard University. For the past twelve years, he has served as scientific director of the Project on Human Development in Chicago Neighborhoods (PHDCN), which has been the source for much of his research on neighborhood effects, crime, inequality, and the social structure of the contemporary city. He is the author of many journal articles and several books, including The Explanation of Crime: Context, Mechanisms, and Development *(Cambridge University Press 2006);* The Social Ecology of Crime *(Springer-Verlag 1996); and the award-winning* Crime in the Making: Pathways and Turning Points through Life *(Harvard University Press 1993) and* Shared Beginnings, Divergent Lives: Delinquent Boys to Age 70 *(Harvard University Press 2003).*

Moynihan was writing in the prefeminist era and producing an internal memo whose purpose was to attract attention to a critical national issue. While his language is certainly sexist by today's standards, it was nonetheless successful in getting the attention of one particular male chauvinist, President Johnson, who drew heavily on the Moynihan Report for his celebrated speech at Howard University on June 4:

> Negro poverty is not white poverty. Many of its causes and many of its cures are the same. But there are differences—deep, corrosive, obstinate differences—radiating painful roots into the community, and into the family, and the nature of the individual.
>
> Perhaps most important—its influence radiating to every part of life—is the breakdown of the Negro family structure. For this, most of all, white America must accept responsibility. It flows from centuries of oppression and persecution of the Negro man. It flows from the long years of degradation and discrimination, which have attacked his dignity and assaulted his ability to produce for his family.
>
> So, unless we work to strengthen the family, to create conditions under which most parents will stay together—all the rest: schools, and playgrounds, and public assistance, and private concern, will never be enough to cut completely the circle of despair and deprivation. (Johnson 1965)

President Johnson went on to note that solving the problem would not be easy and would involve bold new programs on a variety of fronts. Following Moynihan's analysis, first and foremost among the solutions he listed was the provision of jobs, followed by improvements in housing, education, welfare, and health. Sure enough, in the ensuing "War on Poverty," the president launched Medicare and Medicaid to move forward on health, food stamps and community action agencies to enhance welfare, Head Start and the National Education Corps to improve education, the Fair Housing Act and Model Cities Program to deal with housing, and the Job Corps and neighborhood youth corps to address employment.

The latter programs offered training and education to improve the skills of disadvantaged workers, thereby addressing supply-side labor issues noted by Moynihan, but the public effort to generate jobs for low-income workers on the demand side was conspicuously absent, especially given the report's focus on steady work as *the* most important step in breaking the tangle of pathology. The closest Johnson ever came was creating VISTA—Volunteers in Service to America—as a kind of domestic version of the Peace Corps.

Perhaps a major effort to generate employment for low-income, minority workers was never in the cards. Even LBJ was skeptical of government work programs. But something else also transpired to seal the fate of Moynihan, his report, and its emphasis on federal employment programs. Immediately after the president's speech at Howard University, someone leaked the Moynihan Report to journalists, who naturally published the florid language and incendiary prose that was *meant* to stir passions within the administration while ignoring the more prosaic but critical structural analysis embedded in the report.

Soon, headlines blared that Moynihan was calling the black family pathological and blaming it for the problems of the ghetto, which suggested that he was laying the onus of black educational failure, joblessness, and criminality on female matriarchs. Moynihan-bashing quickly became a boom industry in the liberal press, led by the journalist William Ryan, who in *The Nation* coined the term "blaming the victim" to describe the report (Ryan 1971). Moreover, in the context of an emergent black power movement, Moynihan's emphasis on humiliated black men could not have been less timely, and in the context of a coalescing feminist movement, his pairing of matriarchy and pathology could not have been less welcome. Young black militants and newly self-aware feminists joined in the rising tide of vilification, and Moynihan was widely pilloried not only as a racist, but a sexist to boot.

A great irony is that few of his vociferous critics had actually read Moynihan's report. It was still an internal document with a very limited number of copies. Most people had only read selective extracts published in columns and stories about the report, which when combined yielded a bowdlerized version of its arguments. One wonders, for example, whether critics who claimed Moynihan was racist had read even the first page of the report, where it was claimed that "the racist virus in the American blood stream still afflicts us." The report was not actually "published" and widely distributed until 1967, when Rainwater and Yancey included a facsimile in their analysis of "the politics of controversy." By then, of course, it was too late; Moynihan's report had been consigned to the netherworld of the politically incorrect, where it would remain for decades. One can only imagine the even more vociferous reaction that would have ensued had the Moynihan Report been leaked in the technological world of today, with its capacity for instantaneous and frenzied distribution the world over.

Legacies of the Controversy

By the end of 1965, President Johnson himself had disowned the Moynihan Report and Moynihan had left the administration scarred and somewhat bitter over his glib portrayal as a bigot by liberal colleagues in and out of political power. To this day, the source of the leak is unknown. Some point to a jealous official at the Department of Health and Human Services who sought to defend the agency's turf against an interloper from outside the agency who dared to speak up on family issues. Others point to a racist civil servant who was adamantly opposed to empowering and advancing the economic status of the black community. Whatever the source, by the end of 1965, a crucial moment had passed, and the episode left several unfortunate and entirely dysfunctional legacies.

Zero-sum integration

A major factor behind the remarkable integration of the descendants of European immigrants from 1945 to 1975 was the sustained economic expansion and the structural transformation of the postwar period (Massey 1995). In an era when employment was steadily rising, earnings were effortlessly growing, and the entire occupational distribution was shifting upward, economic mobility became a non-zero-sum game (Alba forthcoming). In this context, advances by the descendants of earlier Italian, Polish, Slavic, and Jewish immigrants did not come at the expense of the descendants of earlier arrivals from Northern and Western Europe (Alba and Nee 2003). As Danziger and Gottschalk (1995) pointed out, a rising economic tide lifted all boats, which made it relatively painless for WASP elites in the 1950s and 1960s to give up defending formerly bright boundaries between themselves and ethnic out-groups.

Being a shrewd politician, Lyndon Johnson instinctively realized this logic and in many ways the Great Society was an attempt to create a non-zero-sum context for civil rights. If he could somehow expand the economic pie enough so that the incorporation of blacks did not come at the economic expense of working- and middle-class whites, then his civil rights project just might succeed. In the end, of course, his failure to commit to a federal jobs program and his fateful course on the Vietnam War rendered the goal of non-zero-sum integration impossible, putting young African Americans and older white workers on a collision course (Quadagno 1996).

Despite President Johnson's initial reluctance to embrace a jobs program, as the cycle of summer race riots escalated in the late 1960s officials searched desperately for some way to quell the violence; in this context, finding jobs for young black males became a national priority. Given the fiscal impossibility of a federal jobs program by 1968, when the Vietnam War was at its height, white leaders inside and outside of government were forced to develop an alternative strategy that would somehow break the white monopoly on skilled and semiskilled occupations and facilitate the hiring of African Americans. The expedient they developed was affirmative action (Skrentny 1996), which pushed employers to set goals and timetables for hiring African American workers in rough proportion to their share in the population.

As the economy faltered in the 1970s, however, and as unemployment rose and wages declined, this strategy increasingly pitted aspiring blacks against working-class whites, creating precisely the kind of zero-sum mobility that Moynihan had originally sought to avoid (Massey 2007). The inevitable result was a backlash against the civil rights movement and social programs of the Great Society, ushering in a conservative realignment that Krugman (2003) has labeled "the great unraveling," an unraveling that was built into the political economy in the absence of a federal commitment to full employment.

Taboo subjects

Although one would never know it from the negative reaction to his report, Daniel Patrick Moynihan was a New Frontier liberal who came to Washington with the Kennedy administration to act upon his commitment to social equality. Although committed, he was no ideologue but a man of facts and figures. Moynihan was dedicated to the use of social science to build an accurate understanding of social problems from data and analysis rather than dogma, and then applying this understanding intelligently to develop policies that would improve society and, particularly, improve the well-being of its less fortunate members.

He had a particular soft spot for denigrated minorities and knew all too well how his own and other groups had been treated historically in the United States. Decades before the advent of "whiteness studies" and the publication of such titles as *How the Irish Became White* (Ignatiev 1995), *How Jews Became White Folk* (Brodkin 1998), and *Working toward Whiteness* (Roediger 2006), Moynihan was acutely aware of the legacy of racialization and exploitation that the Irish, Italians, Poles, and Slavs had each, in turn, been forced to overcome to gain access to American society. He also knew historically how important the programs of the New Deal had been in helping these groups face and ultimately overcome the barriers they encountered on the way up (see Katznelson 2005).

More than most, Moynihan was also personally aware of the disadvantages of poverty and of the difficulties associated with growing up in a single-parent family in a bad neighborhood (Hodgson 2000). His father had abandoned the family, and as a child, he grew up shining shoes for money in some of New York City's tougher neighborhoods before graduating from high school in Harlem. He also personally knew what a critical role government could play in moving someone from poverty to affluence, as he and his family directly benefited from many of the programs of the New Deal and he owed his education at least partly to the GI Bill.

As assistant secretary for policy, planning, and research, he therefore immersed himself in the social science literature of the day, focusing particularly on issues involving race, ethnicity, and poverty (see Glazer and Moynihan 1963; Moynihan 1969). It was with this personal background and a firm grounding in social science research that Moynihan sat down in late 1964 to craft an agenda to address the "American Dilemma." His respect for data is clearly reflected in the abundance of charts, tables, and figures included in the report, and his regard for social scientific analysis is evident in his effort to place individual and family behaviors in the context of broader social structures. His passion for the issue was reflected in his fulsome and now infamous prose, which was never intended for a public audience.

Given this background, imagine Moynihan's shock and dismay upon finding himself the target of a vicious campaign of demonization by erstwhile friends in the liberal media and academia. Although he later grew into public life and came to understand the inevitable price of taking public positions on controversial issues, the episode was nonetheless painful at the time. Even though in economic or career terms he can hardly be considered to have suffered, personally, he seems never to really have gotten over the experience. In his biography of the senator, Hodgson (2000) simply refers to it as Moynihan's "dark hour."

Whatever his personal feelings about the report's reception, a more important legacy is what others concluded from the reaction it garnered. Having seen what happened to a well-known liberal who had in good faith tackled a sensitive issue from a well-grounded social scientific perspective, people could not help but conclude that addressing combustible racial issues was a dangerous enterprise. The high public and reputational price paid by Moynihan for his apostasy yielded

a decided chilling effect in public debate and social science research. As Massey
put it in a 1995 review,

> As research into the causes of racial disadvantage and urban poverty progressed during
> the 1960s, sociologists came face-to-face with a series of emotionally charged, method-
> ologically intransigent but important and unavoidable issues, such as culture, intelli-
> gence, sex, marriage, and childbearing. . . . In a variety of ways, the field actively
> discouraged the examination of social differences with respect to [these issues]. For
> those who were slow to catch on, object lessons were made of Oscar Lewis and Daniel
> Patrick Moynihan, and, after the treatment these two prominent social scientists
> received, no one could miss the point. . . . [They had] implied that under certain cir-
> cumstances, the behavior of poor people might contribute to the perpetuation of their
> poverty, and for this heresy both men were excoriated by liberals throughout the social
> science establishment. The calumny heaped on these two distinguished social scientists
> had a chilling effect on social science over the next two decades. Sociologists avoided
> studying controversial issues related to race, culture, and intelligence, and those who
> insisted on investigating such unpopular notions generally encountered resistance and
> ostracism. (Pp. 747-48)

During the 1970s and 1980s, therefore, liberal scholarship shied away from
many of the unpleasant realities of ghetto life and sought instead to project a positive image of African Americans by showing the resilience of black families in the
face of adversity and the creativity of black women in developing survival strategies that enabled them and their children to negotiate a difficult social world (see,
for example, Stack 1974). The idea that behavioral repertoires, interpersonal
scripts, and cultural understandings developed to cope with the extreme circumstances of poverty, segregation, and concentrated disadvantage might themselves
have deleterious consequences was a line of thinking no one dared to pursue. The
possibility that family disruption, multipartner childbearing, and tenuous attachment by fathers might have negative effects on children became taboo. In the
end, the hypothesis that single parenthood might interact with structural features
of American society to exacerbate the detrimental effects of joblessness, discrimination, and segregation was set aside.

A boon to conservatives

Whereas liberal social scientists learned one thing from the furor over the
Moynihan Report, conservatives with an axe to grind in the emerging culture
wars learned another lesson entirely: that there were certain subjects that liberal
pundits and social scientists would not touch, which opened up a vast and fertile
conceptual terrain for them to cultivate with their own ideological seeds. With a
very few notable exceptions, instead of studying the causes of single parenthood
and measuring the consequences for children and the community, researchers
extolled the virtues of single motherhood and hailed the resilience of children in
families they headed. Rather than acknowledging that unwed childbearing,
family disruption, delinquency, crime, and violence might be endogenous to the
reproduction of poverty, liberal analysts downplayed the problems of the ghetto
and attributed the growing prevalence of negative outcomes to the all-powerful

and single cause of systemic racism. "Blaming the victim" was an all-too-easy put-down for an entire class of work that sought to make broader structural, cultural, and historical connections.

The refusal to grapple with the mounting array of serious problems in ghetto communities played into the hands of conservatives in several ways. First, as rates of unwed childbearing, violence, welfare dependency, and drug dealing continued to rise in the 1970s and were broadcast widely and, indeed, exaggerated by the media, the reluctance of liberals to even acknowledge the existence of, much less study, behavioral problems like interpersonal violence in urban black communities put them on the wrong side of public opinion and left them open to caricature and ridicule by pundits on the right. Considering that homicide is one of the leading causes of death in the black community and most violence is intraracial, the widespread avoidance of this topic in particular was almost scandalous (Sampson and Wilson 1995).

Second, by suppressing research on sensitive subjects such as single parenthood and crime, a strong record of facts and analysis connecting negative behaviors to structural conditions never accumulated and a clear delineation of the direction and strength of the various causal effects was never made, which left the field clear for conservatives to spin their own plausible explanations backed by sometimes questionable evidence that attributed black socioeconomic problems to such conservative favorites as an overly indulgent welfare system (Murray 1984; Mead 1985), maladaptive cultural values (Steele 1990; Sowell 1994), or inherited intellectual inferiority (Herrnstein and Murray 1994).

The ultimate irony was the conservative appropriation of Moynihan's focus on family instability to explain black poverty. Whereas his report clearly viewed family instability as an *endogenous* component in a long causal chain that moved from macro structures to micro behaviors, conservatives ignored the macro structures and portrayed family instability itself as an exogenous force linked to personal weaknesses and failings (Dobson 1977, 1997). Whereas Moynihan's analysis sought to justify policy interventions to change structural relations in society, the analysis of conservatives led more often to moralistic hectoring and cheap sermonizing to individuals ("Just say no!"). For decades, the terms of public debate were skewed away from structural issues such as segregation, discrimination, and economic restructuring and toward individual issues such as values, culture, and morality.

An untested hypothesis

Despite obfuscation from both the right and the left, Moynihan's core argument was really rather simple: whenever males in any population subgroup lack widespread access to reliable jobs, decent earnings, and key forms of socially rewarded status, single parenthood will increase, with negative side effects on women and children. Although he believed that African Americans were uniquely vulnerable to this scenario because the black family had already been weakened by generations of racial subordination, the basic logic of the argument nonetheless applies to any group in which males experience a systematic loss in jobs and earnings over time.

Under these circumstances, Moynihan would predict an increase in unwed child-bearing, falling rates of marriage, rising rates of divorce, more frequent separation, and lower rates of remarriage, all with deleterious effects on the well-being of women and children.

At the time, Moynihan encountered great resistance to this idea from people who should have been his allies because it implied that family instability and the proliferation of female-headed households were somehow implicated in the reproduction and intergenerational transmission of poverty. Although Moynihan was forthright in arguing that family instability was an endogenous product of exogenous structural conditions, and his proposed solution was a major structural intervention to raise black employment rates, these features of his argument were generally ignored, and most observers, both liberal and conservative, instead focused obsessively on the black family as the major source of problems within the black community, arguing either for or against a view he never held.

At the time Moynihan published his report, in 1965, high and rising rates of single parenthood were confined to the black and Puerto Rican communities. Given the sensitivities of race in the United States, it was perhaps inevitable that any blunt discussion of these issues would prove controversial. Because the principal subjects in question were black and female, and given the report's appearance at the beginning of the surging black power and feminist movements, Moynihan's rather blunt analysis received little empirical scrutiny for years. As social scientists dithered, however, a real-world experiment was already under way that would provide a strong confirmation of the basic thrust of Moynihan's hypothesis, for ironically the backlash against civil rights and the War on Poverty had fractured the political coalition supporting the New Deal and had led to a conservative realignment.

During the 1980s, Republicans in Congress and the White House undid many of progressive policies implemented in the 1930s and rewrote the rules of the U.S. political economy to favor the wealthy over the middle and working classes (Krugman 2007). As a result, income inequality, which had fallen steadily throughout the postwar period, began to rise in the mid-1970s and by 2005 had reached heights not seen since the late 1920s. Unlike the period from 1945 to 1975, however, when inequality was structured along the lines of race, ethnicity, and gender (see Massey 2007), inequality in the new political economy was increasingly structured along the lines of class, which meant that poor and working-class *whites*, as well as minorities, were now subject to the conditions that Moynihan had posited as forerunners of family instability. In the three decades since 1975, for example, male earnings stagnated and fell in real terms, unionization levels plummeted, health insurance coverage disappeared, hours of work decreased, part-time work proliferated, and firms increasingly shifted from direct hiring to labor subcontracting. The net effect of these changes was a clear deterioration in the economic position of poor and working-class white men, especially compared to white women (Blau and Kahn 2002; Massey 2007).

If Moynihan was right, these exogenous structural shifts in the economic circumstances of whites should have produced a marked upswing in the prevalence of white single-parent households, and as several articles in this volume show, this is exactly what we observe. Over the past several decades, rates of teenage child-bearing, unwed fertility, divorce, and separation have all risen among whites while marriage rates have fallen, to the point where a quarter of white births now occur out of wedlock—the very same rate that Moynihan observed among blacks in 1965. Moreover, if we look at the rate of single parenthood among poor and working-class whites only, the rates are much higher and are now beginning to approach levels formerly observed only among blacks. Paradoxically, the conservative realignment that followed the demise of the Great Society ended up reengineering the American economy to produce a natural time-series experiment that offered a real-world test of the Moynihan hypothesis. Although this empirical test had been postponed by ideological turmoil in the 1960s, ultimately, it could not be prevented as trends evolved to vindicate Moynihan and confirm his basic argument. One wonders whether this natural experiment would even have been allowed to go forward if Moynihan's original subjects had been white instead of black.

The Moynihan Report Then and Now

Much has changed in the United States since Moynihan wrote his report. In society at large, America has grown far more diverse socially, economically, and culturally, and the nature and thrust of its public policies have changed dramatically. Within academia, the reluctance of social scientists to face up to difficult, racially sensitive questions has given way to a new willingness to measure and model unflattering behaviors and to consider their consequences for women, children, and society at large.

A new political economy

As already noted, shortly after Moynihan wrote his report the progressive New Deal coalition led by Democrats was replaced by a conservative coalition led by Republicans, a realignment that witnessed and arguably helped produce a rather sharp increase in U.S. economic inequality (McCarty, Poole, and Rosenthal 2006), whether measured in terms of income (Levy 1999) or wealth (Keister 2000). In rough terms, conditions deteriorated for those in the bottom 20 percent of the income distribution, stagnated for those in the middle 60 percent, and rose among those in the top 20 percent. Even in the top fifth of the distribution, however, the economic gains were distributed very unevenly. The higher up the income distribution one goes, the greater the improvement between 1975 and 2000 (Piketty and Saez 2003), with those at the 10th percentile outpacing those at the 20th, those at the 5th outpacing those at the 10th, those in the 1st outpacing those at the 5th, and so on all the way up to the top one-tenth of 1 percent of earners. Distributions of income and wealth have not been this skewed in nearly a century.

These changes were brought about by a combination of technological changes that increasingly rewarded those skilled in the "information economy" and delib erate changes in public policy that created new political economies of poverty and affluence (Massey 2007). In the new political economy of affluence, taxes were dramatically slashed, especially on sources of income enjoyed dispropor- tionately by the wealthy. In the new political economy of poverty, the minimum wage was allowed to drop, and social spending on housing and families was slashed. In 1996, Congress also ended welfare as a social entitlement and replaced it with a time-limited program of cash support that was contingent on work effort (Grogger and Karoly 2005; Blank and Haskins 2001). These policy changes, interacting with an increase in returns to education and technological skills, led to a changing social dynamic of inequality that disproportionately hurt low-income minorities, especially those living in concentrated poverty.

Socially, as Moynihan feared, the crisis of black male employment deepened in the 1970s and 1980s, but rather than meeting the challenge with a massive federal intervention to create jobs, a different and in many quarters unexpected govern- ment intervention occurred—the rapid and historically unprecedented increase in the prison population, yielding a new criminal justice complex that incarcerated an unprecedented share of black males (Tonry 1995). Remarkably, the run-up began just after Alfred Blumstein, a renowned criminologist, published "The Stability of Punishment" (Blumstein and Cohen 1973), an analysis showing the great stability in rates of punishment over the course of U.S. history. But from that point onward, history would prove Blumstein's hypothesis wrong, as rates of incar- ceration skyrocketed almost continuously over the past thirty years even when crime rates declined. Of course, the lower down in the class distribution one goes, the greater the likelihood of involvement in the criminal justice system, to the point where for a black male high school dropout, the lifetime odds of going to prison vastly exceed those of getting married, joining a union, attending college, or maintaining a career (Western 2006). Overall, then, rather than spending tax- payer money to create jobs for marginally employable black males, the U.S. embarked on a taxpayer-funded experiment that, in effect, locked them up, para- doxically at a higher marginal cost when considered over the long run.

In the social realm, mass incarceration only served to exacerbate the marriage squeeze faced by black females, and the 25 percent rate of unwed childbearing that so alarmed Moynihan ultimately rose to the point where more than two-thirds of all black births now occur outside the confines of marriage. Moreover, the shortage of marriageable males is now just as great, if not greater, for black women in the middle and upper classes as for those in the lower classes. In their survey of blacks entering selective colleges and universities in 1999, for example, Massey et al. (2003) found that black women outnumbered black men by two to one.

Another critical change since Moynihan wrote his report is the dramatic revival of immigration to the United States. Although no one perceived it at the time, 1965 stood at the very end of a long hiatus in immigration extending back to the 1920s (Massey 1995). After that year, immigration began to increase, slowly at first but at an increasing pace as new legislation opened the door to immigration from Asia and Africa for the first time in eight decades (Zolberg 2006) and cancelled a large guest worker program to transform Mexican immigration into an increasingly illegal flow (Massey, Durand, and Malone 2002). At the same time, political and economic turmoil in the rest of Latin America spurred new movements northward (Alba forthcoming; Durand and Massey 2008).

The scale of the transformation is suggested by a comparison of data from 1965 and the present. In the year Moynihan published his report, 297,000 immigrants entered the United States legally and 110,000 illegal migrants were arrested at the border. In 2006, 1.3 million immigrants entered the country legally, 1.2 million illegal migrants were arrested at the border, and another 12 million were estimated to be living in the country without authorization (U.S. Department of Homeland Security 2007). The latter brought the total number of foreigners to 37.5 million, or 12.5 percent of the population, and made Hispanics the nation's largest minority, exceeding African Americans by 44.3 million to 36.4 million (Pew Hispanic Center 2008).

Thus, whereas Moynihan contemplated an overwhelmingly white society composed mainly of the descendants of European immigrants, today, the share of non-Hispanic whites is rapidly falling while the share of Hispanics and Asians is rising and African Americans are no longer the nation's largest minority. Accompanying this shift in racial composition has been a corresponding shift in white racial attitudes characterized by the progressive abandonment of principled racism (Schuman et al. 1998). In the early 1960s, 68 percent of all white Americans still thought that blacks and whites should attend separate schools, 54 percent supported racially segregated public transportation, 60 percent said that whites had a right to keep blacks out of their neighborhoods, and 62 percent supported laws prohibiting racial intermarriage. By the 1980s, only 4 percent supported school segregation whereas just 12 percent supported segregated transportation, and the share saying that whites had a right to keep blacks out of their neighborhood had fallen to 13 percent, the same share that favored laws against racial intermarriage.

Although whites have largely abandoned principled racism, however, they have not necessarily given up negative racial stereotypes; nor do they feel comfortable interacting with African Americans within social settings such as schools, offices, and neighborhoods; and they tend not to support government measures to integrate these domains (Schuman et al. 1998). In the post–civil rights era, racism has not disappeared but has grown more complicated. The new attitudinal structure has been studied under various rubrics, such as symbolic racism (Kinder and Sears 1981), modern racism (McConahay 1983), laissez faire racism (Bobo, Kluegel, and Smith 1997), color-blind racism (Bonilla-Silva 2003), and aversive racism (Dovidio and Gaertner 2004). What all these terms have in common is the recognition that white attitudes are now segmented—between a conscious rejection of principled racism, on one hand, and the persistence of negative sentiments and beliefs about African Americans, on the other.

Turning point in academia

With liberal voices intimidated and quiescent, during the 1970s and 1980s, a host of right-leaning nongovernmental organizations and institutes arose to put forth a steady stream of ideas and research to back conservative and libertarian views on American social problems and government policies (Massey 2005), which led to a series of high-profile publications that garnered widespread attention in the media as well as academia. The prominence and voice given to these broadside attacks on liberal ideas finally seemed to shake social scientists out of their torpor and persuade them to take on risky shibboleths that were formally taboo.

The key turning point was the publication of William Julius Wilson's landmark book *The Truly Disadvantaged* (1987), written largely in response to Charles Murray's book *Losing Ground* (1984), which blamed family instability on a welfare system that rewarded unwed childbearing, and Lawrence Mead's book *Beyond Entitlement* (1985), which blamed black poverty on welfare's discouragement of work. In contrast, Wilson traced black poverty and family instability to the structural transformation of the urban economy and a resultant growing concentration of poverty in the inner city.

Rather than evading the unpleasant realities of the ghetto, Wilson (1987) addressed them head-on, speaking directly about the proliferation of unwed childbearing, female-headed families, joblessness, drugs, and violence that by the 1980s was very much in the news. In fact, Wilson's scholarly intervention actually began earlier in the decade, including an influential article in *The Annals* (1981) that paved the way for *The Truly Disadvantaged*, which in turn paved the way for other scholars to approach sensitive topics, the editors of this volume included. On the heels of Wilson's work, for example, Robert Sampson was able to publish "Urban Black Violence: The Effect of Male Joblessness and Family Disruption" (Sampson 1987), and Douglas Massey was able to publish "American Apartheid: Segregation and the Making of the Underclass" (Massey 1990), both in the *American Journal of Sociology*. Neither of these papers would likely have been published just a few years earlier in such a prominent journal. Massey and Denton's (1993) follow-up, which dealt frankly with the unpleasant realities of ghetto life and linked the growing concentration of poverty to an insidious interaction between the transformation of the urban economy and high levels of segregation, was soon followed by Sara McLanahan and Gary Sandefur's (1994) *Growing Up with a Single Parent*, which objectively assessed the positive and negative effects of family dissolution on children. After the publication of Richard Herrnstein and Charles Murray's treatise on the genetic limitations on black intelligence in *The Bell Curve* (1994), social scientists even began to address the persistent shortfall in cognitive skills long evinced by African Americans on standardized tests (Fischer et al. 1996; Jencks and Phillips 1998).

Not only was new research being done on controversial issues, but innovative data sets were being assembled to measure and model the causes and consequences of family instability in ways that Moynihan in 1965 could scarcely have imagined. Richard Udry and Peter Bearman launched the National Longitudinal

Survey of Adolescent Health in the mid 1990s, a multiwave longitudinal survey administered in 1994, 2001, and 2007 that sought "to examine how social contexts (families, friends, peers, schools, neighborhoods, and communities) influence adolescents' health and risk behaviors" (see National Longitudinal Survey of Adolescent Health 2008). Also in the mid 1990s, Felton Earls, Stephen Raudenbush, Robert Sampson and colleagues launched the Project on Human Development in Chicago Neighborhoods, a multilevel interdisciplinary study to examine how families, schools, and neighborhoods interact to influence child and adolescent development (see Project on Human Development in Chicago Neighborhoods 2008). Finally, in 1998, Sara McLanahan and Irwin Garfinkle initiated the Fragile Families and Child Wellbeing Study to measure the capabilities of unmarried fathers and mothers and the relationship between them and to assess how children born into single-parent families fare (see Fragile Families and Child Wellbeing Study 2008). Many of the articles in this volume draw upon these large-scale projects.

Lessons Learned

More than four decades after Moynihan wrote his prophetic report, the good news is that social scientists have never been in such a good position to document and analyze various elements in the "tangle of pathology" he hypothesized. The bad news is that many of the negative trends that Moynihan feared would come to pass have done so. Moreover, the long-standing problems of poverty, segregation, discrimination, and family instability now unfold in a very different societal context, one characterized by hyperinequality, mass incarceration, large-scale immigration, and white ambivalence about race, all of which have greatly complicated, if not exacerbated, the reproduction of poverty in the United States.

An important goal of the present volume is to reinforce the shift in social scientific and liberal opinion that has occurred since the mid-1980s to encourage systematic study of the sorts of difficult, sensitive, and often explosive issues that Moynihan first addressed in his 1965 report. Looking back over the past four decades, it is clear that the demonization of Moynihan and the denunciation of his report served no useful purpose. As we have argued, these actions cast a pall on a generation of social scientists and had a chilling effect that discouraged important research, leaving the field imbalanced and in many cases dominated by ideologues with axes to grind. We do not mean to argue, however, that conservative scholarship or conservative scholars are illegitimate—quite the opposite. Several leading conservative scholars of political thought were invited to publish in this volume. Rather, our point here and throughout is that if liberal intellectuals are unwilling to discuss sensitive, uncomfortable issues, and liberal social scientists refrain from investigating them, then by definition the only parties to the public debate will be conservative, which ironically undercuts diversity of thought and is certainly counterproductive to the forthright evaluation of a full range of policy options.

A second purpose of this volume is to provide a general audience with a sample of some of the best social scientific work now being done on the thorny issues raised by Moynihan and his report, particularly in light of the changed social, economic, and political circumstances of the early-twenty-first century. The stage is set by two distinguished professors named Wilson, who offer their separate reflections on Moynihan and his report. James Q. Wilson begins the contributions by underscoring the extent to which the man and the report were marginalized and ignored by the Johnson administration, how inaccurately both were described in the media, and how subsequent research and experience have largely confirmed Moynihan's grim warnings. Drawing on his close association with Moynihan, Wilson outlines the biographical roots of his interest in the family and concludes by noting, sadly, that toward the end of his life, Moynihan was at a loss to describe how government might act to strengthen the family.

William Julius Wilson, in turn, focuses on the report's hostile reception in the black community and attributes the caustic reaction to an "atmosphere of racial chauvinism" associated with the black power movement. He views the categorical dismissal of the report not simply as a lost opportunity, but as a real setback for social policy analysis, which for decades strenuously avoided facing up to the escalating maladies of ghetto life and refused to consider a possible interplay between structure and culture in perpetuating them. There is an interesting parallel to today in that some critics of Wilson himself have taken the same tack by suggesting that Wilson is "conservative" for delving into social structural and cultural explanations beyond simple racism.

The next two chapters take up Moynihan's core structural concern—the state of the labor market for young black men. Harry J. Holzer reviews trends since 1965 to show just how prescient Moynihan was in foreseeing not only future patterns of black labor force participation, but also their causes and consequences. Moynihan correctly predicted that a rising demand for skills would combine with a widening black-white educational gap to exacerbate joblessness among black men, and he accurately foresaw the consequences in terms of rising unemployment, labor force withdrawal, crime, and unwed childbearing. He could not foresee, of course, the revival of immigration that would increase the number of unskilled workers, the crack epidemic that would accelerate the turn toward crime, or the subsequent wars on crime and drugs that would lead to the mass incarceration of poor black men. Holzer concludes by noting that the tangle of pathology identified by Moynihan will not be solved by one single policy, but by a set of policies to improve educational outcomes; strengthen links to the labor market; create stronger incentives for work; and lower barriers to employment stemming from discrimination, segregation, and social isolation.

In the next article, Devah Pager and Diana Karafin review recent research to show quite clearly that racial stereotypes are still very much alive in American labor markets. They argue that discrimination is actually greater with the more skills and education one possesses, which occurs not only in response to race but also to a criminal record that black males are increasingly likely to possess. Their research showed that a black noncriminal had about the same odds of receiving a callback for a potential job as a white criminal; the odds that a black criminal would get a callback were virtually nil. Qualitative interviews they conducted with employers revealed that discrimination of this sort stems from widespread negative stereotyping about the desirability of African Americans as employees. More ominous, these negative stereotypes are not revised in light of actual positive experiences with black workers, making the employers what they term "Bayesian bigots" for refusing to update their initial estimates.

The next article, by Frank F. Furstenberg, shifts the focus of the volume from jobs to the family. Although Moynihan may have been correct in his overall reading of the data and his prediction of future trends, Furstenberg argues that his analysis was needlessly racialized—and made more controversial—by his neglect of the influence of social class. As generations of sociologists had clearly demonstrated, black family patterns at the time differed markedly by socioeconomic status, with middle- and upper-class African Americans being, if anything, more attuned than whites to the values and mores of conventional society. When it came to marriage and childbearing, low-income blacks and whites had much in common with each other and little in common with high-income blacks or whites who, in turn, also had much more in common with each other. Recognizing the conditioning effect of class would have enabled Moynihan to engage in analyses that were less explicitly racial. The irony is that the labor market conditions common to working-class black men in 1965 increasingly pertained to working-class white men after 1975, with similar effects on the family, to the point where the percentage of children born to unwed white mothers is now the same as that born to unwed black mothers in 1965.

Furstenberg's ultimate conclusion is that "efforts to promote marriage without changing the economic and social conditions that foster stable unions are destined to be ineffective," a point that is bolstered by the analysis of Sara McLanahan in her chapter based on data from the Fragile Families Project. Just as Moynihan postulated, she demonstrates that nonmarital childbearing is both a cause and a consequence of poverty. Socioeconomic disadvantage lowers the chances of forming a stable union after a nonmarital birth, while the presence of nonmarital children increases the risk of poverty. Her data also confirm Moynihan's suspicion that single parenthood reduces the life chances of children, not only by lowering parental resources but also by undermining the quality of parenting. She shows that partnership instability and multipartnered fertility together create considerable stress and reduce a mother's prospects of forming a stable union by contributing to jealousy and distrust between parents. This distrust, in turn, reduces the willingness of fathers to pay child support, whereas multipartner childbearing reduces fathers' commitment by spreading their limited time and money across multiple households.

The ensuing article by Linda M. Burton and M. Belinda Tucker fleshes out the reasons poverty and marital instability are so closely interconnected. The salient feature in the lives of poor black women, they argue, is uncertainty, a fact that powerfully frames their perceptions, attitudes, assessments, decisions, and behavior and places strong constraints on their control of and access to time. In such a context, low-income African American women's marital and romantic behavior may be viewed not as "pathological," but as logical and consistent with the behavior of similarly situated white women. They argue that reducing poverty will ultimately require ameliorating the time binds experienced by poor women and recalibrating gender-linked behavioral expectations.

In their article, Kathryn Edin, Laura Tach, and Ronald Mincy look at the issue of single parenthood from the viewpoint of the father. They find little evidence for the stereotype of "hit-and-run fathers." Most men are present and involved at the time children are born and strongly desire an ongoing relationship with their off-spring and fully intend to provide material and emotional support for them as they grow up. The authors' quantitative analysis of Fragile Families data revealed that rates of father involvement are quite high even five years after the birth—provided that the father was still romantically involved with the mother. This is a major proviso, since once a romantic relationship ends, father involvement drops sharply. Their analysis of qualitative data gathered through interviews with low-income men in Philadelphia suggests that even though most fathers reject the notion that father-hood is part of a "package deal" that depends on maintaining a relationship with the mother, they behave otherwise. Owing to the prevalence of multipartner fertility, the children of unmarried parents rarely experience an involved father throughout childhood and adolescence. Once again, context matters.

The next set of articles explores the changes in American society that have unfolded since Moynihan wrote his report. A major difference is the radical transformation of the American welfare regime from a system based on entitle-ment to one based on contingency. The 1996 Personal Responsibility and Work Opportunity Reconciliation Act (PRWORA) set a five-year time limit to the receipt of welfare and instituted work requirements and other restrictive rules. Drawing data from a systematic, three-city study of what happened to poor, welfare-dependent women in the wake of this change, Andrew Cherlin and his colleagues find that, consistent with congressional intentions, six years after the time limits came into force a large majority of welfare mothers had left the system, though only half of these women were employed. On average, African American welfare-leavers experienced a modest decline in poverty, whereas Hispanics fared somewhat better. As one might expect, however, the fortunes of women who left welfare diverged sharply depending on whether they were employed or unemployed. Whereas the employed mothers experienced substantial gains in household income and a narrowing of the gap with respect to the poverty line, unemployed mothers saw a decline in income and rising poverty. Jobless African American women, in particular, experienced an increase of one-third in the gap between their average income and the poverty line. As Moynihan might have predicted, because black women were less likely than Hispanic women to share a household with other adults, they were less able to draw on the financial support of others, most notably husbands.

Making a comparison between black and Hispanic women would probably not have occurred to Moynihan, as Hispanics were a small share of the U.S. population in 1965. Now, of course, they have overtaken African Americans to become the nation's largest minority group, largely because of immigration. The presence of a relatively impoverished brown-skinned minority in between blacks and whites naturally complicates issues of race, family, and poverty in the United States. After surveying recent evidence, Frank Bean and his colleagues conclude that despite facing many disadvantages, on the whole Hispanics do not seem to be following African Americans into a tangle of pathology. Mexicans, in particular, have low rates of welfare use, relatively stable families, high intermarriage rates with whites, and a marked propensity to identify themselves in multiracial terms compared with blacks. They suggest that a new black-nonblack divide is forming in the United States. Rather than erasing racial boundaries, Hispanic immigration has led to a reworking of the traditional color line to situate Latinos and Asians on the lighter side of a new black-nonblack divide.

Although Hispanics have been swept into the criminal justice system along with blacks, their rate of incarceration does not begin to approach that of African Americans. In their chapter, Bruce Western and Christopher Wildeman lay out the consequences of life in a mass incarceration society, a brave new world created by deliberate policy decisions made in the 1970s and 1980s. Owing to legislation passed to prosecute the War on Crime and the War on Drugs, the number of African Americans behind bars has exploded, but not because the rate at which black men are committing crimes has increased over time. Rather, it is because the crimes they do commit are more likely to result in an arrest; an arrest is more likely to yield a conviction; a conviction is more likely to result in jail time; a prison sentence is likely to be longer; and finally, a sentence is less likely to be shorted by judicial discretion, probation, or parole.

As a result of legislative changes, going to prison has become a normative feature of life for low-income black men, putting the black family under greater pressure than Moynihan ever imagined. A third of noncollege black men end up in prison by their midthirties, which separates them from wives, girlfriends, and children who somehow have to cope with the loss of material and emotional support. Moreover, Western and Wildeman argue that having a prison record reduces quite significantly the likelihood that a black male will ever marry, finish school, or hold a job, further limiting the supply of "marriageable males" in urban black communities and increasing the likelihood of unwed childbearing. Consistent with Sampson and Wilson's (1995) argument, we cannot ignore the enormity of crime's reach into the black community, extending as it does across the board.

As the articles in this volume clearly indicate, race remains a fundamental cleavage in American society, a conclusion that may perplex white Americans who generally reject racist principles and think the United States is, or at least should be, a race-blind society. In their chapter on white racial attitudes, Lawrence D. Bobo and Camille Z. Charles account for this paradox by explaining the new contours of racism in the post–civil rights era. Their data indicate that, despite rejecting racial segregation and discrimination in principle, whites continue to hold a variety of negative racial stereotypes and to be quite uncomfortable in settings that involve close interactions with significant numbers of black people. Whites generally attribute the low socioeconomic status of blacks to their own weaknesses and failings rather than to structural factors such as discrimination or segregation, and consistent with this attribution they are unwilling to support government efforts to benefit African Americans.

The racial divide is perhaps nowhere as discouraging as in the realm of housing, where racial residential segregation persists at very high levels and, as Sampson demonstrates in his chapter, blacks and whites occupy very different residential environments. He points out that in much of the debate over the black family and its role in the cycle of poverty, Moynihan's emphasis on segregation and neighborhood context has largely been forgotten. Drawing on data from the Project on Human Development in Chicago Neighborhoods, Sampson marshals evidence to suggest that Moynihan's "tangle of pathology" is ecologically embedded in the residential structure of American cities. Specifically, high rates of black poverty combine with high residential segregation to concentrate disadvantage geographically, thereby creating an intercorrelated constellation of social and economic problems that is unique to African Americans. In essence, Sampson updates and expands upon Moynihan by arguing that the tangle of pathology is, in fact, socially reproduced over time and across generations by an ecological dynamic in which blacks are unwilling or unable to leave disadvantaged neighborhoods while whites and Hispanics studiously avoid them. Absent government interventions at the neighborhood level, this dynamic is unlikely to be interrupted.

Despite this rather bleak conclusion, however, Sampson does describe evidence of the change that is possible in distressed communities, and in the last article, Ron Haskins draws on the findings of well-controlled evaluations to offer concrete recommendations that address several of Moynihan's fundamental concerns. The volume thus ends on a positive note. Haskins specifically outlines four sets of recommendations to answer the question, "If Moynihan was right, now what?" First, he recommends increasing the Earned Income Tax Credit and extending it to unmarried fathers to increase their attachment to the labor force. Second, to reduce unwed fertility and strengthen marriage, he advocates the teaching of both abstinence and birth control to teens while expanding marriage counseling programs and reducing marriage penalties now embedded in the tax code and transfer programs. Third, consistent with the Nobel laureate James Heckman's (2006) call to increase human capital development among disadvantaged children, Haskins proposes to expand preschool education by enlarging several promising demonstration projects and increasing funding to Head Start. Finally, he advocates reducing incarceration rates by eliminating the sentencing discrepancy between crack and powdered cocaine and restoring judicial discretion by repealing mandatory minimum sentencing and three strikes laws while at the same time funding ex-felon reintegration programs.

Conclusion

The hackneyed saying that "the more things change the more things stay the same" is an apt description of the situation four decades after the appearance of the Moynihan Report. On one hand, American society is very different now compared with then. The country has more immigrants, more convicts, greater inequality, and proportionately fewer welfare mothers than it did in the 1960s. On the other hand, despite some progress, segregation and discrimination continue in American life, employment among black men lags, unwed childbearing is all too common, child poverty is high, and the black family remains fragmented. Durable inequality reigns, in other words. Moreover, now as in the past, marriage and the family lie at the core of heated debates about the causes, consequences, and reproduction of poverty in the United States. Moynihan's blunt assessment offended many people at the time, and his public humiliation inhibited research and discussion for decades. Although this volume may not have resolved the contentious issues surrounding Moynihan and his report, we hope that it has opened the way for a more open, honest, and civil debate on America's very real and continued social problems.

References

Alba, Richard D. Forthcoming. *Blurring the color line*. Cambridge, MA: Harvard University Press.

Alba, Richard D., and Victor Nee. 2003. *Remaking the American mainstream: Assimilation and contemporary immigration*. Cambridge, MA: Harvard University Press.

Blank, Rebecca M., and Ron Haskins, eds. 2001. *The new world of welfare*. Washington, DC: Brookings Institution.

Blau, Francine D., and Lawrence M. Kahn. 2002. *At home and abroad: U.S. labor-market performance in international perspective*. New York: Russell Sage Foundation.

Blumstein, Alfred, and Jacqueline Cohen. 1973. A theory of the stability of punishment. *Journal of Criminal Law and Criminology* 64:198-207.

Bobo, Lawrence D., James R. Kluegel, and Ryan A. Smith. 1997. Laissez-Faire racism: The crystallization of a kinder, gentler, antiblack ideology. In *Racial attitudes in the 1990s: Continuities and change*, ed. Steven J. Tuch and Jack A. Martin, 15-44. Westport, CT: Praeger.

Bonilla-Silva, Eduardo. 2003. *Racism without racists: Color-blind racism and the persistence of racial inequality in the United States*. Lanham, MD: Rowman & Littlefield.

Brodkin, Karen. 1998. *How Jews became white folks and what that says about race in America*. New Brunswick, NJ: Rutgers University Press.

Danziger, Sheldon, and Peter Gottschalk. 1995. *America unequal*. New York: Russell Sage Foundation.

Dobson, James C. 1977. *Dare to discipline*. New York: Bantam.

———. 1997. *Solid answers: America's foremost family counselor responds to tough questions facing today's families*. Carol Stream, IL: Tyndale.

Dovidio, John F., and Samuel L. Gaertner. 2004. Aversive racism. *Advances in Experimental Social Psychology* 36:1-51.

Durand, Jorge, and Douglas S. Massey. 2008. Patterns and processes of international migration in Latin America. Paper presented at the Conference on International Migration in Latin America, Vanderbilt University, Nashville, TN, May 5-6.

Fischer, Claude S., Michael Hout, Martin Sanchez Jankowski, Samuel R. Lucas, Ann Swidler, and Kim Voss. 1996. *Inequality by design: Cracking the bell curve myth*. Berkeley: University of California Press.

Fragile Families and Child Wellbeing Study. 2008. Home page of the Fragile Families and Wellbeing Study. Center for Research on Child Wellbeing, Princeton University, Princeton, NJ. http://www.fragilefamilies.princeton.edu/.

Glazer, Nathan, and Daniel P. Moynihan. 1963. *Beyond the melting pot: The Negroes, Puerto Ricans, Jews, Italians, and Irish of New York City*. Cambridge, MA: Harvard University Press.

Grogger, Jeffrey, and Lynn A. Karoly. 2005. *Welfare reform: Effects of a decade of change*. Cambridge, MA: Harvard University Press.

Heckman, James J. 2006. Skill formation and the economics of investing in disadvantaged children. *Science* 312:1900-1902.

Herrnstein, Richard J., and Charles Murray. 1994. *The bell curve: Intelligence and class structure in American life*. New York: Free Press.

Hodgson, Godfrey. 2000. The gentleman from New York: Daniel Patrick Moynihan—A biography. New York: Houghton-Mifflin.

Ignatiev, Noel. 1995. *How the Irish became white*. New York: Routledge.

Jencks, Christopher, and Meredith Phillips, eds. 1998. *The black-white test score gap*. Washington, DC: Brookings Institution.

Johnson, Lyndon Baines. 1965. President Lyndon B. Johnson's commencement address at Howard University: "To fulfill these rights." June 4. http://www.lbjlib.utexas.edu/johnson/archives.hom/speeches.hom/650604.asp.

Katznelson, Ira. 2005. *When affirmative action was white: An untold history of racial inequality in twentieth-century America*. New York: Norton.

Keister, Lisa A. 2000. *Wealth in America: Trends in inequality*. New York: Cambridge University Press.

Kinder, Donald R., and David O. Sears. 1981. Prejudice and politics: Symbolic racism versus threats to the good life. *Journal of Personality and Social Psychology* 40:414-31.

Krugman, Paul. 2003. *The great unraveling: Losing our way in the new century*. New York: Norton.

Krugman, Paul. 2007. *The conscience of a liberal*. New York: Norton.

Levy, Frank. 1999. *The new dollars and dreams: American incomes and economic change*. New York: Russell Sage Foundation.

Massey, Douglas S. 1990. American apartheid: Segregation and the making of the underclass. *American Journal of Sociology* 96:329-57.

———. 1995. The new immigration and the meaning of ethnicity in the United States. *Population and Development Review* 21:747-53.

———. 2005. *Return of the "L" word: A liberal vision for the new century*. Princeton, NJ: Princeton University Press.

———. 2007. *Categorically unequal: The American stratification system*. New York: Russell Sage Foundation.

Massey, Douglas S., Camille Charles, Garvey Lundy, and Mary J. Fischer. 2003. *Source of the river: The social origins of freshmen at America's selective colleges and universities*. Princeton, NJ: Princeton University Press.

Massey, Douglas S., and Nancy Denton. 1993. *American apartheid: Segregation and the making of the underclass*. Cambridge, MA: Harvard University Press.

Massey, Douglas S., Jorge Durand, and Nolane J. Malone. 2002. *Beyond smoke and mirrors: Mexican immigration in an era of economic integration*. New York: Russell Sage Foundation.

McCarty, Nolan, Keith T. Poole, and Howard Rosenthal. 2006. *Polarized America: The dance of ideology and unequal riches*. Cambridge, MA: MIT Press.

McConahay, J. B. 1983. Modern racism and modern discrimination: The effects of race, racial attitudes, and context on simulated hiring decisions. *Personality and Social Psychology Bulletin* 9:551-58.

McLanahan, Sara, and Gary Sandefur. 1994. *Growing up with a single parent: What hurts, what helps*. Cambridge, MA: Harvard University Press.

Mead, Lawrence. 1985. Beyond entitlement: The social obligations of citizenship. New York: Free Press.

Moynihan, Daniel P. 1965. *The Negro family: The case for national action*. Washington, DC: Office of Policy Planning and Research, U.S. Department of Labor.

———, ed. 1969. *On understanding poverty*. New York: Free Press.

Murray, Charles. 1984. *Losing ground: American social policy 1950-1980*. New York: Basic Books.

National Longitudinal Survey of Adolescent Health. 2008. Add health: The National Longitudinal Survey of Adolescent Health. http://www.cpc.unc.edu/addhealth.

Pew Hispanic Center. 2008. Factsheet: Statistical portrait of Hispanics in the United States, 2006. Washington, DC: Pew Hispanic Center. http://pewhispanic.org/factsheets/factsheet.php?FactsheetID=35.

Piketty, Thomas, and Emmanuel Saez. 2003. Income inequality in the United States, 1913-1998. *Quarterly Journal of Economics* 158:1-16.

Project on Human Development in Chicago Neighborhoods. 2008. Homepage of the project on Human Development in Chicago Neighborhoods. http://www.icpsr.umich.edu/PHDCN/.

Quadagno, Jill. 1996. *The color of welfare: How racism undermined the war on poverty*. New York: Oxford University Press.

Rainwater, Lee, and William L. Yancey. 1967. *The Moynihan Report and the politics of controversy*. Cambridge, MA: MIT Press.

Roediger, David R. 2006. *Working toward whiteness: How America's immigrants became white: The strange journey from Ellis Island to the suburbs*. New York: Basic Books.

Ryan, William. 1971. *Blaming the victim*. New York: Pantheon.

Sampson, Robert J. 1987. Urban black violence: The effect of male joblessness and family disruption. *American Journal of Sociology* 93:348-82.

Sampson, Robert J., and William Julius Wilson. 1995. Toward a theory of race, crime, and urban inequality. In *Crime and inequality*, ed. John Hagan and Ruth Peterson, 37-56. Stanford, CA: Stanford University Press.

Schuman, Howard, Charlotte Steeh, Lawrence D. Bobo, and Maria Krysan. 1998. *Racial attitudes in America: Trends and interpretations*. Cambridge, MA: Harvard University Press.

Skrentny, John D. 1996. The ironies of affirmative action: Politics, culture, and justice in America. Chicago: University of Chicago Press.

Sowell, Thomas. 1994. *Race and culture: A world view*. New York: Basic Books.

Stack, Carol. 1974. All our kin: Strategies for survival in a black community. New York: Harper & Row.

Steele, Shelby. 1990. The content of our character: A new vision of race in America. New York: St. Martin's.

Tonry, Michael. 1995. *Malign neglect: Race, crime, and punishment in America*. New York: Oxford University Press.

U.S. Department of Homeland Security. 2007. *2006 yearbook of immigration statistics*. Washington, DC: Government Printing Office.

Western, Bruce. 2006. *Punishment and inequality in America*. New York: Russell Sage Foundation.

Wilson, William Julius. 1981. The black community in the 1980s: Questions of race, class, and public policy. *The Annals of the American Academy of Political and Social Science* 454:26-41.

———. 1987. The truly disadvantaged: The inner city, the underclass, and public policy. Chicago: University of Chicago Press.

Zolberg, Aristide R. 2006. *A nation by design: Immigration policy in the fashioning of America*. New York: Russell Sage Foundation.

FOREWORD

Keywords: Daniel Patrick Moynihan; *The Negro Family*, race; single-parent families; welfare

Pat Moynihan Thinks about Families

By
JAMES Q. WILSON

The work and thinking of one of my oldest and best friends, Pat Moynihan, is dear to my heart. We knew each other for forty years. I helped bring him to Harvard University. I lamented when he left Harvard but was relieved to learn that he was leaving only to become a United States Senator from the state of New York.

In March 1965, Pat Moynihan, then assistant secretary of labor for public policy research, finished an internal memorandum, of which fewer than one hundred copies were printed, designed to guide the Johnson administration in the aftermath of the Civil Rights Act of 1964. It was leaked to the press. No one quite knows by whom, but the best suspicion points to middle managers in the Department of Health, Education, and Welfare who, I think, felt offended that the family problem would be raised outside of their context and approval. When this report was leaked to the press, to quote Charles Dickens, "It was the best of times; it was the worst of times." It was the best of times in the sense that the Civil Rights Act had just been passed in 1964, setting in motion finally an effort to redress the legal and political difficulties under which African Americans had labored so long in this country. But it was the worst of times because in 1964, there were riots involving blacks and whites in both Rochester and Philadelphia.

James Q. Wilson has been the Shattuck Professor of Government at Harvard University and the Collins Professor of Management at the University of California, Los Angeles. He now teaches at Pepperdine University. He is the author or coauthor of fifteen books about politics, crime, marriage, and morality. In 2003, he received the Presidential Medal of Freedom, the nation's highest civilian award.

DOI: 10.1177/0002716208324606

In 1965, shortly after the report was leaked to the press, there was the Watts riot in Los Angeles, and in 1966 there was a riot in Cleveland. The good news continued, however briefly, because Moynihan's report provided the inspiration for Lyndon B. Johnson's address to Howard University in June 1965.

When the report appeared, it received a great deal of criticism—criticism that in my view reflects either an unwillingness to read the report or an unwillingness to think about it in a serious way. William Ryan, writing in *The Nation* magazine, said that the Moynihan Report was "a new form of subtle racism" because "it seduces the reader into believing that it is not racism and discrimination but the weaknesses and defects of the Negro, himself, that accounts for the present status of inequality" (Ryan 1965, 380). These were sharp words and totally at odds with what Moynihan wrote in the report, a matter on which I will dwell briefly in a moment.

> *[W]hen the [Moynihan Report] appeared, it received a great deal of criticism—criticism that in my view reflects either an unwillingness to read the report or an unwillingness to think about it in a serious way.*

Many people stepped forward and endorsed the release of the report or the reading of the report, and that included Roy Wilkins, Whitney Young, and the Reverend Martin Luther King Jr. But soon the left in American politics was seized with an anti–Pat Moynihan passion. James Farmer at the Congress of Racial Equality and the leaders of many of the mainline Protestant churches began to denounce it and urged that the report be repudiated. There was to be a White House Conference on Civil Rights presided over by President Johnson. A planning meeting was called, which I attended, and there the prospective executive director of the White House Conference on Civil Rights, Berl Bernhard, stood up and said with a wide smile on his face, "I have been reliably informed that no such person as Daniel Patrick Moynihan exists." And when the conference was in fact held, the report was absent, Moynihan was not invited, and the subject was never mentioned.

Now we skip ahead twenty years. Pat Moynihan, by then a senator, was invited to give the 1985 Godkin Lectures at the John F. Kennedy School of Government at Harvard. His 1985 speech was very similar to his 1965 report, updated with new statistics but making essentially the same argument. He received a standing ovation. His remarks were widely praised in the press. Editorials complimented him on his insightfulness. Why the difference between 1965 and 1985? I don't think it's because Harvard University or the mass media liked senators better than they liked obscure subcabinet officers. And I don't think it's because his critics had become converted to his cause. But perhaps one of the reasons was the following: in 1965, one-quarter of African American children were born out of wedlock. In 2005, one-quarter of *white* children were born out of wedlock (Child Trends 2008). When white readers realized that the problem was not confined to a race, but was the problem of a nation and of a culture, they became aware that this was a serious issue.

There was never, between 1965 and now, a decent reason for rejecting his argument. If you read the report, you realize he never blamed the victim. Quite the contrary, he blamed slavery. He did not ignore segregation. Quite the contrary, he called attention repeatedly to segregation in the occupational, residential, and educational markets. He wrote that African Americans were the victims of the segregation. He did not ignore urban life or ignore the enormous strains placed on recent migrants to cities. He pointed out in detail the effects of urbanization.

He certainly did not ignore unemployment. He emphasized unemployment but said that unemployment had to be understood in a somewhat broader context. It was a tragedy that so many African Americans were unemployed; the cure for this unemployment must address not simply the availability of jobs, not simply the training for jobs, but the culture in which employment occurs. He believed that the fundamental problem facing African Americans was "the crumbling" of the black family in urban ghettos, and the root cause of that was slavery.

During the forty years I knew Pat, we met endlessly, talked at great length, and drank a lot. During all of these conversations, the status of the family was always at the forefront of his concerns, perhaps understandably because he was a Catholic and the status of the family is a key issue in Catholic teachings. But he was also the product of a broken family, raised by a mother abandoned by her husband. The family moved from Tulsa, Oklahoma, where Pat was born, to live on the side streets of New York City. He never deviated from the view that the family was the core of culture. He did not deviate in part because he knew personally what it meant to have been the victim of a broken family.

This argument fell on deaf ears among his critics. Many approached his views by saying, in effect, that slavery was not such a bad thing at all. One writer said that slavery provided its victims with "a remarkably stable base for living" (Genovese 1974, 452). Stephanie Coontz said that unmarried black women had "healthy, not pathological qualities" (Coontz 1992, 252). A third scholar, Herbert Gutman, argued that the black family was not, in fact, harmed by slavery (Gutman 1977). Robert Fogel, who won the 1993 Nobel Prize in Economics, in his book on slavery with Stanley Engerman said that it was in the rational interest of slave owners to take care of their slaves because, after all, these slaves were property, and without cultivating and improving this property, the property would depreciate in value (Fogel and Engerman 1974).

We know that all of these arguments were, in important respects, wrong. How could a vicious system of oppression in which blacks were not allowed to sue, own property, marry, or conduct their own religious experiences; who could be sold on a slave block at a moment's notice—how could such a system that lasted for nearly three centuries have any effect other than in weakening a culture? This problem was especially acute in small plantations because there male blacks would often be sent out under orders to work in other locations. The possibility of their enjoying even the company of female slaves, much less the prospect of living together in something approximating marriage, was close to zero.

Steven Ruggles and others have examined the level of marriage formation during those days when some city-level census data were available, generally from the period 1860 to 1880. In this period, single parenthood was three times more common among black than white families (Fitch and Ruggles 2000). If you read Herbert Gutman's book (1977), widely quoted as a criticism of the Moynihan report and described by Professor Gutman as a criticism, we discover that his data support the same conclusion. Single-parent families were roughly three times as common among African Americans as among whites.

Orlando Patterson in his book *Rituals of Blood* (1999) has written that slavery meant that a black man could not offer a black woman security, status, name, or identity. This did not end with the end of slavery, because following slavery came a period of pseudo-slavery in which African Americans became sharecroppers, living on property they did not own, working for people other than themselves, and thus having little or no opportunity to earn savings that could pay for a decent life for their children.

Moynihan in his report was not entirely clear on what effect single-parent families would have on persons experiencing them. But Sara McLanahan and Gary Sandefur (1994) in their book on the single-parent family analyzed four longitudinal data sets (the Panel Study of Income Dynamics [PSID], the National Longitudinal Study of Youth, High School and Beyond, and the National Survey of Families and Neighborhoods and Households) to find out what effect low income, poverty, and single-parent status had on the behavior of children. They concluded that it harmed the children—the boys much more than the girls. Boys were twice as likely to drop out of school and much more likely to be idle on the street corner than boys in two-parent families. Girls were twice as likely to become unmarried teenage mothers compared with girls in two-parent families.

In trying to explain this difference, McLanahan and Sandefur (1994) suggested that income differences make an important contribution, perhaps explaining half the variance, and that living in a single parent family (after controlling for income) also explains about half the variance. Of course, it is difficult to separate income effects and family effects because family status profoundly affects one's income and income status profoundly affects one's opportunities for being married. McLanahan and Sandefur also said that living with a grandmother or a stepfather made little difference.

These problems were not limited to black Americans; they were true of white Americans as well. The only difference between black and white Americans is that there were more black Americans in this condition. That, in my view, was largely the result of slavery. If you look around the world, you will discover that this problem of out-of-wedlock births has become a phenomenon throughout almost the entire Western world. The growth in the proportion of children living with a single parent has grown rapidly in Canada, Germany, Sweden, and the United Kingdom.

A puzzle in analyzing these facts arises from the following difficulty. About 95 percent of the good social science research in the world (and probably also 95 percent of the bad social science in the world) is produced in the United States. We examine ourselves much more fully than other countries examine themselves. I spent a week in Sweden, for example, trying to uncover what information was available about the behavior of children, controlling for the usual independent variables, in single-parent families or that were raised by unmarried parents. The answer was that the Swedes didn't know. My guess is that in many other countries, they don't know.

This absence of data raises the following problem: how important is marriage as opposed to cohabitation? Suppose a man and woman are not married, suppose the woman has a child, suppose the biological father of the mother remains in residence and the two raise the child as if they were married, but they are not. Does this make a difference? In all likelihood, it does. Suppose that the biological father does not remain there, but other relatives participate. Does this make a difference? In some cultures it may; in this culture it does not. We really do not know the answer for these larger questions.

Families do not exist in isolation. As Rob Sampson has pointed out in the important studies he has done for the Chicago Project, families live in neighborhoods, and the characteristics of neighborhoods may affect the behavior of individuals within them. Neighborhoods with a high proportion of single-parent families have more murders and robberies even after adjusting for race and income. Sampson seems to suggest that it is the presence of single-parent families, not differences between blacks and whites, that explains most, if not all, of the difference in black and white rates of criminality (Sampson, Raudenbush, and Earls 1997).

You might wonder what Pat Moynihan thought should be done about the family problem. He didn't know. We kicked around many ideas. He came up with several. Some ideas he liked, some ideas he did not. Welfare reform was tried in 1996 with a bill introduced by President Bill Clinton. Pat Moynihan opposed this bill vigorously on the floor of the Senate because he read an Urban Institute study that erroneously led him to believe that welfare reform would increase dramatically the level of childhood poverty (Zedlewski et al. 1996). In fact, there was a flaw in the Urban Institute study. Welfare reform was passed and it did not lead to an increase in childhood poverty. It also did not lead to an increase in marriage, however, and there is a very simple explanation for this.

It is relatively easy to persuade working-level officials in a welfare department to tell a woman applying for welfare that her first task is to look hard for a job, and if she is unable to find a job, she can come back and fill out the application for welfare. But it is very difficult, if not impossible, to require the same worker to tell a welfare applicant that she should go out and get married and then if she remains poor come back and apply for help. Asking for marriage in a large American bureaucracy is much harder than asking for work. We might, of course, deal with this problem by increasing the cultural support for marriage and increasing the level of shame attached to unwed parents, but how do we do this? Churches might, but governments don't produce shame; they rarely, indeed, produce culture.

Could we rely on family allowances? Pat loved this idea and talked about it endlessly throughout his life. A family allowance means that, as in most European nations, the government would pay an additional income supplement to families that have children. He thought the United States should embrace the European ideal. In time we did, though quite slowly. Our program is called the Earned Income Tax Credit (EITC). Created in 1975, the EITC now goes to 21 million Americans and costs about $35 to $36 billion a year. It is an additional payment to two working parents below a certain income level when they have a child. The problem is that since 1975, the proportion of families producing children who live only with one parent went up.

Toward the end of his career, Pat was asked, What do you think the government should do about it? He answered in what I think is one of his most famous phrases. He said, and I quote, "If you think a government program can restore marriage, you know more about the government than I do." And nobody knew more about the government than Pat Moynihan.

References

Child Trends. 2008. Percentage of births to unmarried women. Child Trends Data Bank. http://www .childtrendsdatabank.org/pdf/75_PDF.pdf.

Coontz, Stephanie. 1992. *The way we never were: American families and the nostalgia trap*. New York: Basic Books.

Fitch, Chatherine, and Steven Ruggles. 2000. Historical trends in marriage formation. In *Ties that bind: Perspectives on marriage and cohabitation*, ed. Linda Waite, Christine Bachrach, Michelle Hindin, Elizabeth Thomson, and Arland Thornton, 59-88. Hawthorne, NY: Aldine de Gruyter.

Fogel, Robert William, and Stanley L. Engerman. 1974. *Time on the cross: The economics of American Negro slavery*. 2 vols. Boston: Little, Brown.

Genovese, Eugene D. 1974. *Roll, Jordon roll: The world the slaves made*. New York: Pantheon.

Gutman, Herbert. 1977. *The black family in slavery and freedom, 1750-1925*. New York: Vintage Books.

McLanahan, Sara, and Gary Sandefur. 1994. *Growing up with a single parent: What hurts, what helps*. Cambridge, MA: Harvard University Press.

Patterson, Orlando. 1999. *Rituals of blood: Consequences of slavery in two American centuries*. New York: Basic Civitas.

Ryan, William. 1965. Savage discovery: The Moynihan Report. *The Nation* 201 (November 22): 380-84.

Sampson, Robert J., Stephen Raudenbush, and Felton Earls. 1997. Neighborhoods and violent crime: A multilevel study of collective efficacy. *Science* 277:918-24.

Zedlewski, Sheila R., Sandra J. Clark, Eric Meier, and Keith Watson. 1996. Potential effects of congressional welfare reform legislation on family incomes. Urban Institute, July 26. http://www.urban.org/ publications/406622.html.

FOREWORD

Keywords: Daniel Patrick Moynihan; *The Negro Family*, race, inequality, single-parent families; poverty

The Moynihan Report and Research on the Black Community

By
WILLIAM JULIUS WILSON

In a *New York Times* obituary for Daniel Patrick Moynihan in March 2003, I was quoted as saying that the Moynihan Report is an important and prophetic document. I still stand by that statement. The report is important because it continues to be a reference for studies on the black family and low-skilled black males. It was prophetic because Moynihan's predictions about the fragmentation of the African American family and its connection to inner-city poverty were largely borne out, and since 1990, social scientists and civil rights leaders have echoed his concerns about black male joblessness.

Yet, it is often said that there was nothing new in the report. After all, people such as Bayard Rustin, E. Franklin Frazier, and Kenneth B. Clark had previously presented arguments highlighted by Moynihan. Like Frazier (1939), Moynihan argued that the problems of the black family, which present many obstacles to black equality, derive from previous patterns of inequality that originated in the experience of

William Julius Wilson is Lewis P. and Linda L. Geyser University Professor at Harvard University. A MacArthur Prize Fellow, Wilson has been elected to the National Academy of Sciences, the American Academy of Arts and Sciences, the National Academy of Education, the American Philosophical Society, the Institute of Medicine, and the British Academy. He is a recipient of the 1998 National Medal of Science and was awarded the Talcott Parsons Prize in the Social Sciences by the American Academy of Arts and Sciences in 2003.

NOTE: Parts of this foreword are based on my book *More Than Just Race: Being Black and Poor in the Inner City* (Norton forthcoming). I would like to thank Michéle Lamont, James Quane, Mario Luis Small, Jessica Houston Su, and Edward Walker for their helpful comments on previous drafts.

DOI: 10.1177/0002716208324625

ANNALS, *AAPSS*, 621, January 2009

slavery and have been maintained and reinforced by years of racial discrimination. Like Rustin (1965), Moynihan asserted that as antidiscrimination legislation breaks down barriers to black liberty, issues of equality will draw attention away from issues of liberty. In other words, concerns for equal resources enabling blacks to live comparably to whites in material ways will exceed concerns of freedom.

Moynihan maintained that the simple removal of legal barriers would not necessarily achieve the goal of equality. African Americans are free in a legal sense, but many social mechanisms perpetuate their subordinate social position. Moreover, like Clark (1964), Moynihan emphasized that family fragmentation, as revealed in urban blacks' rising rates of broken marriages, female-headed homes, out-of-wedlock births, and welfare receipt, was one of the central problems of the black lower class. Thus, far from being a document of original research, the report effectively synthesized the writings of some of the most notable black intellectuals of the twentieth century. Why then was it so controversial?

James Q. Wilson has discussed some of the reasons for the controversy (2008 [this volume]). In addition, controversy was fed by the way the report was written. Bold expressions and attention-grabbing phrases sprinkled throughout the document were frequently quoted and embellished in editorials and media accounts. Given the racial climate in the mid-1960s, these press reports heightened concerns among black leaders about the public's perception of African Americans. Let me briefly review the developments.

The Moynihan Report was an internal document written for officials in the executive branch of government, not for the general public. The report was not edited to reduce the chances of press distortions and the odds of offending civil rights groups. Understandably, Moynihan had no idea it was going to be leaked. Dramatic statements drew press attention and were often taken out of context. For example, in his chapter titled "The Tangle of Pathology," Moynihan boldly stated, "At the heart of the deterioration of the fabric of Negro society is the deterioration of the Negro family. It is a fundamental weakness of the Negro at the present time." And "at the center of the tangle of pathology is a weakness of the family structure. Once or twice removed it will be found to be the principal source of most of the aberrant, inadequate or antisocial behavior that did not establish, but now serves to perpetuate the cycle of poverty and deprivation" (Moynihan 1965).

Also, as Lee Rainwater and William L. Yancey (1967) pointed out in their excellent book on the controversy that surrounded the report, Moynihan's frequent use of words such as "failure" to describe the unsuccessful adaptation of many black men to American society was seen in many eyes to connote individual responsibility rather than the structure of opportunity, racial discrimination, access to quality education, employment prospects, and so on for poor social outcomes. Reporters and columnists organized their coverage around the attention-grabbing statements on the breakdown of the black family and the predicament of black males, and readers who had not read the actual document would often have no idea that Moynihan devoted an entire chapter to the root causes of family fragmentation, including Jim Crow segregation, urbanization, unemployment, and poverty.

Finally, a *Washington Post* article noted, according to White House sources, that the Watts riot in 1965 strengthened President Johnson's "feeling of the urgent need to restore Negro family stability" (Rainwater and Yancey 1967, 144). Accordingly, by the time that many critics, including black critics, got around to reading the report, "they could no longer see it with fresh eyes, but were instead heavily influenced by their exposure to the press coverage, particularly as this coverage tied the report to an official 'explanation' for Watts" (Rainwater and Yancey 1967, 154).

The critical reaction of many African Americans to the report was also influenced by racial sentiments in the black community flowing from the emergence of the black power movement in the mid-1960s. Some blacks were highly critical of the report's emphasis on social pathologies within poor black neighborhoods, not simply because of its potential for embarrassment but also because it conflicted with their claim that blacks were developing a community power base that could become a major force in American society and would reflect the strength and vitality of the black community.

This critical reaction reflected a new definition, description, and explanation of the black condition that accompanied the emergence of the black power movement. This new approach, proclaimed as the black perspective, signaled an ideological shift from interracialism to black solidarity. It first gained currency among militant black spokespersons in the middle 1960s. By the early 1970s, it had become a recurrent theme in the writings of a number of black academics and intellectuals. Although the black perspective represented a variety of views and arguments on issues of race, the trumpeting of racial pride and self-affirmation was common to many of the writings and speeches on the subject.

In this atmosphere of racial chauvinism, a series of scholarly studies proclaiming a black perspective were published. The arguments set forth made clear a substantial and fundamental shift in both the tone and focus of race relations scholarship. Consistent with the emphasis on black glorification and the quest for self-affirmation, analyses that described some aspects of ghetto life as pathological tended to be rejected in favor of those that emphasized black strengths. Arguments that focused on the deterioration of the poor black family were dismissed in favor of those that extolled the strengths of black families. Thus, black perspective proponents reinterpreted behavior described as self-destructive by Moynihan, Kenneth Clark, and Lee Rainwater, and instead proclaimed it as creative—creative in the sense that blacks were displaying the ability to survive and even flourish in a ghetto community. Poor African Americans were described as resilient and were seen as imaginatively adapting to an oppressive society.

The logic put forth by the proponents of the black perspective explanation is interesting because it does not even acknowledge self-destructive behavior in the ghetto. This is a unique response to the dominant American belief system's emphasis on individual deficiencies rather than the structure of opportunity as causes of poverty and welfare. Instead of challenging the validity of the underlying assumptions of this belief system, this approach sidesteps the issue altogether by denying that social dislocations in the inner city represent any special problem. Researchers who emphasized these dislocations were denounced, even those who rejected the assumption of individual responsibility for poverty and welfare, and focused instead on the structure or roots of these problems.

Accordingly, in the early 1970s, unlike in the middle 1960s, there was little motivation to develop a research agenda that pursued the structural and cultural roots of ghetto social dislocations. The vitriolic attacks and acrimonious debate that characterized this controversy proved to be too intimidating to scholars, particularly to liberal scholars. Indeed, in the aftermath of this controversy and in an effort to protect their work from the charge of racism, or of blaming the victim, many liberal social scientists tended to avoid describing any behavior that could be construed as unflattering or stigmatizing to people of color. Accordingly, until the mid-1980s and well after this controversy had subsided, social problems in the inner-city ghetto did not attract serious research attention.

[I]n the aftermath of this controversy and in an effort to protect their work from the charge of racism, or of blaming the victim, many liberal social scientists tended to avoid describing any behavior that could be construed as unflattering or stigmatizing to people of color.

Although research on urban poverty has mushroomed in the past several years, lingering effects of this controversy on the willingness of social scientists to pursue a cultural analysis of life in poverty still remain. I will address this issue shortly, but first let me very briefly put Moynihan's concerns in current perspective to highlight the ways in which the document was prophetic. Several trends that had earlier worried Moynihan have become much more pronounced over time. As indicated in Figure 1, a quarter of all nonwhite births were to unmarried women. I say nonwhite because specific data on non-Hispanic blacks were not available when Moynihan wrote the report. By 1996, the proportion of non-Hispanic black births outside of marriage reached a high of 70 percent and then dipped slightly to 69 percent in 2005. As Figure 2 reveals, in 1965, 25 percent of all nonwhite families were headed by a single woman. However, by 1996, the proportion of all non-Hispanic black families headed by a single woman swelled to 47 percent but dropped slightly to 45 percent in 2006.

FIGURE 1
NON-HISPANIC BLACK NONMARITAL BIRTHS

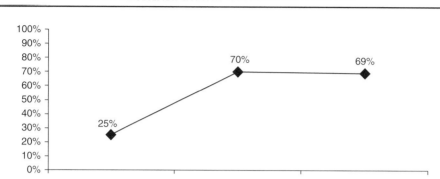

SOURCE: U.S. Department of Health, Education, and Welfare (1974); U.S. Department of Health and Human Services (2000, 2006).

NOTE: Statistics were not available for non-Hispanic blacks in 1965. It is estimated that non-Hispanic blacks composed roughly 90 percent of those classified as "nonwhite."

FIGURE 2
NON-HISPANIC BLACK FAMILIES HEADED BY A SINGLE MOTHER

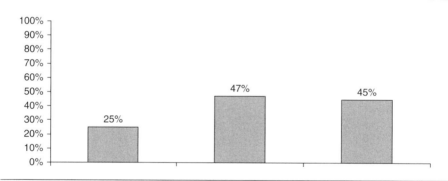

SOURCE: U.S. Census Bureau (1996, 2006).

NOTE: Statistics were not available for non-Hispanic blacks in 1965. It is estimated that non-Hispanic blacks composed roughly 90 percent of those classified as "nonwhite."

Accompanying these trends was a sharp increase in joblessness among low-skilled black men, another one of Moynihan's major concerns. Few serious scholars would maintain that Moynihan's concerns were unjustified even though the percentage of nonmarital births and single mother families has increased among whites and Latinos as well. What continues to be disputed is how we account for the fragmentation of the African American family and the social outcomes of low-skilled black males. As I argued previously, the controversy over the Moynihan

Report resulted in a persistent taboo on cultural explanations to help explain social problems in the poor black community. Allow me to elaborate.

If the leaking of the report to the public was untimely in terms of the changing racial climate, it was also published at the unfortunate time of heated debates over Oscar Lewis's work on the culture of poverty. Indeed, the report quickly became a reference point for debates about the culture of poverty. This was especially true following the publication of an article, and later a book, both titled *Blaming the Victim*, written by psychologist and civil rights activist William Ryan as a critique of the Moynihan Report (Ryan 1971). "Blaming the victim" became a slogan repeatedly used by critics of the culture of poverty thesis, and they made repeated reference to the Moynihan Report when voicing their criticisms.

Relying on participant observation and life history data to analyze Latin American poverty, the anthropologist Oscar Lewis described the culture of poverty as "both an adaptation and a reaction of the poor to their marginal position in a class stratified highly individuated capitalistic society" (Lewis 1968, 188; see also Lewis 1959, 1966). However, he also noted that once the culture of poverty comes into existence, "it tends to perpetuate itself from generation to generation because of its effect on the children. By the time slum children are age six or seven, they have usually absorbed the basic values and attitudes of their subculture, and are not psychologically geared to take advantage of changing conditions or increased opportunities which may occur in their lifetime" (Lewis 1968, 188). Although Oscar Lewis later modified his position by placing more weight on external societal forces than on self-perpetuating cultural traits to explain the behavior of the poor, conservative social scientists embellished the idea that poverty is a product of "deeply ingrained habits" that are unlikely to change following improvements in external conditions.

Although Moynihan devoted an entire chapter to structural causes for the fragmentation of the black family, and the downward spiral of low-skilled black males, a close reading of his report does reveal an implicit culture of poverty explanation as well. Like Oscar Lewis, Moynihan relates cultural patterns to structural factors, and then discusses how these patterns come to influence other aspects of behavior. For example, in the concluding chapter of his report, he states that the situation of the black family "may indeed have begun to feed on itself." To illustrate, he noted that from 1948 to 1962, the black male unemployment rate and the number of new Aid to Families with Dependent Children (AFDC) cases were very highly correlated. However, after 1962, the trend reversed itself for the first time. The number of new AFDC cases continued to rise, but black male unemployment declined. "With this one statistical correlation by far the most highly publicized in the Report," states the historian Alice O'Connor (2001, 205), "Moynihan sealed the argument that the 'pathology' had become self-perpetuating: pathology here measured as welfare 'dependency' was no longer correlated with the unemployment rate, it was going up on its own."

Also like Oscar Lewis, Moynihan discusses the adverse effects of children being exposed to the cultural environment or, as he puts it, to the tangle of pathology in the ghetto. Unlike many conservative social scientists, however, Moynihan does not imply that black family fragmentation and the problems associated with it are immutable and cannot be changed through social policies. And his implicit cultural argument on the impact of black family fragmentation, which many would associate with a culture of poverty, is part of a complex thesis on the African American family that combines structural and cultural factors. Is the integration of the structural and cultural factors of black family fragmentation and the plight of black males reflected in social science studies today?

My colleague Orlando Patterson argues emphatically that in recent years cultural explanations have not received the serious attention normally given to structural arguments in studies of race and poverty. Patterson maintains that since the mid-1960s "a deep-seated dogma" in social science and policy circles has led to "the rejection of any explanation that invokes a group's cultural attributes—its distinctive attitudes, values and predispositions, and the resulting behavior of its members—and the relentless preference for relying on structural factors like low incomes, joblessness, poor schools and bad housing" (Patterson 2006). As Patterson points out, perhaps the main reason liberal social scientists avoid cultural explanations is that reactionary analysts and simpleminded public figures associate the problems of the poor with their values and therefore feel that taxpayers and the government should assume no responsibility for their alleviation. Culture as explanation, states Patterson, "languishes in intellectual exile, partly because of guilt by association" (Patterson 2000, 204).

Patterson argues, and I strongly agree, that this "deep-seated dogma" against cultural analysis of the fragmentation of the black family and the plight of low-skilled inner-city African American males was caused in no small measure by reactions to the Moynihan Report. It has resulted in a lack of attention to possible cultural continuities in the black family that may be traceable back to slavery as well as to the role of culture in accounting for how black people respond to poverty, indeed, how cultural practices may contribute to either the increase or reduction of poverty.

As Patterson correctly points out, scholars such as W. E. B. Du Bois, E. Franklin Frasier, and Kenneth B. Clark had already established a long tradition of African American scholarship that partly explained the distinctive gender and familial patterns of African Americans as a continuity from slavery. However, following the Moynihan Report, he states, "The ideological and scholarly tie turn sharply away from this claim of continuity toward a denial of any such connection" (Patterson 2004, 71).

The most persuasive and widely cited critique of this view was a book by the historian Herbert G. Gutman, who challenged Moynihan's view that the African American family was weak, disorganized, and matrifocal coming out of slavery. Relying on census data and historical documents, including letters and diaries, Gutman argued that far from being weak, black American families had been strong and resilient after emancipation. In the early twentieth century most were in married-couple families, and a majority of the children were born within marriage. "In the 50 years after emancipation," Gutman wrote, "most African American families were headed by a husband and wife, most eventually married, and most children lived with both parents" (Gutman 1976, 80).

However, two major studies by social scientists from the University of Pennsylvania seriously challenged Gutman's thesis: one by Samuel H. Preston and his colleagues and the other by S. Philip Morgan and his colleagues. Each study is based on national census public use samples that were released after, not before, the publication of Gutman's book. As Preston et al. (1992, 1) point out, these new data sets allow for a more fine-grain analysis of the "consistency of various census items, and of the link among marital status, marital history, current fertility and fertility history." Using these data, Preston et al. demonstrate that Gutman's use of straightforward census tabulations obscures the difference between the black and white communities on marriage and childbearing, and therefore, his portrait of stable African American families in the rural south prior to their mass migration to the urban north is overdrawn.

Following this study, S. Philip Morgan and his colleagues found distinct differences in living arrangements between native-born white and black Americans at the turn of the century that "were geographically pervasive, that are unmistakable in the north and south, in both rural and urban areas" (Morgan et al. 1993, 822). Socioeconomic factors such as poverty, female employment, and the lower earnings of African American males accounted for some of these racial differences, but it was clear from this study that these factors, although clearly necessary to consider, were hardly sufficient to explain these differences.

Indeed, both studies argued that more attention should be given to cultural historical factors. For example, Morgan et al. point out that despite studies showing cultural historical continuity in the linguistic and religious behavior of African Americans, and despite studies of Caribbean societies that take historical and cultural influences on family patterns seriously, "most historians of the African American family have gone to great lengths to discount the possibility of cultural continuity between African and African American family systems" (Morgan et al. 1993, 822).

Morgan and his colleagues note that some contemporary historians have argued that antebellum slavery reinforced the Sub-Saharan African pattern of strong ties and obligations to extended kin. "Despite the absence of any legal standing for slave 'marriage,' slaves were able to maintain strong familial bonds, especially kin bonds. These traditions could make spouse absence and separation more acceptable among African Americans than among whites" (Morgan et al. 1993, 823), and persistent residential segregation and the lack of racial interaction in the socioeconomic and cultural spheres tend to maintain or reinforce such differences. However, from a comparative perspective, it is difficult to follow this reasoning. For example, Mexican Americans also value extended family and yet do not have a high tolerance for paternal absence (W. J. Wilson 1996). Morgan and his colleagues do not address such issues, but they do conclude that an adequate explanation of contemporary African American patterns requires carefully "synthesized arguments that weave together the influence of demographic, socioeconomic, and cultural/historical factors" (Morgan et al. 1993, 824).

A few years later, Orlando Patterson made the same point in his provocative book *Rituals of Blood* (1999). However, in his zeal to demonstrate the importance of cultural continuity, he downplays the importance of socioeconomic factors, such as male joblessness, in accounting for family fragmentation among African Americans, leaving unexplored the puzzle raised by David Ellwood and Christopher Jencks (2002, 22): "why these cultural legacies should suddenly have become more important in the last half of the 20th century."[1] Patterson argues that the economic problems experienced by inner-city residents do not suffi-ciently explain current trends in black family formation. Following Patterson's logic, if historical research suggests cultural/historical continuity in the linguistic and religious behavior of African Americans, we should not dismiss cultural con-tinuity in trying to fully explain family patterns in the African American commu-nity. However, cultural continuities are difficult to substantiate. What are the mechanisms that transmit weak family structure across generations? With lin-guistic and religious traditions it is pretty clear how intergenerational continuity is maintained, especially when families are segregated by race and class and have limited contacts with other groups. However, how does one separate factors influenced by cultural continuities from factors derived from situational and con-textual factors such as joblessness and persistent poverty?[2]

Concerns about cultural continuity are even raised by scholars who have urged that more attention be given to the role of culture in the study of human behav-ior. Their major concern is that the proponents of cultural historical continuity tend to define culture as a specific set of orientations and practices characteristic of a particular group. However, in their perceptive paper on how culture matters for the understanding of poverty, Michèle Lamont and Mario L. Small, two prominent cultural sociologists, question the idea that races or ethnic groups have a culture "in the sense of sets of values or attitudes that all or most mem-bers of a racial or ethnic group share" (Lamont and Small forthcoming).

Pointing out that intragroup differences are often larger than intergroup dif-ferences, they maintain that it is not helpful to speak of an African American cul-ture that differs from an Asian culture or Anglo-American culture in the study of racial differences in poverty. "Instead of imputing a shared culture to groups," argue Lamont and Small (forthcoming), it is better to examine empirically "the range of frames through which people make sense of their reality, and how they use them to orient their action." Lamont and Small further argue that cultural frames do not cause behavior so much as make it possible or likely. In other words, cultural frames are necessary but not sufficient explanations for behavior. For purposes of pursuing a cultural analysis of life and poverty, I fully agree.

The cultural continuity thesis may have merit, but there is not enough evi-dence to corroborate or confirm it at this time. In other words, the relative importance of the combination of cultural continuity and contemporary socio-economic factors in accounting for black family patterns remains an open ques-tion that can be best answered through careful empirical research.

Aside from the lack of attention to cultural continuities, as Lamont and Small correctly point out, only a handful of recent studies seriously examine cultural responses to poverty and how they may affect daily life. One major exception is Kathryn Edin and Maria Kefalas's book on low-income, black, white, and Puerto

Rican single mothers in Camden, New Jersey, one of America's poorest cities, and in eight poor neighborhoods in Philadelphia. Edin and Kefalas (2005) point out that unlike more affluent women, the poor women they studied do not view having a child out of wedlock as ruining their lives, because they feel that their future would be even bleaker without children.

For these women, motherhood is the most important social role they believe they will ever play, and it is the surest source of accomplishment within their reach. Many of the women told Edin and Kefalas that they were headed for trouble until they got pregnant and turned their lives around because of the desire to be good mothers. Many of them said that having children was a life-altering experience and that they could not imagine living without children. Whereas middle-class women put off marriage and childbearing to pursue economic goals, poor women have children in the absence of better opportunities, they point out.

The mothers in this study express confidence in their ability to provide for their children. However, because these mothers frequently fail to recognize the disadvantages that will affect their children's chances in life, this confidence is often unjustified. In this sense their cultural framing of marriage and motherhood not only shapes how they respond to poverty but may also indirectly affect their children's odds of escaping poverty.

Edin and Kefalas's (2005) study provides a compelling argument for examining the role of culture under conditions of chronic economic subordination, and its impact on family life. Their findings on the similar views on motherhood and marriage held by poor African American, Puerto Rican, and white women reinforce Lamont and Small's (forthcoming) argument on meaning-making, namely, that the empirical focus should be on cultural frames that develop in different spatial and contextual circumstances and how they orient action rather than on the shared values of members of a particular racial or ethnic group. Nonetheless, by one logic, every woman in Edin and Kefalas's study—black, white, or Latino—is likely to respond to urban poverty by finding positive meaning in having out-of-wedlock children. By a different logic, the unique historic racial experiences of inner-city blacks may have also influenced their cultural framing of marriage and motherhood in ways that were not captured by Edin and Kefalas. I tend to think that both logics apply—that is, all the women in their study could find meaning and purpose in childrearing in spite of serious financial hardship, and black women would, on balance, have particular views on family formed though the unique circumstance tied to racial segregation. However, I would place far more weight on the former because it reveals that not only blacks, but also other ethnic groups, have responded to conditions of poverty in similar ways. How families are formed among America's poorest citizens is an area that cries out for further research, especially ethnographic research.

However, what about a cultural analysis of life in poverty to help understand the experiences of low-skilled black males, a group that also received much attention in the Moynihan Report? Orlando Patterson (2006) addresses this question head on. He asked, "Why do so many young, unemployed black men have children, several of them which they have no resources or intention to support?" Patterson argues that sociologists need to pay more attention to what has been called the "cool pose culture," which for many young black men is "almost like a drug, hanging out on the street after school, shopping and dressing sharply, sexual conquests, party drugs, hip-hop music and culture" (p. 13).

Patterson maintains that "cool pose culture" blatantly promotes the most anomalous models of behavior in urban lower-class neighborhoods including gangsta rap, predatory sexuality, and irresponsible fatherhood. "It is reasonable to conclude," states Patterson (2000, 204), "that among a large number of urban, Afro-American lower class young men these models are now fully normative, and that men act in accordance with them whenever they can." For example, Patterson argues, male pride has become increasingly defined in terms of the impregnation of women. But this is not unique to the current generation of young black males. Several decades ago, the sociologist Lee Rainwater (1966) uncovered a similar pattern. A majority of the inner-city young black male respondents he interviewed not only stated that they were indifferent to the fact that their girlfriends were pregnant, but some even expressed pride because getting a girl pregnant proves that you are a man. The fact that Elijah Anderson and others discovered identical models decades later suggests the possibility of a pattern of cultural transmission (Anderson 1990; Majors and Billson 1992; Nightingale 1993).

Finally, Patterson (2006) argues that a cultural explanation of black male self-destructiveness not only speaks to the immediate relationship between their attitudes and behavior and the undesirable outcomes, but it also examines their brutalized past, perhaps over generations, to investigate the origins and changing nature of these attitudes. Patterson maintains that we cannot explain the predatory sexuality and irresponsible paternity of young black males without a deep examination of their collective past. But the problem is not simply a lack of attention to culture. The problem is developing a framework that allows one to capture the complexity and multidimensionality of culture.

As Lamont and Small (forthcoming) point out, studies of poverty need to go beyond vague conceptions of culture in terms of group norms, values, and attitudes toward family and work. We also need to examine the micro-level processes of decision making and meaning-making among the poor to not only determine how cultural frames as well as cultural repertoires (habits, styles and skills) are shaped by poverty but also how they, in turn, shape responses to poverty, including those responses that may contribute to the reproduction of poverty.

In many respects, Daniel Patrick Moynihan was trying to move us in the latter direction. His presentation certainly lacked elegance, but it was an attempt to synthesize structural and cultural analyses to understand the dynamics of poor black families and the plight of low-skilled black males. If the work of Lamont and Small is any indication, we may finally be seeing the beginning of a much more sophisticated synthesis of structure and culture, more than forty years after the public release of the Moynihan Report.

Notes

1. Ellwood and Jencks (2004, 52).

2. I thank Tommie Shelby for some of the points raised in this paragraph, private communication, July 10, 2008.

References

Anderson, Elijah. 1990. *Streetwise: Race, class and change in an urban community*. Chicago: University of Chicago Press.

Clark, Kenneth B. 1964. Youth in the ghetto: A study of the consequences of powerlessness and a blueprint for change. Harlem Youth Opportunities (HARYOU) Report, New York.

Edin, Kathryn, and Maria Kefalas. 2005. *A promise I can keep: Why poor women put motherhood before marriage*. Berkeley: University of California Press.

Ellwood, David T., and Christopher Jencks. 2002. The spread of single-parent families in the United States since 1960. Harvard Multidisciplinary Program in Inequality and Social Policy. http://www.hks .harvard.edu/inequality/Seminar/Papers/ElwdJnck.pdf.

———. 2004. The uneven spread of single parent families in the United States. What do we know? Where do we look for answers? In *Social inequality*, ed. Kathryn Neckerman, pp. 3-77. New York: Russell Sage Foundation.

Frazier, E. Franklin. 1939. *The Negro family in the United States*. Chicago: University of Chicago Press.

Gutman, Herbert G. 1976. *The black family in slavery and freedom, 1750-1925*. New York: Pantheon.

Lamont, Michèle, and Mario L. Small. Forthcoming. How culture matters for the understanding of poverty: Enriching our understanding. In *The colors of poverty: Why racial and ethnic disparities exist*, ed. David R. Harris and Ann Chih Lin. New York: Russell Sage Foundation.

Lewis, Oscar. 1959. *Five families: Mexican case studies in the culture of poverty*. New York: Basic Books.

———. 1966. *La Vida: A Puerto Rican family in the culture of poverty in San Juan and New York*. New York: Random House.

———. 1968. The culture of poverty. In *On understanding poverty: Perspectives from the social sciences*, ed. Daniel Patrick Moynihan, 187-220. New York: Basic Books.

Majors, Richard, and Janet Billson. 1992. *Cool pose*. Lexington, MA: Heath.

Morgan, S. Philip, Antonio McDaniel, Andrew Miller, and Samuel Preston. 1993. Racial differences in household and family structure at the turn of the century. *American Journal of Sociology* 98:798-828.

Moynihan, Daniel P. 1965. *The Negro family: The case for national action*. Washington, DC: Office of Policy Planning and Research, U.S. Department of Labor. http://www.dol.gov/oasam/programs/history/ webid-meynihan.htm.

Nightingale, Carl. 1993. *On the edge: A history of poor black children and their American dream*. New York: Basic Books.

O'Connor, Alice. 2001. *Poverty and knowledge: Social science, social policy, and the poor in twentieth-century U.S. history*. Princeton, NJ: Princeton University Press.

Patterson, Orlando. 1999. *Rituals of blood: Consequences of slavery in two American centuries*. New York: Basic Books.

———. 2000. Taking culture seriously: A framework and Afro-American illustration. In *Culture matters: How values shape human progress*, ed. Lawrence E. Harrison and Samuel P. Huntington, 202-218. New York: Basic Books.

———. 2004. Culture and continuity: Causal structures in socio-cultural persistence. In *Matters of culture: Cultural sociology in practice*, 71-109. New York: Cambridge University Press.

———. 2006. A poverty of the mind. *New York Times*, March 26. http://www.nytimes.com/2006/03/26/ opinion/26patterson.html.

Preston, Samuel H., Irma T. Elo, Mark E. Hill, and Ira Rosenwaike. 1992. *The demography of African Americans, 1930-1990*. New York: Springer.

Rainwater, Lee. 1966. Crucible of identity: The Negro lower-class family. *Daedalus* 95 (Winter): 176-216.

Rainwater, Lee, and William L. Yancey. 1967. *The Moynihan report and the politics of controversy.* Cambridge, MA: MIT Press.

Rustin, Bayard. 1965. From protest to politics: The future of the civil rights movement. *Commentary* 39:25-31.

Ryan, William. 1971. *Blaming the victim.* New York: Pantheon.

U.S. Census Bureau. 1996. Current Population Survey. Washington, DC: Government Printing Office.

———. 2006. Current Population Survey. Washington, DC: Government Printing Office.

U.S. Department of Health and Human Services. 2000. *Nonmarital childbearing in the United States, 1940-1999.* National Vital Statistics Reports, vol. 48, no. 16. Washington, DC: Government Printing Office.

———. 2006. *Births: Preliminary data for 2005.* Washington, DC: Government Printing Office.

U.S. Department of Health, Education, and Welfare. 1974. *Trends in illegitimacy: 1940-1965.* National Vital Statistics System, series 21, no. 15. Washington, DC: Government Printing Office.

Wilson, James Q. 2008. Foreword: Pat Moynihan thinks about families. *The Annals of the American Academy of Political and Social Science* 621:28-33.

Wilson, William Julius. 1996. *When work disappears: The world of the new urban poor.* New York: Knopf.

The Labor Market and Young Black Men: Updating Moynihan's Perspective

By
HARRY J. HOLZER

This article reviews Daniel Patrick Moynihan's views on employment and young black men in his 1965 report. The author then updates the evidence on their employment status and reviews the causes and policy implications of these trends. Moynihan was extremely insightful and even prescient in arguing that the employment situation of young black men was a "crisis . . . that would only grow worse." He understood that these trends involve both limits on labor market opportunities that these young men face as well as skill deficits of and behavioral responses by the young men themselves. Policies that deal with a wide range of disadvantages and behaviors are needed to reverse these trends.

Keywords: Daniel Patrick Moynihan; *The Negro Family*; employment; black men; labor market

In his 1965 report on the status of black families in America, Daniel Patrick Moynihan referred to the employment situation of young black men as an "unconcealable crisis. . . . This problem will now become steadily more serious." He also identified this situation as a primary cause of the instability of black families that he documented in the report and as a priority for any public policies that

Harry J. Holzer is a professor of public policy at Georgetown University and a senior fellow at the Urban Institute in Washington, D.C. He is a former chief economist for the U.S. Department of Labor, a senior affiliate of the National Poverty Center at the University of Michigan, and a research affiliate of the Institute for Research on Poverty at the University of Wisconsin–Madison. His books include The Black Youth Employment Crisis *(coedited with Richard Freeman; University of Chicago Press 1986);* What Employers Want: Job Prospects for Less-Educated Workers *(Russell Sage Foundation 1996);* Employers and Welfare Recipients: The Effects of Welfare Reform in the Workplace *(with Michael Stoll; Public Policy Institute of California 2001:);* Reconnecting Disadvantaged Young Men *(with Peter Edelman and Paul Offner; Urban Institute Press 2006); and* Reshaping the American Workforce in a Changing Economy *(coedited with Demetra Nightingale; Urban Institute Press 2007).*

DOI: 10.1177/0002716208324627

might seek to stabilize black families. How correct was Moynihan's prognosis of a steadily growing crisis in the employment of young black men? Was his analysis of the problem accurate, both in the mid-1960s and in subsequent decades? What additional factors that he did not foresee affect the employment outcomes of young black men? And what does all of this imply for public policy?

In this article, I review Moynihan's perspective on the employment problems of young black men in 1965 and what we have learned from empirical research on this topic since then. I begin in the next section by documenting Moynihan's perspective, and then in subsequent parts of the article I review more recent trends and empirical evidence on their causes. I conclude with some thoughts on what all of this implies for public policy. I argue that Moynihan's views in 1965 were insightful and stunningly prescient, as the employment situation of young black men has steadily deteriorated since then. He correctly identified many of the causes of this problem, though some economic and social forces and trends were impossible to foresee at that time. The appropriate policy prescriptions today are thus somewhat broader than what he argued for at the time, though still fairly consistent with his overall views.

Moynihan's Perspective on Black Male Employment

Chapter 3 of the Moynihan Report (1965) focuses on "The Roots of the Problem," and in a subsection titled "Unemployment and Poverty," he focuses on employment issues involving young black men. He continues this focus in chapter 4 ("The Tangle of Pathology"). Moynihan first documents the growing rate of black male unemployment (especially relative to white males) from 1930 to 1963. He notes that, despite the overall prosperity of the economy during the year 1963, "29.2 percent of all Negro men in the labor force were unemployed at some time during the year. Almost half of these men were out of work 15 weeks or more." While he focuses primarily on *unemployment* throughout the report, Moynihan later notes an additional trend of rising *nonparticipation* in the labor force among these men—and the emergence of a small gap in the participation rate of black men relative to white men (75.8 vs. 78 percent in 1964).

Moynihan documents the extent to which black men were falling behind black women in the 1960s (and earlier) in educational attainment and occupational status. He notes that young black men were more likely to drop out of high school, less likely to attend college, and less likely to enter white-collar occupations than young black women as of the 1960s.[1] He also notes (though without much empirical documentation) a deteriorating knowledge of the world of work and of informal connections to the labor market, and especially to jobs in and training for the skilled crafts and other well-paying blue-collar jobs, among young men growing up in fatherless families. A rising trend in crime and "delinquency" among these young men receives a fair amount of attention as well, and of course, he emphasizes a strong empirical correlation between trends in joblessness and other social indicators for black men, on one hand, and the growth of female-headed families in the black community, on the other, throughout the report.

Moynihan notes, of course, that educational attainment and occupational status were rising for the black community overall in the aftermath of the "Negro American Revolution" that culminated in the passage of the Civil Rights Act of 1964. But to what does he attribute the growing employment problems of young black men in America, especially among those who are not growing up in middle-class families? At various places in the report, Moynihan argues that "jobs became more and more difficult to find" (chap. 3) and further that "discouragement about finding a job" has driven the downward trends in labor force participation among young black men (chap. 4). But in the middle of a great postwar boom, why should their abilities to find work have declined?

In the report, Moynihan attributes employment problems to a "lack of training and opportunity," which he also argues grows more serious over time as the occupational structure of the economy changes and jobs require more education. He also repeatedly acknowledges the important role of discrimination and various ills associated with growing up in segregated urban environments. He notes a growing "alienation" among young men along with a set of psychological and emotional issues (such as a lack of a "minimal sense of competence," a "low tolerance for frustration," and the like). Thus, Moynihan notes the effects of employer characteristics and behavior in the broader labor market as well as those of the young men themselves in accounting for employment trends over time.

Also, Moynihan clearly regards the deterioration of the black family as a very serious force leading to less opportunity for young black men. In his view, fatherless families in the black community are initially rooted in the experience of slavery and then northern urbanization in twentieth-century America. Over time, the absence of fathers in so many households leads to weaker skill attainment, growing participation in crime, and growing "alienation" among young black men. These forces, along with the persistence of discrimination and racism, lead to a further deterioration of the position of black men in the labor market and the family, thus creating a continuing downward cycle of pathology. In this view, fatherless families are both an effect and a major cause of the growing deterioration of employment opportunities among low-income urban young black men in the United States.

The Trends since 1965 and Their Causes

How have the trends in employment outcomes among young black men evolved since 1965? What are the major causes of these trends? To what extent was Moynihan's prognosis of growing employment problems accurate, as well as his diagnosis of their origins? I address these questions below.

Employment trends and other outcomes

Unfortunately, it is clear that Moynihan's prognosis of steadily deteriorating employment outcomes among young black men was stunningly accurate, perhaps

TABLE 1
EMPLOYMENT AND UNEMPLOYMENT RATES AMONG BLACK AND WHITE
MALE YOUTH, 1964-1981

Age	Blacks and Other Nonwhites				Whites			
	1964	1969	1977	1981	1964	1969	1977	1981
Percentage of the population employed								
16–17	27.6	28.4	18.9	17.9	36.5	42.7	44.3	41.2
18–19	51.8	51.1	36.9	34.5	57.7	61.8	65.2	61.4
20–24	78.1	77.3	61.2	58.0	79.3	78.8	80.5	76.9
25–54	87.8	89.7	81.7	78.6	94.4	95.1	91.3	90.5
Percentage of the labor force unemployed								
16–17	25.9	24.7	38.4	40.1	16.1	12.5	17.6	19.9
18–19	23.1	19.0	35.4	36.0	13.4	7.9	13.0	16.4
20–24	12.6	8.4	21.4	24.4	7.4	4.6	9.3	11.6
25–54	6.6	2.8	7.8	10.1	2.8	1.5	3.9	4.8

SOURCE: Adapted from Freeman and Holzer (1986, 7).

to an even greater extent than he realized at the time. Table 1 documents the decline of employment and rise of unemployment for black men in various age groups between 1964 and 1981.[2] The table indicates very clearly that employment rates are declining and unemployment rates rising among black men throughout this period, to some extent regardless of the state of the aggregate U.S. economy.[3] While labor force outcomes of prime-age black men improve with the economy between 1964 and 1969, they deteriorate afterward to a greater extent than do those of white men. All of this occurs despite the general improvement in relative earnings for blacks that has been well documented for this period, at least for the decade after 1964.[4]

But the declines are greatest among *young* black men, especially relative to those of young white men. Although school enrollment rises for young men of both racial groups in this period, employment rates hold steady or improve somewhat for young white men, while they deteriorate dramatically for their black counterparts. The data also imply that labor force participation, both in absolute and relative terms, is declining for young black men throughout this period.[5]

Trends in employment and labor force activity for young black and white men (as well as Hispanics) between approximately 1980 and 2005 are further documented in Figure 1. The samples here are limited to those in the civilian noninstitutional population, aged sixteen through twenty-four, who are not enrolled in school and have attained only a high school diploma or less.[6] Part A presents trends in employment/population rates, while part B presents trends in labor force participation.

The results show that both the employment and labor force activity of young black men have deteriorated since 1980. While employment rates show some

FIGURE 1
A. EMPLOYMENT RATES OF SIXTEEN-
TO TWENTY-FOUR-YEAR-OLDS, 1979-2005

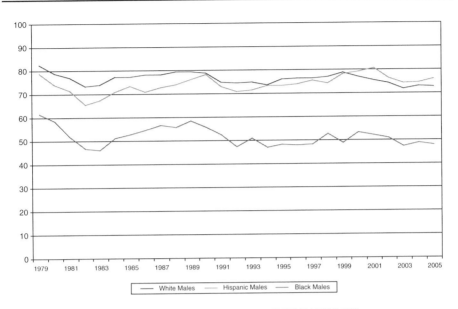

B. LABOR FORCE PARTICIPATION RATES OF
SIXTEEN- TO TWENTY-FOUR-YEAR-OLDS, 1979-2005

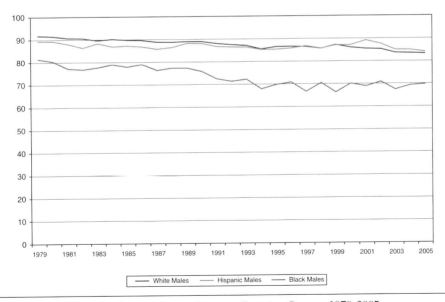

SOURCE: Current Population Surveys, Outgoing Rotation Groups, 1979-2005.
NOTE: The samples include only those not enrolled in school and with a high school diploma
or less.

sensitivity to the business cycle (with downturns in the early 1980s, early 1990s, and early 2000s that correspond to periods of recession), clearly a secular decline in employment occurs for young blacks as well as a widening gap between their employment rates and those of less educated whites and Hispanics. The trends are even more noticeable when considering labor force participation, which is a less cyclical outcome for young men.

If anything, the downward trends in employment and labor force activity are even stronger in the 1990s than in the 1980s—despite the very strong economy of the latter period.[7] Furthermore, the 1990s were a decade of dramatic improvement in labor force activity of young black women, due to welfare reform and the growth of work supports like the Earned Income Tax Credit (Blank 2002). These trends were most dramatic for the least-educated black women, especially single mothers. In other words, while these women were pouring into the labor market, their male counterparts continued to pour out.[8] And if anything, the trends in Figure 1 understate the deterioration of employment among young black men, as the surveys are limited to the civilian noninstitutional population, thereby omitting the growing fraction of the black male population that was incarcerated during this time period; had they been included in the denominators of the measured outcomes, the observed downward trends would have no doubt been worse.

Before moving on to consider the causes of these developments, we briefly review some other trends. Table 2 presents data on educational and behavioral outcomes among youth born between 1980 and 1984. These data are drawn from the 1997 cohort of the National Longitudinal Survey of Youth (NLSY97). All outcomes are presented separately by race and gender.[9] The outcomes considered include the likelihood of dropping out of high school, enrolling in a four-year college, or attaining a four-year college degree; grade point averages and percentile scores on standardized tests; the likelihood of having children outside of marriage; and rates of incarceration.[10]

The data in Table 2 indicate, not surprisingly, that educational outcomes among minority youth lag behind those of whites. Interestingly, these outcomes for young women are better than those of young men in each age group—indicating a growing "gender gap" in education in favor of females (Jacob 2002). Minority youth are also more likely to have children outside of marriage and to become incarcerated. But the data also indicate that, for virtually each outcome considered, young black men now lag behind every other race and gender group in the United States.[11] Indeed, young black men are the group most likely to drop out of high school and least likely to attend (and graduate from) college; their achievement, as measured by grades and test scores, is the lowest; and they are most likely to become incarcerated for criminal activity.

These facts are striking, especially given that the Hispanic population is now heavily populated by first-generation immigrants with fairly little formal schooling, at least some of whom are captured in the NLSY97. The growing gaps in many outcomes between young black men and women are also quite striking; and of course, the tendency of young black men to be incarcerated is not even fully captured here, as data from the Bureau of Justice Statistics (BJS) indicate that

TABLE 2
MEAN EDUCATIONAL AND BEHAVIORAL OUTCOMES OF YOUTH: NLSY97

	Males			Females		
	White	Black	Hispanic	White	Black	Hispanic
High school GPA	2.47	1.86	2.05	2.66	2.18	2.34
ASVAB (percentile)	57.34	28.14	39.39	58.20	32.01	38.76
Not enrolled in school (%)						
High school dropout/GED	13.37	27.60	20.79	12.03	19.00	20.55
Bachelor's degree	12.81	5.57	3.63	18.15	6.89	5.52
Enrolled in four-year college (%)	17.17	9.66	10.11	18.97	14.40	13.21
Unmarried, has children (%)	9.9	30.8	17.9	17.3	47.5	29.6
Ever incarcerated (%)	7.6	14.8	9.6	2.7	3.1	2.4

SOURCE: Hill, Holzer, and Chen (forthcoming).
NOTE: Samples include respondents ages twenty-two to twenty-four at the time of the interview. Variables were measured in round 8 of the 1997 cohort of the National Longitudinal Survey of Youth (NLSY97), from October 2004 to July 2005. Enrollment is measured in the month of November. The percentages of young people enrolled and not enrolled in school, including some categories not listed in the table (like those out of school with high school diplomas or some college and those enrolled in two-year colleges), all sum to one. The ASVAB, or Armed Service Vocational Aptitude Battery score, is measured as a percentile of the overall distribution of scores.

more than a third of all young black men are now incarcerated, on parole, or on probation at any point in time (Raphael 2007). At least some comparisons with data from the earlier cohorts of the NLSY (i.e., from 1979) indicate a greater relative deterioration in outcomes among young black men than for any other group (Hill, Holzer, and Chen forthcoming).

The NLSY97 data also indicate that, by the end of the twentieth century, only about 20 percent of all black youth are growing up in two-parent families (compared to more than half of young whites and Hispanics).[12] And the outcomes observed among those growing up without both parents, and especially those with never-married mothers, clearly lag behind those observed for those growing up in two-parent families. Table 3 presents the estimated effects of growing up without both biological parents on the observed outcomes of youth blacks, from regressions that include a variety of control variables, estimated both without and with controls for family income. In other words, these results show the estimated effect of youth growing up in some type of single-parent family at age twelve, relative to growing up with both biological parents, on the probability of achieving a certain outcome.[13]

The results indicate that those growing up without both biological parents have less education, less achievement, greater likelihood of parenting out of marriage, and greater likelihood of becoming incarcerated than those growing up with both parents. The observed outcomes are generally worst among those with

TABLE 3
EFFECTS OF HOUSEHOLD STRUCTURE ON OUTCOMES FOR YOUNG BLACKS: COEFFICIENTS FROM ESTIMATED REGRESSIONS WITHOUT AND WITH CONTROLS FOR PARENTAL INCOME

	High School Dropout/GED		Enrolled in Four-Year College or Not Enrolled, Bachelor's Degree or More		High School GPA	
	1	2	1	2	1	2
At age twelve, sample member lived with (omitted: two biological parents)						
Mother, never married	0.124***	0.088**	−0.153***	−0.109***	−0.291***	−0.204***
	(0.033)	(0.034)	(0.030)	(0.032)	(0.066)	(0.066)
Mother, had been married, no spouse in household	0.110***	0.078**	−0.114***	−0.072**	−0.130**	−0.060
	(0.030)	(0.032)	(0.033)	(0.035)	(0.062)	(0.062)
Mother and her spouse	0.039	0.021	−0.099***	−0.077**	−0.127**	−0.093
	(0.029)	(0.029)	(0.033)	(0.033)	(0.062)	(0.062)
Father	0.039	0.026	−0.071	−0.056	−0.362***	−0.341***
	(0.053)	(0.052)	(0.059)	(0.058)	(0.105)	(0.102)
Other	0.090**	0.061	−0.122***	−0.086**	−0.060	0.003
	(0.039)	(0.040)	(0.036)	(0.037)	(0.077)	(0.078)
Average family income included	No	Yes	No	Yes	No	Yes
Observations	1,964	1,964	1,964	1,964	1,521	1,521
R-squared	.155	.164	.139	.152	.189	.203

(continued)

TABLE 3 (CONTINUED)

	ASVAB		Unmarried with a Child		Ever Incarcerated	
	1	2	1	2	1	2
At age twelve, sample member lived with (omitted: two biological parents)						
Mother, never married	-8.217°°°	-4.258°°	0.089°°	0.055	0.079°°°	0.073°°°
	(1.821)	(1.816)	(0.036)	(0.037)	(0.018)	(0.019)
Mother, had been married, no spouse in household	-7.456°°°	-3.502°	0.144°°°	0.109°°°	0.054°°°	0.049°°°
	(1.933)	(1.933)	(0.036)	(0.037)	(0.018)	(0.018)
Mother and her spouse	-3.461°	-1.379	0.065°	0.045	0.040°°	0.037°°
	(1.858)	(1.789)	(0.034)	(0.035)	(0.016)	(0.016)
Father	-3.747	-1.479	0.084	0.062	0.047	0.045
	(3.323)	(3.056)	(0.066)	(0.066)	(0.037)	(0.038)
Other	-5.356°°	-2.108	0.107°°	0.077°	0.073°°°	0.069°°°
	(2.210)	(2.228)	(0.044)	(0.044)	(0.024)	(0.025)
Average family income included	No	Yes	No	Yes	No	Yes
Observations	1,793	1,793	1,960	1,960	2,028	2,028
R-squared	.206	.240	.110	.117	.367	.368

SOURCE: Hill, Holzer, and Chen (forthcoming).

NOTE: Robust standard errors clustered by family are shown in parentheses. The outcomes are drawn from the variables listed in Table 2; all are dichotomous except for grade point average (GPA) and Armed Service Vocational Aptitude Battery (ASVAB) percentile score. Variables are measured in round 8 of the 1997 cohort of the National Longitudinal Survey of Youth (NLSY97), from October 2004 to July 2005. Average family income is measured from ages fourteen to fifteen for the 1982 to 1984 birth cohorts and from sixteen to seventeen for the 1980 to 1981 birth cohorts. Control variables include respondent's age at round 8 interview, mother's age when she had her first child, whether mother is an immigrant, number of siblings in the respondent's household at age sixteen, mother's educational attainment, mother's hours worked, month of round 8 interview, and respondent's household structure at age twelve. Missing data dummies were included for all explanatory variables except for race/gender.

°p < .10. °°p < .05. °°°p < .01.

55

never-married mothers. Adjusting for family income accounts for some, though by no means all, of these results.[14] Given the very large fraction of young blacks growing up in these families—for reasons that are discussed below—these results suggest that changing family structure contributes somewhat to negative employment, educational, and behavioral outcomes in the black community overall.[15]

Of course, the extent to which the observed effects of family structure on these outcomes are causal remains very controversial. In my view, some parts of the observed estimates are clearly causal and some are not (Hill, Holzer, and Chen forthcoming).[16] Furthermore, young black girls and women are growing up in the same families as are young boys and men, though their outcomes show some relative improvement. We have some evidence that any negative effects of household structure on black young males may be more serious than those for black young females.[17]

In sum, the data indicate that employment outcomes of young black men continue to deteriorate over time, while their educational and behavioral outcomes lag behind those of all other demographic groups in the United States. Outcomes for those growing up in single-parent families are worst of all, and the rising fraction of young blacks growing up in such families likely contributes somewhat to these outcomes. Moynihan certainly foresaw many of these trends and developments, although even he was likely surprised and dismayed by their extent at the close of the twentieth century.

What explains the trends?

If Moynihan was disconcertingly prescient in his prediction that employment outcomes of young black men would steadily worsen over time, especially for those in fatherless families, how do his explanations of these trends hold up over time, in light of several decades of subsequent empirical analysis by social scientists? Implicit in Moynihan's discussion is the notion that, broadly speaking, two sets of forces affect employment opportunities and outcomes for young black men: (1) *labor demand factors*, including employer attitudes and hiring behaviors toward black men, and (2) *labor supply factors*, including family formation and skill development, which themselves can be responsive to characteristics of and/or changes in the demand side of the labor market.

My view of how these factors interact, and their resulting effects on employment outcomes, appears in Figure 2. The chart denotes an inward shift in labor demand for a set of workers along a labor supply curve that is elastic—that is, responsive to available wages. The inward shift in demand can reflect a gap in employer demand across groups of workers (such as whites and blacks) at a point in time or a downward shift in demand for a particular group (such as less educated black men) over time. Either way, black men respond to their (increasingly) weak employment opportunities by withdrawing from the labor market altogether—perhaps before they even enter the market.

Furthermore, a range of additional behaviors seems to characterize these young men as they withdraw—such as growing participation in illegal activities,

FIGURE 2
LABOR DEMAND SHIFTS AND LABOR SUPPLY RESPONSE

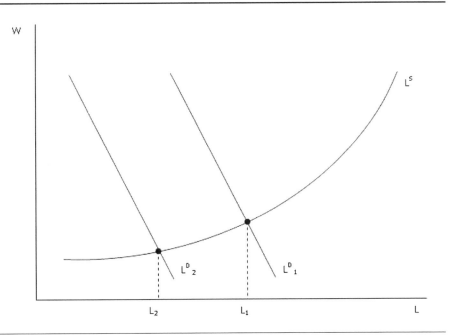

a declining tendency to marry, and even a tendency to "disconnect" from school and other mainstream behaviors at a relatively early age (Edelman, Holzer, and Offner 2006). The elastic labor supply curve reflects the tendency of these young men to withdraw from the labor market, and from other mainstream behavioral norms and institutions, as the labor market opportunities they face lag behind those of other groups or further deteriorate.

Moynihan's report clearly notes some factors that cause employer demand for blacks to lag behind that for whites, and some of these factors are worsening over time. They include

- employer demand for skills, which are growing over time (through an evolving occupational structure);
- employer discrimination against black men;
- the effects of urban segregation on employer demand; and
- employer reliance on informal networks to generate job applicants and trainees.

On all of these issues, empirical research has borne out Moynihan's analysis. For example, my earlier cross-sectional analysis of employers (Holzer 1996, 2001) documents that employers are generally more averse to hiring black male applicants than those from any other racial/gender group, especially in jobs requiring social/verbal skills and in service (relative to blue-collar) occupations; that the tendency of employers to locate farther away from the central city generates a "spatial mismatch" for those blacks who continue to reside in segregated, central-city neighborhoods and who lack transportation to and information about suburban opportunities; and that employers frequently use informal methods, especially employee referrals, to fill jobs that require relatively little formal education, often to the detriment of young blacks. The work of many other authors in this body of literature tends to corroborate these findings.[18]

But Moynihan clearly did not foresee—nor did anyone else, for that matter—the dramatic changes in the structure of labor demand that would further curtail labor market opportunities for less educated black men, especially in the 1970s and beyond. William Julius Wilson (1987) and John Kasarda (1985) were among the first to note that rapidly declining employment in manufacturing was disproportionately hurting employment of less educated urban black men, though this occurred more in the Midwest than elsewhere (Bound and Holzer 1993).

But the wages of less educated men in all race/gender groups were falling in that period, even within manufacturing and other industries, for reasons (such as technological change, globalization, and changing institutions) that have been widely analyzed in the past two decades (e.g., Levy and Murnane 1992; Danziger and Gottschalk 1995).[19] Juhn (1992) has shown that declining wages of less educated men in the 1970s and 1980s have led to significant labor market withdrawals for all of these groups. Were these wage effects larger for black men than for those in other racial groups? In a labor market that increasingly rewards cognitive skills, even a modestly declining but still substantial achievement gap between blacks and other groups might generate a growing wage gap between them and other groups—as Derek Neal has argued (Neal and Johnson 1996).

Most analyses show that wages for less educated black men fell no more than did wages of other less educated groups in that period; and Juhn (1992) documents a much greater decline in labor force activity among black men than among others in response to a given wage decline. But it is also likely that wage data understate the relative deterioration for black men, given the growing truncation of the bottom of the wage distribution for this group (Chandra 2003). Once we account for this truncation, the deterioration of opportunities for young black men were likely larger than those that occurred for other groups—and any deterioration of wage opportunities for black men occurred on top of a lengthy list of continuing disadvantages in the labor market that are noted above, implying perhaps that the demand shifts pushed many young black men beyond a threshold below which many were simply unwilling to continue working in regular jobs.

The tendency of less educated young men, and especially black men, to withdraw from the workforce in response to declining wages is another area where Moynihan's analysis falls somewhat short. Indeed, Moynihan clearly notes that labor force withdrawals occur due to "discouragement" about finding employment. But labor market withdrawal might occur not only in response to declining job opportunities in general, but especially those at wages considered minimally acceptable to the potential jobseeker. As wage opportunities decline relative to the "reservation wages" of those seeking work, labor market withdrawal becomes more likely—perhaps before labor market entrance even occurs.

Furthermore, it is likely that reservation wages (the lowest wage rate at which a worker would be willing to accept a particular type of job) of young black men also rose over time (Holzer 1986)—especially during the 1960s, as their own expectations rose;[20] and then in the 1980s, as alternative means of generating income for young men became relatively more lucrative and also more acceptable.[21] In particular, Freeman (1991) first noted that, as the wages to legal work for less educated men were declining in the 1970s and 1980s, those to illegal work were rising—particularly during the boom in the crack cocaine trade. Consistent with Becker (1968), most economists would expect that, all else equal, more men would choose "employment" in the illegal relative to the legal sector under these circumstances. And this is exactly what occurred during the 1980s.[22]

In Moynihan's view, growing crime and delinquency represented a "tangle of pathology" and some deterioration in the psychological well-being of many young men. More recently, others (e.g., Ferguson 2001; Patterson 2006; Mead 2007) have noted the growth of an "oppositional culture" among young black boys and adolescents that precedes or precludes their entrance in the labor market and correspondingly leads them to engage in crime, out-of-wedlock fatherhood, and other nonmainstream behaviors. The fact that so many more of these young men are growing up in families and neighborhoods in which fathers are absent might further contribute to the development of these behaviors, in this view.

Indeed, such a deterioration in attitudes, values, and "culture" has probably occurred among young black men—although the few attempts I know of to directly measure these characteristics have generated mixed evidence.[23] But if it has occurred, it also seems quite likely that this development is not completely exogenous to labor market developments. In other words, as the relative rewards to mainstream legal work of less educated young black men have declined, so has their own attachment to the mainstream worlds of school and work and to mainstream behaviors and values more broadly (Wilson 1987, 1996).

This view implies that behavioral and cultural trends among urban black men are fueled by the perception that legitimate economic opportunities are disappearing. These perceptions, in turn, encourage young black boys and adolescents to disengage from mainstream institutions very early in life and to engage in behaviors that ultimately foreclose their future options. These behaviors are thus not necessarily economically rational for any given individual over the long run, or for the community as a whole. But declining marriage rates over time and rising rates of births outside marriage, as well as rising crime and incarceration, might be at least partly explained within this context.[24]

Of course, as the rewards to educational attainment grow, so do their incentives to gain *more* education—which has occurred, to some extent, among young blacks as well as other demographic groups. But for those who become skeptical, at an early age, of their ability to attain labor market success at any level of education—perhaps because of the poor and segregated schools that they attend and the complete absence of successful male role models in their families and neighborhoods—the social and economic inducements to withdraw might outweigh those to remain attached to school and work (Edelman, Holzer, and Offner 2006). Under these circumstances, an "oppositional culture" is especially likely to develop, which then generates self-defeating behaviors and a self-fulfilling prophecy of failure in the mainstream world, thus reinforcing the economic factors leading to disengagement in the first place.

["Oppositional cultures" can generate] self-defeating behaviors and a self-fulfilling prophecy of failure in the mainstream world, thus reinforcing the economic factors leading to disengagement in the first place.

The 1990s and Beyond

The list of labor market demand shifts and supply responses noted above seem broadly consistent with labor market trends of young black men over time and fairly consistent with Moynihan's original (though somewhat incomplete) formulation. But these explanations alone have some difficulty fully explaining the most recent trends in employment among young black men—especially during the 1990s. For one thing, the 1990s—and especially the latter half of the decade—generated the strongest and tightest labor markets in thirty years. Real wage growth resumed for all workers and particularly for those at the bottom of the earnings distribution (Autor, Katz, and Kearney 2005). Furthermore, crime rates dropped precipitously, and other measures of black disadvantage (such as residential segregation and associated spatial mismatch in the labor market) showed some modest improvement as well. All else equal, this should certainly have produced rising employment and labor market activity among young blacks—not only relative to that observed in the slack labor markets of the early 1990s (Freeman and Rodgers 1999) but also relative to the 1970s and 1980s.

Despite some cyclical improvement in employment rates, however, the long-term secular decline in employment and labor force activity among less educated young black men continued and perhaps even accelerated (Holzer and Offner 2006). So what else might have accounted for these trends? My coauthors and I (Holzer, Offner, and Sorenson 2005) largely attribute these continuing secular trends to two new forces that became much more salient in the 1990s than earlier: (1) the growing percentage of young black men with criminal records and (2) work disincentives associated with the child support system.

The rising tendency of young black men to become involved in illegal activities, along with changes in criminal justice policy, have generated a dramatic rise in incarceration rates for this population. These developments have also generated a new phenomenon: a dramatic rise in the prevalence of ex-offenders in the black male population. Absent strong data on this phenomenon, Freeman (2003) has estimated that more than 20 percent of the black male population might have criminal records at this point. The rates might well be considerably higher among young men in their thirties and forties, who are most likely to have been incarcerated by the mid-1990s. And while many of these men recidivate and become incarcerated once again after their initial release, ultimately most are released again and eventually age out of serious crime (Travis 2005).

Employers are extremely reluctant to hire men with criminal records, especially for jobs that require contact with customers, handling cash, or other skills requiring employer trust (Holzer, Raphael, and Stoll 2004; Pager 2003). Employer fear of legal liabilities no doubt reinforces this behavior, as do a variety of state laws that prohibit employers from hiring those with criminal records into particular sectors of the economy. Employers increasingly can check criminal records online at little cost, though questions remain about the accuracy of these checks.

Employers who do not check backgrounds and have more difficulty distinguishing offenders from nonoffenders have a tendency to avoid hiring young black men more broadly, in a form of "statistical discrimination" based on a lack of individual-specific information (Holzer, Raphael, and Stoll 2006). Indeed, such an aversion might well account for Pager's (2003) finding that young black male applicants who do not directly report having criminal records and young white men who do report them are treated similarly by employers, and though it is not always clear that such employer aversion and discrimination actually reduce observed employment outcomes for the affected groups, most recent empirical analysis on this subject suggests that it does for young black men with criminal records.[25]

Of course, these demand-side factors only reinforce the many supply-side factors that also tend to drive these men out of the labor market—such as their very poor skills, substance abuse problems, lack of informal networks and supports, and personal feelings of discouragement and alienation. With some assistance, many or even most of these men can find some employment—but usually at very low wages and with little hope of advancement. Under these circumstances, rates of job retention are low and ultimate labor market withdrawal is frequent.

As for the child support system, recent estimates suggest that up to half of all young black men have become noncustodial fathers by their early thirties (Holzer, Offner, and Sorenson 2005). The much more strenuous enforcement of child support laws over the past two decades might certainly provide incentive for many noncustodial fathers to participate more frequently in the labor market, rather than less; much depends on the effectiveness of enforcement activities at the state level.

On the other hand, for low-income young men who have fallen into "arrears" on their payments, the "tax rate" on their legitimate earnings is enormous—in fact, up to 50 percent of their gross earnings. Moreover, if some or all of these payments are not "passed through" to their families, the analogy of child support orders to taxes become even more accurate. In these cases, the incentives might be for low-income men to avoid work—especially if they can escape detection and enforcement activities—because their labor supply is responsive to net wages.

Of course, these explanations seem most convincing for men in their thirties and beyond, but they might have little direct relevance to the teens and youth whose behavior has been captured in the NLSY. Given the terrible price ultimately paid by somewhat older black men who disconnect from school and work and eventually become incarcerated, why do the behaviors of younger black men in their adolescent and teen years not respond and become more positive? Should not the examples of older men generate enough incentive for their younger counterparts to go a different route?

The recurrence of disconnection among young black men, given the experiences of their older male counterparts, remains something of a conundrum. But I would speculate that, as these very young men develop expectations of their future labor market prospects, based in part on what they observe among their fathers, uncles, older brothers, and neighbors, they come to regard the odds of their own future success as being very low, regardless of what they do. If so, their tendency to withdraw from the mainstream world, and to generate a reality of failure, is further reinforced.

Conclusion and Policy Implications

The analysis above suggests that Daniel Patrick Moynihan was quite prescient about trends in the employment of young black men beyond 1965. His view at the time was quite pessimistic—he perceived a crisis in employment for this group, one that would only worsen with time. Subsequent trends have certainly borne out his pessimism, despite the huge gains associated with the civil rights movement in the period from 1965 to 1975.

Daniel Patrick Moynihan was quite prescient about trends in the employment of young black men beyond 1965.

Moynihan also understood, and implicitly acknowledged in his report, that observed employment outcomes of young blacks represent a range of factors and trends on the demand side of the labor market, those involving employers and their hiring patterns. They also reflect those on the supply side, involving the skills and behaviors of the young men themselves and how they responded to these demand trends. He correctly noted the effects of growing employer skill needs (and continuing racial gaps in skills), persisting discrimination, urban segregation, and informal networks on black male employment; and he correctly foresaw growing participation in crime and noncustodial fatherhood in this population, as well as a tendency for young black men to withdraw from the labor market altogether.

On the other hand, neither Moynihan nor anyone else of that time could foresee the extent to which legitimate labor markets would deteriorate for all less educated young men, and especially black men, in the 1970s and beyond. He also did not foresee the booming of the market for illegal activities, especially the crack cocaine trade, in the 1980s—and the distortion of incentives to work that would be generated by these developments. Although he predicted growing joblessness and crime over time, the magnitude of these developments—and the ultimate entanglement of a third of all young black men in the criminal justice system, as well as up to one-half of them in the child support system—no doubt surprised (and depressed) him as well. The "tangle of pathology" that he described for a minority of these young men ultimately became a much broader phenomenon, involving economic rewards and behaviors, and associated attitudes and values, for entire communities.

What does all of this imply for public policy? In the 1960s, Moynihan argued for public jobs programs for less educated men on a large scale—a recommendation that President Lyndon B. Johnson largely rejected in formulating his War on Poverty programs.[26] Ultimately, he argued for a program of guaranteed annual incomes through a negative income tax, though welfare reform took a very different path in the 1990s. Even job training programs, and especially their public employment components, shrank in scale and scope after the 1970s and have not recovered to date (Spence and Kiel 2003).

What is now needed, in my view, is a more comprehensive set of policies designed to counter the negative trends in labor force opportunities and behaviors that have come to pass since that time (Edelman, Holzer, and Offner 2006). The goal of these policies would be to enhance both the perceptions and the reality of greater opportunity for young people, through a variety of pathways to success, which would then encourage more responsible behavior on their part. This set of policies would begin very early in the life cycle of young black children, and initially seek to counter the "achievement gaps" that develop so early in life for them (Fryer and Levitt 2004; Ludwig and Sawhill 2007) and would focus on early childhood interventions and reforms in the K-8 years of school.

By the time these young people reach their adolescence and teen years, policies must enhance their educational and labor market opportunities in ways that the young people themselves can clearly perceive and believe. Such a set of policies would emphasize three goals: (1) improving their education and early links to the labor market, while helping them avoid early "disconnection"; (2) improving the incentives of less educated young men to take available jobs; and

(3) addressing the specific barriers and disincentives faced by ex-offenders and low-income noncustodial fathers.

Improving education and early links to the labor market would require a broad set of community-based youth development and mentoring efforts targeted at adolescents,[27] and then a range of options in high school that lead more young people either to higher education, or directly to the labor market, or both. Combining better financial aid policies with other supports might improve the enrollment and completion of college by young blacks (Dynarski and Scott-Clayton 2007), while expansion of high-quality career and technical education options (like career academies and apprenticeships) would generate earlier labor market attachment, especially to firms and jobs that pay better wages and provide careers (Lerman 2007).[28]

Greater support for a variety of labor market intermediaries that connect out-of-school youth to training and jobs in higher-paying firms and sectors would help as well and could be useful for countering employer skepticism about these youth.[29] And of course, school- and neighborhood-based interventions that emphasize personal responsibility would also fit into this package and would likely be more powerful when young people can clearly perceive some chances of mainstream success if they do not disengage.

No doubt, some young people will continue to withdraw from the labor market and run afoul of the law. For them, improving their incentives to accept low-wage employment—perhaps before but especially after one or more spell of incarceration—would primarily involve an extension of the Earned Income Tax Credit to low-income workers without custody of children and perhaps other efforts (such as higher minimum wages or more collective bargaining) to raise the wages available for these workers.[30]

Finally, the kinds of efforts needed to help ex-offenders and noncustodial fathers include greater funding for programs that seek to overcome the many personal barriers that they face, such as "prisoner reentry" and "fatherhood" programs. They also include efforts by states to review and adjust many of their policies on incarceration, legal barriers to employment of those with criminal records, enforcement of antidiscrimination laws for those with records, and child support orders and arrearages among low-income noncustodial fathers.[31] Generating better incentives for participation for those with huge arrears is particularly important, as the current set of disincentives likely drive underground many noncustodial fathers who are otherwise ready to begin to play more positive roles in the lives of their children. Such a set of programs and policies would no doubt go well beyond what Moynihan first envisioned in 1965 but are quite consistent with his vision and how that vision has played out over the past four decades.

Notes

1. For example, Moynihan notes that the dropout rates of nonwhite (mostly black) males and females in 1963 were 66.3 and 55.0 percent, respectively. He also notes that the percentages of women among those aged twenty-five and over with a college degree were 39 percent and 53 percent among whites and nonwhites, respectively.

2. I have adapted this table from Freeman and Holzer (1986).

3. 1969 was a very strong economic year and 1977 was a moderate one, with aggregate unemployment rates of 3.5 and 7.1 percent, respectively. In contrast, 1981 was the beginning of a major economic downturn, in which the unemployment rate averaged 7.6 percent. Employment and unemployment rates for black men were clearly deteriorating more rapidly than the overall economy in this period.

4. See Freeman (1981) for an early analysis of the impact of the Civil Rights Act on relative earnings of blacks and Heckman and Payner (1989) for further analysis. The end of the relative improvements in earnings for blacks, and the deterioration for young blacks that occurred afterward, was documented in Bound and Freeman (1992).

5. Given the changes in unemployment rates, along with the magnitudes of labor force participation rates, the declines in employment observed for black men in this table are generally too large to be explained only by the observed changes in unemployment within the labor force alone. The employment changes therefore imply that labor force activity must have declined as well.

6. These data have been tabulated from the outgoing rotation groups of the Current Population Survey (CPS). They essentially update the tabulations first presented in Holzer and Offner (2006). While the quality of those who are high school graduates or less has likely changed (and perhaps deteriorated) as enrollment rates grow, this is likely less true for young black men than for others, as their enrollment rates have grown by less over time. Our analysis of data across states and metro areas shows little effect of relative enrollment rates on the trends we document.

7. Holzer and Offner (2006) report that the coefficient on a time trend in a regression equation for employment for the 1990s is more negative than one for the 1980s, during the period 1979 to 2000.

8. There is very little evidence that the growth of the black female labor force in these areas caused employers to shift employment away from black men. See Blank and Gelbach (2006).

9. These data are drawn from Hill, Holzer, and Chen (forthcoming). The outcomes are measured in round 8 of the survey, administered in 2004 to 2005.

10. The test scores reported are those on the Armed Services Vocational Aptitude Battery (ASVAB). The measured rate of incarceration includes those who report an episode of incarceration as well as those interviewed in jail or prison. Other self-reported measures of criminal activity in the National Longitudinal Survey of Youth (NLSY) are notoriously underreported, especially among blacks (Hindelang, Hirschi, and Weiss 1981).

11. The one exception to this statement is in the area of youth having children out of wedlock, which are reported more frequently by young black women than their male counterparts. The higher tendency of young women to report having children might simply reflect a greater tendency on their part to report the presence of a given child or that some of these children have been fathered by older men.

12. See Hill, Holzer, and Chen (forthcoming, chap. 3). These data represent a snapshot of living arrangements at age twelve for these youth, though they correlate very highly with those observed at earlier ages.

13. The regressions also include controls for age, mother's education and hours worked per year, number of children in the house, mother's age at time of first child's birth, immigrant status, and year.

14. These results are fully consistent with those of McLanahan and Sandefur (1994), among many other authors.

15. The estimated effects on probabilities presented in Table 3, when multiplied by the changes in the fractions of young blacks growing up in the different kinds of single-parent families, suggest that family structure changes over the past four decades have reduced high school graduation and college enrollment, and raised incarceration, by several percentage points each. See Hill, Holzer, and Chen (forthcoming).

16. Our results show that those in single-parent families have many disadvantages—like low parental education and lack of enrichment materials in the home—that are likely not caused by single parenthood per se. On the other hand, some differences in family income and in parenting behaviors that help predict youth outcomes and are correlated strongly with household structure (such as degree of parental supervision and various measures of household organization) are likely more causally related to household structure. Also, some individual and sibling fixed effects models that we estimated suggest at least some causal effects of household structure on these outcomes. See Hill, Holzer, and Chen (forthcoming).

17. We have estimated these regressions separately for young black males and females using the NLSY data, and coefficients for the males tend to be larger than for females—though small sample sizes generate fairly large standard errors in most cases.

18. For instance, see Neal and Johnson (1996) on the importance of cognitive skills in determining the relative earnings of blacks, Kirschenman and Neckerman (1991) and Fix and Struyk (1993) on employer attitudes and discrimination, Kain (1992) and Ihlanfeldt and Sjoquist (1998) on "spatial mismatch," and Ionnides and Loury (2004) on informal networks. For a broad assessment of demand-side factors based on small samples and in-depth interviews with employers, see Moss and Tilly (2001).

19. Whether the *real* wages of less educated men actually fell during that period in absolute terms, or simply *relative* to those of more educated and/or female workers, depends on how we adjust for inflation over time. Since the Consumer Price Index (CPI) has a tendency to overstate inflation, by nearly a percentage point a year, we tend to understate real wage growth when we use it. At best, the real wages of less educated young men have been stagnant over a period of roughly three decades and have certainly fallen in relative terms.

20. The declining employment of black men that Moynihan documented well before the 1960s might be associated with the disappearance of low-wage jobs in southern agriculture on which so many relied in earlier decades and their replacement by northern jobs that paid more but were somewhat fewer in number. See Cogan (1982).

21. Rising expectations and alternative income sources might be viewed either as factors that shift the supply of labor inward or that make it more elastic at the low end of the wage distribution. The effects on employment of less educated black men are the same either way.

22. Fryer et al. (2005) have also noted the negative impact of the crack trade not only on employment but also on an entire range of outcomes observed among urban blacks during that period.

23. For instance, the notion that mainstream academic or labor market success is viewed as "acting white" among young urban black males was rejected by Cook and Ludwig (1998) but more recently supported by Fryer and Torelli (2005).

24. See Ellwood and Jencks (2004) for a review of evidence on why marriage rates and childbearing behavior have evolved differently over time for more and less educated women. See also Edin and Kefalas (2005) for evidence on how low-income women see their prospects for stable marriage. Evidence on the responsiveness of marriage rates to employment outcomes of men also appears in Blau, Kahn, and Waldfogel (2000) and Moffitt (2001). Strong evidence on the responsiveness of criminal activity of young black men to market wages appears in Grogger (1998).

25. See Becker (1971) and Heckman (1998) for a discussion of how job applicants of a particular race can avoid discriminating employers and perhaps find sufficient employment opportunities among nondiscriminators—assuming that there are sufficient numbers of the latter relative to the former, there is sufficient information available to the jobseekers about who they are, and there are no other barriers limiting their employment options. Of course, each of these conditions is unlikely to hold for ex-offenders, especially among low-income black men. See Holzer (2007) for a review of these arguments and the empirical evidence on this issue. Analysis of data from the NLSY uniformly leads to the conclusion that criminal records impede subsequent labor market success. Analysis of various state-level data sets in which Unemployment Insurance earnings data are merged with incarceration data generate more mixed results, though these efforts are somewhat less convincing than those based on the NLSY.

26. See, for instance, Rainwater and Yancey (1967).

27. The Harlem Children's Zone is one fairly large attempt to create a comprehensive set of developmental, educational, and employment-oriented efforts for low-income youth. The Youth Opportunities program of the U.S. Department of Labor was another attempt to generate comprehensive policies at the neighborhood level, though this effort was discontinued in 2003.

28. Evaluations of the Career Academies (see Kemple 2004) show that those enrolled ultimately obtained postsecondary education at the same rate as those in the control group, while also having higher employment rates and earnings. The latter gains were especially impressive for at-risk young men.

29. Intermediaries that work with employers to help them meet their labor needs can often provide information about job candidates that might overcome the "statistical discrimination" against black men in which they might otherwise engage; they can also help overcome the weak informal networks and spatial mismatch that limit worker access to these jobs. These activities can be considered complements to more traditional equal employment opportunity (EEO) law enforcement. The latter alone is unlikely to successfully counter the growing tendency of young black males to fail to attach to employers in the labor market at all and to generate the necessary early work experience for successful earnings growth in the first place.

30. Various proposals for expanding the Earned Income Tax Credit (EITC) to adults without children appear in Edelman, Holzer, and Offner (2006); Berlin (2007); and Raphael (2007). The positive effects of earnings supplementation on the work effort of young black men was also demonstrated in the New Hope demonstration project (Duncan, Huston, and Weisner 2007).

31. See Edelman, Holzer, and Offner (2006, chap. 6) as well as Travis (2005). Many of these ideas are incorporated in "fatherhood" legislation that has recently been proposed by Senators Bayh and Obama.

References

Autor, David, Lawrence Katz, and Melissa Kearney. 2005. The polarization of the U.S. labor market. NBER Working Paper no. 11986, National Bureau of Economic Research, Cambridge, MA.

Becker, Gary. 1968. Crime and punishment: An economic approach. *Journal of Political Economy* 76:169-217.

———. 1971. *The economics of discrimination*. Chicago: University of Chicago Press.

Berlin, Gordon. 2007. Rewarding the work of individuals: A counterintuitive approach to reducing poverty and strengthening families. *The Future of Children* 17:17-39.

Blank, Rebecca. 2002. Evaluating welfare reform in the United States. *Journal of Economic Literature* 40:1105-66.

Blank, Rebecca, and Jonah Gelbach. 2006. Are less-educated women crowding less-educated men out of the labor market? In *Black males left behind*, ed. Ronald Mincy, 87-120. Washington, DC: Urban Institute Press.

Blau, Francine, Lawrence Kahn, and Jane Waldfogel. 2000. Understanding young women's marriage decisions. *Industrial and Labor Relations Review* 53:624-47.

Bound, John, and Richard Freeman. 1992. What went wrong? The erosion of relative earnings and employment among young black men in the 1980s. *Quarterly Journal of Economics* 108:201-32.

Bound, John, and Harry J. Holzer. 1993. Industrial shifts, skill levels, and the labor market for white and black males. *Review of Economics and Statistics* 75:387-96.

Chandra, Amitabh. 2003. Is the convergence of the racial wage gap illusory? Working Paper no. 9476, National Bureau of Economic Research, Cambridge, MA.

Cogan, John. 1982. The decline in black teenage employment: 1950-70. *American Economic Review* 72:621-38.

Cook, Philip, and Jens Ludwig. 1998. Weighing the burden of acting white: Are there race differences in attitudes towards education? In *The black-white test score gap*, ed. Christopher Jencks and Meredith Phillips, 375-400. Washington, DC: Brookings Institution.

Danziger, Sheldon, and Peter Gottschalk. 1995. *America unequal*. New York: Russell Sage Foundation.

Duncan, Greg, Aletha Huston, and Thomas Weisner. 2007. *Higher ground: New hope for the working poor and their children*. New York: Russell Sage Foundation.

Dynarski, Susan, and Judith Scott-Clayton. 2007. College grants on a postcard: A proposal for simple and predictable federal student aid. Hamilton Project Paper, Brookings Institution, Washington, DC.

Edelman, Peter, Harry J. Holzer, and Paul Offner. 2006. *Reconnecting disadvantaged young men*. Washington, DC: Urban Institute Press.

Edin, Kathryn, and Maria Kefalas. 2005. *Promises I can keep*. Berkeley: University of California Press.

Ellwood, David, and Christopher Jencks. 2004. The spread of single-parent families in the U.S. since 1960. In *Social inequality*, ed. Kathryn Neckerman, 3-78. New York: Russell Sage Foundation.

Ferguson, Ronald. 2001. Test score trends along racial lines, 1971-96: Popular culture and community academic standards. In *America becoming: Racial trends and their consequences*, vol. 1, ed. Neil Smelser, William J. Wilson, and Faith Mitchell, 348-90. Washington, DC: National Academy Press.

Fix, Michael, and Raymond Struyk. 1993. *Clear and convincing evidence*. Washington, DC: Urban Institute Press.

Freeman, Richard B. 1981. Black economic progress after 1964: Who has gained and why. In *Studies in labor markets*, ed. Sherwin Rosen, 247-94. Chicago: University of Chicago Press.

———. 1991. Employment and earnings of disadvantaged young men in a labor shortage economy. In *The urban underclass*, ed. Christopher Jencks and Paul Peterson, 103-21. Washington, DC: Brookings Institution.

————. 2003. Can we close the revolving door? Recidivism vs. employment of ex-offenders in the U.S. Presented at the Urban Institute Reentry Roundtable on Employment Dimensions of Reentry. New York University, May 19-20.

Freeman, Richard B., and Harry J. Holzer. 1986. *The black youth employment crisis*. Chicago: University of Chicago Press.

Freeman, Richard B., and William Rodgers. 1999. Area economic conditions and the labor market outcomes of young men in the 1990s expansion. NBER Working Paper no. 7073, National Bureau of Economic Research, Cambridge, MA.

Fryer, Roland, Paul Heaton, Steven Levitt, and Kevin Murphy. 2005. Measuring the impact of crack cocaine. NBER Working Paper no. 11318, National Bureau of Economic Research, Cambridge, MA.

Fryer, Roland, and Steven Levitt. 2004. Understanding the black-white test score gap in the first two years of school. *Review of Economics and Statistics* 86:447–64.

Fryer, Roland, and Paul Torelli. 2005. An empirical analysis of "acting white." NBER Working Paper no. 11334, National Bureau of Economic Research, Cambridge, MA.

Grogger, Jeff. 1998. Market wages and youth crime. *Journal of Labor Economics* 16:756-91.

Heckman, James. 1998. Detecting discrimination. *Journal of Economic Perspectives* 12:101-16.

Heckman, James, and Brook Payner. 1989. Determining the impact of government policy on the economic status of blacks: A case study of South Carolina. *American Economic Review* 79:138-77.

Hill, Carolyn, Harry J. Holzer, and Henry Chen. Forthcoming. *Against the tide: Household structure, opportunities, and outcomes among white and minority youth*. Kalamazoo, MI: W.E. Upjohn Institute for Employment Research.

Hindelang, Michael, Travis Hirschi, and Joseph Weis. 1981. *Measuring delinquency*. Beverly Hills, CA: Sage.

Holzer, Harry J. 1986. Reservation wages and their labor market effects for white and black male youth. *Journal of Human Resources* 21:157-77.

————. 1996. *What employers want: Job prospects for less-educated workers*. New York: Russell Sage Foundation.

————. 2001. Racial differences in labor market outcomes among men. In *America becoming: Racial trends and their consequences*, vol. 2, ed. Neil Smelser, William J. Wilson, and Faith Mitchell, 98-123. Washington, DC: National Academy Press.

————. 2007. Collateral costs: The effects of incarceration on employment and earnings of young men. Unpublished manuscript.

Holzer, Harry J., and Paul Offner. 2006. Trends in employment among less-educated young men, 1979-2000. In *Black males left behind*, ed. Ronald Mincy, 11-38. Washington, DC: Urban Institute Press.

Holzer, Harry J., Paul Offner, and Elaine Sorensen. 2005. Declining employment among young black men: The role of incarceration and child support. *Journal of Policy Analysis and Management* 24:329-50.

Holzer, Harry J., Steven Raphael, and Michael Stoll. 2004. Will employers hire former offenders? Employer preferences, background checks and their determinants. In *Imprisoning America: The social effects of mass incarceration*, ed. Mary Pattillo, Davjd Weiman, and Bruce Western, 205-46. New York: Russell Sage Foundation.

————. 2006. Perceived criminality, background checks, and the racial hiring practices of employers. *Journal of Law and Economics* 49:451-80.

Ihlanfeldt, Keith, and David Sjoquist. 1998. The spatial mismatch hypothesis: Empirical evidence and implications for welfare reform. *Housing Policy Debate* 9:849-92.

Ionnides, Yannis, and Linda Datcher Loury. 2004. Job information networks, neighborhood effects, and inequality. *Journal of Economic Literature* 42:1056-93.

Jacob, Brian. 2002. Where the boys aren't: Non-cognitive skills, returns to education, and the gender gap in higher education. *Economics of Education Review* 21:589-98.

Juhn, Chinhui. 1992. Decline of male labor market participation: The role of declining market opportunities. *Quarterly Journal of Economics* 108:201-32.

Kain, John. 1992. The spatial mismatch hypothesis: Three decades later. *Housing Policy Debate* 3:371-462.

Kasarda, John. 1985. Urban change and minority opportunities. In *The new urban reality*, ed. Paul Peterson, 33-65. Washington, DC: Brookings Institution.

Kemple, James J., with Judith Scott Clayton. 2004. *Career academies: Impacts on labor market outcomes and educational attainment*. New York: Manpower Development Research Corporation.

Kirschenman, Joleen, and Kathryn Neckerman. 1991. We'd Love to hire them but . . . . In *The urban underclass*, ed. Christopher Jencks and Paul Peterson, 203-34. Washington, DC: Brookings Institution.

Lerman, Robert. 2007. Career-focused education and training for youth. In *Reshaping the American workforce in a changing economy*, ed. Harry Holzer and Demetra Nightingale, 41-90. Washington, DC: Urban Institute Press.

Levy, Frank, and Richard Murnane. 1992. U.S. earnings levels and earnings inequality: A review of recent trends and proposed explanations. *Journal of Economic Literature* 30:1332-81.

Ludwig, Jens, and Isabel Sawhill. 2007. Success by age ten. Hamilton Project Paper, Brookings Institution, Washington, DC.

McLanahan, Sara, and Gary Sandefur. 1994. *Growing up with a single parent*. Cambridge, MA: Harvard University Press.

Mead, Lawrence. 2007. Testimony before the Subcommitee on Income Support, Ways and Means Committee, U.S. House of Representatives, 110th Cong., 1st sess., April 26.

Moffitt, Robert. 2001. Welfare benefits and female headship in U.S. time series. In *Out of wedlock: Causes and consequences of nonmarital fertility*, ed. Lawrence Wu and Barbara Wolfe, 143-72. New York: Russell Sage Foundation.

Moss, Philip, and Chris Tilly. 2001. *Stories employers tell*. New York: Russell Sage Foundation.

Moynihan, Daniel P. 1965. *The Negro family: The case for national action*. Washington, DC: Office of Policy Planning and Research, U.S. Department of Labor. http://www.dol.gov/oasam/programs/history/webid-meynihan.htm.

Neal, Derek, and William Johnson. 1996. The role of pre-market factors in black-white wage differentials. *Journal of Political Economy* 104:869-95.

Pager, Devah. 2003. The mark of a criminal record. *American Journal of Sociology* 108:937-75.

Patterson, Orlando. 2006. A poverty of the mind. *New York Times*, March 26.

Rainwater, Lee, and William Yancey. 1967. *The Moynihan Report and the politics of controversy*. Cambridge, MA: MIT Press.

Raphael, Steven. 2007. The impact of incarceration on the employment outcomes of former inmates: Policy options for fostering self-sufficiency and an assessment of the cost-effectiveness of current corrections policy. Presented at the Conference on Pathways to Self-Sufficiency, Institute for Research on Poverty, Madison, WI, September 7.

Spence, Robin, and Brendan Kiel. 2003. *Skilling the American workforce "on the cheap": Ongoing shortfalls in federal funding for workforce development*. Washington, DC: The Workforce Alliance.

Travis, Jeremy. 2005. *But they all come back: Facing the challenges of prisoner Reentry*. Washington, DC: Urban Institute Press.

Wilson, William J. 1987. *The truly disadvantaged: The inner city, the underclass, and public policy*. Chicago: University of Chicago Press.

———. 1996. *When work disappears: The world of the new urban poor*. New York: Knopf.

Bayesian Bigot? Statistical Discrimination, Stereotypes, and Employer Decision Making

By
DEVAH PAGER
and
DIANA KARAFIN

Much of the debate over the underlying causes of discrimination centers on the rationality of employer decision making. Economic models of statistical discrimination emphasize the cognitive utility of group estimates as a means of dealing with the problems of uncertainty. Sociological and social-psychological models, by contrast, question the accuracy of group-level attributions. Although mean differences may exist between groups on productivity-related characteristics, these differences are often inflated in their application, leading to much larger differences in individual evaluations than would be warranted by actual group-level trait distributions. In this study, the authors examine the nature of employer attitudes about black and white workers and the extent to which these views are calibrated against their direct experiences with workers from each group. They use data from fifty-five in-depth interviews with hiring managers to explore employers' group-level attributions and their direct observations to develop a model of attitude formation and employer learning.

Keywords: racial discrimination; employment; employer interviews; African Americans; stereotypes

The continuing significance of race in the minds of employers has been demonstrated in numerous contexts. Interviews with employers reveal the persistence of strong negative associations with minority workers, with particularly negative characteristics attributed to African American men (Kirschenman and Neckerman 1991; Moss and Tilly 2001; Wilson 1996). Studies of hiring behavior likewise suggest that employers strongly prefer white (and Latino) workers to otherwise similar African

NOTE: We thank Bruce Western for his contributions to the original interview schedule and for valuable comments on the article. Thanks also to Susan Fiske and Jeremy Freese for helpful comments and suggestions. Support for this project came from grants from NSF (SES-0547810), NIH (K01-HD053694), and a William T. Grant Foundation Scholar's Award. Direct all correspondence to Devah Pager, Department of Sociology, Princeton University, Princeton, New Jersey 08544; e-mail: pager@princeton.edu.

DOI: 10.1177/0002716208324628

Americans (Pager 2003; Pager, Western, and Bonikowski 2007; Bertrand and Mullainathan 2004; Bendick, Brown, and Wall 1999; Fix and Struyk 1993). Where the continuing existence of discrimination is a matter of little controversy, however, the underlying causes remain widely contested.

Much of the debate over the causes of discrimination centers on the rationality of employer decision making. Economic models of statistical discrimination, for example, emphasize the cognitive utility of group estimates as a means of dealing with the problems of uncertainty (Phelps 1972; Arrow 1972). Group-level estimates of difficult-to-observe characteristics—such as productivity, reliability, or willingness to submit to authority—can provide useful information in the screening of individual applicants. If employers can accurately estimate differences in the skills or disposition of blacks and whites on average, this information can be helpful in guiding decisions about individual black and white candidates for whom these characteristics are more difficult to observe directly.

Sociological and social-psychological models, by contrast, question the degree to which group-level attributions reflect accurate assessments (Bielby and Baron 1986; Tomaskovic-Devey and Skaggs 1999). Although mean differences may exist between groups on some productivity-related characteristics, these differences may be inflated in their application, leading to much larger differences in individual evaluations than would be warranted by actual group-level trait distributions (Rothschild and Stiglitz 1982).[1] Furthermore, estimates of group characteristics may reflect outdated associations, with factors such as occupational segregation, imperfect information flows, and negative feedback effects reducing awareness of changing distributions (Whatley and Wright 1994; Arrow 1998; Farmer and Terrell 1996). It thus remains unclear whether employers' assessments of various racial groups represent accurate representations and to what extent these assessments are responsive to novel or competing sources of information.

In this study, we take one step toward investigating these questions by measuring the nature of employer attitudes about black and white workers and the extent to which these views are calibrated against their direct experiences with workers from each group. Using data from fifty-five in-depth interviews with hiring managers, we explore employers' group-level attributions and their direct observations to develop a model of attitude formation and employer learning.

Devah Pager is an associate professor of sociology and a faculty associate of the Office of Population Research at Princeton University. Her research focuses on institutions affecting racial stratification, including education, labor markets, and the criminal justice system. Her current research has involved a series of field experiments studying discrimination against minorities and ex-offenders in the low-wage labor market. Recent publications include Marked: Race, Crime, and Finding Work in an Era of Mass Incarceration *(University of Chicago Press 2007) and "Walking the Talk: What Employers Say versus What They Do" (with Lincoln Quillian), in* American Sociological Review 70, *no. 3 (2005): 355-80.*

Diana Karafin is a PhD candidate at Ohio State University whose research focuses on consequences of neighborhood integration, racial democracy and crime, and discrimination in the housing and labor markets.

Prior Research on Discrimination

Direct observations of employer behavior suggest that race continues to shape employment opportunities in important ways. A recent field experiment of employment discrimination in New York City, for example, provided a rare glimpse into the pervasiveness of discrimination in low-wage labor markets (Pager, Western, and Bonikowski 2007). Across hundreds of applications for entry-level jobs, blacks were half as likely to receive a callback or job offer as equally qualified white applicants. Furthermore, blacks with clean records fared no better than a white man just released from prison. The results of this and earlier audit studies provide vivid illustration of the degree to which racial considerations continue to actively shape the employment opportunities available to young black men (Bendick, Brown, and Wall 1999; Fix and Struyk 1993; Bertrand and Mullainathan 2004; Pager 2003; see Pager [2007] for a review).

Although the foregoing studies provide an important measure of the demand side of the labor market, audit methods offer little insight into the motivations or attitudes that shape employer behavior. Does discrimination typically reflect racial animus? Have employers had negative experiences with African American employees in the past that have led them to shy away from hiring blacks? Or do other factors shape employer decision making?

Previous research leaves these questions only partially answered. The classic study by Kirschenman and Neckerman (1991) indicates that race is indeed salient to employers in their hiring decisions. Results from a large sample of in-depth interviews reveal employers' blatant admission of their avoidance of young inner-city black men, attributing characteristics such as "lazy" and "unreliable" to this group (p. 213; see also Wilson 1996; Moss and Tilly 2001; Waldinger and Lichter 2003).[2]

At the same time, while this study has been widely cited as evidence of employers' deep biases about African Americans, especially young black inner-city men, the findings themselves present a more complicated picture. While some employers spoke only in general terms about the assumed characteristics of black inner-city men, suggestive of the role of broad cultural stereotypes, others made specific reference to negative experiences with their own black employees, indicating that employer attitudes may be heavily shaped by direct observation of racial differences among their workers.

The underlying sources of employer attitudes thus remain somewhat unclear. Indeed, in framing their analysis with the concept of statistical discrimination, Kirschenman and Neckerman (1991) remain agnostic as to whether employers' comments represent accurate depictions or exaggerated stereotypes. Employers are clearly using race as a proxy for employment-relevant characteristics, but the degree to which the use of this proxy is informed by empirical realities remains uncertain.

Moss and Tilly (2001) also find employers readily referring to negative characteristics among African American workers, with pervasive concerns about dependability, motivation, attitude, and skill. Many of these employers cite concrete experiences with their own black employees as the basis of their attitudes, though some also cite media representations and more general observations of African Americans as the source of their racial attributions (pp. 138-40). At the same time, Moss and Tilly note that a "silent majority" of employers claim not to notice racial differences among their employees. The authors speculate that these responses are due to some combination of social desirability bias, effective screening or training techniques (rendering a population-level racial skills gap irrelevant for the particular firm), or an honest experience of black and white workers as comparable. Among the largest group of employers, then, it is difficult to assess to what extent perceptions of racial differences are relevant for employers' decision making.

While the present study can move no closer to assessing the accuracy (or honesty) of employers' racial assessments, it does attempt to provide a more explicit understanding of the connection between employers' direct experiences and their more general racial attitudes. Following in the footsteps of the important employer-interview studies from the 1990s, this project seeks to better understand the degree to which employers' extensive experience with black and white workers generates assessments of racial differences that reflect their own empirical observations. In exploring the link between experience and beliefs, we hope to provide some insight into the dynamic process by which racial attitudes are constructed and reinforced.

A Rational Actor Model of Hiring

Economic models of statistical discrimination suggest that race offers a useful proxy for difficult-to-observe characteristics. Because productivity is difficult to observe directly, particularly for new hires, employers rely on indirect information inferred from group membership. This model can represent rational action on the part of employers, provided that the information they have about groups is accurate, and provided that there is a mechanism for updating estimates of group characteristics over time. Where discussions of statistical discrimination typically focus on accounting for single-point hiring decisions, the theoretical propositions can be readily extended to a dynamic process. Figure 1 represents such a model schematically, in its simplest form.

The model starts with information about *known group characteristics*: for example, employers may be aware of racial differences in graduation rates, test scores, incarceration rates, and other relevant disparities. Employers may also have direct *prior experiences* to which they refer in shaping their own beliefs. These antecedent sources of information then shape the employers' general *beliefs about blacks*—about their productivity, reliability, intelligence, and other

FIGURE 1
A RATIONAL ACTOR MODEL OF HIRING DECISIONS

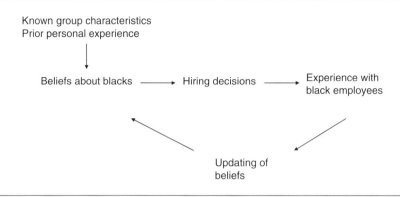

relevant characteristics. Those beliefs will then guide individual *hiring decisions*. Once hiring decisions are made, employers are exposed to a range of black employees, and to the extent that these *experiences with black employees* do not fit the assumptions of the employer about members of that group, employers will revise their beliefs in a sort of Bayesian *updating process* to reflect a more accurate set of expectations.[3]

This equilibrium model of statistical discrimination describes the mechanisms by which employers can incorporate their direct observations into more general assessments of group characteristics. This feedback loop provides an efficient means of calibrating expectations, observations, and behavior. Consistent with such a model, some research does indeed point to evidence of employer updating. Altonji and Pierret (2001), for example, show that as firms acquire more information about a worker (through posthire observation), their evaluations (as reflected in wage offers) rely less on general (noisy) characteristics, such as educational attainment, and more on individual-specific characteristics, such as cognitive skill (see also Oettinger 1996; Farber and Gibbons 1996).[4] These studies provide compelling evidence that employers weigh their direct observations more heavily than inferences based on group proxies and that employer learning can improve on initial estimates. Nonetheless, this line of research applies specifically to learning about individual workers, whereby group-based estimates are replaced with the observed characteristics of individuals. It remains unclear, however, whether an employer's learning about an individual employee affects the employer's expectations about the broader group to which that individual employee belongs.

Indeed, Farmer and Terrell (1996) provide an elegant theoretical analysis of employer learning and statistical discrimination in which initial employer beliefs are revised through an updating process similar to that described above.

According to the authors, however, the updating process might apply only to the specific employees under observation, rather than to members of the larger group. "Higher than expected output of one worker provides much information about individual ability, but only a single data point to estimate the average ability of a population of millions. In addition to observation of workers, an employer receives an abundance of information on average group ability from other sources. Observations of average output, or perhaps occupations, of other members of the group influence the assessment of group ability" (p. 206). The process by which employers generate estimates of group characteristics and update those estimates over time thus remains unknown. In the following analysis, we seek to make headway in understanding this dynamic process.

Source of Data

This research is based on in-depth, in-person interviews with 55 New York City employers. The employers in this study represent a subsample of firms advertising for entry-level positions in 2004.[5] In selecting respondents, we aimed to capture the full range of entry-level employers according to industry, occupation, and other types of characteristics thought to be associated with discrimination. In all, we made 243 in-person contacts with 152 firms to solicit participation in our study, 55 of whom agreed, rendering a response rate of 36 percent. The majority of respondents were male (70 percent); white (59 percent); located in Manhattan (82 percent); and managing a firm in the retail industry (46 percent), the restaurant industry (31 percent), or the service industry (11 percent).[6] Furthermore, 47 percent of respondents represented independent firms, 40 percent national chains, and 13 percent local New York City chains.

Interviews ranged in length from thirty minutes to two hours, with the average interview lasting fifty minutes. Content of the interviews reflected a wide range of topics, including recruitment strategies; screening procedures; concerns about entry-level workers; and criteria for selection, placement, and promotion decisions. The questions we focus on here come from a module focusing on employers' racial attitudes. This core segment of the interview probed three primary sets of issues related to (1) employers' general attitudes about the employment problems of black men, (2) their specific experiences with black applicants and employees, and (3) the relationship between employers' concrete experiences and their general attitudes. In the following discussion, we examine the pattern of responses that emerged from our conversations with employers, focusing specifically on the link between employers' general attitudes about blacks and their specific experiences.

The use of qualitative data is well suited to investigating complex processes given its ability to capture the nuance and depth of personal attitudes (Orbuch 1997). But this approach also has its limitations. The relatively small sample prevents us from drawing strong conclusions about the attitudes of employers more generally. More important, the validity of findings from interview data depends on respondents' willingness to provide truthful answers to questions. Given the sensitive nature of this investigation, concerns over social desirability bias are highly relevant. As we discuss below, the candid answers we received from employers about their negative racial attitudes offer some reassurance that employers were not entirely self-censoring. At the same time, we must remain aware of the possibility that some responses may be affected by these concerns.

Despite these limitations, in-depth interviews provide a rare window into employers' thought processes and offer some leverage in understanding the complex process of attitude formation among this group. While we cannot conclusively adjudicate among theories based on the results from this study, we hope that our findings will be generative of hypotheses for further testing.

How Do Employers Think about Young Black Men?

In talking about race, and in particular the employment problems of black men, employers' responses represented a range of views.[7] Some employers emphasized the structural barriers facing African Americans, including poverty, a lack of education, disadvantaged neighborhood contexts, and prejudice and discrimination. For example, one employer from a courier company emphasized the problems of residential segregation, discrimination, and incarceration as key barriers to black men's employment opportunities.

> Well, there are of course the obvious problems of racial profiling where people don't want to hire them. They won't tell you that and you don't really think it happens as much in society. People think all of that segregation has ended, but it really hasn't. . . . Another problem, as a good example in terms of hiring people that have criminal backgrounds, a lot of people are not looking to take the chance, and unfortunately the number of African American men that have been incarcerated has just, in the past few years, been phenomenal. And so people don't stop to think that, let's say someone wasn't really involved in something. Maybe they just got caught up, so to speak. Some people may just think that, well you have been in trouble and so I don't want to hire you. So that is another aspect that keeps people from hiring black men.

Another employer from a retail chain pointed to a range of factors, from racism to a lack of education, that disadvantage black men in the labor market:

> Racism is still a huge issue in America. . . . Especially like black men have been repressed for so many years, like due to every, like due to racial issues, a lot of them are very like limited in their, their work experience, or in their education levels, because the education system in New York City is terrible, like in public schools especially, like in the inner city, and you know, in the poorer neighborhoods, so . . . there . . . is a lack of education . . . and so many people can't, you know, afford to go to college. . . . And therefore there's so many jobs that so many people are trying to compete for. . . . You know I think that that's what a lot of the problem is for, for, for especially black men in, in this city.

Overall, more than 40 percent of employers commented on structural issues, about 15 percent of whom emphasized these factors as their primary explanation for the employment problems of black men.

By far, the most common explanations for black men's employment problems, however, focused on the individual shortcomings of black men themselves. More than three-fourths of employers mentioned individual explanations at some point in their discussion of black men's employment problems, with well over half (60 percent) emphasizing individual factors as their primary explanation. A wide range of perceived shortcomings were identified as primary explanations for black men's employment troubles, including concerns over work ethic, attire, and attitude, which we discuss in detail below.

Of course, we know from other research that Americans tend to give individualistic explanations for inequality in general, whether racial or otherwise (Schuman and Krysan 1999; Kluegel and Smith 1985; Jackman 1994; Bobo 2004). For example, in his analysis of General Social Survey data collected between 2000 and 2004, Hunt (2007) finds that at least half of Americans believed contemporary racial inequality to be caused by a "lack of motivation," relative to less than a third who cited discrimination as an important problem.[8] To some extent, then, the distribution of responses we observe reflects a more general reluctance to view inequality in structural terms.

At the same time, however, the content in these interviews goes beyond the standard narrative of "pull yourself up by your bootstraps." Certainly we also heard comments of this sort. One employer from a local restaurant chain, for example, insisted, "If you are persistent, something will eventually pan out for you. I am sure of it. If you really want a job, you will eventually find one." The comments we focus on in this analysis, by contrast, go well beyond these generic beliefs in individualism to reveal far more specific attributions about black men.

In asking employers to reflect on their experiences with workers from different racial groups, we are not simply asking them about their general beliefs about inequality; we are asking them to draw from their expertise as *employers* to help us better understand why the economic outcomes for some groups are systematically better/worse than others. Given their unique vantage point, we might expect employers to express attitudes about the characteristics of black and white workers that diverge from mainstream American racial attitudes. Because of highly segregated social networks, many white Americans' exposure to African Americans is limited to casual observation, brief encounters, and media representations. Most employers, by contrast, have had extensive contact with black workers and have had the opportunity to observe these workers perform specific tasks and responsibilities.

Under these conditions, then, we might expect employers' direct experiences to play a larger role in shaping their racial attitudes relative to other white Americans. Previous research provides only partial insight into this question. Bobo, Johnson, and Suh (2002), for example, find that employers' racial stereotypes are indistinguishable from those of the general public, suggesting that workplace power or experience does little to shift generalized racial associations.[9]

At the same time, close-ended survey measures capture only one dimension of attitudes, potentially overlooking some of the complexities and contradictions embedded in employers' ideas about the characteristics of racial groups. The present study uses in-depth interviews to investigate employers' attitudes about and experiences with black men. We begin with an investigation of employers' general characterizations of black men, and then explore the degree to which these characterizations are rooted in direct experiences and observations.

Lack of a work ethic

One of the most common themes we heard from employers centered on the perceived lack of a work ethic among black men (fully 55 percent mentioned this issue). Some of these employers referred to a general lack of motivation to work among African American men. Others described a desire among black men to take advantage of the system instead of working. One employer at a retail store said simply, "I will tell you the truth. African Americans don't want to work." A manager of a retail store said similarly, "They don't want to work—you can tell by the attitude, clothing, the general body language." The owner of a dry-cleaning store commented, "They just don't have any drive. No get up and go attitude." Likewise, a young male employer working in a national clothing chain stated, "I think for a lot of them they are too lazy to work so they are not going to work."

A human resources manager at a national retail chain, when asked what she thinks explains the employment problems of black men, explained,

> Employer (E): They are not as motivated as other races to, you know, to get out and do more and to improve or make themselves better. ... [T]hey are not as motivated or determined to move up or to even do anything to improve themselves.
> Interviewer (I): What do you think this lack of motivation stems from?
> E: I don't know how to say this but probably laziness. Just being lazy and not wanting to work.

When asked the same question, the manager of a local restaurant chain in New York City first argued that more black men are employed than the statistics indicate because many work off the books. However, the employer then refined his initial explanation, stating, "Listen, I also think there is a degree of being lazy." As with many of the other employers interviewed, this manager seemed to believe that if black men were motivated to search for employment in a responsible manner, their employment problems would be resolved.

In several cases, employers attributed the lack of work ethic to a complex history of racism and paternalism. For example, the long-term manager of an industrial supply store in the Bronx noted, "In America blacks believe the golden opportunity is to be taken care of." Another employer who earlier had asserted that "African Americans don't want to work" elaborated on his initial comment:

> Maybe they think that this country owes them so much. Because of slavery and all of that. They, they tend to forget that was a couple of years ago. Instead of catching up with

the world, they still keep that anger. . . . So African American men feel like they deserve something. That is basically why they don't want to work. They feel that if they can get things for free, why not?

The manager of a national restaurant chain expressed a similar view, differentiating between black men and black women. "I think the mentality is changing. I think [black men] are more accepting of letting the female work and they stay home." He went on to explain,

> I think, you know, a percentage of it, probably has to do with them figuring out how to take advantage of the system. You know, with welfare or something like that. I do think that a lot of them have the mentality of: I'm black and the government doesn't help. So, let me do what I can to get from the government. Though Martin Luther King has changed the world, a lot of them have the mentality that it is still a white world.

A different employer emphasized that programs exist to help those in need of work but that black men elect to ignore the programs as they want "things handed to them." The main supervisor of a national food chain explained,

> The key is, I think there are great programs out there, but people don't take advantage of them. It is probably laziness. You know, there are programs. But people are lazy. A lot of people want things handed to them.

Another employer focused more specifically on negative consequences of welfare dependence:

> Unfortunately we've bred generations of welfare—of people whose . . . careers are . . . welfare and social agencies. And, uh, and it's unfortunate. A lot of these people just don't have any work values.

Applying a similar line of reasoning, the young manager of a local telemarketing firm expressed frustration with black men playing the "race card" as a way of escaping responsibility:

> I mean, I do understand that sometimes the black man is racially profiled. So it is something they are always going to deal with. This is unfortunate for them, but I think they shouldn't even go there with playing the race card. I mean, a lot of them are like, "You treat me this way because I am black," and "I can't do this and I can't do that." I just think for a lot of them, it is that they just don't want to do things. They want to smoke weed and be a rapper.

Although this employer does see racial discrimination as a reality, he views it as more often used as a convenient excuse for failure than a direct cause. Underlying the employment problems of black men, according to this employer, is more often a simple lack of motivation and effort.

According to each of these employers, a lack of work ethic, motivation, and personal responsibility is pervasive among African American men, and together, these factors represent the primary causes of this group's employment problems. Historical social policies (e.g., slavery and welfare) are seen less as explanations for these patterns and more as convenient excuses available for African Americans in the abdication of responsibility.

Self-presentation

A second persistent theme in the interviews was the issue of black men's self-presentation (45 percent of employers mentioned this issue). In particular, employers highlighted problems of unsuitable appearance, negative attitude, and inappropriate conduct among black men. Particularly for positions involving customer service, employers expressed concern about the image projected by black men in their attire and attitude. An employer representing a local New York City clothing chain remarked,

> Sometimes these people looking for a job, why would they have a do-rag on and jeans? Why would they? You know, just the way you present yourself, it's how you are. . . . The black male, yes. It's just the way they carry themselves.

Another employer, the manager of a children's clothing store, when explaining why black men have difficulty securing employment, stated,

> The way they present themselves in the store. If they come in, and excuse the word, but they are all thugged out, it is not somebody I want on my sales floor.

Also placing significant weight on the role of appearance in securing employment, an employer representing a popular local New York City retail chain commented,

> If you go out looking for a job with caps, baggy pants and triple x t-shirts or whatever, you can't expect someone to hire you like that. Why don't you put on some decent clothes and go look for a job? That is the mistake minorities, black and Hispanics tend to do. They look for a job, and when they don't get hired, they automatically say it is discrimination.

The manager of a retail clothing chain complained, "[Black men are] usually, like very urban looking, baggy pants, you know, just like baggy clothes, hat." Likewise, an employer for a moving company said, "I think people who come in wearing baggy pants or something like that just make a bad impression. You can be green, orange, purple, or whatever. It doesn't matter, it isn't good."[10] For these employers, the problems of attire—and specifically the issue of baggy pants—signaled a lack of professionalism or an ignorance about appropriate work attire, something they often associated with black men.

In addition to matters of appearance, employers' comments about the self-presentation of black men also emphasized issues of attitude and conduct. Black men were often perceived as having a "bad attitude" about work or relations of authority, or at times behaved in ways considered inappropriate for mainstream work environments. When considering the employment problems of black men, an employer from a national clothing chain explained, "It's just the way they carry themselves." Another described black men's tendency to present "language and the attitude, like gangsta or street."

The manager of a large national retail chain noted that differences in the self-presentation and conduct of black and white men affected the way they are perceived by employers and customers:

> I have heard people say that it is easier to deal with a white person more than a black person. I guess because they feel black people are always loud and hyper. Which is true. White people may know how to carry themselves a little better than black people. Black people always want to make a scene and always want to be heard.

A manager of a national retail store emphasized the distinction between qualifications and self-presentation, with the latter undermining the former in the case of black men:

> You know, I know a lot of black males and I know how they react to things and I know why they don't get jobs. I kind of know why. Some of them are actually qualified for jobs but they go in with that attitude. It is all in how they present themselves.

Several employers commented on the attitude problems they perceived among young black men as reflecting a sense of hostility or resistance to authority. An employer from a small, independent retail store stated, "[Black men have] this kind of attitude that is, is umm, resentful. It is hard. It is not an attitude that is favorable for business." An employer representing a large national clothing chain emphasized that black men don't present themselves to employers appropriately because they have a chip on their shoulder:

> I: Why do you think they are not presenting themselves in what you think is the best way? Where does this stem from?
> E: Um, ego and insecurity. The insecurity part is that they don't feel that they are right for the job. They lack that confidence but yet their ego won't let them admit it so they have a chip on their shoulder.

The owner of a local garment factory echoed some of the same concerns:

> [Black men] act a little more belligerent than others. There is the attitude and pattern of animosity with this group. They have a chip on their shoulders. They think, man, you are white and that is why you don't give me a job. That kind of thing. . . . The black male will come and say I am better than this and better than that and so on. So there is more of a macho type of attitude with the black male. When you go for a job you have to be, besides appearing decent and trustworthy, you can't look macho or act like you are better than other people.

Another employer at a retail store found it difficult to advise young black men about appropriate attire because of their resistance to authority.

> I think that it is hard for these men because they are too proud. Especially the younger guys, the eighteen- and nineteen-year-old black guys that come in here, are like, "Who are you to tell me no?" They have a real problem with authority.

These employers perceive black men to exhibit styles of dress or demeanor that present barriers to their mainstream involvement in the labor market. Concerns about the self-presentation of black men, ranging from baggy pants to bad attitudes, were viewed as a key obstacle to employment for this group.

A threatening or criminal demeanor

A final major theme in employers' general comments about black men focused on a perceived threatening or criminal demeanor. Extending comments about the "hardness" or "animosity" of black men discussed above, roughly a third of employers mentioned concerns of this sort. According to an employer from a local garment factory,

> I find that the great majority of this minority group that you are talking about either doesn't qualify for certain jobs because they look a little bit more, they come on as if, well, they are threatening.

An employer from a popular national clothing chain dismisses the racial frame initially but ultimately reached a similar conclusion:

> I don't know if I consider it on a race level. I just consider it more on approachability. And if someone seems intimidating, you know, and which, stereotypically might be, you might consider like a Hispanic person or a black person more intimidating than like a white person.[11]

Other employers focused more specifically on concerns about criminality. According to one employer from an ice cream chain, for example,

> I notice here working in the store, sometimes, a group of young black males will come in. And sort of, a red flag goes up. Everything stops, and you wonder, what are they going to do? Are they here to buy something? There is a general belief that, because of the way they dress and how they carry themselves, that they are trouble.

An employer from a retail store explained, "I mean, black males are not expected to go out and work, because they are doing other illegal things in the neighborhood." Likewise, an employer for a moving company pointed to the lure of criminal activity among African Americans:

> They see the drug dealer who is driving around in a Lexus, and then they see me in a Chevy, and they say I don't need to be a mover. I don't need to work sixty hours a week. I can go hustle stuff on the corner and drive a Lexus.

Another explained simply, "Half of them are in jail." These employers associate black men with danger, crime, and the criminal justice system, factors that appear incompatible with legitimate work.

Overall, then, we find fairly pervasive negative attitudes about black men as a group. While some employers did place more emphasis on lack of opportunity, prejudice, or other more structural factors, the majority of employers pointed to specific deficiencies among black men that led them to have difficulty in the job market. Our next set of questions seeks to investigate to what extent these negative attitudes are a function of employers' direct experiences.

Are Employers' Perceptions Informed by Experience?

In discussing their general attitudes about black men, many employers inevitably referred to specific observations or experiences in their own workplace. These anecdotes point to one potential source of employers' general attitudes, though they tell us little about the overall distribution of experiences. Our next set of interview questions, then, attempted to elicit more systematic information about employers' experiences with applicants and employees from various racial groups.[12] In particular, we asked employers to consider the extent to which the characteristics they had described to us were reflected in the black applicants or employees they had encountered over the past year.

In some cases, there was clearly a link between employers' general attitudes and their direct experiences. For example, one employer who had expressed negative views of blacks generally ("basically these people are lazy") went on to describe the differences he has observed between black and white applicants.

> Black people, mostly, yeah I can say that they come in, and "Are you hiring?" That's their question, and then that's it. They don't have, they are not prepared at all. I give them an application and they don't show up back with it. It's like, "I'm taking it, but let's see what happens. . . ." White people . . . they mostly come with resume already done, the paper with them.

Another employer who had commented earlier on dysfunctional culture affecting "people that come from two or three generations that are on welfare" described the differences he observed:

> Well for my business I am looking for somebody that comes dressed for the interview. If you walk in with baggy jeans it is not even worth talking to you. This is something I have observed with black men. I mean, yeah, I definitely have noticed that a lot of black male applicants typically don't know how to properly talk to me, or they leave messages on the phone that aren't really what I am looking for. I mean, they just don't seem energetic or like they really want this job.

An employer from a national service organization commented on her experiences with black applicants who seemed to take job opportunities for granted, not demonstrating suitable interest or seriousness of purpose.

> People will call here and you will try to schedule them for an interview. So you will offer them an interview, and they call up asking for one, and they say things like, "Yeah, I don't know if that time works for me." You know what I mean? It is just not proper etiquette.

While we were conducting an interview with the manager of a local telemarketing firm, a black male job applicant entered the room, dressed in baggy clothing, and asked to schedule an interview. The manager replied that the individual would have to come back later in the week, to which the applicant stated, "Gotcha. See you then." After the applicant left, the manager stated, "Not gonna hire him. See what I mean? Where did he learn that 'gotcha' was the right thing to say to a potential boss? And see what I mean about attire?"

A number of the employers we spoke to reported at least some negative experiences with black applicants and/or employees, ranging from comments about individual workers to descriptions of more general patterns. Overall, among our sample of white respondents, employers were more likely to note racial difference among their applicant pool (46 percent) than among their employees (34 percent).[13] This suggests that employers are doing an effective job at weeding out good employees from a more heterogeneous applicant pool. At the same time, note that more than half of employers claim not to notice racial differences in the quality of their applicants, and fully two-thirds of employers notice no racial differences among their own employees. In these cases, there is often little relationship between the impressions they report about African Americans generally and their own direct observations of black employees.

For example, one employer earlier emphasized the lack of work ethic among blacks ("just being lazy and not wanting to work") as the major factor for their employment problems; but when asked if she had observed these problems in her workplace, she replied, "Well no. . . . Of course once in a while they goof off, but that is across the board. I don't see any differences between groups." A video store employer acknowledged that stereotypes were often quite different from reality: "There are people that say there are differences in work ethics of black men, but I have no specific thing like that that I have noticed. Absolutely not. The worst employees have been the non people of color. They have been the worst."

An employer who earlier had alluded to the problems black men have with "presentation" and "attitude," went on to describe his employees with the following comments:

> I: Among your employees, have you noticed differences in the work performance of blacks and whites?
> E: Um, do you mean in terms of work ethic?
> I: Sure.
> E: They really have a nice work ethic.
> I: What about comparing whites to blacks?
> E: In my experience blacks will outdo them.
> I: Blacks will outdo whites?
> E: Yeah, once you get the right person. Sometimes with an entry-level, they don't seem as committed.
> I: You mean your white employees?
> E: Yeah. It is like they think they are above this. I don't find this with the black employees.

An employer for a retail clothing store (who had referred to blacks as being more "intimidating" than whites) came to a similar assessment about her own employees: "It's hard to compare because it's different types of work that they're doing, but I would say that the people who are not of Caucasian descent work a little harder than the white kids."

In several cases, employers did acknowledge differences among workers but accounted for them along nonracial lines. We asked an employer who had earlier emphasized the importance of attire for her workers:

> I: Do you observe that black male applicants are more likely than white male applicants to present themselves to you inappropriately?
> E: No not really. I think it is a problem for all of them. I think just men in general.

In another case, the employer started out describing the problematic applicants she deals with. When we pressed her to consider whether these characteristics were more prevalent among black men, she thought about the question and then reframed her comments in terms of age.

> E: They don't come in dressed, they don't come in and speak to you in a correct way. They speak like they are hanging out and not looking for a job.
> I: Okay, so do you notice that black males come in not prepared or dressed appropriately more often than white males that are looking for jobs?
> E: I think it is about the same honestly. It is more about the age. The high school kids are the ones that don't come in dressed like they are looking for a job. As they get older you can see the difference because they are coming in in slacks and they are coming in in a shirt and they are speaking to you. They aren't just like, "Here is an application," and then they walk out the door.

These employers appear to have identified a cluster of behaviors or styles of presentation that signal poor performance, some of which are often associated with African American men, but when pressed to make sense of their observations, they focus on a different set of categories. Of course, it may be the case that employers feel uncomfortable making racial attributions and thus retreat to a language of gender or age out of social desirability concerns. We have no way of conclusively ruling out this possibility. At the same time, given the extremely candid racial remarks made by these employers just moments before, we feel some reassurance in taking these responses at face value. These comments lead us to believe that employers felt sufficiently at ease to speak in racial terms, and thus, we see little reason that they would suddenly retreat into a more politically correct style of discourse. In fact, we were concerned with the opposite effect, that employers would feel some pressure to come up with specific examples of poor performance among their black employees, if only to maintain consistency with their earlier comments. Quite the contrary, we found employers repeatedly emphasizing the lack of clear distinctions between black and white applicants and employees, even as these comments appear to contradict earlier statements about the generalized characteristics of black men.

As a final example of the disconnect that often appeared between employers' expectations and outcomes, one employer from a small retail store describes her recent experience with a black man she had hired for a stockperson position in her retail store:

Like, last year. I had this guy come in, with a big hat and a big jacket. I don't know if he had a criminal record, but he looked like it. But I was so desperate that I hired him. [Laughs] He was OK. But the way he dressed. Sometimes the way they dress. It is bad. I mean, a big hat. You try to be nice, but at the same time, I don't need a guy with a big hat. [Laughs] I was surprised that he worked out well. He finished the season very nicely."

In this case, despite the fact that the employer viewed this man as poorly dressed and potentially criminal, he ultimately wound up being a reliable employee. Indeed, employers frequently acknowledged that their first impressions of applicants were often completely off base. Here, the employer recognized her misjudgment, and yet, there is little sign that this experience caused her to rethink her more general, negative impressions of black men. Earlier in the interview, this employer had characterized black men as having attitude problems. "Socially there is a difference. In the neighborhood [black men] have a kind of attitude, that is, is um, resentful. It is hard. It is not an attitude that is favorable for business." Although here (and in other comments), she insists that her own experiences with black employees have been overwhelmingly positive, she retains strong negative impressions about black men "in the neighborhood," the source of which remains unknown.

[E]mployers frequently acknowledged that their first impressions of applicants were often completely off base.

How to Explain the Gap between Employers' Perceptions and Experience?

Whereas most of the employers in our sample expressed consistent negative attitudes about black men, far fewer could identify specific patterns or experiences among their own applicants or employees to fit these characterizations. How can we account for this surprising disconnect? While the results of this study cannot provide a definitive answer, we consider several plausible explanations.

The salience of negative events

First, it is possible that while employers' experiences with black applicants or employees *on average* may be similar to those with whites, a small number of negative experiences may hold especially strong weight in shaping attitudes

(Fiske 1998). Indeed, several of the employers in our sample referred to singular experiences that, while not representative of their experiences more generally, seemed to shape their associations of specific groups. According to one employer from a national retail chain,

> You know, everyone has a couple of bad hires. And you remember those very vividly. And who that person is can really impact. [He describes a negative experience with an African American female employee.] That person just stuck in my head. That was the first time I had done hiring during a holiday season, which is pretty stressful. And that person just stuck in my head. And I could see her. It was hard to not see her in other people that you meet.

According to this employer's account, one particularly negative experience with a black employee colored the employers' expectations of blacks in the future. Where this employer also noted a number of positive experiences he had had with African American employees, this negative experience appeared to carry especially strong weight.

In another case, an employer for a retail clothing store spoke about his negative experiences with a few black employees at a previous company.

> One of them in particular was threatening me and telling me after I fired him that he was going to wait for me outside and that he was going to get me. So that kind of thing sometimes gives you a vengeance. So, you know, you become biased a little bit.

Again, this employer acknowledges the ways in which a particularly unpleasant encounter contributed to his biases against black men more generally. It may be the case, then, that where employers may have had only a small number of unusually negative experiences with African Americans, these incidents may be the driving force behind generalized negative attributions. Benign or positive experiences create less salient memories, even if more prevalent overall.

At the same time, only a few of the employers in the sample reported extreme negative experiences, and more than half reported that their experiences with black and white applicants and employees were roughly comparable.[14] Without salient negative experiences coloring attitudes, what then might explain employers' persistent negative racial attitudes?

Selection and screening

A second possible explanation for the disconnect between employers' characterizations of black men in general and their direct experiences has to do with the various selection and screening procedures that weed out the most undesirable members of the group. Indeed, recall that employers were significantly more likely to report noticing racial differences in the characteristics of their job applicants than among their employees (46 versus 34 percent), suggesting that the hiring process leads to a more even distribution of productivity characteristics among black and white employees than exist in the general population. As one employer mentioned, "Yeah, once you get the right person . . . ," indicating that the selection process can yield high-quality black employees, even if there is a great deal of variation within the general population. Recognizing that employees are not picked at random, we asked employers to comment separately on their perceptions of the applicant pool, expecting that racial differences may be more pronounced before the employers' active screening. The fact that more than half of employers claim not to notice racial differences even at this stage suggests that more remains to be explained than employer sorting.

Of course, the hiring process is not the only selection process at work. Showing up to apply for a job itself involves a process of selection, with the search process requiring some degree of organization, motivation, and a commitment to formal work. Particularly in recent years, as we have seen increasing numbers of young black men exit the labor force altogether (Holzer, Offner, and Sorensen 2005), selection into labor force participation may differentiate the types of black men employers encounter among their applicant pool from those in the general population.

This research does not make claims about employers' accuracy in detecting population-level characteristics relative to those observed in the workplace. Rather, we simply note that for many employers, whatever sources of information they use to infer general characteristics of black men, direct experiences with black applicants and employees do not appear dominant.

[F]or many employers, whatever sources of information they use to infer general characteristics of black men, direct experiences with black applicants and employees do not appear dominant.

Updating versus subtyping

A third potential explanation for the disconnect between employers' general attitudes and their specific experiences draws upon the social-psychological concept of subtyping. Where Bayesian models of updating assume that individuals incorporate new information by refining their expectations in ways consistent with their experiences, social psychological models emphasize the cognitive resistance to information that is disconfirming of expectations (Fiske 1998). A wealth of experimental evidence illustrates ways in which individuals are prone to view those who do not conform to stereotypes as exceptions, unrepresentative of the group as a whole, rather than as impetus for stereotype refinement (Taylor 1981; Weber and Crocker 1983). The creation of a subtype allows group stereotypes to remain intact in the face of disconfirming information.

Figure 2 applies the theory of subtyping to the schematic model proposed earlier to reveal a potentially different set of processes shaping racial attitudes. Here, instead of (or in addition to) known group characteristics and prior experiences being the predominant sources of racial attitudes, cultural stereotypes and media imagery play a strong role in shaping group expectations.[15] Those beliefs then translate into hiring decisions, which in turn provide a range of direct experiences for employers with black workers. But instead of positive experiences with black employees—as many of these employers report—leading to an updating of beliefs about blacks in general, we see a process of subtyping. As the saying might go, "*My blacks* aren't like blacks in general." Employers view their own black workers as a special subtype whose characteristics have little bearing on their evaluations of the larger group. Correspondingly, we see no pathway linking direct experiences with general beliefs.

Of course, this simple model does not capture the many nuances of attitude formation and change, which certainly contain a more diverse set of influences and pathways than are represented here. Rather, this basic schematic serves to represent one important alternative to the model proposed earlier, in which information flowed from the general to the specific and back again in ways that enhanced accuracy over time. Here, by contrast, an updating of expectations may occur with respect to specific members of the group (the subtype), but little revision of employers' more general attitudes is expected.

The analysis likewise does not imply that employers are necessarily wrong in their assessments of various group characteristics. It may be the case that employers' information about African Americans as a group is accurate and that the various selection processes at work (with individuals selecting into labor market participation and employers selecting workers) simply yield a more advantaged subgroup to which employers are exposed. This research makes no claims about the relationship between employers' attitudes and the "true" characteristics of African Americans. Rather, the findings suggest that, whatever sources of information they may be drawing from in forming racial attitudes, employers do not seem to draw heavily from their own personal experiences.

Conclusion and Discussion

The findings of this research suggest that, while most employers expressed strong negative views about the characteristics of African American men, fewer than half of these employers reported observations of their own applicants or employees consistent with these general perceptions. Where employers may

FIGURE 2
RESILIENCE OF STEREOTYPES

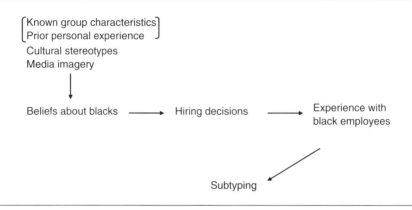

update their expectations regarding individual workers, these experiences do not seem to have noticeable effects on their attitudes about the group as a whole. Rather, employer attitudes appear more consistent with a model of subtyping, in which individuals who do not conform to a stereotype are viewed as exceptions whose characteristics have little bearing on the larger group.

Employers surely receive relevant information about various groups from sources other than direct workplace experience. They observe and interact with people in public spaces, they read newspaper coverage and watch TV news, and they are aware of racial inequality and have their own ideas about how and why this inequality is generated and maintained. These sources of information surely provide valuable complements to direct workplace experience. At the same time, it is surprising that the experiences employers report from their own direct observations do not carry greater weight in their general attitude formation. These results suggest that simple contact and exposure are themselves insufficient to revise deeply embedded racial attributions.

This analysis holds potentially troubling implications for hiring behavior. We know from the results of field experiments that employers consistently avoid black workers, hiring them at roughly half the rate of equally qualified whites. Where models of statistical discrimination might interpret this behavior as the rational response to observed differences in the productivity of black and white workers, the present research questions this conclusion. The majority of employers who report positive experiences with black workers (or no differences between black and white workers) nevertheless maintain strong negative attitudes about black men generally. To the extent that these attitudes shape hiring decisions, even in the scenario of equal productivity among black and white workers, we would expect the problems of hiring discrimination to persist well into the future.

Notes

1. See Armour (1997) for an extensive discussion of the logical, legal, and moral dilemmas of "reasonable racism."

2. Although the results of this study are indeed striking, it is important to keep in mind that more than 50 percent of Kirshenman and Neckerman's (1991) sample "either saw no difference [in the work ethic of whites, blacks, and Hispanics] or refused to categorize in a straightforward way" (p. 210).

3. A similar process of updating is described in the social psychological literature on stereotype change, referred to as a "book keeping model," according to which new information is incrementally incorporated into existing beliefs or attitudes about a group (Weber and Crocker 1983).

4. In this analysis, cognitive ability is observed to the researcher (by the respondent's score on an Armed Forces Qualification Test [AFQT] test measured earlier) but not by the employer at the point of hire. The assumption is that the worker's cognitive ability becomes observable to the employer with time on the job.

5. Roughly 80 percent of the employers in this sample were drawn from a random sample of employers advertising for an entry-level position in 2004 (see Pager, Western, and Bonikowski 2007). The remaining 20 percent were drawn through a purposive sampling technique enabling us to better represent large employers and industries underrepresented by the primary sample.

6. Note that within these industries are represented a wide range of job titles, including stockers, sales assistants, busboys, kitchen staff, waiters, couriers, and customer service positions.

7. The vast majority of employers offered multiple explanations within a single response series. In categorizing employers' sentiments, we distinguish between individual and structural explanations using several coding schemes. The first coding scheme takes into account the "first-mention," or whatever explanation was first proposed by the employer; the second takes into account any factor mentioned by an employer, with most employers being coded into several categories; the third uses a "holistic" approach in which we coded the comments according to what appeared to be the employers' main point. In many interviews, we specifically probed employers who reported multiple explanations with the question, "What do you think is the most important factor?" In other cases, this coding is based on our interpretation of the transcript. The main substantive conclusions are consistent across coding schemes, and where relevant, multiple measures are reported here.

8. An additional 10 percent cited "less inborn ability" as a major explanation, and 43 percent cited a "lack of chance for education." Respondents were allowed to choose more than one explanation, and thus, the categories do not sum to 100 percent (Hunt 2007, 400, Table 2).

9. Bobo, Johnson, and Suh's (2002) study draws data from the Los Angeles Study of Urban Inequality in which respondents were asked to rate members of a series of racial groups according to a range of characteristics (unintelligent, prefer welfare, hard to get along with, poor English).

10. Note that here (and in several other interviews), the job in question requires primarily manual work and few customer interactions. Jobs at a cleaning company or a moving company do not typically require professional dress, and yet, for these employers, a worker's attire sends an important signal about his reliability and commitment to work.

11. A number of other employers emphasized the perceptions of others about blacks as threatening or intimidating. For example, one employer said, "I think a lot of white people are scared of black people for some reason. I think they are scared of them, intimidated by them, they don't feel comfortable around them." Similarly, the manager of a small restaurant expressed concern over the aggressive demeanor of black men, stating that employers may be hesitant to call black applicants back because "immediately a black male is perceived as being aggressive." Although these perceptions may also be highly relevant for hiring decisions, we do not include these responses here as this analysis focuses on employers' own views about African Americans.

12. We asked separately about applicants and employees, given that effective employer screening would lead to a different distribution of characteristics among those seeking employment relative to those who become employed.

13. African American employers appeared slightly more inclined to notice racial differences among applicants but substantially less likely to report racial differences among employees. Immigrant employers noted more racial differences at both stages. Note, however, that our sample of African American and immigrant employers is small and that these indications must be taken as tentative.

14. Even respondents who described just one negative event were coded among those who had observed racial differences.

15. While we cannot measure the influence of cultural stereotypes directly, several employers did explicitly comment on the ways in which cultural representations of black men in the media affected their perceptions of black men. According to one employer, "I'd probably say 90 percent of the crimes you see on TV are African Americans, female or male, and that's something that's in the back of your head, you know." Similarly, another employer commented, "We have the media sending all this negative information about the young black male. All this negative information constantly. . . . We are getting the wrong image of what they look like."

References

Altonji, Joseph G., and Charles R. Pierret. 2001. Employer learning and statistical discrimination. *Quarterly Journal of Economics* 116:313-50.

Armour, Jody David. 1997. *Negrophobia and reasonable racism: The hidden costs of being black in America*. New York: New York University Press.

Arrow, Kenneth J. 1972. Models of job discrimination. In *Racial discrimination in economic life*, ed. Anthony H. Pascal, 83-102. Lexington, MA: D.C. Heath.

———. 1998. What has economics to say about racial discrimination? *Journal of Economic Perspectives* 12:91-100.

Bendick, Marc, Jr., Lauren Brown, and Kennington Wall. 1999. No foot in the door: An experimental study of employment discrimination. *Journal of Aging and Social Policy* 10:5-23.

Bertrand, Marianne, and Sendhil Mullainathan. 2004. Are Emily and Greg more employable than Lakisha and Jamal? A field experiment on labor market discrimination. *American Economic Review* 94:991-1013.

Bielby, William, and James N. Baron. 1986. Men and women at work: Sex segregation, and statistical discrimination. *American Journal of Sociology* 91:759-99.

Bobo, Lawrence D. 2004. Inequalities that endure? Racial ideology, American politics, and the peculiar role of the social sciences. In *The changing terrain of race and ethnicity*, ed. Maria Krysan and Amanda E. Lewis, 13-42. New York: Russell Sage Foundation.

Bobo, Lawrence D., Devon Johnson, and Susan A. Suh. 2002. Racial attitudes and power in the workplace: Do the haves differ from the have-nots? In *Prismatic metropolis: Inequality in Los Angeles*, ed. Lawrence D. Bobo, Melvin Oliver, James H. Johnson Jr., and Abel Valenzuela Jr., 491-523. New York: Russell Sage Foundation.

Farber, Henry S., and Robert Gibbons. 1996. Learning and wage dynamics. *Quarterly Journal of Economics* 111:1007-47.

Farmer, Amy, and Dek Terrell. 1996. Discrimination, Bayesian updating of employer beliefs and human capital accumulation. *Economic Inquiry* 34:204-19.

Fiske, Susan. 1998. Stereotyping, prejudice, and discrimination. In *The handbook of social psychology*, ed. Daniel Gilbert, Susan Fiske, and Gardner Lindzey, 357-411. New York: McGraw Hill.

Fix, Michael, and Raymond J. Struyk, eds. 1993. *Clear and convincing evidence: Measurement of discrimination in America*. Washington, DC: Urban Institute Press.

Holzer, Harry J., Paul Offner, and Elaine Sorensen. 2005. Declining employment among young black less-educated men: The role of incarceration and child support. *Journal of Policy Analysis and Management* 24:330-33.

Hunt, Matthew O. 2007. African American, Hispanic, and white beliefs about black/white inequality, 1977-2004. *American Sociological Review* 72:390-415.

Jackman, Man R. 1994. *The velvet glove: Paternalism and conflict in gender, class, and race relations*. Berkeley: University of California Press.

Kirschenman, Joleen, and Katherine Neckerman. 1991. We'd love to hire them, but . . . : The meaning of race for employers. In *The urban underclass*, ed. Christopher Jencks and Paul E. Peterson, 203-34. Washington, DC: Brookings Institution.

Kluegel, James R., and Eliot R. Smith. 1985. *Beliefs about inequality: Americans' views of what is and what ought to be*. New York: Aldine de Gruyter.

Moss, Philip I., and Christopher Tilly. 2001. *Stories employers tell: Race, skill, and hiring in America*. New York: Russell Sage Foundation.

Oettinger, Gerald S. 1996. Statistical discrimination and the early career evolution of the black-white wage gap. *Journal of Labor Economics* 14:52-78.

Orbuch, Terri L. 1997. People's accounts count: The sociology of accounts. *Annual Review of Sociology* 23:455-78.

Pager, Devah. 2003. The mark of a criminal record. *American Journal of Sociology* 108:937-75.

———. 2007. *Marked: Race, crime, and finding work in an era of mass incarceration*. Chicago: University of Chicago Press.

Pager, Devah, Bruce Western, and Bart Bonikowski. 2007. Discrimination in low wage labor markets. Working Paper, Office of Population Research, Princeton University, Princeton, NJ.

Phelps, Edmund. 1972. The statistical theory of racism and sexism. *American Economic Review* 62:659-61.

Rothschild, Micahel, and Joseph E. Stiglitz. 1982. A model of employment outcomes illustrating the effect of the structure of information on the level and distribution of income. *Economic Letters* 10:231-36.

Schuman, Howard, and Maria Krysan. 1999. A historical note on whites' beliefs about racial inequality. *American Sociological Review* 64:847-55.

Taylor, Shelley E. 1981. A categorization approach to stereotyping. In *Cognitive processes in stereotyping and intergroup behavior*, ed. D. L. Hamilton, 83-114. Hillsdale, NJ: Lawrence Erlbaum.

Tomaskovic-Devey, Donald, and Sheryl Skaggs. 1999. An establishment-level test of the statistical discrimination hypothesis. *Work and Occupations* 26:420-43.

Waldinger, Roger, and Michael Lichter. 2003. *How the other half works: Immigration and the social organization of labor*. Berkeley: University of California Press.

Weber, Renee, and Jennifer Crocker. 1983. Cognitive processes in the revision of stereotypic beliefs. *Journal of Personality and Social Psychology* 45 (5): 961-77.

Whatley, Warren, and Gavin Wright. 1994. Race, human capital, and labour markets in American history. In *Labour market evolution: The economic history of market integration, wage flexibility, and the employment relation*, ed. George Grantham and Mary MacKinnon, 270-91. London: Routledge.

Wilson, William Julius. 1996. *When work disappears: The world of the new urban poor*. New York: Vintage Books.

If Moynihan Had Only Known: Race, Class, and Family Change in the Late Twentieth Century

By
FRANK F. FURSTENBERG

In this article, the author argues that while Daniel Patrick Moynihan's 1965 analysis of the black family was prescient in many respects, it also largely ignored social class variations among black families. This gave the erroneous impression that the changes occurring in the black family were related to distinctive cultural features rather than the economic position of most blacks. Over time, it has become evident that poor economic circumstances would produce comparable effects on whites just as they did for blacks when Moynihan published his findings.

Keywords: Daniel Patrick Moynihan; *The Negro Family*; teen pregnancy; social class; race

In 1965, the year that the Moynihan Report was issued, the American family stood at the precipice of a yawning demographic divide that separated the now legendary postwar family that was in full flower at midcentury from the pluralistic model that superseded it in the final decades of the twentieth century. Although he was a true visionary who observed with remarkable clarity what was happening to the black family, Moynihan, like virtually all of the social scientists of his era, did not adequately appreciate the incipient contradictions in the prevailing family form. Incorrectly assuming that the kinship system in place—referred to at the time as the "isolated nuclear family" or "conjugal family form"—was normatively ideal (rooted in nature), functional for society, and permanent, Moynihan failed to see that the changes taking

Frank F. Furstenberg is the Zellerbach Family Professor of Sociology and a research associate at the Population Studies Center at the University of Pennsylvania. He has written extensively on issues relating to family change over the past four decades. His most recent book, Destinies of the Disadvantaged: The Politics of Teenage Childbearing, *was published by the Russell Sage Foundation in 2007. His current research examines the well-being of middle-income families in Canada and the United States.*

DOI: 10.1177/0002716208324866

place in low-income black families were also happening, albeit at a slower pace, among lower-income families more generally.

If Moynihan had only known what was to become evident in later decades, he might well have structured his analysis and interpretation of the plight of the black family quite differently (see Moynihan, Smeeding, and Rainwater 2005). In fact, as I show in this article, Moynihan might well have been more nuanced in his interpretations had he paid closer attention to a long line of research on both black and ethnic minority families that had been carried out in the United States over the course of the first two-thirds of the twentieth century. Indeed, some of his critics observed as much shortly after the report was published (Rainwater and Yancey 1967).

Moynihan drew only selectively from the literature on the black family in making his case that blacks as a subgroup were uniquely challenged by economic and social conditions in the postwar period. Had he been more attentive to a tradition of research that focused simultaneously on social class and race, the report might have had far different political and social consequences, leading to alternative policy directions. Moynihan's focus on race rather than class continues to dominate policy debates about the family to this day. At least, this is the claim that I try to demonstrate in this article.

The first part sets the stage for my argument that Moynihan chose to structure his argument about the stresses on the black family primarily in terms of racial rather than social class cleavages. Then, I reexamine some of the data that he used to make his case. By updating some of the trends on family change that Moynihan observed, at least in hindsight, it is clear that many of the pressures on marriage and family formation that seemed uniquely relevant to blacks have been felt by low-income populations more generally. Then, I return to the reasons Moynihan was unable to imagine the future trends (other than the fact that he was writing in 1965) and attempt to generalize from some of his observations of why the family abandoned its postwar appearance.

The American Family in Black and White

The postwar family that we now love to love (or love to hate)

The Western family of the mid-twentieth century represented a cultural culmination of values, economic, and demographic forces that had been evident for several centuries (Coontz 2005; Goode 1960; Stone 1977). The decline of the family organized along lines of generation and gender (the patriarchal family) was steadily eroded by religious ideology, humanism, and economic and technological forces, many of which were evident at the very inception of this nation. Edward Shorter (1977) contended several decades ago that the American family was born modern. By this, he meant that the family organized around the control of males and elders took hold only incompletely when our nation was founded.

Even before industrialization, a stream of foreign travelers, de Tocqueville most prominent among them, observed that the American family drew its strength from its voluntary nature, democratic style of relationships, and low reliance on formal authority. They also noted the relatively strong boundaries around the marriage unit in the United States compared to Europe at the time. Later on, this tight family form, emphasizing marital over generational ties, was said to buffer its members from the growing demands of an industrial economy, or, in the words of Christopher Lasch (1977), the family became "a haven in a heartless world."

Even before industrialization, a stream of foreign travelers, de Tocqueville most prominent among them, observed that the American family drew its strength from its voluntary nature, democratic style of relationships, and low reliance on formal authority.

Family experts in the 1950s, when functional analysis in sociology was in its heyday, claimed that the family form that had adapted to the decline of agriculture and the rise of industry was ideally suited to provide the need, support, and socialization required to raise the next generation (Bell and Vogel 1968; Coser 1964). With Mom at home (after being displaced by the war) and Dad at work, the nuclear family was the stripped-down model for producing successful children. This commentary seemed to be widely supported by the huge boom in marriages and childbearing from the end of World War II until the early 1960s—what I have elsewhere called the "era of domestic mass production."

Most family sociologists, like most sociologists of the era, explained the family as a product or adaptation to postindustrial conditions. Talcott Parsons (1964), in several essays on the American family that were widely read in the 1950s and early 1960s, claimed that the bilateral nuclear family system in the West was uniquely equipped to cope with the industrial economic system that had become paramount in the first half of the twentieth century. Dad was the instrumental leader of the family who managed the outside world and connecting his children to the economic system; Mom was the expressive leader, who helped to protect

Dad from the pressures of the economic world and managing the home front. William J. Goode (1963), elaborating on the Parsonian thesis, contended that the conjugal form of the family—based primarily on marriage rather than extended kinship—rendered the family geographically mobile and flexible to respond to economic opportunities.

The framing of the Moynihan Report

It is impossible now to imagine just how pervasive this view was among family scholars in the 1950s and early 1960s, but suffice it to say that Moynihan was greatly influenced by this cultural template in his analysis of the breakdown of the black family. Divorce and nonmarital childbearing were undermining the partnership between parents, but also Moynihan noted how matriarchal practices fostered by slavery, economic exclusion, and racial discrimination were weakening the position of men and boys in black families:

> In essence, the Negro community has been forced into a matriarchal structure which, because it is too out of line with the rest of the American society, seriously retards the progress of the group as a whole, and imposes a crushing burden on the Negro male and, in consequence, on a great many Negro women as well. (Moynihan 1965, chap. 4)

Moynihan assembled a truly remarkable set of data to demonstrate that black families were buckling under the pressures of unemployment, urban ills, and ensuing marital instability. Whereas in the first decade after the Second World War, blacks, if anything, settled down into marriage earlier, there were troubling signs that the institution of marriage was losing its grip in the succeeding decade from the mid-1950s to the mid-1960s. By contrast, there appeared to be no such trend in the white population. Moynihan concluded that this divergence was the result of the declining employment among black men, the rising rates of delinquency and crime, and a cultural change within black communities that decreased commitment to mainstream patterns of family formation.

Moynihan not only drew on demographic data to bolster his argument that the black family was in crisis, but he also cited a number of studies that had been carried out over the course of the century on the black family. Moynihan relied on numerous historical studies and accounts of black family life by W. E. B. Du Bois, Franklin Frazier, and others to make the case that the black family had been uniquely affected by a series of social and economic shocks from slavery to Reconstruction and beyond into the twentieth century. Moynihan concluded that economic pressures and racial segregation in the postwar period were creating undue stresses on the already stressed black family. The black family was especially susceptible to these pressures because of its unique history of slavery and its aftermath that had shaped black culture in ways that undermined marriage and family formation. The report itself, I argue, played a powerful role in directing attention on low-income black families, helping to establish the conventional wisdom that the black family system was and still is distinctively different from the rest of the population.

The Moynihan Report in historical context

Recently, I undertook a review of the major qualitative studies on the black family in the past century (Furstenberg 2007). My readings spanned the period beginning with the classics of Du Bois—the community study in *The Philadelphia Negro* (1899) and his later writings on *The Negro American Family* (1908)—as well as the earliest and best-known ethnographic studies conducted from the 1930s through the early 1960s that preceded the Moynihan Report and the work produced in the wake of its publication during the last third of the twentieth century. I paid particular attention to a cluster of family practices revolving around sexual behavior, family formation, marriage practices, and gender relationships. Virtually all of the ethnographic community studies have extensive discussions of these behaviors that would later become a focus of attention in the Moynihan Report.

From Du Bois's foundational work to Frazier's (1939) monumental historical accounts of black family life beginning in the 1930s, which helped to lay the groundwork for the earliest ethnographic studies of black communities in both the rural South and the urban North, research in the first half of the twentieth century emphasized the influence of social class in shaping family patterns. Indeed, most of the authors of empirical studies closely adhered to the pioneering community research that had been carried out by such luminaries as Robert and Helen Lynd (1929), Lloyd Warner and his associates (Warner and Lunt 1941), and August Hollingshead (1949) on white communities, examining family life through the lens of social class.

Du Bois was explicit in observing that differences among blacks in Philadelphia varied sharply by "social station." Influenced by Du Bois's writing, Frazier, too, structured his historical account of black families by noting that experiences during slavery and Reconstruction created different opportunities for blacks in the twentieth century, which resulted in a pronounced stratification system operating within black communities much as existed in white communities. Research by Hortense Powdermaker (1939), Drake and Cayton (1945, 788), Hylan Lewis (1955), Allison Davis (Davis, Gardner, and Gardner 1941), and John Dollard (1937) among others all embraced a tradition of community research growing out of the Chicago School of sociology that paid close attention to social stratification.

I could not find a single study in my review of the literature that did not report powerful class differences within black communities that paralleled the stratification reported among families in predominately white localities. While the patterns of family life by social class bore a distinct resemblance especially at the lower end, the distribution of families across the social class spectrum, of course, varied enormously for whites and blacks. Nonetheless, descriptions of family life were cast in remarkably similar terms. Drake and Cayton (1945) observe that "all serious students of Negro communities since Du Bois have been concerned with the nature of social stratification among Negroes."

At the top of the social ladder, upper-class black families were very sensitive to propriety, manners, and the acquisition of culture, a cluster of habits that Drake and Cayton (1945) referred to as "the home-centric upper-class." Bourgeois sensibilities, as Frazier previously noted in his trenchant writings about the upper class, were marked by a strong commitment to achieving in the American status system and took some pains to distance themselves from families beneath them. The more socially concerned upper-class families were interested "in trying to speed up the processes by which the lower class can be transformed from a poverty-stricken group isolated from the general stream of American life, into a counterpart of middle-class America" (Drake and Cayton 1945, 563).

The depiction of lower-class life rendered by Drake and Cayton (1945) in their landmark book *Black Metropolis*, perhaps the most notable ethnographic study of an urban, black community carried out in the first half of the twentieth century, bears an uncanny resemblance to the qualitative studies of black family life that were to follow. In a discussion of the "The Hazards of Marriage," Drake and Cayton assert that Bronzeville was "suffering from social disorganization." Citing Frazier, the authors conclude that the legacy of the economic conditions since the Depression had created a high level of instability in lower-class black families, including "high rates of desertion, illegitimacy, and divorce as well as a great deal of violent conflict within the average lower-class household" (p. 582).

Lower-class families were said by the informants of Cayton and Drake (1945) to have a "loose" family life; the poor raised "immoral children," with low ambitions. The poor were promiscuous, drank excessively, were boisterous in public, were violent, and were emotionally unstable. Relationships between men and women were often conflict-ridden and highly unstable. Drake and Cayton discuss how men had become increasingly dependent on women. "Lower-class men are thus in a weak economic position vis-à-vis their women and children. . . . Since she pays the piper, she usually feels justified in calling the tune" (p. 583). Men often compensated by trading love for a living.

Nevertheless, Drake and Cayton (1945, 363) point out that "three out of every five lower-class men and women in Bronzeville claim that they are married." The authors assert, however, that many of these marriages are likely common-law unions that were imported from the South, which long had less concern for "the formalities of law and church." Drake and Cayton describe a "good" man in the lower class as someone who works when able and does not spend money frivolously on gambling, drink, and other women. A good woman is sexually satisfying, loyal, and does not take up with other men. "Some couples manage to stick it out and maintain a stable, unbroken home, but this is not the typical lower-class pattern" (p. 587).

The class gradient of family patterns so vividly depicted in Bronzeville by Drake and Cayton recurs in study after study regardless of date or location. I could find no important substantive differences in descriptions of family life of upper-, middle-, and low-income residents of rural community studies conducted by Powdermaker (1939); Dollard (1937); Davis, Gardner, and Gardner (1941); or Lewis (1955). Clearly, the predominance of lower-income families in black communities made family formation more precarious and marital relations more hazardous, but all writers noted the significant role played by middle- and upper-income black families in setting standards of propriety for family formation.

I also discovered that the family standards reported in black communities bore a notable resemblance to the family practices in white communities carried out during the first half of the twentieth century (see also Jarrett's [1992] discussion of more recent community research.) Hylan Lewis in his community study, *The Blackways of Kent* (1955), for example, undertook his examination of a Piedmont community under the direction of George Simpson, a leading student of race relations in the 1950s. While no explicit comparisons were drawn in the analyses between Lewis's findings and the work in white communities that were being carried out at the same time, Lewis notes that his results about lower-class family patterns are similar to findings in a nearby mill town inhabited by whites. He writes, "It seems clear that both the mill village and the Negro society have cultures that retain significant rural features; both are derived in part from the anxieties of low-status." (p. 320)

A decade before Moynihan, Lewis warned of the dangers of a black subculture "evolving a natural character all of its own based on a 'tough cultural situation' that Negroes face" (p. 311).

Bringing back social class

By this time, the noted anthropologist Oscar Lewis, in a series of studies, had proposed the idea that low-income families throughout the world adapted to their conditions in similar ways. During the same era, research on family life in the Caribbean revealed kinship arrangements that permitted a great deal of sexual latitude, de-emphasized the importance of marriage, and created a strong emphasis on matrifocal lineage. The social anthropologist Hyman Rodman (1971), one of the researchers working in this area, would later argue that the lower-class patterns of family life reflected a "value stretch." While low-income families did not reject marriage as a preferred form, they were forced to settle for less by their limited means. In a similar vein, William J. Goode (1960) proposed that in the absence of tangible inheritance, the rationale for marriage was undermined.

Moynihan was well aware of this literature and borrowed from Oscar Lewis the notion of a "culture of poverty," even though he did not employ the term explicitly in his review. By this, Lewis meant that low-income families created a culture that became an impediment to social mobility because it exposed children to a matrilineal form of family life that threatened to become self-perpetuating. Like his colleague, Lee Rainwater, Moynihan came to believe that lower-class culture in the black community was relatively autonomous and resistant to change, a point that was heatedly debated after the report's publication.

In my examination of qualitative studies of black family life, I discovered a clear shift in the attention of researchers following the publication of the Moynihan Report. Class-comparative studies almost disappeared in the period immediate afterward. During the late 1960s and 1970s, a series of brilliant ethnographic accounts of lower-class communities were carried out by writers such as Camille Jeffers (1967) Eliot Liebow (1968), Ulf Hannerz (1969), Lee Rainwater (1970), Joyce Ladner (1971), and Carol Stack (1974), providing rich accounts of lower-class family life describing how low-income families adapted to their circumstances. In one way or another, all of these studies were motivated by Moynihan's argument that low-income families were embedded in poverty communities that shaped the nature of sexual practices, union formation and dissolution, and childrearing patterns.

All but lost in these accounts was the comparative focus on intraethnic and intraracial class differences and interethnic and interracial class similarities that characterized the family literature before the 1960s. By the late 1960s, the social science literature was dominated by discussions of whether a culture of poverty existed and, if it did, what policy remedies were available to change the values of the poor families in ways that would permit them to enter the mainstream American social system. Conservative social scientists argued that the problem was culture, while liberals maintained that the root of the problem was structural (Banfield 1968, 1984).

This debate continued up until the publication of William Julius Wilson's book on *The Truly Disadvantaged* in 1987, which in some sense represented a peace offering to the warring sides. Wilson acknowledged the existed of what he called a "ghetto specific culture" that represented an adaptation to poverty in response to the growing racial segregation of American urban areas. Wilson also noted the declining opportunities for families in high-poverty communities for employment, adequate education, and services that might permit mobility.

In the past decade and a half, I found evidence that there may again be a shift in the focus of qualitative studies on black family life, indicating a return to the class-comparative perspective. There appears to be evidence that social scientists are returning to cross-racial and ethnic comparisons as well as more studies of class variations within race/ethnic groups (Anderson 1999; Edin and Kefalas 2005; Lareau 2003; Pattillo-McCoy 1999). This work reflects a growing reality based on social demographic studies that white patterns of sexual behavior, family formation, and gender relations among lower-income families increasingly resemble the family patterns that troubled Moynihan nearly a half century ago.

Converging Black and White Family Patterns

The narrowing divide in teenage and nonmarital childbearing

For a decade or two after the publication of the Moynihan Report, public attention initially focused on the level of teenage childbearing and nonmarital childbearing among women in their teens and early twenties. At first, the issue of early and out-of-wedlock childbearing, consistent with Moynihan's observations, was primarily seen as a pattern of family formation occurring almost exclusively among African Americans. It so happened that I began collecting data on a cohort of teenage mothers in Baltimore, the very year that the Moynihan Report appeared. The early findings of my research seemed to support the concerns that Moynihan had voiced.

From interviews with pregnant teens and their parents, I learned that virtually all of the whites in the sample had plans to marry or had already wed by the time that they were interviewed. By contrast, the black teens and their parents were openly ambivalent about the potential benefits of marriage, though more than half eventually married the father of the child. Many black participants, especially the parents of the pregnant teens, were skeptical that early marriage would confer any advantage to their daughters. They preferred for them to remain in school and test the father's commitment to the relationship.

In fact, their assessments were realistic. Of the marriages contracted by the mostly black participants in the first five years of the study, half dissolved. Over time, 80 percent of the mothers who married the child's father and an even higher percentage of those who married a surrogate ultimately separated. I had less success in following the whites in the sample because they married and often moved out of Baltimore, but it appeared that they had somewhat lower rates of marital instability. Consistent with national data, however, they still suffered relatively high rates of dissolution as well.

These doubts about marriage among the black women in my study were reflected in national trends showing a steep decline in teenage marriage and a rising level of nonmarital childbearing among black women younger than twenty occurring in the 1960s (Moore, Simms, and Betsey 1986; O'Connell and Moore 1980). Among all teenagers in 1969, the first year in which racial comparisons can be made, blacks were about ten times more likely than whites to have a child out of wedlock. Of all white teens, less than 1 percent had a child out of wedlock, compared with nearly 10 percent of black teens (Ventura and Bachrach 2000). From the vantage point of the time, there was little reason to question Moynihan's view that out-of-wedlock childbearing among teens demonstrated a striking racial difference in family formation patterns.

Yet, as I have observed in greater detail in a recently published book on the topic of the politics of teenage childbearing, the racial disparity in nonmarital childbearing became less and less pronounced over the decades since the Moynihan Report was published (Furstenberg 2007). The difference between the *rate* of teenage childbearing (per thousand unmarried teens) outside of marriage among blacks and whites (which now constitutes almost all births among women under the age of twenty) has steadily declined over time, as shown in Figures 1, 2, and 3. Indeed, it dropped from a twelvefold difference in the 1960s to slightly more than two to one in the most recent decade. In 2004, the last year for which data are available, approximately 6 percent of black teens and nearly 3 percent of white teens had a child outside of marriage.

Two factors have produced the gradual convergence in levels of nonmarital childbearing among teens. Since the 1960s, black teens have actually *decreased* their rates of teenage fertility, while the rate among white teenagers has steadily

FIGURE 1
BIRTHRATES FOR UNMARRIED WHITE WOMEN BY AGE GROUP, 1965-2005

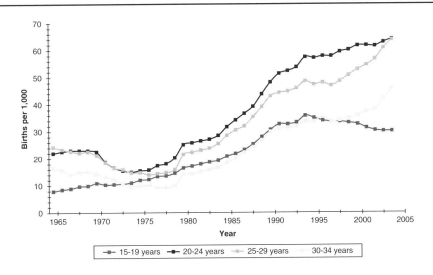

FIGURE 2
BIRTHRATES FOR UNMARRIED AFRICAN AMERICAN WOMEN
BY AGE GROUP, 1965-2005

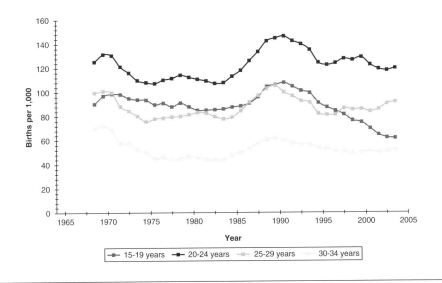

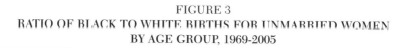

FIGURE 3
RATIO OF BLACK TO WHITE BIRTHS FOR UNMARRIED WOMEN
BY AGE GROUP, 1969-2005

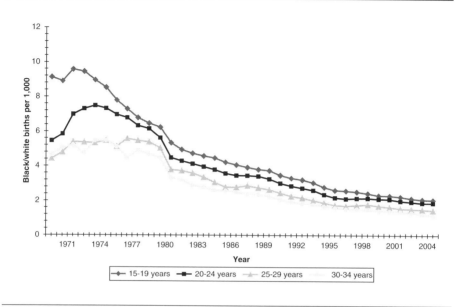

risen until the middle of the past decade, when it has effectively plateaued (see Figures 1 and 2). A number of different potential sources underlie this incompletely understood demographic change. First, just as happened among blacks in the period of late 1950s and early 1960s, white teenagers who became pregnant began to perceive that early marriage was a precarious solution to a premarital conception (Edin and Kefalas 2005). The partners of soon-to-be mothers did not look as appealing as they once had when skilled blue-collar jobs with union wages were more plentiful.

At the same time, the pressure on white women to complete their schooling before marriage and become economically self-sufficient, no doubt, increased as well. There is also strong evidence that the stigma associated with nonmarital childbearing began to decline for young white women just as it had for blacks beginning in the 1950s. The cultural logic that had drawn many white women into shotgun weddings collapsed. Younger white women who would have once married upon learning that they were pregnant now join the ranks of single mothers when they become unintentionally pregnant.

Nonmarital childbearing rates among teenage blacks are now substantially lower than they were when Moynihan published his report. A host of changing conditions, including policies that were designed to make teenage childbearing less attractive, greater availability of effective contraception, and, most particularly, the perceived threat of AIDS and STDs, led young black women to become more adept at managing sexual relationships and avoiding unwanted pregnancies. There is evidence, too, that young men became aware of the requirement of paying child support for the children whom they sired and began to exercise more responsibility in their sexual relationships.

In the intervening decades since the publication of the Moynihan Report, the complexion of teenage childbearing has changed radically in ways that make blacks and whites look far more similar today than they once appeared. In part, I would argue that their behavior has become more similar because their conditions have become more alike in the past forty years. White teenagers no longer are inclined to use marriage as a safety net when faced with an unintended pregnancy, while black women have become less likely to become pregnant due to greater contraceptive vigilance.

Narrowing differences in nonmarital childbearing among older women

Over the past several decades, teenage childbearing has become a smaller and smaller component of the total number of nonmarital births in a given year (Terry-Humen, Manlove, and Moore 2001). When I began the Baltimore study, teenagers accounted for a large and growing share of all nonmarital childbearing. This occurred in part because of the huge baby boom population that came of age in the 1960s but also because rates of nonmarital childbearing were growing among teenagers faster than among older women. Whereas marriage—even for pregnant women—was declining among teens, marriage rates continued to be robust for a decade or so among older women, especially when they experienced an unplanned pregnancy.

In the late 1960s and early 1970s, teenagers produced half or more of the share of all nonmarital births. Since then, the share of nonmarital births occurring to teenagers has steadily declined (Elo, Berkowitz-King, and Furstenberg 1999). Teenagers now account for less than a fourth of all nonmarital births, less than half the share they made up just thirty years ago. Part of this shift in the age distribution of nonmarital childbearing can be explained by the aging of the baby boomers. Teens are now a smaller proportion of all women of childbearing ages. More important, however, older women themselves have become increasingly susceptible to having children out of wedlock. In fact, women over the age of twenty-five have experienced the largest growth in the share of all nonmarital births and now produce almost two-fifths of all nonmarital births in the United States.

Of course, this demographic shift in nonmarital childbearing among older women need not have changed the racial distribution of nonmarital births, but the same pattern of racial convergence evident among teenagers occurred among older women. Whites have now become more likely to defer or postpone marriage indefinitely when pregnancy occurs than they were forty years ago. This trend is evident among both women who never married and those who previously married. Among all women of childbearing ages, the rate of nonmarital childbearing has quadrupled, rising from about fourteen per thousand in 1970 to almost forty-six per thousand in 2004, despite the fact that the rate of nonmarital fertility among black women has declined by a third—from ninety-six to ninety-seven per thousand (Hamilton, Martin, and Ventura 2006; Ventura and Bachrach 2000).

Explaining the narrowing gap

What could possibly account for this remarkable reversal in the racial distribution of nonmarital childbearing over the past several decades? Obviously, the explanation requires understanding both why and how blacks have managed to decrease their nonmarital childbearing and understanding why white nonmarital fertility has grown. I do not as yet have the answer, but I am willing to speculate on some of the reasons for this reversal of trends.

In an important paper about premarital fertility that explores these trends, Scott South (1999) also notes the striking trend toward racial convergence in an analysis of data from the Panel Survey of Income Dynamics, demonstrating that it is not a product of changing demographic conditions within the racial groups. Consistent with earlier studies, South reported sharp class differences in the risk of early childbearing, but he also found that over the life course, the effect of natal family resources eventually declined (though not maternal education). In other words, over time, women's own social class status waned in influence, and life circumstances became more prominent predictors of their likelihood of having a nonmarital birth.

South's (1999) findings are provocative because they suggest that the growth of nonmarital childbearing has been largely at the bottom of the income distribution. By dichotomizing income, roughly at the median, South's findings suggest that the growth of nonmarital childbearing has primarily occurred among lower-income whites in the bottom half of the income distribution. Although higher-income whites have more births, their share of the nonmarital births has not risen over time. Nonmarital births among the better off were extremely rare in the 1960s and early 1970s, and today, they are still proportionally just as rare.

This analysis is completely consistent with work done by Ellwood and Jencks (2005) and Goldstein and Kenney (2001) on marriage trends over roughly the same period of time. Trends in marriage have revealed a pattern bifurcated by socioeconomic status as measured by educational level. Among the less educated, levels of marriage and marital stability have trended sharply downward, whereas rates of marriage and marital stability have remained relatively constant among women who have completed college.

These findings, like those on nonmarital childbearing, indicate a diverging family system. Marriage itself has become more of a luxury good, affordable and sustainable among the better-educated and the more affluent. For those with more limited means, cohabitation that may or may not eventuate in marriage has become an increasingly common practice, especially among white couples. It has long been known that cohabitational unions are less stable. A growing number of less affluent whites who have children may start out as couples, hoping to move toward marriage, but most are unable to sustain the weak bonds of a more provisional and perhaps conditional childbearing relationship. Lower-income blacks may be both less willing to start out as a couple than whites, but in time, both blacks and whites with limited means end up as single parents.

No doubt other factors are implicated in the rise of nonmarital childbearing among lower-income and less educated white women. Over the decades, a growing proportion have experienced parental divorce during childhood; that experience may have made them more wary of marriage just as it did among black women several decades earlier. The experiences of one generation do affect the next, though most research shows that the "transmission" of family instability is modest and could not adequately account for the large-scale retreat from early marriage and the growth of cohabitation. More likely, high rates of marital instability have a direct effect on the children of divorce and affect the attitudes and behavior of children who have grown up in intact families.

We are beginning to witness a sharp divergence in family formation strategies by social class. Young adults from all social strata realize that establishing educational and work credentials are an essential stage in the early part of the life course and may be incompatible with the decision to create a permanent partnership. Among the better-educated and more affluent, cohabitation makes good sense as a way of testing the waters. Less educated couples, too, are inclined to delay. However, they are both less adept at managing their sexual relationships and more inclined to experience an unintended pregnancy. In all likelihood, they are less willing and able to get an abortion when a pregnancy occurs. Abortion has become both more stigmatized and less accessible since the early 1980s, especially to the lower income women. Add to this volatile mix the difficulty of finding a marriageable partner, and one has created the conditions for high levels of nonmarital childbearing among those with limited resources.

Social class has always influenced patterns of family formation. This is not to ignore the racial differences in marriage and fertility that Moynihan wrote about four decades ago. However, these racial differences have waned as a growing number of black women have begun to exercise greater control over their fertility and as white women have started to experience the same sorts of constraints that blacks were feeling about their prospects of forming a lasting marriage when Moynihan focused on their plight. Perhaps it is time then to recognize that Moynihan's contribution to understanding the situation of the black family was historically rooted in the era in which he was writing. Were the Moynihan Report written today, it would, no doubt, be framed more by the disparate conditions created by social class than by racial differences.

Conclusion

Even conceding that the family circumstances of blacks and whites looked very different when Moynihan published his report, I have claimed that he might have been able to do a better job of unpacking the racial differences that he observed in the family had he paid closer attention to the qualitative research produced by social scientists in the decades leading up to his report. Family life was highly structured by social class conditions even within racial groupings. Low-income blacks and whites had much in common, but Moynihan chose to cast his analysis and interpretation of the problems that blacks were experiencing as due to the cultural legacy of slavery and discrimination rather than to the chronic economic conditions that made family formation hazardous. This is not to say that African Americans do not have a greater vulnerability but that much of the vulnerability that they have experienced is due to precarious economic circumstances rather than their disadvantaged historical circumstances or the heritage of family forms from Africa.

[Moynihan] might have been able to do a better job of unpacking the racial differences that he observed in the family had he paid closer attention to the qualitative research produced by social scientists in the decades leading up to his report.

As more and more lower-income whites have faced the same set of precarious economic conditions, they have begun to exhibit the same patterns of family formation behavior as African Americans. The advantages that marriage ostensibly confers become more apparent than real in an era of great inequality, and fewer are willing to commit to or able to maintain stable unions whether they take the form of marriage or de facto marriage. As a result, efforts to promote marriage without changing the economic and social conditions that foster stable unions are destined to be ineffective. There is nothing wrong with attempting to provide skill training for young couples, but such efforts will yield little if low-income couples continue to experience chronic unemployment, underemployment, time pressures due to the need to work extra hours, lack of supportive services, and the like.

I have ignored altogether in this article the circumstances of the Latino population because they were not a part of the Moynihan Report. However, they provide an instructive case for the argument that I have advanced. Growing evidence indicates the Latino population is experiencing a change from a marriage-oriented population among the foreign-born to an American pattern of family formation among the second generation and among those born abroad but reared in the United States. Among Mexicans, in particular, rates of nonmarital child-bearing have risen to levels that exceed those of whites and are beginning to approach those of African Americans.

This pattern suggests that it is insufficient to have strong cultural values about marriage if the economic and social conditions that foster marriage are not maintained. Mexicans, like lower-income blacks and whites, are finding it difficult to form and maintain stable unions that survive the vicissitudes of stressful conditions that continue to undermine the family. To be sure, the story of change over the past forty years is not strictly an economic one. Gender relationships, premarital sexual practices, and social and cultural influences have all played a part in reshaping the family. However, the continuing pattern of class difference, which was in evidence when Moynihan wrote his report, has become more pronounced over the passing decades and cannot be ignored by either scholars or policy makers. Four decades later, it appears that Moynihan's analyses of the reasons that the black family was in crisis has a much wider application than he believed in 1965.

References

Anderson, Elijah. 1999. *Code of the street: Decency, violence, and the moral life of the inner city.* New York: Norton.

Banfield, Edward C. 1968. *The unheavenly city revisited.* Boston: Little, Brown.

———. 1984. *The democratic muse: Visual arts and the public interest.* New York: Basic Books.

Bell, Norman W., and Ezra F. Vogel. 1968. *A modern introduction to the family.* Rev. ed. New York: Free Press.

Coontz, Stephanie. 2005. *Marriage, a history: From obedience to intimacy, or how love conquered marriage.* New York: Viking.

Coser, Rose L. 1964. *The family: Its structure and functions.* New York: St. Martin's.

Davis, Alison, Burleigh Gardner, and Mary Gardner. 1941. *Deep South: A social anthropological study of caste and class.* Chicago: University of Chicago Press.

Dollard, John. 1937. *Caste and class in a southern town.* New Haven, CT: Yale University Press.

Drake, St. Claire, and Horace R. Cayton. 1945. *Black metropolis: A study of Negro life in a northern city.* New York: Harcourt, Brace and Co.

Du Bois, W. E. B. 1899. *The Philadelphia Negro.* Philadelphia: University of Pennsylvania Press.

———. 1908. *The Negro American family.* Atlanta, GA: Atlanta University Press.

Edin, Kathryn J., and Maria Kefalas. 2005. *Promises I can keep: Why low-income women put motherhood before marriage.* Berkeley: University of California Press.

Elo, Irma, Rosalind Berkowitz-King, and Frank F. Furstenberg. 1999. Adolescent females: Their sexual partners and fathers of their children. *Journal of Marriage and the Family* 61:74-84.

Ellwood, David T., and Christopher Jencks. 2005. The spread of single-parent families in the United States since 1960. In *The future of the family,* ed. Daniel Patrick Moynihan, Timothy Smeeding, and Lee Rainwater, 25-65. New York: Russell Sage Foundation.

Frazier, E. Franklin. 1939. *The Negro family in the United States.* Chicago: University of Chicago Press.

Furstenberg, Frank F. 2007. The making of the black family: Race and class in qualitative studies in the 20th century. *Annual Review of Sociology* 33:429-48.

Goldstein, Joshua R., and Catherine T. Kenney. 2001. Marriage delayed or marriage forgone? New cohort forecasts of first marriage for U.S. women. *American Sociological Review* 66:506-19.

Goode, William J. 1960. Illegitimacy in the Caribbean social structure. *American Sociological Review* 25:21-30.

———. 1963. *World revolution in family patterns.* New York: Free Press.

Hamilton, Brady E., Joyce A. Martin, and Stephanie J. Ventura. 2006. *Births: Preliminary data for 2005.* Bethesda, MD: National Center for Health Statistics. http://www.cdc.gov/nchs/products/pubs/pubd/ hestats/prelimbirths05/prelimbirths05.htm.

Hannerz, Ulf. 1969. *Soulside: Inquiries into ghetto culture and community.* New York: Columbia University Press.

Hollingshead, August B. 1949. *Elmtown's youth: The impact of social classes on adolescents.* New York: Wiley.

Jarrett, Robin L. 1992. *A comparative examination of socialization patterns among low-income African-Americans, Chicanos, Puerto Ricans, and whites: A review of the literature.* Evanston, IL: Northwestern University, Center for Urban Affairs and Public Policy.

Jeffers, Camille. 1967. *Living poor: A participant observer study of priorities and choices.* Ann Arbor, MI: Ann Arbor Publishers.

Ladner, Joyce A. 1971. *Tomorrow's tomorrow: The black woman.* Garden City, NY: Doubleday.

Lareau, Annette. 2003. *Unequal childhoods: Race, class and family life.* Berkeley: University of California Press.

Lasch, Christopher. 1977. *Haven in a heartless world: The family besieged.* New York: Basic Books.

Lewis, Hylan. 1955. *Blackways of Kent.* Chapel Hill: University of North Carolina Press.

Liebow, Elliot O. 1968. *Tally's corner.* Boston: Little, Brown.

Lynd, Robert S., and Helen M. Lynd. 1929. *Middletown: A study in contemporary American culture.* New York: Harcourt, Brace & Co.

Moore, Kristin A., Margaret C. Simms, and Charles L. Betsey. 1986. *Choice and circumstances: Racial differences in adolescent sexuality and fertility.* New Brunswick, NJ: Transaction Books.

Moynihan, Daniel Patrick. 1965. *The Negro family: The case for national action.* Washington, DC: Office of Policy Planning and Research, U.S. Department of Labor.

Moynihan, Daniel P., Timothy M. Smeeding, and Lee Rainwater, eds. 2005. *The future of the family.* New York: Russell Sage Foundation.

O'Connell, Martin, and Maurice J. Moore. 1980. The legitimacy status of first births to U.S. women aged 15–24, 1939–1978. *Family Planning Perspectives* 12:16-23, 25.

Parsons, Talcott. 1964. *Essays in sociological theory.* Rev. ed. New York: Free Press.

Pattillo-McCoy, Mary. 1999. *Black picket fences: Privilege and peril among the black middle class.* Chicago: University of Chicago Press.

Powdermaker, Hortense. 1939. *After freedom: A cultural study of the deep South.* New York: Viking.

Rainwater, Lee. 1970. *Behind ghetto walls.* Chicago: Aldine.

Rainwater, Lee, and William L. Yancey. 1967. *The Moynihan Report and the politics of controversy.* Cambridge, MA: MIT Press.

Rodman, Hyman. 1971. *Lower class families: The culture of poverty in Negro Trinidad.* New York: Oxford University Press.

South, Scott. 1999. Historical changes and life course variation in the determinants of premarital childbearing. *Journal of Marriage and the Family* 61:752-63.

Shorter, Edward. 1977. *The making of the modern family.* New York: Basic Books.

Stack, Carol B. 1974. *All our kin: Strategies for survival in a black community.* Chicago: Aldine.

Stone, Lawrence. 1977. *The family, sex and marriage in England 1500–1800.* London: Weidenfield and Nicholson.

Terry-Humen, Elizabeth, Jennifer Manlove, and Kristin A. Moore. 2001. *Births outside of marriage: Perceptions vs. reality.* Washington, DC: Child Trends www.childtrends.org.

Ventura, Stephanie J., and Christine A. Bachrach. 2000. Nonmarital childbearing in the United States, 1940–1999. *National Vital Statistics Report* 48 (16): 1-39.

Warner, W. Lloyd, and Paul S. Lunt. 1941. *The social life of a modern community.* New Haven, CT: Yale University Press.

Wilson, William J. 1987. *The truly disadvantaged: The inner city, the underclass, and public policy.* Chicago: University of Chicago Press.

Fragile Families and the Reproduction of Poverty

In 1965, Daniel Patrick Moynihan warned that non-marital childbearing and marital dissolution were undermining the progress of African Americans. The author argues that what Moynihan identified as a race-specific problem in the 1960s has now become a class-based phenomena as well. Using data from a new birth cohort study, the author shows that unmarried parents come from much more disadvantaged populations than married parents. The author further argues that non-marital childbearing reproduces class and racial disparities through its association with *partnership instability* and *multipartnered fertility*. These processes increase maternal stress and mental health problems, reduce the quality of mothers' parenting, reduce paternal investments, and ultimately lead to poor outcomes in children. Finally, by spreading fathers' contributions across multiple households, partnership instability and multipartnered fertility undermine the importance of individual fathers' contributions of time and money, which is likely to affect the future marriage expectations of both sons and daughters.

Keywords: Daniel Patrick Moynihan; *The Negro Family*; family structure; family instability; poverty; inequality; parenting; child well-being

By
SARA McLANAHAN

In his report on the Negro family, Daniel Patrick Moynihan (1965) noted that nonmarital childbearing was increasing among African Americans and that the root causes of the increase were the legacy of slavery, urbanization, and persistent male unemployment. He

Sara McLanahan is the William S. Tod Professor of Sociology and Public Affairs at Princeton University. She directs the Bendheim-Thoman Center for Research on Child Wellbeing and is Editor-in-Chief of The Future of Children. *Her research interests include family demography, inequality, and social policy. She has written five books, including* Fathers under Fire *(Urban Institute 1998),* Growing Up with a Single Parent *(Harvard University Press 1994), and* Single Mothers and Their Children *(Urban Institute 1986), as well as more than one hundred scholarly articles.*

NOTE: I would like to thank David Bradley, Martin Innes, Susanne Karstedt, Gary LaFree, Clifford Shearing, Richard Sparks, and Neil Walker for their comments on earlier versions of this article.

DOI: 10.1177/0002716208324862

further argued that these forces had led to a self-reinforcing "tangle of pathology," consisting of nonmarital childbearing, high male unemployment, and welfare dependence, which was undermining the progress of African Americans and contributing to the perpetuation of poverty. In the final paragraph of the report, Moynihan stated,

> The policy of the United States is to bring the Negro American to full and equal sharing in the responsibilities and rewards of citizenship. To this end, the programs of the federal government bearing on this objective shall be designed to have the effect, directly or indirectly, of enhancing the stability and resources of the Negro American family. (Moynihan 1965, 48)

Although initially praised by the black leadership for focusing national attention on a serious problem, the Moynihan Report soon become the target of harsh and widespread criticism from liberals (and eventually from black leaders) for using words like *pathology* to describe the black family and for attributing the disadvantages of African Americans to family structure rather than structural factors such as racial discrimination and poverty (Rainwater and Yancey 1967). In contrast, social conservatives praised the report and used it to support a "culture-of-poverty" argument that emphasized values and behaviors rather than poverty as the root cause of intergenerational poverty (Ryan 1976).

In the aftermath of the Moynihan controversy, liberal researchers avoided the topic of family structure, or they wrote only about the positive aspects of the black family (Stack 1974), until the 1980s when William Julius Wilson reopened the debate. In his book *The Truly Disadvantaged*, Wilson (1987) refocused attention on the instability of the African American family and its role in undermining the life chances of black children. Like Moynihan, Wilson distinguished between a black middle class, which he saw as advancing in terms of socioeconomic status, and a black lower class, which he saw as losing ground. Unlike Moynihan, however, Wilson argued explicitly that the best way to strengthen families was to increase men's employment and earnings.

Since the publication of the Moynihan Report, the proportion of African American children born outside marriage has grown dramatically, from 24 percent in 1965 to 69 percent in 2000 (see Figure 1). Nonmarital childbearing has also increased among other racial and ethnic groups, however. The proportion of white children born to unmarried parents has grown from 6 percent in 1965 to 24 percent today, and the proportion of Hispanic children has grown from 37 percent in 1990 to 42 percent in 2000,[1] Yet, after four decades of discussion, the debate over the role of family structure in the reproduction of poverty continues, with the basic positions showing very little change. At one extreme are analysts who argue that nonmarital childbearing is a consequence but not a cause of poverty (Coontz and Folbre 2002); at the other extreme are those who argue it is a cause but not a consequence (Murray 1984; J. Wilson 2002); and in between are those who, like Moynihan and William Julius Wilson, view it as both a cause and a consequence (Massey 2007; Western 2007).[2]

FIGURE 1
TRENDS IN NON MARITAL CHILDBEARING: 1950-2000

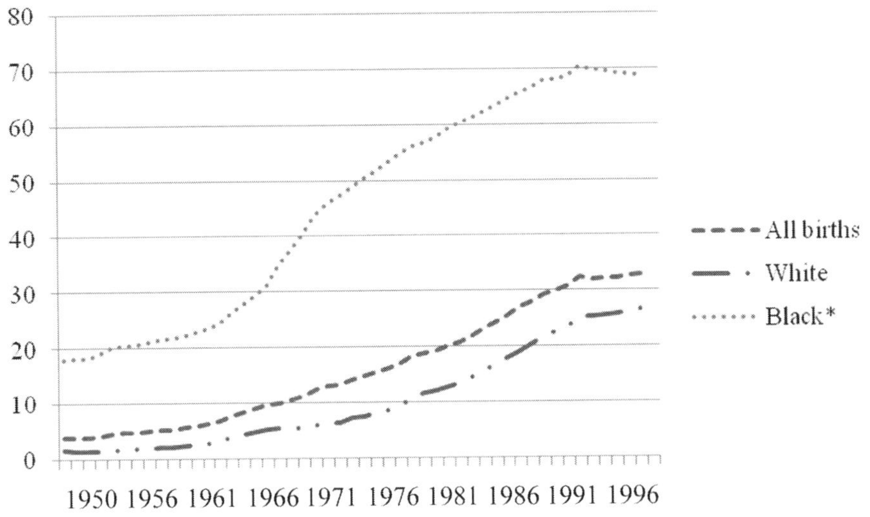

NOTE: °Births before 1969 classified as nonwhite.

Despite the importance of the topic and the intensity of the debate, empirical data pertaining to unmarried parents and their children has been limited until recently. Although we know something about the characteristics of the women who give birth outside marriage, we know much less about the fathers of these children; and although we know something about the role of economic factors in predicting nonmarital childbearing, we have very little data on the role of values and social skills. Finally, although a large body of research exists on the consequences of father absence and single motherhood for parents and children, most of this research is based on divorced families, which are likely to differ in important ways from families formed by unmarried parents (McLanahan and Sandefur 1994).

The Fragile Families Study

To learn more about unmarried parents and their children and to address some of the unanswered questions first raised during the debate over the Moynihan Report, my colleagues and I began work (in 1998) on the Fragile Families and Child Wellbeing Study, a longitudinal survey of about five thousand births, including more than thirty-six hundred births to unmarried parents.[3] The study design called for sampling new parents shortly after the birth of their child, and then reinterviewing both mothers and fathers when the focal child was one, three, and five years old. Child outcomes were assessed at years three and five. To maximize our chances of interviewing fathers as well as mothers, we started at the hospital and sampled new births. In cases where fathers could not be contacted at the hospital, we interviewed them by phone or in person as soon after the birth as possible. Births were sampled in seventy-five hospitals in twenty large cities throughout the United States, and when weighted, the data are representative of births in U.S. cities with populations of two hundred thousand or more people (Reichman et al. 2001). The study was designed to addresses the following questions:

- What are the capabilities of unmarried parents when their child is born, especially fathers?
- What is the nature of relationships in fragile families at birth? How do relationships change over time?
- How do parents and children fare in fragile families?[4]

The answers to these questions are important for resolving the debate over the Moynihan Report. For example, the answer to the first question can tell us the extent to which nonmarital childbearing is selective of people with different human capital and social skills and whether these differences are large enough to account for differences in children's outcomes later on. If poverty and low education are the root causes of nonmarital childbearing, as some people suggest, we would expect to find substantial differences in the human capital and social skills of married and unmarried parents at the time of their child's birth. If poverty is not a cause, we would expect differences to be small.

The answer to the second question can tell us something about whether families formed by unmarried parents are different from families formed by married parents in terms of parental values and commitment. In addition, by following parents over time, we can compare the stability of marital and nonmarital relationships and identify the factors that predict stability. If nonmarital unions are less stable than marital unions and if relationship stability is strongly associated with differences in human capital at birth, this finding would support the argument that poverty and economic insecurity cause family instability; alternatively, if instability is associated with differences in commitment and social-emotional skills, this finding would support the argument that the latter are contributing to family instability.

Finally, the answer to the third question can tell us something about whether a nonmarital birth leads to differences in parental resources and ultimately to poor child outcomes. If parental resources and child outcomes are no different in married- and unmarried-parent families, once socioeconomic status at birth is taken into account, this finding would lend support to the argument that nonmarital childbearing is a marker but not a cause of future poverty. Alternatively, if family structure is associated with poorer parenting, even after controlling for socioeconomic status at birth, or if changes in family structure are associated with changes in parental resources, these findings would lend support to the argument that family structure is a mechanism in the reproduction of poverty. Here, I

TABLE 1
CAPABILITIES OF PARENTS AT BIRTH: SOCIOECONOMIC (IN PERCENTAGES)

	Mothers			Fathers		
	Married	Cohabitating	Single	Married	Cohabitating	Single
Age (mean)	29.6	24.3	22.5	32.0	27.6	25.0
Teen parent	4.2	17.5	33.9	0	9.1	22.2
Child with other partner	13.6	39.5	32.8	16.4	38.5	38.9
Race						
White, non-Hispanic	50.9	22.5	14.9	51.1	16.9	8.8
Black, non-Hispanic	11.6	29.4	49.9	13.0	34.4	59.2
Hispanic	27.0	44.0	31.6	27.7	46.8	26.7
Other	10.6	4.1	3.6	8.2	2.0	5.3
Education						
Less than high school	18.0	41.5	48.0	21.5	40.7	44.3
High school	24.7	39.6	36.1	20.1	39.6	35.5
Some college	21.0	17.5	14.4	25.9	15.9	16.2
College	36.3	1.4	1.4	32.6	3.7	4.0
Weeks worked (mean)	46.2	42.2	42.7	47.5	45.1	40.7
Earnings ($) (mean)	28,507.0	11,446.0	10,792.0	40,125.0	21,166.0	16,393.0
Poverty status	12.3	33.7	52.9	11.4	33.4	53.4

describe what we have learned about these questions during the first five years of the Fragile Families Study, and then move on to discuss how the findings inform our understanding of the processes underlying intergenerational mobility.

What Are Unmarried Parents' Capabilities?

When we began our study in the late 1990s, quite a bit was known about the demographic characteristics of unwed mothers (age, education, parity), thanks to several national surveys that routinely collect information on women's marital and fertility histories. Much less was known about unmarried fathers, however. One reason for the lack of data on fathers was that these men are often omitted from national and local surveys either because they are not identified by standard survey techniques or because they do not report their paternity status (Rendall et al. 1999; Garfinkel, McLanahan, and Hanson 1998). The so-called missing fathers problem is especially serious among low-income men, and a major objective of the Fragile Families and Child Wellbeing Study was to obtain an accurate description of the capabilities of the men who father children outside marriage as well as the values and social skills of unmarried mothers.

Table 1 presents data on the characteristics of new parents at the time of their child's birth.[5] The table distinguishes between unmarried parents who are cohabiting and living apart because we expect these two types of unmarried couples to differ from one another. To date, we have not identified large racial or ethnic differences in our sample, and thus the information reported in the table is based on all parents. Where important differences exist, they will be noted in the text.

A brief comparison of the columns in Table 1 indicates that married and unmarried parents come from very different worlds. As compared with their married counterparts, unmarried parents are disproportionately African American and Hispanic, they are younger and more likely to be teen parents, and they are more likely to have children by other partners. Cohabiting parents are somewhat better off than noncohabiting parents, but the gap with married parents is large for both groups. The high prevalence of "multipartnered fertility"—defined as having children with different partners—is one of several important new findings to have emerged from the study. Whereas between 14 and 16 percent of married parents report having had a child with another partner, between 35 and 40 percent of unmarried parents report having done so (Carlson and Furstenberg 2006, 2007).

Perhaps the most striking difference between married and unmarried parents is the gap in education. Whereas a majority of married parents has attended at least some college, a large minority of unmarried parents has not even completed high school, and although both groups of parents report working a similar number of weeks in the past year, unmarried parents report much lower earnings and much higher poverty rates. The large marital status gap in human capital and earnings underscores the fact that many unmarried parents are poor *prior* to having a child. To make sure that the differences we observe were not due to differences in the stage of the family life cycle, we redid the analyses for parents having a first birth. Limiting the sample in this way does not alter the disparities reported in Table 1.

Table 2 presents data on the mental health and health behaviors of married, cohabiting, and noncoresident parents. We view these measures as good indicators of parents' social-emotional skills and ability to form stable relationships. According to Table 2, unmarried parents—both cohabiting and noncoresident—are more likely to suffer from depression than married parents and somewhat more likely to report more problems with alcohol (DeKlyen et al. 2006). Unmarried fathers are twice as likely as married fathers to have problems with drug use, three times as likely to be violent, and nearly seven times as likely to have been incarcerated in the past. Again, although cohabiting fathers look better than noncoresident fathers on some indicators, the major gap is between married and unmarried fathers.

Drug use and violence are likely to be underreported in these data. However, there is no reason to expect that underreporting differs by marital status, which means that our estimates of the gap between married and unmarried parents is likely to be accurate. The high level of incarceration among unmarried fathers is particularly striking and underscores the fact that the changes in penal policy that occurred after 1980 have played an important role in the lives of these parents (Geller, Garfinkel, and Western 2006; Swisher and Waller forthcoming).

TABLE 2
CAPABILITIES OF PARENTS AT BIRTH: HEALTH (IN PERCENTAGES)

	Mothers			Fathers		
	Married	Cohabiting	Single	Married	Cohabiting	Single
Depression	11.9	15.5	17.8	6.8	9.5	14.8
Heavy drinking	3.9	7.6	7.4	24.0	29.9	23.1
Illegal drug use	0.7	2.0	3.3	3.1	9.1	10.4
Partner violence	—	—	—	2.6	8.0	9.6
Father incarcerated	—	—	—	9.4	36.8	46.2

In sum, we found important race/ethnic differences in three domains: multipartnered fertility, drug/alcohol problems, and fathers' incarceration. In each domain, the marital status gap was smaller among blacks than among whites and Hispanics, primarily because the behaviors were more common among married blacks.

What Is the Nature of Relationships in Fragile Families?

One of the most important questions in the ongoing debate over the role of nonmarital childbearing in the reproduction of poverty is whether the relationship between unmarried parents is committed or casual. When we began our study, much of the existing research on unwed parents' relationships was based on ethnographic studies, which present a rather mixed picture (Waller 2002). Some researchers have reported that unmarried fathers are committed to their families but face serious barriers to forming a stable family because of limited resources (Sullivan 1989); others have argued that nonmarital childbearing is the by-product of a "mating game" in which young (uncommitted) men take advantage of young women's fantasies of marriage and motherhood to gain sexual favors (Anderson 1989), and still others describe a world composed of "good daddies" and "bad daddies" (Furstenberg, Sherwood, and Sullivan 1992).

Thus, a major objective of the Fragile Families Study was to learn more about the nature of parental relationships at birth, including how parents viewed marriage, whether they expected to marry, and whether their relationships were of sufficient quality to sustain a long-term commitment. We also sought to learn more about parents' attitudes toward marriage and the extent to which gender conflict and mistrust were serious problems as some qualitative studies have suggested. By following parents over time, we hoped to gain information about the prevalence of stable relationships as well as the factors affecting stability. We also hoped to learn about new partnerships and new children and the extent to which these new unions represent a gain or a loss for children.

Finally, we were interested in whether unmarried fathers were involved in the lives of their children. Research on divorced fathers had shown that father

FIGURE 2
UNMARRIED PARENTS' RELATIONSHIP STATUS AT BIRTH

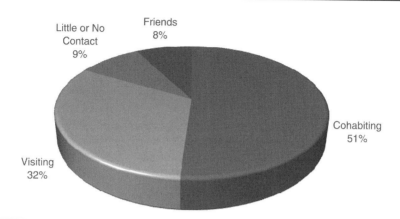

involvement declines rather dramatically during the years following a divorce (Seltzer 1991), but whether this pattern extended to unmarried fathers was an open question. On one hand, we might expect unmarried fathers to be more involved with their children than divorced fathers, given that many of these men are still romantically involved with the child's mother. On the other hand, we might expect them to be less involved given that the rights and obligations of unmarried fathers are less institutionalized (Nock 1998).

Relationships at birth

Figure 2 provides information on the nature of unmarried parents' relationships at the time of the child's birth. As shown in the figure, more than half of parents are cohabiting and another 32 percent are romantically involved. Fewer than 10 percent of mothers say they have "no contact" with the father. Overall levels of romantic involvement are similar for whites, blacks, and Hispanics, although blacks are less likely to be cohabiting at birth.

According to Table 3, most unmarried parents hold positive attitudes toward marriage, although not as positive as those of married parents (Waller and McLanahan 2005). Half of the cohabiting mothers "strongly agree" with the statement "it is better for children if their parents are married," and 90 percent say their chances of marriage are "fifty-fifty or better." Noncohabiting parents also hold positive views toward marriage, although they rate their chances of marriage much lower. Finally, most parents describe their relationships as being "very supportive" and "low conflict" (scales range from 1 to 3, with 3 being high), with cohabiting parents being closer to married parents than to noncoresident parents. Unmarried fathers are slightly more positive and more optimistic about their relationships than unmarried mothers (not shown in table).

TABLE 3
MARRIAGE ATTITUDES AND EXPECTATIONS AT BIRTH (IN PERCENTAGES)

	All Mothers			White Mothers		
	Married	Cohabitating	Single	Married	Cohabitating	Single
Promarriage attitudes	72.6	49.3	49.3	67.7	40.3	27.2
Approval of single mom	57.6	80.7	85.4	46.8	75.2	74.7
Gender distrust	10.4	19.8	33.7	3.3	11.1	20.1
Supportiveness (mean)	2.7	2.7	2.4	2.7	2.7	2.3
Conflict (mean)	1.3	1.4	1.5	1.3	1.4	1.4
Chances of marriage						
Almost certain	—	51.6	13.7	—	72.9	49.8
Good	—	26.0	17.1	—	17.1	17.9
Fifty/fifty	—	14.5	19.7	—	7.9	8.3
Not so good	—	4.0	12.5	—	1.4	5.7
No chance	—	3.9	37.1	—	0.8	18.3

	Black Mothers			Hispanic Mothers		
	Married	Cohabitating	Single	Married	Cohabitating	Single
Promarriage attitudes	81.2	58.9	53.9	74.4	49.1	52.7
Approval of single mom	72.5	83.2	89.1	74.6	80.5	88.2
Gender distrust	7.1	16.4	30.2	25.7	28.3	45.9
Supportiveness (mean)	2.7	2.7	2.4	2.6	2.7	2.4
Conflict (mean)	1.4	1.5	1.5	1.3	1.4	1.4
Chances of marriage						
Almost certain	—	45.5	15.0	—	40.9	11.8
Good	—	30.7	18.1	—	28.9	13.6
Fifty/fifty	—	15.0	22.8	—	6.5	12.6
Not so good	—	3.2	12.9	—	6.5	12.6
No chance	—	5.6	31.3	—	4.4	43.4

We found only two areas in which unmarried parents' attitudes might be described as less than positive toward marriage: first, unmarried mothers are much more likely than married parents to strongly agree with the statement that "a single mother can raise a child alone," and second, unmarried mothers are much more likely to agree with the statement "men cannot be trusted to be faithful." Cohabiting parents are closer to married parents in their beliefs about single mothers and in between married and single parents in gender distrust.

In general, black mothers are more positive about marriage than white mothers, and the gap between married and unmarried parents is also smaller. Black mothers are also less likely than white mothers to believe that their chances of marriage are good. These findings are consistent with the argument that the increase in single motherhood has feedback effects on marriage, not by undermining positive attitudes toward marriage but rather by altering expectations and making single motherhood a more acceptable alternative. Hispanic mothers are the most likely to report distrust.

Relationships at five years

Despite their high hopes for a future together, only a small proportion of unmarried parents (22 percent) ever follow through on their plans, and even fewer (16 percent) are still married by the time of the five-year interview. Counting both cohabiting and married parents, about one-third of unmarried parents were living together five years after the birth of their child. Most of these parents were cohabiting at birth, although some were romantically involved and living apart and a few reported no romantic relationship at birth.

White and Hispanic mothers are more likely than African American mothers to marry the fathers of their children. Indeed, union dissolution overall is higher among blacks than among the other groups, in part because fewer parents are cohabiting at birth and in part because breakup rates are higher among black couples irrespective of status. Much of the postbirth marriage gap between blacks and whites can be accounted for by a shortage of "marriageable men," defined as the ratio of employed men to all women in a city (Harknett and McLanahan 2004). Black mothers are almost as likely to marry as white mothers when marriage market conditions are similar.

To learn more about their motivations for marriage, we conducted in-depth interviews with a subgroup of parents who participated in the core survey. When asked why they were not married, parents often said that they were waiting until they had achieved a certain standard of living that they viewed as necessary for a successful marriage (Gibson-Davis, Edin, and McLanahan 2005). One young Hispanic father in his twenties put it this way:

> I want to be secure. . . . I don't want to get married and be like we have no money or nothing. . . . I want to get my little house in Long Island, you know, white-picket fence, and two-car garage, me hitting the garbage cans when I pull up in the driveway. (McLanahan 2004, 619)

Mothers also emphasized the importance of sexual fidelity as a condition for marriage. Both rationales are supported by the quantitative analyses. Fathers' income increases the chances of marriage, and mothers' distrust reduces the chances (Carlson, McLanahan, and England 2004). Furthermore, fathers (but not mothers) who have had a child by another partner are less likely to marry postbirth. The fact that fathers' multipartnered fertility is more likely to undermine union stability than mothers' suggests that multipartnered fertility creates tension between the parents by causing a drain on fathers' resources (time and money) and by creating conflict between the couple. In the qualitative interviews, mothers often express jealousy over the time fathers spend with a child who lives in another household, including jealousy about the time he spends with the child's mother. This source of conflict is referred to as the "baby mama drama" (Monte 2007).

New partnerships

Many unmarried parents have formed new partnerships by the time their child is age five. About half of mothers who have ended their relationships with the biological father have a new partner (about 30 percent of all mothers), and two-thirds of these are living with a new partner. Whereas we might have expected mothers' new partners to be of lower quality than the original biological fathers—previous research suggests that having a child outside marriage reduces a woman's chances of marriage (Bennett, Bloom, and Miller 2005)—in fact these men are of higher quality (Bzostek, Carlson, and McLanahan 2006). New partners are much more likely to have a high school degree, more likely to be employed, less likely to have problems with drugs or alcohol, less likely to engage in domestic violence, and less likely to have been incarcerated than original biological fathers. Some of this improvement is due to aging and greater maturity, and some is due to mothers being more selective in choosing new partners.

The high prevalence of new partnerships underscores an important feature of fragile families—*high partnership instability*. We estimate that by the time of the child's third birthday, two-thirds of unmarried mothers have experienced at least one partnership change, more than a third have experienced at least two changes, and nearly 20 percent have experienced three or more changes. In contrast, only 13 percent of married mothers have experienced a partnership change by the time their child is three, and only 6 percent will have experienced two or more changes (Osborne and McLanahan 2007).

Interestingly, the difference in partnership stability between married and unmarried mothers is not due to the fact that married mothers have fewer partnerships overall. Indeed, married mothers report having had more partners than unmarried mothers at the time of their child's birth. What is different, however, is that married mothers have not had children with their prior partners, whereas unmarried mothers have. Despite the fact that many mothers are able to improve their living conditions by partnering with a new man, the search process itself can be stressful for both the mother and the child. Thus, the gains associated with improving the quality of mothers' partners may be offset by the losses associated with greater instability.

Biological fathers' commitment

Most unmarried fathers are generally highly involved at birth (see Table 4), with cohabiting fathers showing much higher levels of involvement than non-coresident fathers. According to mothers' reports, more than 90 percent of cohabiting fathers provided financial support and other types of help during the pregnancy, and 95 percent visited the mother at the hospital. Most important, nearly 100 percent of these men told the mothers that they wanted to help raise the child, and nearly 100 percent of mothers said they wanted the father to be involved (Johnson 2001). The proportions are lower for noncoresident fathers, with more than half providing some type of support during the pregnancy, and much higher levels reporting that they wanted to be involved.

TABLE 4
UNMARRIED FATHERS' INVOLVEMENT AT BIRTH (IN PERCENTAGES)

	Cohabitating	Single
Gave money/bought things for child	95.3	64.1
Helped in another way	97.7	56.1
Visited baby's mother in the hospital	96.5	54.9
Child will take father's surname	93.1	63.9
Father's name is on birth certificate	96.0	71.0
Mother says father wants to be involved	99.5	89.3
Mother wants father to be involved	99.5	87.6

Despite their best intentions, just a little more than a third of fathers are living with their children five years later, and there is substantial variation in the involvement of nonresident fathers: a third have no contact and 43 percent have monthly contact with their child. Among the latter, the average number of days a father sees his child is twelve per month (Carlson, McLanahan, and Brooks-Gunn forthcoming). Not surprisingly, the quality of the parents' relationship is a strong predictor of fathers' involvement (Waller and Swisher 2006). When the mother trusts the father and the parents are able to communicate about the child's needs, the father is more likely to visit and engage in activities with the child. Although one might argue that causality is operating in the opposite direction—father involvement is leading to better cooperation—analyses indicate that most of the effect is going from cooperation to involvement (Carlson, McLanahan, and Brooks-Gunn forthcoming). Other factors that predict father involvement include whether a father has a child by another partner, whether he was born outside the United States, and whether he was ever incarcerated, all of which reduce parental cooperation and father involvement.

Just over half of nonresident fathers provide some kind of financial support to their child, and just under half provide in-kind support (Nepomnyaschy and Garfinkel 2006). Informal support is somewhat more common than formal child support at year five, although the proportion of mothers receiving formal support increases over time. Interestingly, stronger child support enforcement does not appear to increase the amount of money the father contributes, at least not during the first five years after birth. Rather, strong enforcement simply replaces informal payments with formal payments. When a mother receives welfare, formal child support payments are taken by the state to offset welfare costs, which means that the mother has less income overall.

How Do Parents and Children Fare?

Marriage is expected to increase parents' resources (financial, health, and social), which, in turn, is expected to improve children's home environments and future life chances. In theory, marriage increases family income by creating economies of scale and by encouraging parents to work harder and more efficiently (for example, through specialization—see Becker 1981). Marriage also increases parents' mental health by promoting social integration and emotional support (Gove, Hughes, and Style 1983). Finally, marriage increases access to social support by increasing neighborhood quality and residential stability and by expanding family networks and reinforcing family commitments (Coleman 1988). Each of these resources is important for the quality of the child's home environment.

The theoretical arguments for the benefits of marriage are supported by a large body of empirical research, including research on parents' economic and social resources as well as research on outcomes for children and young adults (Waite 1995). Most of this research, however, is based on samples of adults (parents) who were married at birth and subsequently divorced. Thus, many questions remain about whether the benefits of marriage and the costs of union dissolution are as great for children born to unmarried parents. More important, perhaps, research on the benefits of marriage and the costs of divorce is frequently criticized for making causal inferences from evidence of correlations.

Part of our rationale for following a cohort of new parents and their children was to determine whether the correlations between family structure and child outcomes found in previous studies were due to the number of parents in the household, the marital status of the parents, and/or the stability of the household. Specifically, we wanted to know whether the benefits of marriage extended to children raised in stable cohabiting parent families and whether the benefits of stability extended to households headed by a single mother.

A second motivation was to address the issue of causality by collecting better data on the specific mechanisms that are expected to mediate (or account for) the association between family structure and child outcomes. By starting with the birth of the child and by collecting data on a wide range of parental and relationship characteristics at the time of the birth, we hoped to be able to rule out some of the alternative arguments for why divorce and marital instability might be correlated with poor outcomes in children. For example, many analysts argue that divorce is a proxy for high conflict between parents. Thus, we measured this construct at birth so that we could include it in our analyses. We also measured prior relationship instability, alcohol and drug abuse, antisocial behavior, and incarceration history.

Finally, by identifying and measuring the key theoretical pathways linking family structure with child outcomes, we sought to test specific hypotheses about the causal processes underlying the correlation between family structure and outcomes, including hypotheses about the effects of nonmarital childbearing on family income, parental health, social support, and parenting quality. While observational data can never provide conclusive evidence of causal effects, a more detailed description of the mechanisms that link family structure with particular outcomes is better than a simple correlation.

FIGURE 3
TRAJECTORIES OF PARENTS' INCOME AND HEALTH

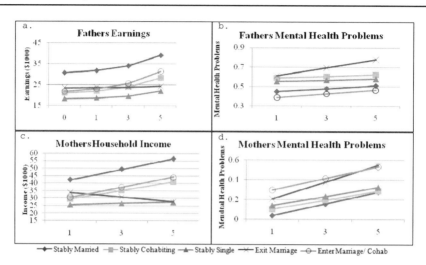

Fathers' earnings and health trajectories

Figure 3 presents data on the trajectories of parents' economic status and mental health during the first five years after the child's birth. Figure 3a provides data on fathers' earnings, Figure 3b provides data on fathers' mental health, Figure 3c provides data on mothers' family income, and Figure 3d provides data on mothers' mental health. Parents are grouped according to their relationship status at birth and changes in relationships after birth. Thus, we have couples in stable marriages, stable cohabiting relationships, relationships that break up, and so on.

In examining the figures, two pieces of information are important: the starting point for each group (measured at birth) and the slope for each group. Both are adjusted for differences in fathers' age, education, race/ethnicity, and immigrant status. Looking first at the starting points in Figure 3a, we see that fathers who are stably married report the highest earnings of all groups in the year prior to the birth.[6] Below are married fathers who subsequently divorce, and next in line are unmarried fathers, followed by fathers who marry after the birth, fathers who are stably cohabiting, and fathers who never cohabit (stably single). Note that all fathers experience earnings growth over time, but fathers who divorce experience less of an increase than fathers who remain married, a finding consistent with previous research. Note also that fathers who marry after their child's birth experience a greater gain in earnings than unmarried fathers who remain single (Garfinkel et al. 2008).

In separate analyses, we found that much of the relatively lower earnings growth of fathers who are stably single is due to the fact that these men have more mental health problems and are more likely to have been incarcerated than other fathers. When these factors are taken into account, the difference in earnings growth between those who marry and stably married fathers and stable single fathers is cut in half. The lower earnings growth of single fathers is consistent with the argument that marriage increases fathers' earnings. It is also consistent with the argument that women are less likely to marry men whom they view as having poor earnings trajectories.

The lower earnings growth of single fathers is consistent with the argument that marriage increases fathers' earnings. It is also consistent with the argument that women are less likely to marry men whom they view as having poor earnings trajectories.

The pattern for fathers' mental health is somewhat different. Married fathers and fathers who subsequently marry report the fewest mental health problems at birth; fathers who subsequently divorce report the most mental health problems. Cohabiting and single fathers fall in between (Meadows 2007). All fathers experience increases in mental health problems over time, but there is no evidence of growing disparities. These results do not support the argument that marriage after birth helps close the gap in mental health between married and unmarried fathers.

Mothers' economic status and health

As was true for fathers, married mothers are in a much better economic condition than other mothers at the time their child is born. Single mothers who never marry report the lowest incomes. Most mothers experience improvements in economic status over time; divorced mothers are an exception. However, some groups of mothers experience smaller gains than others. Mothers who are stably single experience growing gaps with married mothers. Otherwise, unmarried mothers, including those who marry or move in with the father, experience income gains similar to those of stably married mothers. Regarding mental health, married mothers in stable unions report the fewest mental health problems at birth, whereas mothers who eventually divorce (or separate) report the most problems (Meadows, McLanahan, and Brooks-Gunn 2007). Mental health problems increase among all women after birth regardless of relationship status. In other analyses (not shown in the figure), we find that all partnership changes (entrances as well as exits) have short-term negative effects on mothers' mental health. The only exception is mothers who marry the fathers of their child before the child's first birthday; these mothers experience no short-term increase in mental health problems.

Social support

Social support, defined as instrumental and emotional assistance from family or friends, is an important family resource, especially for new parents and single mothers (Cowan and Cowan 1992; Eggebeen 1992). Social support serves as a form of insurance against poverty and economic hardship and is expected to improve the quality of the child's home environment by reducing parental stress. The Fragile Families and Child Wellbeing Study asked parents whether they knew someone who would lend them money, provide them with a place to live, and/or provide child care in case of an emergency. Using these measures, researchers find that unmarried mothers have less access to social support in the form of housing and cash assistance than married mothers. The disparity in support is due to several factors: First, access to support is higher in neighborhoods with higher median incomes (Turney and Harknett 2007), and unmarried parents are less likely than married parents to live in such neighborhoods. Second, access to support is positively associated with residential stability, and unmarried parents are less likely than married parents to have stable housing ("The Frequency and Correlates of Mothers' Residential Mobility" 2007). Indeed, unmarried parents are twice as likely as married parents to move during the five years following their child's birth and three times as likely to move three or more times.[7] Finally, mothers who have children by different partners report having less access to support, especially financial support (Harknett and Knab 2007).

Parenting quality

Nonmarital childbearing reduces the quality of parenting by contributing to partnership instability and multipartnered fertility. Just as partnership changes reduce mothers' income and increase mental health problems, we find that most types of instability (marriage to the biological father is an exception) increase maternal stress (Cooper et al. 2007). The negative effects of instability persist even after controlling for predisruption characteristics and parental resources. Importantly, the negative effects of partnership instability appear to be limited to mothers with a high school degree or less. Mothers with some college education do not report increases in maternal stress unless they experience multiple transitions.

Multipartnered fertility also undermines the quantity and quality of parenting by reducing parents' ability to get along and to cooperate in raising their child. Mothers report less support from the nonresident father and lower overall relationship quality when either parent has a child by another partner. Mothers also report less shared parenting and less cooperation in raising their child when the father has a child with another partner (Carlson and Furstenberg 2007).

Child well-being

Insofar as families formed outside marriage are quite diverse—ranging from stable cohabiting parent families to highly unstable families—distinguishing among these different types of households is likely to be important. Although we have only recently begun to examine how being born to unmarried parents affects child outcomes, the evidence garnered thus far suggests that both instability and material hardship have negative effects. Children who live with stably single mothers and children who live with mothers who experience multiple partnership changes show higher levels of aggression and anxiety/depression than children who live with stably married parents (Osborne and McLanahan 2007). In contrast, children who live with parents who are stably cohabiting do not differ from children raised by married parents. Half of the negative association between children's family context and behavioral problems can be accounted for by the fact that single mothers and mothers in unstable partnerships report higher levels of maternal stress and are more likely to exhibit poor parenting.

Does Nonmarital Childbearing Help Reproduce Poverty?

For nonmarital childbearing to be a mechanism in the reproduction of poverty, it must be both a consequence and a cause of poverty. With respect to the first question, the findings from the Fragile Families and Child Wellbeing Study are consistent with the argument that unmarried mothers come from disadvantaged backgrounds and that low education reduces a mother's chances of forming a stable union after a nonmarital birth. Although attitudes toward marriage and single motherhood also affect union stability, these differences do not negate the fact that factors associated with poverty play an important role in family formation.

With respect to the second condition, the evidence is also consistent with the argument than nonmarital childbearing reduces children's life chances by lowering parental resources and the quality of parenting. Unmarried mothers experience less income growth, more mental health problems, and more maternal stress than married mothers. They also receive less help from the fathers of their children, and they have less access to much-needed social support from family and friends. Each of these factors increases the risk of poor parenting.

Finally, these data highlight the importance of two causal mechanisms in the link between family structure and child outcomes: *partnership instability* and *multipartnered fertility*. Both conditions, which are inevitable consequences of a process in which women have children while they continue to search for a permanent partner, create considerable stress for mothers and children and reduce a mother's prospects of forming a stable union by contributing to jealousy and distrust between parents. Moreover, multipartnered fertility increases the costs of children to fathers and thus reduces their willingness to pay child support (Willis 2000). Finally, by spreading fathers' contributions across multiple households, partnership instability and multi-partnered fertility undermine the importance of individual fathers' contributions of time and money to the family economy, which is likely to affect the future marriage expectations of both sons and daughters. In sum, the processes described above have important feedback effects on family formation, which retard upward mobility for children born to disadvantaged parents.

What Is the Solution?

In his report on the family, Moynihan argued that government policy should be directed toward enhancing the stability and resources of the African American family. Twenty years later, William Julius Wilson (1987) argued that government could strengthen the family by increasing employment opportunities and wages of low-skilled men. For many years, neither message was heeded. Cash and in-kind benefits for poor families were highly income-tested and thus not available to most two-parent families, which created large disincentives for marriage among low-income parents. Moreover, the plight of poor unmarried fathers was virtually ignored except insofar as they were the target of child support enforcement.

Conditions changed in the early 1990s, however, beginning with the rapid expansion of the Earned Income Tax Credit, which represented a substantial earnings subsidy for many two-parent families, and followed up by welfare reform legislation in 1996, which made it harder for a single woman to raise a child alone. Most recently, the federal government has begun funding programs designed to promote marriage by enhancing parents' relationship skills and ability to manage disputes. While some portion of unmarried (and married) couples are likely to benefit from this new initiative, many will need additional help to form stable families, including mental health services, employment services, and help with reentry into their communities after incarceration (Garfinkel and McLanahan 2003).

Most important, none of these programs are likely to have a large effect as long as mothers continue to have children before they find a long-term partner. Although wage subsidies and relationship counseling may ameliorate some of the problems associated with nonmarital childbearing, they are likely to be limited in what they can accomplish. Thus, to break the intergenerational cycle of poverty, we will need to find a way to persuade young women from disadvantaged backgrounds that delaying fertility while they search for a suitable partner will have a payoff that is large enough to offset the loss of time spent as a mother or the possibility of forgoing motherhood entirely.

Notes

1. Trends—National Center for Health Statistics, http://www.cdc.gov/nchs/data/nvsr/nvsr55/nvsr55_01.pdf.

2. What is new about the current debate is the argument that nonmarital childbearing is *not* a problem but just an alternative family form (Stacey 1998; Coontz 1997). This position is based on the fact that non-marital childbearing is growing in all Western industrialized countries and that in many countries (e.g., Sweden and France) a large proportion of nonmarital births are to parents in stable cohabiting relation-ships (Chase-Lansdale, Kiernan, and Friedman 2004).

3. The Fragile Families Study is supported by grants from NICHD and a consortium of private foun-dations. See http://www.fragilefamilies.princeton.edu/.

4. A fourth question was, "How do policies affect family formation and child well-being?"

5. Thanks to Kevin Bradway and Kate Bartkus for producing these numbers.

6. Sarah Meadows supplied the data for Figure 3.

7. Rebecca Casciano provided these numbers.

References

Anderson, E. 1989. Sex codes and family life among poor inner city youths. *The Annals of the American Academy of Political and Social Science* 501:59-78.

Becker, Gary S. 1981. *A treatise on the family*. Cambridge, MA: Harvard University Press.

Bennett, Neil G., David E. Bloom, and Cynthia K. Miller. 1995. The influence of nonmarital childbearing on the formation of first marriages. *Demography* 32:47-62.

Bzostek, Sharon, Marcia Carlson, and Sara McLanahan. 2006. Does mother know best? A comparison of biological and social fathers after a nonmarital birth. Working Paper no. 2006–27-FF, Center for Research on Child Wellbeing, Princeton, NJ.

Carlson, Marcia J., and Frank F. Furstenberg. 2006. The prevalence and correlates of multipartnered fer-tility among urban U.S. parents. *Journal of Marriage and Family* 68:718-32.

———. 2007. The consequences of multi-partnered fertility for parental involvement and relationships. Working Paper no. 2006–28-FF, Center for Research on Child Wellbeing, Princeton, NJ.

Carlson, Marcia, Sara McLanahan, and Jeanne Brooks-Gunn. Forthcoming. Co-parenting and nonresident fathers' involvement with young children after a nonmarital birth. *Demography*.

Carlson, Marcia, Sara McLanahan, and Paula England. 2004. Union formation in fragile families. *Demography* 41:237-61.

Chase-Lansdale, Lindsay P., Kathleen Kiernan, and Ruth J. Friedman, eds. 2004. *Human development across lives and generations: The potential for change*. New York: Cambridge University Press.

Coleman, James S. 1988. Social capital in the creation of human capital. *American Journal of Sociology* 94:S95-S120.

Coontz, Stephanie. 1997. *The way we really are: Coming to terms with America's changing families*. New York: Basic Books.

Coontz, Stephanie, and Nancy Folbre. 2002. Marriage, poverty and public policy. Discussion Paper from the Council on Contemporary Families (CCF), Prepared for the Fifth Annual CCF Conference, New York.

Cooper, Carey, Sara McLanahan, Sarah Meadows, and Jeanne Brooks-Gunn. 2007. Family structure tran-sitions and maternal parenting stress. Working Paper no. 2007–16-FF, Center for Research on Child Wellbeing, Princeton, NJ.

Cowan, Carolyn P., and Philip A. Cowan. 1992. *When partners become parents: The big life change for cou-ples*. New York: Basic Books. (Republished by Lawrence Erlbaum Associates, Mahwah, NJ, 2000)

DeKlyen, Michelle, Jeanne Brooks-Gunn, Sara McLanahan, and Jean Knab. 2006. The mental health of married, cohabiting, and non–coresident parents with infants. *American Journal of Public Health* 96:1836-41.

Eggebeen, David J. 1992. Family structure and intergenerational exchanges. *Research on Aging* 14: 427-47.

The frequency and correlates of mothers' residential mobility. 2007. Fragile Families Research Brief no. 40. Center for Research on Child Wellbeing, Princeton, NJ.

Furstenberg, Frank F., Kay E. Sherwood, and Mercer L. Sullivan. 1992. Daddies and fathers: Men who do for their children and men who don't. In *Report on parents' fair share demonstration*, 34-56. New York: Manpower Development Research Corporation.

Garfinkel, Irwin, and Sara McLanahan. 2003. Strengthening fragile families. In *One percent for the kids: New policies, brighter futures for America's children*, ed. I. Sawhill, 76-92. Washington, DC: Brookings Institution.

Garfinkel, Irwin, Sara McLanahan, and Thomas L. Hanson. 1998. A patchwork portrait of non-resident fathers. In *Fathers under fire: The revolution in child support enforcement*, ed. Irwin Garfinke, Sara McLanahan, Daniel Meyer, and Judith Seltzer, 31-60. New York: Russell Sage Foundation.

Garfinkel, Irwin, Sarah Meadows, Sara McLanahan, and R. Mincy. 2008. Unmarried fathers' earnings trajectories. Manuscript, Princeton University, Princeton, NJ.

Geller, Amanda, Irwin Garfinkel, and Bruce Western. 2006. The effects of incarceration on employment and wages: An analysis of the Fragile Families Survey. Working Paper no. 2006–01-FF, Center for Research on Child Wellbeing, Princeton, NJ.

Gibson-Davis, Christina, Kathryn Edin, and Sara McLanahan. 2005. High hopes, but even higher expectations: The retreat from marriage among low-income couples. *Journal of Marriage and Family* 67:1301-12.

Gove, Walter R., Michael Hughes, and Carolyn Briggs Style. 1983. Does marriage have positive effects on the psychological well-being of individuals? *Journal of Health and Social Behavior* 24:122-31.

Harknett, Kristen, and Jean Knab. 2007. More kin, less support: Multipartnered fertility and kin support among new mothers. *Journal of Marriage and the Family* 69:237-53.

Harknett, Kristen, and Sara S. McLanahan. 2004. Racial and ethnic differences in marriage after the birth of a child. *American Sociological Review* 6:790–811.

Johnson, Waldo E. 2001. Paternal involvement among unwed fathers. *Children and Youth Services Review* 23:513-36.

Massey, Douglas S. 2007. *Categorically unequal: The American stratification system*. New York: Russell Sage Foundation.

McLanahan, Sara. 2004. Diverging Destinies: How Children Are Faring Under the Second Demographic Transition. *Demography* 41:607-627

McLanahan, Sara, and Gary Sandefur. 1994. *Growing up with a single parent: What hurts, what helps*. Cambridge, MA: Harvard University Press.

Meadows, Sarah. 2007. Family structure and fathers' well-being: Trajectories of physical and mental health. Working Paper no. 2007–19-FF, Center for Research on Child Wellbeing, Princeton, NJ.

Meadows, Sarah O., Sara S. McLanahan, and Jeanne Brooks-Gunn. 2007. Parental depression and anxiety and early childhood behavior problems across family types. *Journal of Marriage and the Family* 69:1162-77.

Monte, Lindsay. 2007. Blended but not the Bradys: Navigating unmarried multiple partner fertility. In *Unmarried couples with children*, ed. Paula England and Kathryn Edin, 183-203. New York: Russell Sage Foundation.

Moynihan, Daniel Patrick. 1965. *The Negro family: The case for national action*. Washington, DC: U.S. Department of Labor, Office of Policy Planning and Research.

Murray, Charles. 1984. *Losing ground: American social policy, 1950–1980*. New York: Basic Books.

Nepomnyaschy, Lenna, and Irwin Garfinkel. 2006. Child support enforcement and fathers' contributions to their non-marital children. Working Paper no. 2006–09-FF, Center for Research on Child Wellbeing, Princeton, NJ.

Nock, Steven L. 1998. The consequences of premarital fatherhood. *American Sociological Review* 63: 250-63.

Osborne, Cynthia, and Sara McLanahan. 2007. Partnership instability and child wellbeing. *Journal of Marriage and the Family* 69:1065-83.

Rainwater, Lee, and William L. Yancey. 1967. *The Moynihan Report and the politics of controversy*. Boston: MIT Press.

Reichman, Nancy E., Julien O. Teitler, Irwin Garfinkel, and Sara McLanahan. 2001. Fragile Families: Sample and design. *Children and Youth Services Review* 23:303-26.

Rendall, Michael S., Lynda Clarke, H. Elizabeth Peters, Nalini Ranjit, and Georgia Verropoulou. 1999. Incomplete reporting of men's fertility in the United States and Britain: A research note. *Demography* 36:135-44.

Ryan, William. 1976. *Blaming the victim.* New York: Vintage Books.

Seltzer, Juditha A. 1991. Relationships between fathers and children who live apart. *Journal of Marriage and the Family* 53:79-101.

Stacey, Judith. 1998. *Brave new families: Stories of domestic upheaval in late twentieth century America.* Berkeley: University of California Press.

Stack, Carol B. 1974. *All our kin: Strategies for survival in a black community.* New York: Harper & Row.

Sullivan, M. L. 1989. Absent fathers in the inner city. *The Annals of the American Academy of Political and Social Science* 501:59-78.

Swisher, Raymond, and Maureen Waller. Forthcoming. Confining fatherhood: Incarceration and paternal involvement among unmarried white, African-American and Latino fathers. *Journal of Family Issues.*

Turney, Kristin, and Kristen Harknett. 2007. Neighborhood disadvantage, residential stability, and perceptions of instrumental support among new mothers. Working Paper no. WP07–08-FF, Center for Research on Child Wellbeing, Princeton, NJ.

Waite, Linda J. 1995. Does marriage matter? *Demography* 32:535-51.

Waller, Maureen R. 2002. *My baby's father: Unmarried parents and paternal responsibility.* Ithaca, NY: Cornell University Press.

Waller, Maureen R., and Sara S. McLanahan. 2005. "His" and "her" marriage expectations: Determinants and consequences. *Journal of Marriage and the Family* 67:53-67.

Waller, Maureen R., and Raymond Swisher. 2006. Fathers' risk factors in fragile families: Implications for "healthy" relationships and father involvement. *Social Problems* 53:392-420.

Western, Bruce. 2007. *Punishment and inequality in America.* New York: Russell Sage Foundation.

Willis, Robert. 2000. The economics of fatherhood. *American Economic Review* 90:378-82.

Wilson, James Q. 2002. *The marriage problem: How our culture has weakened families.* New York: HarperCollins.

Wilson, William Julius. 1987. *The truly disadvantaged: The inner city, the underclass, and public policy.* Chicago: University of Chicago Press.

Romantic Unions in an Era of Uncertainty: A Post-Moynihan Perspective on African American Women and Marriage

By
LINDA M. BURTON
and
M. BELINDA TUCKER

This article provides a brief overview of how African American women are situated in and around the thesis of the Moynihan Report. The authors take the lens of uncertainty and apply it to a post-Moynihan discussion of African American women and marriage. They discuss uncertainty in the temporal organization of poor women's lives and in the new terrains of gender relationships and how both influence African American women's thoughts and behaviors in their romantic relationships and marriages. They argue that much is to be learned from by focusing the lens in this way. It allows us to look at the contemporary romantic relationship and marriage behaviors of African American women in context and in ways that do not label them as having pathological behaviors that place them out of sync with broader societal trends.

Keywords: African American women; stereotypes; relationships; choices; gender roles; poverty; uncertainty

I don't know what life is going be like from one day to the next day. Everything is up in the air . . . my job, my children's sickness, my sickness, my mother's sickness, where we're going to live, how I'm going to get a ride to where I got to go. I don't have no time for a *for-real* relationship. I know that a *for-real* relationship takes time and more [time] than I can give on any day. You have to talk about things [with a partner] and have an understanding to make things work. You have to make some decisions about what the man will do and what [a woman] is suppose to do. It's not always about the woman running things, you know. You have to make a man feel like a man. Jesus, I don't have that kind of energy . . . I'm too busy worrying, fixin' to do something, going and coming, running around, taking care of things . . . no time to be still. All I have sometimes is one second to breathe. Besides that, I can't count on nothing from one time to the next, but maybe, the Lord. And, I think sometimes he forgets about me too.

Nadine, a low-income African American twenty-nine-year-old, single mother of three children, and participant in the ethnographic component of the Three-City Study,[1] provided the above

DOI: 10.1177/0002716208324852

commentary on her experiences in sustaining a romantic union while managing day-to-day family life in the context of long-term poverty. Demographically, she fits the stereotype of the young, poor, and never-married mothers featured in and around the discourse on low-income African American women and marriage spawned by Daniel Patrick Moynihan's report, *The Negro Family: The Case for National Action* (see Rainwater and Yancey 1967). However, Nadine's personal reflections on the "how-comes" and "why-nots" of marriage embody a slightly different tone and emphasis. Nadine's tenor about relationships is ambivalent and, unlike the Moynihan Report, does not characterize African American women as matriarchs who dominate romantic unions and emasculate unemployed male partners. Rather, Nadine gives voice to what has become a quagmire for most contemporary American women—how uncertainty influences the potential for and success of romantic and marital relationships.

Nadine's uncertainty is closely tied to her life course experiences with poverty but also is rooted in broader societal transformations that have reconfigured the temporal dimensions of everyday life and gender relations for individuals across all socioeconomic and cultural segments of the American population (Bauman 1991, 1995; Clark 1991; Giddens 1991, 1992; Johnson-Hanks 2006; Mills and Blossfeld 2005). Temporal uncertainty involves women's presumed infractions against socially prescribed moral codes of time use, their expectations and behaviors around the number of "years of life" they pray are available to them, and how they synchronize the daily rhythms of their family's needs with institutional timetables (e.g., business hours of social service agencies) (Abbott 2001; Burton and Sorensen 1993; Daly 1996). Gender role uncertainties derive, in large part, from the changing structural and relational dynamics of male and female labor market and educational experiences, as well as the tenuous nature of norms that govern the distribution of domestic tasks (Cherlin 2004; Franklin 1997; Hochschild 1989, 1997; Taylor, Tucker, and Mitchell-Kernan 1999).

Linda M. Burton is the James B. Duke Professor of Sociology at Duke University. She directed the ethnographic component of the Three-City Study and is currently principal investigator of a multi-site team ethnographic study (Family Life Project) of poverty, family processes, and child development in six rural communities. Her research examines how contextual forces (e.g., community norms) and familial circumstances (e.g., multi-partner fertility) influence accelerated life course transitions of children, adolescents, and adults.

M. Belinda Tucker is Associate Dean for the Graduate Division and Professor of Psychiatry and Biobehavioral Sciences at the University of California, Los Angeles. A social psychologist, she conducts both quantitative and qualitative research on marriage, couple relationships, interethnic relations, and the impact of incarceration on families. Tucker cites data in this article from a 21-city national panel study she directed on the social context and psychological correlates of family formation behaviors and attitudes.

NOTE: We thank the Administration on Children and Families for supporting our research on marriage and relationships among low-income families through grant 90OJ2020. We also wish to acknowledge core support to the Three-City Study from the National Institute of Child Health and Human Development through grants HD36093 and HD25936 and the National Science Foundation through grant SES-07–03968, as well as the support of many government agencies and private foundations.

In this article, using findings from our own programs of research as a base, we take the lens of uncertainty and apply it to a post-Moynihan discussion of African American women and marriage. We discuss uncertainty in the temporal organization of poor women's lives and in the new terrains of gender relationships and how both influence African American women's thoughts and behaviors in their romantic relationships and marriages. We argue that much is to be learned from focusing the lens in this way. It allows us to look at the contemporary romantic relationship and marriage behaviors of African American women in context and in ways that do not label them as having pathological behaviors that place them out of sync with broader societal trends. As we have learned from the Moynihan Report, interpreting demographic trends as having a dysfunctional base is easy to do when a group is studied in isolation and when their behaviors are interpreted out of context. Indeed, the legacy of pathologized ascriptions has discouraged the development of more mature analytical frames that consider the ordinary features of life that eventually emerge for all groups as a function of broader societal changes.

From Pathology to Uncertainty: Shifting the Lens

While it is a demographic fact that low-income African American women represent the leading edge in the rise of single-motherhood in the United States, social scientists have made little progress in understanding what is happening on the ground level in their romantic relationships. Low-income African American women are not marrying at high rates, but they are continuing to become involved in romantic unions that produce children (Lincoln, Taylor, and Jackson 2008). How are the romantic relationships of African Americans created, situated, and experienced in contemporary American society? How do the trends discussed in the Moynihan Report help us to interpret current patterns?

To address these questions, we begin by acknowledging points made in the Moynihan Report about these issues. The report asserted that a determining factor in the increasingly "desperate" situation of so-called "lower-class" Negroes was family instability as displayed by the growing prevalence of out-of-wedlock childbearing, female-headed families, and the decreasing reliance on men's earnings for family support. The stated and unstated implications of these trends were clear. Although black women were not responsible for the joblessness and underemployment of black men, their apparent assumption of economic and social responsibilities for their households served to emasculate their men and undermine men's efforts to be proper husbands and fathers.

Moynihan argued that female dominance itself was not necessarily problematic, but given that the male breadwinner model was the prevailing paradigm in the United States and Western societies at that time, any marriage pattern that deviated from that model was bound to lead to trouble for mothers, fathers, their children, and the larger society. The misappropriated term "matriarch," divorced from its true anthropological meaning, came to dominate characterizations of

African American women as a result of the report (Collins 1991; Dickson 1993). This perception was not confined to the domains of policy or social science (from whence it came) but became equally pervasive in popular culture through written, visual, and spoken work (Bensonsmith 2005; Franklin 1997).

This way of thinking about trends in marriage and childbearing among low-income African American women sheds very little light on the inner workings of their intimate unions and continues to linger as a dominant paradigm as we consider the romantic relationships of low-income African American women today. To circumvent the conceptual bindings of this perspective, we contend that a more fruitful analytical paradigm for understanding the intimate unions of African American women is to interrogate the role of uncertainty as context, engine, and barrier in relationship formation and maintenance.

Poverty and uncertainty

Our foray into a discussion of uncertainty begins with its place in poverty. The lives of impoverished African American women, and to a certain extent black women more generally, are steeped in uncertainty and its corollary, risk. Geof Wood, a British sociologist and specialist in international development, argues that uncertainty *is* the determining condition for impoverished persons (Wood 2001, 2003). Individuals and families with economic means and more or less stable sources of income can formulate strategic plans with a fair degree of confidence that those plans will come to fruition. For individuals living in poverty, however, it makes little sense to strategize in this way when you have little control over the forces that determine the viability of your plans.

Uncertainty, in the form of unreliability and insecurity, permeates the lives of impoverished African American women in a number of specific ways. Clearly, of course, the fundamental problem is limited income generation; the relegation to low-wage, intermittent employment; and the lack of meaningful access to alternative sources of income (e.g., "finding a rich husband"). In addition, reliance on government subsidies as a safety net is no longer possible with federally mandated limits on the extent of such support. These conditions create a cascade of instability for families. For example, the lack of income dictates transience in living situations given the gap between the price of housing and a low-income person's ability to pay (National Low Income Housing Coalition 2008). These concerns, however, are not limited to those at the bottom of our economic rungs. Even today, many middle-class African Americans (as well as others) have emerged from backgrounds of relative deprivation and, given the vicissitudes of the labor market, may harbor very rational fears of economic loss and an uncertain life.

Wood (2001) also argues that in response to the pervasive absence of predictability about the future, people with limited means strive for risk reduction across multiple domains of life. This point extends to intimate relationships. A study from one of our research programs (Tucker, Taylor, and Mitchell-Kernan 1993) showed that older women eschewed serious romantic relationships to avoid the risks associated with involvement at that stage of life: financial (many had finally obtained some degree of financial stability and were concerned that monetary entanglements with another would deplete their resources), physical (older men were more likely to become infirm, require care, and become dependent), and psychological (they preferred a life of independence, finally free from the demands of others—something they had been denied in the past in every aspect of their lives).[2]

Conversely, in a fundamental and practical sense, having children conveys stability and risk reduction. As others have noted, a child is a permanent attachment (no matter what transpires with the child's father or other family members) and is also an investment in the future and a symbol of hope (Burton 1990; Edin and Kefalas 2005). Having a child is the creation of a stable, enduring, perhaps lifelong, emotional and physical bond. Moreover, children can structure the hours, days, years of one's life, unlike any other social phenomenon or event.

[I]n a fundamental and practical sense, having children conveys stability and risk reduction.

The lens of uncertainty also allows us to reconceptualize other dimensions of African American women's lives that have been mischaracterized or demonized in some previous writings but are pertinent to interpreting patterns in romantic relationships and marriage. In the next section, we explore uncertainty and notions of time and their potential impact on intimacy and union formation among African American women.

Temporal Uncertainty and Romantic Relationships

We have studied and lived the lives of African American women, mothers, and wives for well over a quarter of a century. Our personal and scientific experiences have revealed to us that uncertainties about the nature of time in the lives of African American women, particularly low-income women, complicate and compromise their romantic relationships. Temporal uncertainty can be seen across several domains in African American women's lives. First, it is apparent in the struggles women, particularly those receiving welfare, face in debunking negative stereotypes and moral judgments about how they supposedly use time (e.g., watching soap operas rather than working). It underlies the ways some policy makers have judged African American women and is occasionally intimated in the "cracks" regular folks make about them.

For example, several social service workers in the Three-City Study offered the following comments: "Poor black women operate on colored people's time. . . . They are lazy and can't read a clock for the life of them"; "A black woman don't know a thing about being on time but she does know about maxing and relaxing"; and "They know how to waste time on other peoples' dime." In some circles, these opinions suggest that poor African American women are not entitled to discretionary time or to occasionally being late. Rather, their time use, en masse, is subject to public scrutiny and approval in ways that are nonnegotiable (Tubbs, Roy, and Burton 2005). The undergirding mantra in these opinions is that poor women have not earned the right to use their time in any way other than working to get off welfare.

Such characterizations have followed women into many domains of their lives, including intimate unions. For example, we have observed in the Three-City Study ethnography that low-income women often experience uncertainty concerning their temporal worthiness and are occasionally chastised by their partners about their time use based on images that are not in line with their actual behaviors. Sandra, a thirty-five-year-old African American participant in the study, recounted this story concerning her boyfriend's perception about her time use:

> I was at home laying on the couch yesterday evening. I was tired from working a twelve-hour shift and taking care of my children and my mother. My boyfriend walks in the door and starts fussing [and said,] "Get your lazy ass up off that couch. You just like them lazy women who lay around, wanting to get their nails and hair done, and watching soap operas all damn day. You ain't no white woman, you ain't got time for that stuff. You betta' get up. I don't want no lazy, welfare-getting Black women. If I'm spending my time working you betta' be doing the same."

What is interesting about Sandra's comments is that her boyfriend is superimposing a stereotype about African American women's time use on her that in no way approximates her real-time behaviors. Ethnographic data from three years of interviews and participant observations with Sandra, her children, and occasionally her boyfriend indicate that she is hardworking, spends most of her waking hours tending to the needs of others, is on time for appointments, and rarely ever takes time to relax or engage in self-care. Thus, African American male partners occasionally subscribe to misconstrued behaviors attributed to black women via the Moynihan Report. We are personally familiar with these attributions. Although we both were adolescents at the time of the report's release, we came into womanhood ever mindful of the derisive images of African American women that it propelled into popular use in both public and private spheres. We have witnessed, over time, that a legitimate temporal infraction by an African American woman can quickly evoke charges of shiftlessness, disorganization, or "stealing time that you have not earned."

Second, uncertainty is reflected in women's reckonings with their temporal limitations of their life expectancies—specifically their premonitions about the length of their's and their partners' lives. Current health disparities data reveal that poverty reduces the life expectancies of low-income African American men and women (House 2002; National Center for Health Statistics 2001). Overall, black Americans live far fewer years than whites—the mortality differential attributed to multiple chronic fatal diseases that emerge for African Americans in childhood and young adulthood and ending death interceding to the preponderance of homicide and risk behaviors (e.g., drug addiction) among low-income African American males (Elo 2001; Hayward et al. 2000).

Given the realities of high early death rates for African Americans, it is plausible for some to envision survival to a "ripe old age" an unlikely prospect. These truncated views of length of life can heighten uncertainty in ways that directly impact romantic relationships and marriage (Burton 1990). For example, when both a woman and her partner believe that *he* will not live past the age of twenty-five, the intensity of their relationship can escalate quickly, with coresidential living arrangements and a pregnancy ensuing before the couple has taken the time to really get to know one another. We also have seen in our research how contextual cues (e.g., neighborhood violence) hasten some African American women to anticipate the early demise of their partners, and how, to reduce uncertainty and potential grief, women will severely limit their attachment and romantic commitment (Burton et al. 2007; Tucker 2005).

In addition, low-income women's health and their family caregiving responsibilities also place them in a temporal bind that compromises the amount of time they can invest in relationships (Roy, Tubbs, and Burton 2004). Some African American women, as with their men, become aware, at very early ages, of the fact that they have a diminished life expectancy due to poor health. For example, Yvonne, a Three-City Study participant, stated,

> Me and my mom talk about how many problems I've had. I'm only twenty-one and I've had all these problems [asthma, gynecological tumors, and depression] and I worry about in coming years what's going to happen. There's women out there in their thirties having hysterectomies. Is that going to be me? Am I going to die at forty-five?

Women must decide how they will allocate their time based on their health and the health of others. We see the dilemmas women face in doing so in the case of Francine, another Three-City Study participant. Francine, a thirty-year-old mother of three children aged four, six, and eight, also had too many other responsibilities to focus on her own health. As a baby and toddler, she was often hospitalized with pneumonia; she was not expected to live into the school years. She was hospitalized every year with pneumonia until her freshman year of high school. When Francine joined the ethnographic study, she had just received a "temporary diagnosis of stomach cancer," but Francine did not return to the doctor until the pain was unbearable and she "didn't have other folks to take care of." Her six-year-old asthmatic son required constant attention. Francine's mother suffered a recent stroke, a heart attack, and had an "orange-sized" tumor in her chest. Francine, like many of the mothers in the study, was her own mother's primary caregiver. With no alternatives for caring for her mother or children, Francine had no time for treatment for her own medical conditions. And she had no time for marriage.

Finally, temporal uncertainty rests in women's attempts to manage the daily rhythms of their families while adhering to institutional timetables, notably the nine-to-five business hours of social service agencies (Burton and Sorenson 1993). These temporal incongruencies heighten feelings of uncertainty for women as the capricious nature of work schedules, child care, garnering reliable transportation, and the anticipation of long waits in line punctuate their lack of control over time and the fact that they are at the mercy of others' schedules. These features of time and uncertainty were not considered in the Moynihan debates, nor, some forty years later, have they been systematically used to explore and inform interpretations of marriage and romantic relationship patterns among low-income African American women.

In summary, in the lives of low-income African American women there is massive uncertainty about time—uncertainty created by stereotypes, truncated life expectancies, failing health, and the adherence to incongruent institutional timetables. Within these domains, African American women are often forced to operate outside of the normative boundaries of time. In some cases, these demands can foster the self-reliance and creative problem solving that have ensured African American women's and their families' survival over time. But these temporal quagmires also challenge the sustainability of long-term romantic relationships and marriage. Perhaps there is truly not enough time left in the day to nurture a romantic relationship, especially when one also has to negotiate another source of uncertainty—namely, the new terrains of gender roles.

Gender Relationships: Negotiating New Terrains, Roles, and Obligations

With uncertainty as a guiding principle in our analysis of intimate union formation and maintenance among African American women, we recognize that in a more general societal sense, the foundation for romantic relationships is today anything but terra firma. Although social relationships in the United States have evolved in some remarkable and substantive ways since the 1960s, perhaps the most consequential change has been the manner in which women and men relate to each other (Solomon and Knobloch 2001). Men and women have significantly realigned expectations regarding gender-specific behaviors across settings, although consensus about proper conduct for each has apparently diminished. Concerning romantic unions, Cherlin (2004) argues that Americans in general are uncertain and confused about appropriate behavior for partners—part of the process he views as the "deinstitutionalization of marriage."

In recent years, both academic and more literary treatments have signaled unusual strain in relationships between African American men and women (e.g., Aborampah 1989; McMillan 1992; Pinderhughes, 2002). We argue that even greater ambiguity surrounds African American family roles, as structural forces coupled with experientially induced sociocultural tendencies drive new attitudinal and behavioral patterns. We view these new relationship challenges as being rooted in a complex interplay between new economic and resource realities;

changing conceptualizations of appropriate gender-specific behavior; and changing society-wide beliefs about the nature, value, and function of marriage.

New economic realities

African American women have always played essential economic roles within
their families. Throughout the past century, formal labor force participation has
steadily increased—especially for married women. Landry (2000) views African
American women as the vanguard of a "revolution" in the construction of domestic relationships in male-female headed families, arguing that the employment of
black wives fueled the changes in household gender dynamics that idealized
more egalitarian modes of conduct. Only a quarter of married African American
women worked in the 1940s (compared to 8 percent of white wives) (U.S. Census
Bureau 1961). By 2004, working wives had become the dominant paradigm in
the United States, as 70 percent of black and 60 percent of white married women
held jobs (U.S. Department of Labor 2005).

These statistics obscure the extent of black women's economic engagement: they
have been more likely than white women to be employed full-time (Harrison
2003), to return to work more quickly after childbearing (Smith and Amachu 1999),
and to endure significantly longer commutes to work (Johnston 1998). As Mason
(2005) notes, between 1964 and 2000, African American women's labor market
earnings improved relative to black men but declined relative to white women
(Newsome and Dodoo 2002). In 2000, black women's average weekly wage was 79
percent of black men's and 90 percent of white women's wages; the comparable
proportion for white women to men was 61 percent (Mason 2005), which demonstrates greater familial reliance on the income of African American women.

Beneath these new economic realities is the constant of employment uncertainty. Although African American women and men have consistently been more
vulnerable than other racial groups to layoffs and plant closings, they have been
especially susceptible during national economic upheavals (Kletzer 1991; Elvira
and Zatzick 2002; Fairlie and Kletzer 1996). Dorman (2005) reports that during the
major recession of the early 1980s, more than 7 percent of black workers were displaced,[3] compared to not quite 5 percent of white workers. Job loss is more debilitating for blacks, since they have greater difficulty securing new jobs (Dorman
2005; Kletzer 1991; Yang 2007). Due in large part to a concentration of employment in the sectors hit hardest by the recession of the early 1980s, embodied by
deindustrialization of large urban centers, the impact on black men was especially
severe (Johnson and Oliver 1991; Kletzer 1991; Spalter-Roth and Lowenthal 2005;
Wilson 1987). The negative impact of economic strain on marital relationships has
been well documented (Conger et al. 1990; Cutrona et al. 2003). Clara, a participant in the Three-City Study, agrees: "It is hard to keep a relationship together
when most of your time is spent worrying about which one of us is gonna' have a
job the next day. It's like flying blind everyday, never knowing what to expect."

Growing male-female resource gap

Despite the context of erratic employment prospects, the latter half of the twentieth century witnessed great educational gains for African Americans overall. The proportion of African Americans earning high school diplomas rose from 13.7 percent in 1950 to 72.3 percent in 2000; those with college degrees went from 2.2 to 14.3 percent (U.S. Census Bureau 2006a, 2006b). However, although fairly equal proportions of black men and women were college-educated through 1990, since then the educational trajectories of men and women have diverged (*Journal of Blacks in Higher Education* 2007). In 2000, 13.1 percent of black men held bachelor's degrees, relative to 15.2 percent of black women. Enrollment data portend a deepening crisis: in 2005, 45 percent of black women and 35 percent of black men aged eighteen to nineteen were enrolled in college; the comparable figures for ages twenty-two to twenty-four were 31 and 20 percent (U.S. Census Bureau 2007). Since a college education is a foundational resource for many upper-level jobs, the employment prospects of women and men are also becoming more divergent—further complicating male-female romantic relationship formation and maintenance.

Although African American women have always been far more likely than white women to marry men with less education and lower occupational status (e.g., Spanier and Glick 1980; Lichter, Anderson, and Hayward 1995), the increasing gender gap in labor market placement and education has placed black female-male relationships on even more uncertain contextual grounds. Arguably a husband-wife educational gap of high school diploma versus less than high school (which was more characteristic of earlier generations) is more socioculturally congruent than college/professional degree versus high school/trade school.

Although the effect of the latter incongruence on African American relationships has rarely been addressed, a recent study from one of our research programs raises a number of issues: Furdyna, Tucker, and James (2008) found that marital income disparities favoring wives did *not* have the direct, negative effect on the happiness of black wives that has been observed for white wives. Rather, black wives' happiness was compromised when the educational gap between partners was large, which suggested to the authors that although black marriages have historically accommodated more egalitarian economic roles, the growing educational gap between women and men poses a formidable threat for intimate relationships.

Inasmuch as postsecondary educational experiences are, in effect, cultural socializations as well as status markers, large differences in education may affect a couple's way of relating to and engaging one another. For example, several of the women in the Three-City Study noted that their partners were more apprehensive about their going to school and getting an education than working. Partners typically argued that "their women" would outgrow them if they got more education and would be "too smart for the relationship."

Societal change in the status of women

Concurrent with these developments, the women's movement has driven society-wide changes in gender relationships by giving women greater voice and structural power in many domains as well as a greater tolerance for and valuation of female independence. Although couples across the nation were struggling to redefine the terms of the marital bond and find the most appropriate ways to handle the responsibilities of managing homes and families, the task for African American couples was more complex and delicate. Studies have shown that African American men display a greater willingness to share domestic tasks (Hossain and Roopnarine 1993; Xu, Hudspeth, and Estes 1997), yet they do not display an ideological commitment to such arrangements (Kane 2000).

[A] delicate dance is required of women to balance what is viewed in many African American communities as the need to elevate and honor manhood (especially those who have committed to families) while carrying out necessary obligations and tasks.

African American women are also more likely than white women to report a preference for males' having primary economic responsibility (Taylor, Tucker, and Mitchell-Kernan 1999), despite the remoteness of such a prospect. Hatchett, Veroff, and Douvan (1995) have argued that for many African Americans, a more traditional alignment of household responsibilities is viewed as an achievement in the larger society's terms. Haynes (2000) observed a similar phenomenon in middle-class African American marriages but noted that women, in particular, have difficulty maintaining hard-won autonomy (via work and educational status) and at the same time protecting and preserving male ego and authority. These studies suggest (consistent with our personal observations) that a delicate dance is required of women to balance what is viewed in many African American communities as the need to elevate and honor manhood (especially those who have committed to families) while carrying out necessary obligations and tasks. A woman's task is to be strong, but not to overshadow her man. Nadine's opening comments in this article suggest that she has taken this point to heart.

Evolving perspectives on the nature, value, and function of marriage

The set of circumstances described above affect union behavior through the prism of dynamic views on the nature, value, and function of marriage. Cherlin

(2004) has argued that social norms concerning the behavior of marital partners have so weakened that one cannot rely on community understandings for knowledge of proper conduct. Americans irrespective of ethnicity and gender continue to value the institution of marriage (Thornton and Young-DeMarco 2001; Tucker 2000) but also show greater tolerance of an array of behaviors that formerly were negatively sanctioned, including divorce, nonmarital childbirth, cohabitation, same-sex unions, and infidelity (Thornton and Young-DeMarco 2001). Although these trends have been observed society-wide, evidence also shows that this expansion of tolerance occurred earlier and has been much more broadly adopted, in the African American community (Tucker and James 2005).

Is something else especially unusual about current conditions? Empirical data on the complex forces affecting the likelihood of entering into and the ability to maintain relationships are lacking. We nonetheless suggest that the meaning and influence of shifts in resources and values are complicated by a new and widely embraced emphasis on female independence. This respect for female independence preceded the feminist movement of the 1960s and corresponds with contemporary cultural trends. The cultural elevation of highly successful single (even if sometimes partnered) African American women (e.g., Oprah Winfrey, Condoleezza Rice) has demonstrated the possibilities and benefits of going solo. Many songs by popular all-female African American groups celebrate female independence and reliance on self (e.g., "Independent Women" by Destiny's Child; "Control" by Janet Jackson; "Depend on Myself" by TLC).

We strongly assert, though, that the elevation of women's independence must not be viewed through the distorted lens and constraints of Moynihan's sense of "matriarchy." Moynihan misapplied the anthropological term to connote domination of marriage, men, and households by women, not coincidentally while conveniently ignoring the role of welfare policy in isolating or banishing men from Aid to Families with Dependent Children (AFDC)–supported households. The emphasis in the new conceptualization of African American womanhood is self-reliance and self-discovery—not control of others (Giddings 1984). As such, African American successful relationship formation and nurturance is likely to require a novel vision and appreciation of what partners can and should bring to a union. This new compact will also require new forms of negotiation, including a reconstruction of the basis of power and privilege and a new language of process.

Stevenson (1996) and Hill (2005) remind us that the marital contract among African Americans has always differed in significant ways from that embraced by the dominant white society. Marriage has not been protective for black women and has rarely provided the substantial economic benefits that white wives could expect. It is also clear that while more privileged African American women are capable of exercising their independence, the circumstances of poor women are only growing worse, given the disintegration of societal safety nets, the disappearance of low-skill jobs that pay a living wage, and the "demise of female-centered support systems" (Hill 2005). Because the men these women would have access to as potential partners have fared no better in this global economic market, it is difficult to see how marriage would be to either's benefit.

Conclusion

In this discussion, we have attempted to provide an alternate lens through which to view past and current patterns of intimate union formation and maintenance by African American women. We have made uncertainty the framework for our analysis and considered how poverty creates a context of insecurity for women and families, how temporal dimensions of peoples' lives are reconfigured in contemporary society and compromise the potential for long-term relationships, and how changing gender roles increase ambiguity about proper role enactment in female-male relationships. We also have sought to demonstrate how uncertainty frames perceptions, attitudes, assessments, decision making, and behaviors about marriage and intimate unions for African Americans and how it renders contextually relevant interpretations that were sorely missing from the Moynihan discourse and, to some extent, from comparable discussions today.

Unlike what the Moynihan Report suggested, we do not see low-income African American women's trends in marriage and romantic unions as pathologically out of line with the growing numbers of unmarried women and single mothers across all groups in contemporary American culture (Stacey 1998). We are hopeful that the uncertainty that is the foundation of romantic relationships today will reinforce the adaptive skills that have sustained African American women and their families across time. However, the tasks for reducing poverty, reconciling time binds, and recalibrating gender-linked behavioral expectations is an urgent challenge for many groups and nations. Perhaps interrogating the course of African American women and marriage using the uncertainty lens will yield insights that are relevant for resolving those challenges for others.

We close with the words of Eleanor Holmes Norton (1970, p. 404), who made an especially astute observation when societal changes around marriage and romantic relationships first became evident: "With children no longer the universally accepted reason for marriage, marriages are going to have to exist on their own merits. Marriages are going to have to exist because they possess inherent qualities which make them worthy of existing, a plane to which the institution has never before been elevated." It may be that marriage as we have known it in contemporary times will not survive "on its own terms" as Norton warned, but the need for human companionship and love remains intrinsic to the human condition. As subsequent generations are being socialized to enter romantic relationships and to form families, serious community-wide conversations about how to address the current dilemma in this era of uncertainty are essential.

Notes

1. The Three-City Study (Welfare, Children, and Families: A Three-City Study) is a multilevel, multimethod longitudinal project designed to examine, in great detail, the lives of urban African American, Mexican American, Puerto Rican, and non-Hispanic white low-income families with children in Boston, Chicago, and San Antonio. The study comprises three interrelated components: a longitudinal survey of about 2,400 low-income families; a more intensive study of about 700 young children and their caregivers in a subsample of the survey families, which is called the Embedded Developmental Study (EDS); and an

ethnographic study of 256 families with young children (including 42 families of a child who has a disability) and of the neighborhoods in which they reside. For a detailed description of the Three-City Study, see http://web.jhu.edu/threecitystudy

2. This theme can be generalized to older middle-class women across race and ethnicity who also hesitate to risk their freedom and independence for caretaking of new partners in old age (Carol Stack, personal communication, 2008)

3. The Bureau of Labor Statistics (2008) defines displacement as losing or leaving a job due to plant or company closure or moves, insufficient work, or abolition of position or shift.

References

Abbott, Andrew. 2001. *Time matters*. Chicago: University of Chicago Press.

Aborampah, Osei-Mensah. 1989. Black male-female relationships: Some observations. *Journal of Black Studies* 19:320-42.

Bauman, Zygmunt. 1991. *Modernity and ambivalence*. Oxford, UK: Polity.

———. 1995. *Life in fragments: Essays in postmodern morality*. Oxford, UK: Blackwell.

Bensonsmith, Dionne. 2005. Jezebels, matriarchs, and welfare queens: The Moynihan Report of 1965 and the social construction of African American women in welfare policy. In *Deserving and entitled: Social constructions and public policy*, ed. A. L. Schneider and H. M. Ingram, 247-60. Albany: State University of New York Press.

Bureau of Labor Statistics. 2008. Displaced worker summary. http://www.bls.gov/news.release/disp.nr0.htm (accessed March 1, 2008).

Burton, Linda M. 1990. Teenage childbearing as an alternative life-course strategy in multigeneration black families. *Human Nature* 1:123-43.

Burton, Linda M., Andrew Cherlin, Donna-Marie Winn, Angela Estacion, and Clara Holder-Taylor. 2007. The role of trust in low-income mothers' intimate unions. Paper presented at the annual meeting of the American Sociological Association, New York, August.

Burton, Linda M., and Silvia Sorensen. 1993. Temporal dimensions of intergenerational care giving in African-American multi-generation families. In *Care giving systems: Informal and formal helper*, ed. Steven H. Zarit, Leonard I. Pearlin, and K. Warner Schaie, 47-66. New York: Erlbaum.

Cherlin, Andrew J. 2004. The deinstitutionalization of American marriage. *Journal of Marriage and Family* 66:848-61.

Clark, David, ed. 1991. *Marriage, domestic life, and social change*. New York: Routledge.

Collins, Patricia H. 1991. Black feminist thought: Knowledge consciousness, and the politics of empowerment. New York: Routledge.

Conger, Rand D., Glen H. Elder Jr., Frederick O. Lorenz, Katherine J. Conger, Ronald L. Simons, Les B. Whitbeck, Shirley Huck, and Janet N. Melby. 1990. Linking economic hardship to marital quality and instability. *Journal of Marriage and the Family* 52:643-56.

Cutrona, Carolyn E., Daniel W. Russell, W. Todd Abraham, Kelli A. Gardner, Janet N. Melby, Chalandra Bryant, and Rand D. Conger. 2003. Neighborhood context and financial strain as predictors of marital interaction and marital quality in African American couples. *Personal Relationships* 10:389-409.

Daly, Kerry J. 1996. *Families and time: Keeping pace in a hurried culture*. Thousand Oaks, CA: Sage.

Dickson, Linda. 1993. The future of marriage and family in black America. *Journal of Black Studies* 23:472-91.

Dorman, Peter. 2005. Globalization, the transformation of capital, and the erosion of black and Latino living standards. In *2005 African Americans in the U.S. economy*, ed. C. A. Conrad, J. Whitehead, P. Mason, and J. Stewart, 185-92. Lanham, MD: Rowman & Littlefield.

Edin, Kathryn, and Maria J. Kefalas. 2005. *Promises I can keep: Why poor women put motherhood before marriage*. Berkeley: University of California Press.

Elo, Irma T. 2001. New African American life tables from 1935–1940 to 1985–1990. *Demography* 38:97-114.

Elvira, Marta M., and Christopher Zatzick. 2002. Who's displaced first? The role of race in layoff decisions. *Industrial Relations* 41:329-61.

Fairlie, Robert W., and Lori G. Kletzer. 1996. Race and the shifting burden of job displacement: 1982–93. *Monthly Labor Review* 119 (9): 13-23. http://www.bls.gov/opub/mlr/1996/09/art3abs.htm (accessed March 24, 2008).

Franklin, Donna L. 1997. Ensuring inequality: The structural transformation of the African American family. New York: Oxford Press.

Furdyna, Holly, M. Belinda Tucker, and Angela James. 2008. Relative spousal earnings and marital happiness among African American and white women. *Journal of Marriage and Family* 70:332-44.

Giddens, Anthony. 1991. *Modernity and self-identity: Self and society in the late modern age*. Stanford, CA: Stanford University Press.

———. 1992. *The transformations of intimacy: Sexuality, love, and eroticism in modern societies*. Stanford, CA: Stanford University Press.

Giddings, Paula. 1984. *When and where I enter: The impact of black women on race and sex in America*. New York: Bantam.

Harrison, Roderick. 2003. Part-time/full-time employment: Fact sheet. Joint Center for Political and Economic Studies, August. http://www.jointcenter.org/DB/factsheets/parttime2.htm (accessed March 26, 2008).

Hatchett, Shirley, Joseph Veroff, and Elizabeth Douvan. 1995. Marital instability among black and white couples in early marriage. In *The decline in marriage among African Americans: Causes, consequences and policy implications*, ed. M. Belinda Tucker and Claudia Mitchell-Kernan, 177-218. New York: Russell Sage Foundation.

Haynes, Faustina E. 2000. Gender and family ideals: An exploratory study of black middle-class Americans. *Journal of Family Issues* 21:811-37.

Hayward, Mark, D. Eileen, M. Crimmins, Toni P. Miles, and Y. Yu. 2000. The significance of socioeconomic status in explaining the racial gap in chronic health conditions. *American Sociological Review* 65:910-30.

Hill, Shirley A. 2005. Black intimacies: A gender perspective on families and relationships. Walnut Creek, CA: AltaMira.

Hochschild, Arlie R. 1989. *Working parents and the revolutions at home*. New York: Viking Penguin.

———. 1997. The time bind: When work becomes home and home becomes work. New York: Henry Holt and Company.

Hossain, Ziarat, and Jaipaul L. Roopnarine. 1993. Division of household labor and child care in dual-earner families with infants. *Sex Roles* 29:571-83.

House, James S. 2002. Understanding social factors and inequalities in health: 20th century progress and 21st century prospects. *Journal of Health and Social Behavior* 43:125-42.

Johnson, James H., and Melvin Oliver. 1991. Economic restructuring and black male joblessness in U.S. metropolitan areas. *Urban Geography* 12:542-62.

Johnson-Hanks, Jennifer. 2006. *Uncertain honor: Modern motherhood in an African crisis*. Chicago: University of Chicago Press.

Johnston, Ibipo. 1998. Location, race, and labor force participation: Implications for women of color. Women's Travel Issues: Proceedings from the Second National Conference, Baltimore. http://www.fhwa.dot.gov/ohim/womens/wtipage.htm (accessed March 26, 2008).

The Journal of Blacks in Higher Education. 2007. Black student college graduation rates inch higher but a large racial gap persists. Winter (preview). http://www.jbhe.com/preview/winter07preview.html (accessed March 10, 2008).

Kane, Emily W. 2000. Racial and ethnic variations in gender-related attitudes. *Annual Review of Sociology* 26:419-39.

Kletzer, Lori G. 1991. Job displacement, 1979–86: How blacks fared relative to whites. *Monthly Labor Review* 114 (7): 17-25.

Landry, Bart. 2000. *Black working wives: Pioneers of the American revolution*. Berkeley: University of California Press.

Lichter, Daniel T., Robert N. Anderson, and Mark Hayward. 1995. Marriage markets and marital choice. *Journal of Family Issues* 16:412-31.

Lincoln, Karen D., Robert J. Taylor, and James S. Jackson. 2008. Romantic relationships among unmarried African Americans and Caribbean blacks: Finding from the National Survey of American Life. *Family Relations* 57:254-66.

Mason, Patrick L. 2005. Persistent racial discrimination in the labor market. In *African Americans in the U.S. economy*, ed. Cecilia A. Conrad, John Whitehead, Patrick Mason, and James Stewart, 103-8. Lanham, MD: Rowman & Littlefield.

McMillan, Terri. 1992. *Waiting to exhale*. Bergenfield, NJ: Viking Penguin.

Mills, Melinda, and Hans-Peter Blossfeld. 2005. Globalization, uncertainty, and the early life course. In *Globalization, uncertainty, and youth in society*, ed. Hans-Peter Blossfeld, Erik Klijzing, Melinda Mills, and Karin Kurtz, 1-24. New York: Routledge.

National Center for Health Statistics. 2001. *Health, United States, 2001, with urban and rural health chartbook*. DHHS Publication no. PHS 01–132. Hyattsville, MD: National Center for Health Statistics.

National Low Income Housing Coalition. 2008. Out of reach 2007–2008. http://www.nlihc.org/oor/oor2008/ (accessed May 22, 2008).

Newsome, Yvonne D., and F. Nii-Amoo Dodoo. 2002. Reversal of fortune: Explaining the decline in black women's earnings. *Gender & Society* 16:442-64.

Norton, Eleanor Holmes. 1970. For Sadie and Maude. In *Sisterhood is powerful: An anthology of writings from the women's liberation movement*, ed. Robin Morgan, 353-59. New York: Random House.

Pinderhughes, Elaine B. 2002. African American marriage in the 20th century. *Family Process* 41:269-82.

Rainwater, Lee, and William L. Yancey. 1967. *The Moynihan Report and the politics of controversy*. Cambridge, MA: MIT Press.

Roy, Kevin, Carolyn Y. Tubbs, and Linda M. Burton. 2004. "Don't have no time": Daily rhythms and the organization of time for low-income families. *Family Relations* 53:168-78.

Smith, Kristin E., and Bachu Amachu. 1999. Women's labor force attachment patterns and maternity leave: A review of the literature. Population Division Working Paper no. 32, U.S. Census Bureau, Washington, DC. http://www.census.gov/population/www/documentation/twps0032/twps0032.html (accessed October 27, 2005).

Solomon, Denise H., and Leanne K. Knobloch. 2001. Relationship uncertainty, partner interference, and intimacy within dating relationships. *Communication Monograph* 61:345-60.

Spalter-Roth, Roberta, and Terri A. Lowenthal. 2005. Race, ethnicity, and the American labor market: What's at work? American Sociological Association Series on How Race and Ethnicity Matter. http://www2.asanet.org/centennial/race_ethnicity_labormarket.pdf (accessed February 24, 2008).

Spanier, Graham B., and Paul C. Glick. 1980. Mate selection differential between whites and blacks in the United States. *Social Forces* 58:707-25.

Stacey, Judith. 1998. *Brave new families*. Berkeley: University of California Press.

Stevenson, Brenda. 1996. *Life in black and white: Family and community in the slave South*. New York: Oxford University Press.

Taylor, Pamela L., M. Belinda Tucker, and Claudia Mitchell-Kernan. 1999. Ethnic variations in perceptions of men's provider role. *Psychology of Women Quarterly* 23:759-79.

Thornton, Arland, and Linda Young-DeMarco. 2001. Four decades of trends in attitudes toward family issues in the United States: The 1960s through the 1990s. *Journal of Marriage and the Family* 63:1009-37.

Tubbs, Carolyn Y., Kevin Roy, and Linda M. Burton. 2005. Family ties and constructing family time in low-income families. *Family Process* 44:77-91.

Tucker, M. Belinda. 2000. Marital values and expectations in context: Results from a 21 city survey. In *The ties the bind: Perspectives on marriage and cohabitation*, ed. Linda J. Waite, Christine Bachrach, Michelle Hindin, and Arland Thornton, 166-87. New York: Aldine de Gruyter.

———. 2005. Intimate relationships and psychological well-being. In *In and out of our right minds*, ed. Diane R. Brown and Verna M. Keith, 139-59. New York: Columbia University Press.

Tucker, M. Belinda, and Angela D. James. 2005. New families, new functions: Postmodern African American families in context. In *Emerging issues in African American life: Context, adaptation, and policy*, ed. Vonnie C. McLoyd, Nancy E. Hill, and Kenneth A. Dodge, 86-108. New York: Guilford.

Tucker, M. Belinda, Robert J. Taylor, and Claudia Mitchell-Kernan. 1993. Marriage and romantic involvement among aged African Americans. *Journal of Gerontology: Social Sciences* 48:S123-S132.

U.S. Census Bureau. 1961. U.S. census of the population 1960 subject reports: Employment status and work experience. Final Report PC(2)-6A. Washington, DC: Government Printing Office.

———. 2006a. A half-century of learning: Historical statistics on educational attainment in the United States, 1940 to 2000, Table 3: Percent of the population 25 years and over with a high school diploma

or higher by sex, race, and Hispanic origin, for the United States: 1940 to 2000. http://www
.census.gov/population/www/socdemo/education/phct1.html (accessed March 1, 2008).

———. 2006b. A half-century of learning: Historical statistics on educational attainment in the United
States, 1940 to 2000, Table 4: Percent of the population 25 years and over with a bachelor's degree or
higher by sex, race, and Hispanic origin, for the United States: 1940 to 2000. http://www
.census.gov/population/www/socdemo/education/phct41.html (accessed March 1, 2008).

———. 2007. School enrollment, CPS 2005, Table 1: Enrollment status of the population 3 years old and
over, by sex, age, race, Hispanic origin, foreign born, and foreign-born parentage: October 2005.
http://www.census.gov/population/www/socdemo/school/cps2005.html (accessed March 1, 2008).

U.S. Department of Labor. 2005. Bureau of Labor Statistics data extraction from the Current Population
Survey. http://www.bls.gov/data/home.html (accessed July 1, 2005).

Wilson, William Julius. 1987. *The truly disadvantaged: The inner city, the underclass, and public policy.*
Chicago: University of Chicago Press.

Wood, Geof D. 2001. Desperately seeking security. *Journal of International Development* 13:523-34.

———. 2003. Staying secure, staying poor: The Faustian bargain. *World Development* 31:455-71.

Xu, Xiaohe, Clark D. Hudspeth, and Selena Estes. 1997. The effects of husbands' involvement in childrearing activities and participation in household labor on marital quality: A racial comparison. *Journal
of Gender, Culture and Health* 2:187-209.

Yang, Song. 2007. Perceived job insecurity of white and black workers: An expanded gap in organizations
with layoff prevention commitment. Paper presented at the annual meeting of the American
Sociological Association, New York. http://www.allacademic.com/meta/p174716_index.html (accessed
March 27, 2008).

Claiming Fatherhood: Race and the Dynamics of Paternal Involvement among Unmarried Men

By
KATHRYN EDIN,
LAURA TACH,
and
RONALD MINCY

In 1965, Daniel Patrick Moynihan argued that the black family was nearing "complete breakdown" due to high rates of out-of-wedlock childbearing. In subsequent decades, nonmarital childbearing rose dramatically for all racial groups and unwed fathers were often portrayed as being absent from their children's lives. The authors examine contemporary nonmarital father involvement using quantitative evidence from the Fragile Families and Child Wellbeing Study and qualitative evidence from in-depth interviews with 150 unmarried fathers. The authors find that father involvement drops sharply after parents' relationships end, especially when they enter subsequent relationships and have children with new partners. These declines are less dramatic for African American fathers, suggesting that fathers' roles outside of conjugal relationships may be more strongly institutionalized in the black community. The challenges Moynihan described among black families some forty years ago now extend to a significant minority of all American children.

Keywords: Daniel Patrick Moynihan; *The Negro Family*; unmarried parents; paternal involvement; race

In 1965 Daniel Patrick Moynihan, then assistant secretary of labor for President Lyndon Johnson, penned the now-infamous report *The Negro Family: A Case for National Action*. In this document, Moynihan claimed that owing to the sharp increase in out-of-wedlock childbearing—a condition affecting only a small fraction of white children but one in five African Americans at the time—the black family was nearing what he called "complete breakdown," particularly in America's inner cities. Over the next two decades, the rate of unwed childbearing tripled for the nation as a whole. Its prevalence among whites is now as high as it was for African Americans when Moynihan released his report.

In the wake of this dramatic increase in so-called fatherless families, public outrage grew and policy makers responded. Liberals wanted to help supplement the incomes of single mothers, who were disproportionately poor, yet

DOI: 10.1177/0002716208325548

conservatives believed this would only reward their behavior and lead to more female-headed families. Meanwhile, taxpayers increasingly demanded to know why their hard-earned dollars were going to support what many saw as an unfortunate lifestyle choice, not unavoidable hardship.

Scholars responded by devoting a huge amount of attention to studying single mothers and children, detailing the struggles of the parents and documenting the deleterious effects on the children. These studies offered the American public a wealth of knowledge about the lives of the mothers and their progeny, yet told us next to nothing about the fathers of these children. Part of the problem was that surveys provided very little systematic information from which to draw any kind of representative picture. Unwed fathers' often tenuous connections to households made them hard to find, and many refused to admit to survey researchers that they had fathered children. Thus, vast numbers of fathers have been invisible to even the largest, most carefully conducted studies (Hofferth et al. 2002).

From this mix of scholarly ignorance and public indignation, a compelling yet distorted image of unwed inner-city fathers emerged and captured the American public's imagination: the "hit-and-run" father. According to this portrayal, men who father children outside of a marital bond are interested only in sex, not

Kathryn Edin is a professor of social policy at the John F. Kennedy School of Government at Harvard University. Her research focuses on urban poverty and family life, social welfare, public housing, child support, and nonmarital childbearing and the economic lives of the poor. Her most recent publication is Promises I Can Keep: Why Poor Women Put Motherhood before Marriage *(with Maria J. Kefalas; University of California Press 2005). She is also coauthor of* Making Ends Meet: How Low Income Single Mothers Survive Welfare and Low Wage Work *(Russell Sage Foundation 1997). Current projects include an in-depth study nested within the interim evaluation of the Moving to Opportunity Experiment and an in-depth longitudinal study of the Gautreaux Two program.*

Laura Tach is a doctoral candidate in sociology and social policy at Harvard University. Her research examines how various social contexts, particularly family structures and neighborhoods, influence the well-being of individuals. She is presently involved in projects studying mixed-income neighborhoods, multiple-partner fertility and father involvement, and trajectories of marital quality.

Ronald Mincy is the Maurice V. Russell Professor of Social Policy and Social Work Practice at the Columbia University School of Social Work and director of the Center for Research on Fathers, Children, and Family Well-Being. He has published widely on the effects of income security policy on child and family poverty, family formation, child well-being, responsible fatherhood, the urban underclass, and urban poverty. His most recent book is Black Males Left Behind *(Urban Institute 2006). He is currently working on a multiyear study of the New York State Non-custodial Parent Income Tax Credit and a random clinical trial of an intervention that uses nonresident fathers to delay sexual debut among African American males.*

NOTE: The authors wish to thank Julien Tietler, Marcia J. Carlson, Jean Knab, Judith Seltzer, and Frank Furstenberg for helpful comments on earlier tables and drafts. The qualitative study was funded by the William T. Grant Foundation. The Fragile Families and Child Wellbeing Study was supported by Grant Number R01HD36916 from the National Institute of Child Health and Human Development. The contents of the article are solely the responsibility of the authors and do not represent the official views of the W. T. Grant Foundation or the National Institute of Child Health and Human Development.

fatherhood. When their female conquests come up pregnant, they quickly flee the scene, leaving the expectant mother holding the diaper bag. "[Unwed fathers] never signed on to anything," wrote marriage movement founder David Blankenhorn in 1995 in *Fatherless America*. "They never agreed to abide by any fatherhood code. They do not have—they have never had—any explicit obligation to either their children or to the mothers of their children" (pp. 134–35).

In the same spirit, well-known conservative William Bennett, in his 2001 book *The Broken Hearth*, raged, "It is unmarried fathers who are missing in record numbers, who impregnate women and selfishly flee. . . . Abandoning alike those who they have taken as sexual partners, and whose lives they have created, they . . . traduce generations yet to come, and disgrace their very manhood" (pp. 93–94). In 2004, an infuriated Bill Cosby publicly indicted unwed fathers for merely "inserting the sperm cell" while blithely eschewing the responsibilities of fatherhood. "No longer is a boy considered an embarrassment if he tries to run away from being the father of the unmarried child," Cosby declared.[1] Two days before Father's Day in 2007, democratic presidential candidate Barack Obama admonished the congregants of Mt. Moriah Baptist Church in Spartanburg, South Carolina: "There are a lot of men out there who need to stop acting like boys, who need to realize that responsibility does not end at conception, who need to know that what makes you a man is not the ability to have a child but the courage to raise a child."[2]

This image of unwed fatherhood as a hit-and-run encounter plays a dominant role in the public discourse about poverty, family structure, and race. However, a growing body of evidence from the social sciences suggests that unwed fathers who "hit and run" are much rarer than the public assumes. We evaluate the accuracy of this view using evidence from a recent nationally representative longitudinal survey of nonmarital births in large cities—the Fragile Families and Child Wellbeing Study. We find that even by a child's fifth birthday, rates of father involvement are quite high, especially when compared to public perceptions.

We find that even by a child's fifth birthday, rates of father involvement are quite high, especially when compared to public perceptions.

These relatively high levels of involvement mask considerable variation in involvement based on the parents' relationship status, however. After relationships between parents end, father involvement drops sharply. We also find that declines are particularly dramatic when the father and mother enter subsequent relationships and have children with new partners. These declines are less dramatic for African American fathers, suggesting that the role of the father outside the context of a conjugal relationship may be more strongly institutionalized in the black community.

We then draw on qualitative interviews with 150 low-income white, black, and Hispanic fathers from high-poverty neighborhoods in the Philadelphia metropolitan area, all of whom have had a child outside of marriage, to understand the complex social processes that may underlie these statistical associations. We find that contrary to public perceptions, for the large majority of unwed fathers, the father role has high salience, and most strive to be highly engaged with their progeny. Ironically, though we find that the majority of fathers strongly reject traditional notions that the father–child bond should be conditioned upon the state of the relationship between the father and mother, they nonetheless typically enact it. Due to a variety of challenges, especially those stemming from transitions into new partner and parenting roles, children born to unmarried parents only rarely have a stably involved father throughout childhood and adolescence.

Theory and Research on Father Involvement

In the American context, fatherhood has traditionally been viewed as part of a "package deal" (Furstenberg and Cherlin 1991; Townsend 2004). Fatherhood is a relationship that is not independent of, but largely flows through and is contingent upon, the relationship between the father and the child's mother. This explanation is often used to account for the surprisingly low levels of father–child contact and child support payment following a divorce (Furstenberg and Cherlin 1991). To the extent that notions of "the package deal" are still strongly institutionalized within American society, men attempting to father outside of the context of a marriage, a coresidential union, or a romantic relationship will have more difficulty staying involved with their children.

Beyond the additional transaction costs fathers must pay to retain contact with children after a coresidential or romantic partnership ends, the package deal hypothesis holds that there are normative barriers to investment as well. As Cherlin has repeatedly reminded family scholars (1978, 2004), much of family behavior is "automatic"—it relies on ready-made solutions to daily problems based on widely shared normative expectations. These normative expectations not only guide and constrain the behavior of the father but also of the mother, who, as the custodial parent, must cooperate for father–child contact to occur. Following Furstenberg (1995), we extend the application of the package deal hypothesis, arguing that it not only predicts declines in involvement after breakup, but also that subsequent transitions into new partner and parenting roles may pose significant added barriers to involvement. As the father and mother of a child enter into new "family-like" relationships, they may feel considerable pressure to enact the cultural norm of the package deal with the new family without the interference of prior partners or children from past partnerships.

Not all subgroups in American society are equally influenced by this overarching cultural ideal, however. Ronald Mincy and Hillard Pouncy (2007) draw on data from the Caribbean (Brown, Anderson, and Chevannes 1993; Clarke 1957; Senior 1991) and evidence from surveys and focus group interviews with unwed African American fathers and mothers in Louisiana to argue that the role of the father among men who are no longer in a conjugal union with the mother—the "baby father" role—may have achieved a higher degree of institutionalization among African Americans than among other U.S. racial and ethnic groups.

In the Caribbean, for example, where rates of nonmarital fertility and multiple-partnered fertility have been high for decades, the institutionalization of the roles and relationships between parents and children is indicated through the existence of a system of kinship terms that are used to describe the roles and relationships between parents and children in these situations (Senior 1991; Brown et al. 1997; Brown, Anderson, and Chevannes 1993; Roopnarine, et al. 1995, 2004). Mincy and Pouncy's (2007) survey and focus group data drawn from African American residents of Louisiana likewise suggest that a similar process of institutionalization may be occurring in the United States (see also Anderson 1996; Hamer 1998, 2001; Waller 2002). If ongoing father involvement outside of a romantic relationship with the mother is more normative among African Americans than other groups, father involvement should decline less for black fathers than for other fathers after the parents' romantic involvement ends, as subsequent relationships are taken on, and after subsequent childbirth with new partners.

Despite the dominant image of unwed fatherhood as a hit-and-run encounter, the wealth of the evidence, whether qualitative or quantitative, suggests otherwise. Over the past three decades, a number of in-depth qualitative studies have focused on behaviors and attitudes among young unmarried fathers, and with only a few exceptions (Anderson 1993; Bell Kaplan 1997), they have found that the salience of the father role and engagement in fathering activities is high (for example, see Anderson 1996; Hamer 2001; Sullivan 1993; Waller 2002; Young 2003). Similarly, two panel studies—the National Longitudinal Survey of Youth, which began to follow a sample of youth aged fourteen to nineteen in 1979; and the National Survey of Families and Households, a national probability sample of all U.S. households that was launched in 1981—offered much the same portrait using nationally representative samples (Lerman 1993; Seltzer 1991; Mott 1990).

Specifically, by the mid-1980s, we learned that, consistent with qualitative studies that focused mainly on men who were new fathers, unmarried fathers with very young children were usually quite involved. These statistical portraits demonstrated, however, that involvement declined quite dramatically as the children got older (Lerman 1993; Seltzer 2000). Additional surveys conducted in the 1990s showed consistent evidence of a downward trend in involvement as the children aged, although the rates differed considerably across the studies (Argys et al. 2007). By the time nonmarital children reach adolescence, their chances of having a regularly involved father appear to be very low (Argys and Peters 2001).

This decline is somewhat puzzling, given recent evidence from the Fragile Families and Child Wellbeing survey, launched in twenty large U.S. cities in between 1998 and 2000, which showed that the vast majority of nonmarital fathers were present at the time of the birth and said they wished to remain involved in the child's life. This survey of a nationally representative cohort of nonmarital births in large cities found that nine in ten children born to an unwed father were *not* subject to a hit-and-run father's indifference, but welcomed into the arms of someone who said he was committed to "being there" for his child. When the surveyors interviewed the mothers of these children just after the birth, eight in ten said the father had been supportive during pregnancy (McLanahan et al. 2003). Furthermore, nearly all—99.8 percent—of the fathers interviewed said they intended to stay involved (Center for Research on Child Wellbeing 2000).

Studies that consider all nonresidential children find lower rates of involvement for nonmarital than marital children. Father involvement also varies by race and ethnicity, with rates for Africans American being higher and those for Hispanics lower than the average American father (Danziger and Radin 1990; Huang 2006; King 1994; King, Harris, and Heard 2004; Mott 1990; Seltzer 1991; but see Seltzer and Bianchi 1988). Father involvement is also predicted by parental education (Argys and Peters 2001; Huang 2006; King, Harris, and Heard 2004), fathers' age (Lerman and Sorensen 2000) and earnings (Lerman and Sorensen 2000; Seltzer 1991), work status (Danziger and Radin 1990); child gender (King, Harris, and Heard 2004; Manning and Smock 1999; but see Cooksey and Craig 1998), the presence of additional children, father's current marital status, the number of years since the father left the home (Argys and Peters 2001), payment of child support (Seltzer 1991), and the quality of the coparenting relationship (Sobolewski and King 2005; but see Amato and Rezac 1994). Waller and Swisher (2006) focus solely on unmarried fathers and find that a wide array of risk behaviors, such as physical abuse, drug and alcohol use, and incarceration are associated with lower odds of father–child contact.

The literature has shown that for fathers with noncustodial children, living with a new biological child is related to lower support payments (Manning and Smock 2000; Manning, Stewart, and Smock 2003), but findings on involvement are inconsistent (Manning, Stewart, and Smock 2003; Juby et al. 2007). The effect of subsequent partnerships is also examined by Stephens (1996), who looks at nonresident fathers' behavior following divorce and finds that a father's remarriage reduces both payment and visitation. Stewart (1999), who considers nonresident fathers' transitions into both cohabiting and marital relationships, finds that the dampening effect of a father's new partnerships is stronger for cohabitation than for marriage. Other analyses find that when mothers remarry and children acquire a new stepfather, they see less of their biological fathers (Juby et al. 2007; Seltzer and Bianchi 1988), although the effect of mother's remarriage may be weak (Stephens 1996).

These studies, though closely related to ours, have several limitations. First, the data sources they use all suffer from significant underrepresentation of nonmarital fathers, a problem that is minimized in the data set we use. Second, none of the studies considers all possible subsequent partner and parental transitions, including those of fathers as well as mothers. Third, no study focuses specifically on fathers of nonmarital children, and many studies do not even include them at all.

The lack of attention to the effect of subsequent relationship transitions among unmarried fathers is somewhat surprising, as levels of multipartner fertility are dramatically higher among them. Recent data suggest that about 40 percent of all fathers of nonmarital children born between 1998 and 2000 already had at least one child by another partner at the time of this child's birth (Carlson and Furstenberg 2006). Given that the average father surveyed was only in his midtwenties at the time, the proportion of unmarried fathers who will eventually split up, repartner, or have subsequent children with a new partner is likely to be very high.

For this large and growing subset of parents, we expect that transitions into subsequent relationships, and subsequent fertility within those relationships, are the key mechanisms though which father involvement declines over time. First, it is likely that as fathers move on to subsequent partners and parental roles, the demands inherent in working to enact the cultural model of the package deal in these new relationships could supersede obligations to children from prior relationships. Second, it is equally likely that as mothers enter into subsequent partnerships and parent roles, they might respond similarly and seek to exclude the biological father in favor of the new father figure in the home. We also expect that white and Hispanic fathers are somewhat more vulnerable to the threat of new relationships than African American fathers are, due to the greater degree of institutionalization of the "baby-father" role in black communities.

Quantitative Data

In the analyses that follow, we use four waves of the Fragile Families and Child Wellbeing Study to examine levels and changes in father involvement by race among fathers who had a nonmarital birth, focusing on how subsequent partnerships and new parental roles of both mothers and fathers affect this involvement. The Fragile Families and Child Wellbeing Study followed a cohort of nearly five thousand children born in twenty U.S. cities between 1998 and 2000. The study interviewed mothers and fathers at the time of the child's birth and again after one year, three years, and five years. The survey oversampled nonmarital births and, when weighted, is representative of births in all U.S. cities with populations larger than two hundred thousand. Both the mother and father were interviewed at each follow-up, regardless of their relationship status. These data are ideal for the study of father involvement not only because of the large sample of unmarried and nonresidential fathers, but also because they contain detailed longitudinal economic, attitudinal, and behavioral information collected independently from both the mother and the father.

At each survey wave, our analyses are based on the subsample of children in the Fragile Families Study who were born outside of marriage, who lived with their biological mother, whose mother responded to the survey, and for whom we have nonmissing data on parents' relationship status and father involvement from mothers' surveys. This results in sample sizes of 3,243 at the one-year survey, 3,123 at the three-year survey, and 3,050 at the five-year wave of the study. Nonresponse and attrition were higher for unmarried mothers and fathers than for married parents. At baseline, 87 percent of eligible mothers and 75 percent of the fathers agreed to participate in the survey. In subsequent surveys, response rates for unmarried mothers were 90 percent at wave 2, 88 percent at wave 3, and 87 percent at wave 4. The mothers who dropped out of the study tended to be white or Latino, were less likely to be married to the father when the child was born, and had lower average socioeconomic status (Cooper et al. 2007). Fathers had higher attrition rates, at 70 percent, 68 percent, and 66 percent for waves 2, 3, and 4, respectively. Fathers who dropped out of the study were less likely to be involved with their children and were less likely to be residing with the mother of the focal child.

Because fathers' attrition is nonrandom and correlated with our outcome of interest, we use mothers' reports of father involvement. For fathers' independent variables, we use fathers' reports if they are available, mothers' reports if fathers' reports are unavailable, and single imputation if neither mothers' nor fathers' reports are available.[3] Item nonresponse for our analysis variables was generally low, in most cases less than 5 percent. The items for which nonresponse was higher include whether the father repartnered (9 percent), whether the father was employed (8 percent), and whether the father had subsequent children (10 percent).

The main dependent variable in our study is father involvement. We use mothers' reports of fathers' involvement because fathers have higher rates of attrition, which are systematically related to their level of involvement. Fathers are coded *as seeing child several times weekly* if they saw their child for at least eight out of the past thirty days.[4] All fathers who were living with the mother (either married or cohabiting) were coded as *seeing child daily*. Fathers were coded as *seeing child monthly* if they saw their child at least once in the past thirty days, as *seeing the child yearly* if they had seen the child since the previous interview, and as having *no contact* if they had not seen the child since the previous interview.

A father's race and ethnicity was determined using his own report if available and the mother's report if his own was not available. Fathers were classified into four mutually exclusive categories: *non-Hispanic white*, *non-Hispanic black*, *non-Hispanic other*, and *Hispanic*. Based on mothers' reports at each wave, their relationship status was categorized as *married*, *cohabiting*, *romantically involved*, or *no relationship* with the child's father. Couples were defined as *cohabiting* if they were romantically involved and living together all or most of the time, as *living together* if mothers reported they lived together all or most of the time, and as *not living together* otherwise.

Several demographic and background characteristics of fathers are also included as control variables in some analyses. *Father's earnings* were measured by a dummy variable for whether the father earned more than $15,000 in the past year, and *father's age* was measured in years at the time the child was born. *Father's education* was coded as a series of dummy variables indicating *less than high school*, *high school or GED*, *some college*, and *college plus*. Fathers were coded as *father employed* if they reported doing any regular work for pay during the week prior to the interview. For each of these variables, we relied on the fathers' reports if they were available and the mothers' reports if they were not available from the fathers.

Several other relationship characteristics were also used in the following analyses. We measured the *time since parents stopped coresiding* as an ordinal index of the number of survey waves the parents had not lived together. For example, in the fourth survey wave, parents were coded as 0 if they still lived together, 1 if they were living together at the third wave but were not living together at the fourth, 2 if they were living together at the second wave but not in the third or fourth wave, and 3 if they were living together at the first wave but not any of the subsequent ones. Parents who never lived together during the study period were coded as 4. This indexing was repeated for each of the survey waves. *Time since parents stopped romantic involvement* was indexed in the same way. We also measured whether the *father had a new partner*, the *mother had a new partner*, the *father had subsequent children with different partner*, and the *mother had subsequent children with different partner*. Again, fathers' relationship and fertility measures were taken from their own reports if available and from mothers' reports if they were unavailable.

Table 1 shows descriptive statistics for black, white, and Hispanic fathers who had a nonmarital birth and who were not living with their child by the five-year follow-up, weighted by national sampling weights. The majority of fathers who fell into the nonresidential category were black. White fathers were more likely to have a college degree, earn more than $15,000, and be employed. On average, black fathers had spent the longest time not living with their child by the child's fifth birthday, but there were few racial differences in the amount of time since parents were romantically involved. This discrepancy reflects the fact that black fathers were more likely to be romantically involved with mothers when they were not living together than white or Hispanic fathers were. By the time the child was five years old, repartnering and subsequent fertility were common among both mothers and fathers of all races. About half of mothers and fathers had a new romantic partner, and more than a quarter had a subsequent child with a new partner. Men were more likely than women to have children with new partners.

Qualitative Data

Between 1995 and 2001, Timothy Nelson, Kathryn Edin, and a team of graduate students conducted in-depth repeated intensive interviews with 165 low-income fathers who had at least one nonmarital child younger than eighteen.

TABLE 1
DESCRIPTIVE STATISTICS FOR FATHERS WHO HAD A NONMARITAL
BIRTH AND ARE NONRESIDENT BY WAVE 4

	Overall	White	Black	Hispanic
Baseline characteristics				
Age (in years)	26.2	24.6	25.9	27.1
Education				
Less than high school	45.4	41.4	43.5	49.7
High school or GED	36.7	41.2	37.9	33.5
Some college	15.7	12.2	17.1	15.7
College or more	2.2	5.2	1.5	1.1
Child is male	53.8	56.7	55.5	51.6
Wave 4 characteristics				
Earned less than $15,000	53.9	34.9	61.1	52.1
Employed	65.5	79.5	61.2	69.4
Survey waves since stopped coresiding	3.2	2.9	3.3	2.9
Survey waves since relationship ended	2.6	2.6	2.6	2.5
Mom has new partner	51.3	52.3	51.4	49.4
Dad has new partner	50.4	51.6	49.6	47.5
Mom has new children by different partner	24.8	17.9	26.1	24.6
Dad has new children by different partner	37.6	44.9	36.4	34.5
N	2,019	183	1,301	455

NOTE: All figures weighted by national sampling weights. The overall descriptive statistics include the three major racial and ethnic groups and a residual "other race" group. All values are percentages, unless otherwise noted.

These fathers were drawn from three high-poverty communities within the Philadelphia metropolitan area: East Camden, Kensington, and North Philadelphia. Roughly equal numbers of African American, white, and Puerto Rican fathers (Philadelphia's dominant Hispanic group) were interviewed. The sample was also stratified by age: roughly equal portions within each racial and ethnic group were thirty or younger, while the remainder were older than thirty. The inclusion of fathers of multiple racial and ethnic groups and both younger and older fathers offers a considerable advantage over most prior qualitative work, which has typically focused only on black fathers and/or on very young fathers.

Unmarried fathers in these neighborhoods were often not stably attached to households. Rather than employ a random sample in each of the three neighborhoods, researchers contacted a wide range of third parties who could act as trusted intermediaries. These included leaders of a variety of local nonprofit and government sector organizations, including churches, settlement houses, and social service agencies. The intermediaries reported that most men were not attached to their organizations, however, so researchers also recruited subjects through street contacts and via referrals from fathers who had already participated in the study. No more than five referrals came from any given source.

Most fathers were interviewed at least twice at a place and a time of their choosing. Interviews were semistructured to ensure consistency across cases, but interviewers were encouraged to change the order and wording of questions to fit with the flow of the conversation. The first portion of the interview was focused on the father's life history, focusing specifically on transitions into and out of schooling, employment, romantic relationships, and fatherhood roles. In the second part of the interview, fathering views and behaviors as well as father's financial situations were captured. Interviews ranged from one and a half to seven hours and were transcribed verbatim and electronically coded by topic. The results presented here rely on analyses of full transcripts.

Survey Findings on Father Involvement

Table 2 details the proportions of nonmarital children who have contact with their biological father at one, three, and five years. Overall, involvement rates among unmarried fathers begin high but decline for all racial groups throughout the first five years of a child's life. The high initial rates of involvement reflect relatively high rates of coresidence among parents of nonmarital children at first, mostly in the context of cohabiting unions, although some eventually marry. But the table also reveals large declines in coresidence over time. More than half of nonmarital children reside with their father around the time of their first birthday, but this figure declines to only 35 percent by the time of their fifth birthday.

The second panel of the table considers only nonresident fathers and shows that by the child's first birthday, 36 percent see their fathers several times each week, and nearly six in ten saw their father in the past month. By the child's third birthday, these figures have fallen to 30 percent with several visits each week, with rates of monthly involvement at about 50 percent. By the time children reach age five, only about a quarter (26 percent) still see their father several times a week, though 45 percent still have regular contact. At each survey wave, African American children are less likely to live with their fathers than are Hispanics and whites. Thus, fewer African American children experience "automatic" fatherhood—a situation where there are few, if any, impediments to frequent father-child contact.

Although coresident and romantically involved fathers' involvement is "automatic"—an almost inevitable result of maintaining a coresidential romantic relationship with the mother—men outside of a coresidential or romantic bond with the mother must negotiate a fathering relationship, making each hour of father–child contact more "expensive" in terms of transaction costs (see McLanahan 2008 [this volume]). This is particularly true if the father's children live in multiple households. Because nonmarital African American children are significantly less likely to live in a coresidential union with both of their biological parents than their Hispanic or white counterparts, black fathers must work harder to maintain similar levels of intensive and regular contact, which they do. In fact, among nonresidential fathers, African Americans have higher rates of at least weekly, at least monthly, and at least yearly contact with their child until age

TABLE 2
FATHER INVOLVEMENT AFTER A NONMARITAL BIRTH, BY RACE AND ETHNICITY

	Year 1				Year 3				Year 5			
	Overall	White	Black	Hispanic	Overall	White	Black	Hispanic	Overall	White	Black	Hispanic
Resident fathers	52.1	58.8	46.9	57.9	43.9	48.1	39.4	49.2	35.5	39.7	29.3	41.5
Nonresident fathers	47.9	41.2	53.1	42.1	56.1	51.9	60.6	50.8	64.5	60.3	70.7	58.2
All nonresident fathers												
Saw child since previous survey	87.2	89.3	92.8	79.9	73.3	72.7	78.3	67.2	66	69.6	73.1	56.5
Saw child in past month	63.2	58.5	67.4	59.7	49.0	53.1	51.6	42.9	45.9	56.3	52.4	36.6
Saw child at least eight days in past month	36.4	28.7	35.6	39.4	29.8	32.2	30.2	27.7	25.8	35.1	28.1	20.6
Mean number of days father saw child in past month	8.9	6.8	9.3	8.5	6.6	5.9	7.2	6.1	5.8	7.1	6.7	4.3
Fathers who saw child in past month												
Saw child at least eight days in past month	57.6	49.1	52.8	65.8	60.7	65.9	59	64.6	56.3	62.4	53.6	56.3
Mean number of days father saw child	13.7	11.8	13.8	14.2	13.4	11.3	13.9	14.1	12.6	12.5	12.8	11.7

NOTE: Weighted by national sampling weights for each survey year. All values are percentages unless otherwise indicated.

three, after which the racial differences diminish. In sum, African American fathers accomplish their high overall rates of involvement mainly through negotiated visitation, while white and Hispanic fathers are more likely to achieve high rates of involvement through coresidence.

Thus far, we have not taken into consideration the amount of elapsed time since the father lived with the mother or was romantically involved with her. whether the "breakup" is defined as the point at which the father stopped coresiding with the mother or when romantic involvement ended, Table 3 shows that father involvement drops very dramatically in the aftermath of breakup, as the package deal hypothesis would predict. For fathers of all racial and ethnic groups, involvement in the first year after breakup is relatively high, but these rates decline rapidly as more time passes.

Interestingly, the decline in father involvement after coresidence ends is steeper for white and Hispanic fathers than for African American fathers. This difference is in part an artifact of the fact that black fathers are more likely to maintain romantic involvement outside of a coresidential union. The decline in involvement by the number of waves since the parents were romantically involved is even larger, and this large decline is of about the same magnitude for all racial groups.

Next, we consider what accounts for the decline in involvement over time once the relationship ends. If traditional notions of fatherhood as a package deal hold sway, we would expect that much of the decline in involvement could be traced to entry of mothers and fathers into subsequent romantic partnerships, especially those containing children, for fathers in such arrangements could once again father the children in these households—either social or biological children—"automatically."

Table 4 shows the predicted probability of father involvement by subsequent relationship status for white, black, and Hispanic fathers. These predicted probabilities are calculated from logistic regressions that control for exogenous characteristics including father's age, education, employment, earnings, and time since parents stopped coresiding. Coefficients for the full logistic regression models are included in the appendix. These calculations show the steep drop-off in the probability of intensive father involvement for all groups as parents become involved with new partners and have new children with these partners. The declines in involvement are especially drastic for whites and Hispanics. It is important to note, however, that in this study and others like it, the direction of causality is unclear.

Table 4 reveals other interesting differences by race. Among African Americans, for example, a father's subsequent partnerships and parental roles are less strongly associated with declining involvement than the mother's subsequent relationships are, particularly if the mother goes on to have an additional child. This gendered pattern suggests a willingness on the part of the father to remain involved regardless of his other familial commitments, but less willingness on the part of the mother to facilitate that involvement once she establishes a new family. For Hispanics, the story is much the same, but the declines are more dramatic. For whites, it is the fathers' own subsequent partnerships and especially their new parental roles that are associated with the strongest declines.

TABLE 3
INTENSIVE FATHER INVOLVEMENT FOR NONMARITAL CHILDREN
BY TIME SINCE RELATIONSHIP ENDED

	Overall	White	Black	Hispanic
Time since parents stopped coresiding				
1 wave	49.1	47.1	52.1	44.7
2 waves	34.2	26.9	37.8	29.5
3 waves	24.4	20.6	26.8	19.7
4 waves	17.9	17.2	19.2	14.9
Time since parents were romantically involved				
1 wave	42.1	43.2	42.4	40.9
2 waves	25.6	22.7	27.8	23.4
3 waves	19.5	16.8	21.1	16.7
4 waves	8.1	13.8	9.5	3.6

NOTE: Percentages are unweighted and pooled across survey waves in person–period format.
Intensive father involvement is defined as seeing child at least eight days in past month.

TABLE 4
PREDICTED PROBABILITY OF INTENSIVE FATHER
INVOLVEMENT BY PARENTS' SUBSEQUENT RELATIONSHIP
STATUS AT FIVE-YEAR FOLLOW-UP

	Overall	White	Black	Hispanic
Parents are single	.29	.24	.30	.27
Mom repartnered	.20	.18	.21	.18
Dad repartnered	.22	.19	.23	.20
Mom had subsequent children by someone else	.14	.15	.17	.07
Dad had subsequent children by someone else	.20	.08	.24	.15

NOTE: All parents were unmarried at focal child's birth and father is presently nonresidential.
Predicted probabilities are based on logistic regressions that control for father's earnings, age,
education, current employment status, child gender, and time since parents stopped living
together, and are evaluated at the sample means for these variables. Full model parameters are
listed in the appendix.

In sum, we have shown that for urban children born outside of marriage,
ongoing rates of involvement are relatively high among all racial and ethnic
groups. Black nonmarital children are far less likely to have parents living in
coresidential unions, but are somewhat more likely to have parents in an ongoing,
romantic partnership that is not coresidential. Once we limit our focus to only
children whose parents are no longer living together or romantically involved, we
see that the longer the father and the mother have been apart, the more father
involvement wanes, though all else equal, this tendency is stronger for white and
Hispanic fathers than for their African American counterparts. Finally, there is
strong evidence that subsequent partners and parental relationships can account

for a large portion of the decline, but again the impact is larger for whites and Hispanics than for African Americans.

Qualitative Findings on Father Involvement

We now turn to the qualitative data drawn from 165 low-income noncustodial fathers in the Philadelphia metropolitan area. Using these life history narratives, we explore the mechanisms that underlie the strong statistical associations between both men's behaviors and men's and women's transitions into subsequent relationships. We begin by presenting 3 of the 165 cases in some detail, and then discuss broader themes derived from the qualitative analysis, drawing on these cases as examples.

William's story

"We were friends for all our life," said William, a white twenty-seven-year-old father, describing his relationship with Tiffany, the mother of his eleven-year-old daughter Brittney. "Then when I was about twelve or thirteen years old we started seeing each other. We were seeing each other for a while; then we broke up. Six months later," William recounted, "she comes around saying 'I'm pregnant, it's yours.' Of course I denied it. I was young. I said, 'It's not my kid. . . .' I wasn't there for the pregnancy. I wasn't there for the childbirth, nothing. I guess after a while, [I admitted to myself that she was my child]."

"For seven years I didn't have the right to see my child," William told us, as he described how Tiffany retaliated in the face of his initial denials by refusing to allow William to have any contact with his child. William admitted that given his ongoing drug habit and the repeat incarcerations for petty drug offenses and parole violations during these years, her reluctance was perhaps justified. As Brittney was approaching her seventh birthday, however, William was remanded to a residential drug rehabilitation program and, newly clean and sober, began writing and calling his daughter, apologizing for the years he was absent and asking for another chance. "I started writing letters and calling my daughter all the time when I was at the rehab. [Then Tiffany] let my mom bring my daughter up once a week [to visit], so we started building a relationship. . . . We had a relationship when I left . . . that was really tight."

Just before William's release, Tiffany broke up with the father of her five-month-old infant son, BJ. William and Tiffany decided to try again, and after one month in a halfway house, he moved in with her and the two children. They spent nearly two years together parenting Brittney and BJ while he worked as a packer in a tropical fish warehouse. He quickly took on the father role with BJ, which was intensely meaningful to William since he was able to participate more fully in fatherhood as the baby grew. "Like BJ, when he was growing up that was great, because I wasn't there for Brittney. [I loved] being able to see him do things and stuff like that, seeing him grow up."

Meanwhile, BJ's biological father was proving to be a problem. William boasts about how he quickly intervened when the man tried to work his way back into his son's life, an attempt that William saw as a flimsy excuse for trying to rekindle his relationship with Tiffany. "It got to the point where he was harassing her all the time, calling on the phone calling her all kinds of names and stuff like that. So I had to get a restraining order against him." Once, when William found Tiffany and BJ's father together in his car, talking amorously in his view, "I got into a big fight with him . . . and tried to kill him." Not surprisingly, the visits between BJ and his father ended.[5] William, meanwhile, became closer than ever to BJ. William explains, "I have a son, but he's not mine. She had a baby by some-body else and he was only like six months old when I came home and I practi-cally raised him. . . . So he knows me as his father. He knows me as his daddy."

Just after BJ's second birthday, William was again locked up on a drug charge and served nearly two years. Tiffany told him she was through with him and did not want the kids around him either. Nonetheless, when William was released, Tiffany allowed him to spend two to three hours each day with the children after his work shift ended at 3:30, helping them with homework and taking them to the park. Eager to have his children on overnight and weekend visits, he used his first month's wages from a warehouse job to rent a two-bedroom second-floor apart-ment. For several months, he saw his children daily and had them with him most weekends.

Then William became romantically involved with the first-floor tenant, a woman with daughters aged two and five. This relationship had its ups and downs as the new woman, Jessica, was not sure she should trust a repeat drug offender. But eventually Jessica asked William to move in with her. Six months later, when Jessica announced that she was pregnant, William planned to propose marriage, seeing his chance to finally do fatherhood right. "I want to be there for the preg-nancy. I want to be there through everything. When she goes to the doctor, when she has the baby, to wake up with the baby in the middle of the night. It's just something that I've been wanting for a long time."

However, William's happiness was marred by how his hopeful new life had come into conflict with his old. Tiffany, outraged that William's attempts to rekin-dle their romance stopped abruptly when Jessica invited him to move in, began to deny him visitation, threatening to get a restraining order if he approached her apartment building. Tiffany and Jessica did not get along and had a few violent fights. Tiffany did not approve of Jessica, and said she was unwilling to let her children come under Jessica's influence. William considered going to court to establish paternity so he could demand visiting rights, yet he hesitated—this would only allow him access to Brittney, his biological child, and not to BJ, and he did not want to gain legal access to Brittney only to lose out on contact with the boy he insisted on calling his son.

Brittney, age eleven, also played a role. "We were sitting down talking and she started running her mouth about me stepping in and out of her life. 'You want to be a father to the little girl downstairs!' [she said]. I said, 'I'm not being a daddy, I'm just there to support her because her father's not there.'" Thus, within six months of his relationship with Jessica becoming serious, his visits with Brittney and with BJ, as well as his financial contributions, fell to zero.

Like the vast majority of fathers in his situation, William was heartbroken by this state of affairs. "I can't see my kids and I really hate it because I want a relationship with them. . . . My kids are the world. . . . I love doing their homework with them. I love being there for them. . . . Being a father's great. They have [changed my life], they really have. They gave me a sense of responsibility. [Without them] I probably would be goofing off, hanging around on the corner or something like that. Now that I got responsibilities and things like that, it kind of keeps me in line, you know what I'm saying . . . ? My dad wasn't there for me. My dad's dad wasn't there for him. . . . I don't want to repeat the cycle again."

Apple's story

Apple, a twenty-six-year-old African American father, was proud that he was "in love and everything" with Gloria, the mother of his three children (ages eleven, nine, and five), during the eight and a half years the two were together. At first, they saw each other only casually, but within eight months she was pregnant with his daughter Vanessa. Apple, who had to repeat both seventh and eighth grade, had dropped out of school by this point and worked full-time as a drug dealer, but stopped two months shy of Vanessa's birth. His determination to "go straight" was solidified when the baby was born, and as there was an outstanding warrant for his arrest, he decided that the right thing to do was to turn himself in. He and Gloria fought violently over this decision, which she saw as a desertion, and the altercation landed him in the emergency room from a knife wound in the cheek.

When Apple returned home after serving his sentence in a juvenile facility, he moved with Gloria and Vanessa, now nine months old, into a North Philadelphia row house that Gloria inherited from her grandmother. Everything was "lovey dovey" for a brief period of time—long enough for the conception and birth of a second child. During this time Apple worked twelve-hour days as a sandwich maker at a convenience store. During a store robbery he was injured with a gunshot wound and, because he had no insurance, was left with a large debt to the hospital. There was also some trouble in the relationship—Gloria admitted that she had been seeing another man and was pregnant by him, though she terminated the pregnancy—but she also soon conceived a third child by Apple.

Around the time this third child was born, Gloria became a Muslim and prohibited any drinking in the couple's home. Things went well for a while, but a fourth child was then born that looked nothing like Apple. For a while, Apple convinced himself that he was the child's father, but then Apple was caught failing to comply with the drinking prohibition. Another violent fight ensued and Gloria revealed the truth: Apple was not the fourth baby's father. During this fight, a broken bottle used as a weapon caused serious wounds to his hands and arms that landed him in the emergency room again. Several weeks later, the two had yet another altercation on a trip to the Jersey shore with the kids in Gloria's car. This time, Gloria called the police and accused Apple of carjacking. Apple's bail was set at $35,000, and since he did not know anyone with enough money to pay a bail bondsman, he spent two weeks in jail before the charges were dropped.

Because of these two weeks in jail, Apple lost both jobs. Desperate for money, he decided to sell marijuana and was caught and incarcerated briefly, as this was his first adult conviction. Meanwhile, Gloria abruptly married a fellow Muslim, which devastated Apple, who still insists that Gloria was his "first love." Upon his release, Apple moved in with his mother and began searching for work, finally securing a full-time job making sandwiches at a hoagie shop. He also found a new girlfriend, Jennifer, who had a job and her own apartment nearby. Apple moved in with Jennifer, and fourteen months later they conceived a child, who was born with a heart condition that qualified her for a disability payment of just over $1,000 a month. Jennifer quit her job to take care of the child full-time. With the $200 or more Apple cleared each week from the job plus the disability benefits, the two could cover their living expenses.

Meanwhile, Gloria, who left her husband and began to collect welfare, named Apple as the father of the oldest three children. Given Gloria's history, his family suggested that he demand a blood test, but Apple decided against it. "I just never wanted to get the blood work just in case one of the [children wasn't mine]. I would not have felt good about that. Then depression would have set in. So I guess I waived my rights." Meanwhile, once Apple became involved with Jennifer, any direct contact between Gloria and Apple seemed to result in violent fighting. "I wish I could see all four, you know. I pray . . . we can work it out. But [Gloria], she just talk vicious to me like, threatens me." Thus, he visits his children only rarely, though his daughter, the oldest, calls him daily. In fact, the last time he saw them was at a Father's Day barbecue Gloria threw three months prior, a party to which Jennifer and the baby, Jade, were not invited.

Apple could barely contain his joy over life with his baby daughter. He felt his relationship with Jennifer, who was staying home full time with the baby, was "airtight," and he gloried in his relationship with Jade, the eight-month-old. Despite his troubles with Gloria, Apple said, "I am glad I had four children, regardless [of whether] I'm with their mother or whatever. I'm not a rich daddy or the best daddy, but I'm still entitled, still have four children."

Holloway's story

Holloway was a thirty-nine-year-old African American father of a six-year-old. He showed up six days a week at 6:00 a.m. at a day labor agency in North Philadelphia. About four times a week, he succeeded in getting work and was transported to a work site where he did manual labor for $5.15 per hour. The son of a stably employed brick mason whose older brother—a welder—had a union job, this laborer still viewed his situation as better than average, as his two younger brothers were both serving substantial prison sentences. "They were out hustling man. They wanted me to hustle with them [but] I never really did. I'm the only one [in my family] that never really did. I've never been to jail. Not even locked up. I never been arrested at all."

After dropping out of high school because he could not keep up with the work, Holloway began to train for a trade through Job Corps. "They sent me to Gary, Indiana and I stayed out there for about five months. I [got] in hot water, 'cause by me being from Philly, I had to hang with the guys from Philly 'cause if I didn't, there was no protection for me. People would be like, not killed but stabbed, beat up real bad. They end up kicking [the Philly guys] out." At nineteen, Holloway returned to Philadelphia and moved back in with his mother, picking up day labor work. At twenty-two, he joined the National Guard, but quit due to "problems with finishing stuff. I'm messed up like that."

At twenty-three, Holloway had a stroke of luck and landed a full-time job with a building management and janitorial firm cleaning downtown office buildings for $6.75 an hour, plus double pay for plentiful overtime hours. A year later, he met Linda at a downtown club, a woman with two sons aged eight and ten. They moved into a row home that Linda's aunt owned, and the three years that followed were Holloway's best. "It was like I was the man of the house. Bringing in my little pay and stuff like that, it was a family. She made me feel like I was the boss. [I was] giving her half of my check when I had it."

Though Holloway and Linda stopped using birth control early on, it took two years for them to "accidentally" conceive a child. Eight months into the pregnancy, two crises ensued that drove this relatively stable couple apart. First, a Thanksgiving weekend turned tragic when faulty wiring sparked a house fire. Holloway saved himself, jumping out the second-story window onto the fire escape, while the rest of the occupants fled onto the roof, where they were later rescued by firefighters. Linda screamed to Holloway that another child—the son of a cousin who was staying with them overnight—was still in the house. Holloway attempted to go back into the burning building, but the smoke and the heat were so intense that he quickly abandoned his search for the child, who eventually suffocated while hiding in a closet. Holloway spent the next three days in the hospital.

A week later Holloway received the news that his company had decided to downsize, and Holloway, along with many of the other more experienced workers, received a pink slip. This job loss, and the failure to quickly find a substitute, had devastating consequences. By the time the baby was born, Linda and her family, who already blamed Holloway for the death of the four-year-old child in the house fire, had firmly decided that he was "a loser," and Linda gave Holloway "the boot."

Over the next six years, Holloway made valiant attempts to stay connected with his child, and came by whenever he had enough in his paycheck to buy her a treat or go shopping for something she needed. As he lived with his brother and had modest living expenses, he expended the majority of his resources on these outings. "I like seeing her grow up. Smile. I guess it makes me feel . . . it's like I've achieved something. 'Cause like for me, I didn't think I could make something as pretty as my daughter. That's what I think, it's great to see something that you made to grow up."

But these visits stopped abruptly once Linda acquired a new "friend." Linda stopped letting Holloway come around the house to visit anymore, afraid her new man would think that she and Holloway "are up to something." And because he lived with his brother—his mother moved to New York—she would not let her visit there either because his brother was once charged with the rape of a former girlfriends' daughter—charges that were later dropped. Now the only time Holloway sees his daughter is through a chance neighborhood encounter.

As Linda's new romance progressed, it became clear to Holloway that these were not the only threats to his parenthood: Linda's new boyfriend "happens to have taken a liking to my daughter," he confided. "He seems like he's trying to take my daughter from me." Just before we met him, Holloway walked around the corner in hopes of encountering the child and spied Linda's boyfriend buying ice cream for his daughter. According to Holloway, "[I felt like saying,] 'I have a couple of dollars, I might wanna buy ice cream. . . .' I wanted to talk to him several times, and pull him to the side and say, 'Look man, she's my daughter, you don't really gotta buy her ice cream. You know, I do work sometimes.'" Holloway continued, "And this guy she's with, he got kids somewhere else. . . . He lost his family, so he gotta take mine. [And] he has the power [to] because he has a good job. He's like a big shot."

"I suppose every father that's not with his kids' mother or whatever, probably go through the same thing I go through. . . . Being like broke up from the family, I feel abandoned. That's maybe because I had a baby by the wrong person. . . . My brother, he talking about don't go see my daughter or nothing, leave them both alone. But see I got a problem with that. I don't want to abandon them. I ain't much, but at least she knows that she has a father."

Themes from the qualitative analyses

The narratives offered by William, Apple, and Holloway illustrate several themes that are common in our analysis in the 165 in-depth interviews with unmarried fathers in Philadelphia.

Salience of the father role. For all three men, the importance of their role as a father was high. All but William embraced fatherhood from the beginning. William, who denied paternity initially, is more the exception than the rule in our data. If anything, like Apple, the men in our study seemed eager to claim as many children as they could, even when they had some reason to believe that a child might not be theirs biologically. This is perhaps another indication of the salience of the father role.

Rejection of the package deal. Most fathers, but especially African American fathers, firmly rejected the "package deal" noting that a father's parental relationship is contingent upon his relationship with the mother, although many end up living by it nonetheless. This is reflected in the high rates of contact after breakup. Holloway's disdain of Linda's new partner, who had abandoned responsibility for his own biological children, was typical. As Sullivan (1993) also found, men who "step off" from their responsibility as fathers are nearly uniformly condemned, while those who continue to care for their children are generally valued by their peers.

Declines in involvement as unintended consequence of new relationships. No father in our study entered into a new relationship with the intention of shedding commitments to children from past relationships. Instead, the decline in involvement was an unintended consequence of the transition to the new partnership. Faced with real limitations of resources and time, fathers often found that if they wished to make a go of the new relationship, and particularly if they wanted to play the father role to their full satisfaction, the new relationship required most of the resources they had to invest.

Increased transaction costs. Subsequent partnerships can dramatically increase the transaction costs of visiting children from past relationships. As Apple's story richly illustrates, romantic relationships among unmarried parents with children are often quite volatile even from the beginning (Reed 2006; Hill 2007). Sexual jealousy between new and old partners is often a theme, as is evident in both William's and Holloway's cases, but these stories also richly illustrate how many different people have to cooperate for visitation to occur—not only the mother and father but the new partner and the children themselves.

[T]hese stories . . . richly illustrate how many different people have to cooperate for visitation to occur—not only the mother and father but the new partner and the children themselves.

Contradictory definitions of fatherhood. On one hand, when claiming father status with nonbiological children they live with and help raise, many of these fathers firmly rejected the notion that fatherhood is primarily biological. This is most evident among our African American fathers. As we listened to these men talk about their roles as social fathers, and sometimes had an extended opportunity to watch them enact these roles, we became convinced that in some cases, men's roles as social fathers may be as meaningful to them as those with their biological children, as was the case for Apple. However, when it came to their own children by blood, these same men claimed the primacy of the biological tie, and were outraged when their ex-partner and the new man in her life failed to respect him as such.

Motivations to claim social children. As both William's and Holloway's stories show, albeit from different angles, men who enter into new relationships with women who have children by prior partners have strong motivation to claim fatherhood for the children in that household, or have another child by the new partner, especially if they can "do fatherhood right" by participating in their upbringing from an early age. As we see in Linda's relationship with her new "friend," in the typical courtship scenario men tend to woo women by wooing their children as well, in part because women often use the way a man treats "another man's child" as a test of his worthiness as a partner (Edin and Kefalas 2005).

Although many men who play this role insist that their intent was not to push out the biological father, this is sometimes a consequence. A parallel study of low-income single mothers in Philadelphia (Edin and Kefalas 2005) shows a similar pattern for women—though they rarely take on new partners with the intent of displacing the father, the time and attention bestowed on the children by a new romantic partner often creates an unfavorable comparison.

As Elliot Liebow (1967) argued four decades ago, our research shows that even if both men are making equal contributions, the offerings of the man without the biological child are valued more because they are not measured against his obligation to the child, a mental accounting that almost always places the biological father's performance in the red and the nonbiological father's performance in the black. When the new partner is a "big shot" like Linda's new partner and biological fathers like Holloway are only minimally employed, the contest can seem impossible to win.

A portrait of continuous fathering. Except for periods in men's life course when they are struggling with addiction or are incarcerated, an examination of the 165 cases reveals a portrait of almost continuous intensive fatherhood. This portrait is consistent with Lerman and Sorensen's (2000) analysis of data from six waves of the NLSY79, collected between 1984 and 1992, which assesses how many fathers of nonmarital children are intensively involved with any of their biological children at any point in time. They conclude that "the striking reality is that about two of three fathers (under 35 years old) who have fathered a child out of wedlock have a close involvement with at least one of their nonmarital children. Many of those who do not . . . have married someone else and are living with a marital child" (p. 145).[6] Similarly, most fathers in our study felt they were living out the high value they placed on fatherhood by intensively involving themselves in fathering activities for at least one child—whether biological or social—at any given time. Ironically, these narratives often show that part of the motivation to enter subsequent relationships is to enact the father role in a more complete and satisfying way.

Conclusion and Discussion

International comparisons show that among U.S. couples, cohabiting unions among parents with children are extraordinarily fragile—far more fragile than marital unions and far more fragile than unmarried parental unions in other countries in the industrialized world (Andersson 2001). The findings in this paper support the theory that this may, in part, be due to strong norms that support the traditional notion of fatherhood as a "package deal," especially for Hispanics and whites. This support is not only evident in the strong falloff in father involvement after breakup but in the large effect of mothers' and fathers' subsequent partner and parenthood roles in declining father involvement.

As both the mother and the father of a child born outside of marriage move further away from their failed partnership and enter new partnerships and new parental roles, the qualitative data show that new normative expectations are often set into motion that are in sharp competition with the old. Especially for mothers, new partnerships seem to provide a strong motivation to give the new partner the role of father, particularly once the mother has a child with that partner. For his part, the father may be under considerable pressure to use his scarce emotional and financial resources to fulfill the demands of his new partner and parenting roles, which he can enact within the context of a conjugal relationship.

Thus, while the conventional wisdom might assume that unmarried fathers are uninvolved because they are eager to evade responsibility for their progeny, our results suggest a very different story. This analysis suggests that declining rates of fathers' involvement are primarily due to unmarried women's and men's eagerness to enact a cultural ideal of parenting that views it as part of a package deal. Indeed, it may, in part, be women's and men's desire to demonstrate competence in subsequent partner relationships and parenting roles that leads to diminished involvement with children from other relationships.

The findings also support the Mincy and Pouncy (2007) hypothesis of greater institutionalization of the "baby father" role among African Americans than among other U.S. racial and ethnic groups. It may be that stronger norms guide unmarried African American fathers as they enact the father role, which sustain their involvement with the child even after the relationship with the child's mother ends. African American fathers are therefore more likely to remain in regular contact with their children even after entering into relationships with new partners and having children with them.

Past analyses have considered a wide array of factors correlated with the large decline in father involvement among the fathers of nonmarital children over time, but less attention has been paid to the mechanisms involved. No other analysis of unwed parents we know of has focused on the role of men's and women's subsequent romantic relationship transitions, whether marital or not, and their subsequent transitions to new parenting roles. Nor has any study we are aware of looked at mothers' and fathers' relationship transitions simultaneously, so that the relative importance of each can be ascertained. Our analysis suggests that the ways in which fatherhood is defined, both in the culture at large and within racial and ethnic subcultures, hold significant sway.

So was Moynihan right to worry about the impact of rising rates of nonmarital childbearing on future generations? On one hand, we document relatively high rates of father involvement with nonmarital children, which contradicts common conceptions of the "hit-and-run" father. But answering this question requires us to go beyond the father's view and to look at the situation from the point of view of the children. From this vantage point, we concur with Moynihan, though clearly the impact now reaches beyond African American children to encompass a significant minority of all American children. Because fatherhood is generally enacted in a meaningful way within the context of a conjugal union, because the fragility of these unions is high, and because repartnering and subsequent childbearing is common, children are likely to experience fatherhood as a game of musical chairs, a series of temporary commitments rather than a lifelong obligation.

As stability is critical for child well-being, the shifting cast of fathers and father figures in children's lives is likely to detract from, not add to, their well-being (Fomby and Cherlin 2007). Although social fathers might sometimes add to the well-being of their nonbiological children, comparisons of children in single and married stepfather homes suggest that this is not typical (McLanahan and Sandefur 1994). It is unlikely that many children in this situation will receive the same level of emotional or financial investment enjoyed by those who live stably with both their biological mothers and fathers.

APPENDIX

COEFFICIENTS FROM LOGIT REGRESSION MODELS PREDICTING AT LEAST WEEKLY FATHER INVOLVEMENT AT FIVE-YEAR FOLLOW-UP

	Parents Single	Mom Repartnered	Dad Repartnered	Mom Subsequent Children by New Partner	Dad Subsequent Children by New Partner
Race					
Non-Hispanic black	0.59°°	0.62°°	0.66°°	0.69°	1.34°°
	(0.26)	(0.29)	(0.29)	(0.36)	(0.63)
Hispanic	0.11	0.10	0.09	−0.66	0.49
	(0.29)	(0.33)	(0.33)	(0.59)	(0.68)
Non-Hispanic other race	0.53	0.26	1.19°°	0.75	1.05
	(0.61)	(0.72)	(0.56)	(0.93)	(1.03)
Education					
High school or GED	0.17	0.12	0.08	0.37	−0.05
	(0.18)	(0.21)	(0.21)	(0.31)	(0.29)
Some college	0.33	0.40	0.13	0.69	−0.27
	(0.22)	(0.27)	(0.29)	(0.43)	(0.39)
College or more	0.29	0.43	1.09	0.43	—[a]
	(0.51)	(0.65)	(0.72)	(1.17)	
Earned less than $15,000	−0.31	−0.79°°°	−0.82°°°	−0.25	−0.22
	(0.24)	(0.28)	(0.26)	(0.41)	(0.36)
Employed	0.99°°°°	0.78°°°	0.37	1.32°°°	0.84
	(0.19)	(0.25)	(0.25)	(0.38)	(0.33)

(continued)

173

APPENDIX (CONTINUED)

	Parents Single	Mom Repartnered	Dad Repartnered	Mom Subsequent Children by New Partner	Dad Subsequent Children by New Partner
Age (in years)	-0.004	-0.03	-0.01	-0.01	0.02
	(0.01)	(0.02)	(0.02)	(0.03)	(0.02)
Child is male	-0.02	0.07	0.04	0.10	-0.06
	(0.15)	(0.19)	(0.19)	(0.29)	(0.27)
Survey waves since parents stopped coresiding	-0.43°°°°	-0.45°°°°	-0.48°°°°	-0.29°	-0.37°°°
	(0.07)	(0.09)	(0.09)	(0.17)	(0.14)
Constant	-0.64	0.13	0.10	-2.05°	-2.08°°
	(0.49)	(0.63)	(0.63)	(1.08)	(1.04)
N	944	810	684	439	389
Pseudo R^2	.10	.09	.08	.10	.07

NOTE: Omitted reference categories are Non-Hispanic white and less than high school. All parents were unmarried at focal child's birth and dad is presently nonresidential.

a. There are no college-educated fathers in this cell.

°$p < .10$. °°$p < .05$. °°°$p < .01$. °°°°$p < .001$.

Notes

1. The text of Bill Cosby's speech can be found at http://www.mishalov.com/bill-cosby-naacp.html.

2. The text of Barack Obama's speech can be found at http://www.barackobama.com/2007/06/16/a_fathers_day_message_from_oba.php.

3. Single imputation was conducted using Stata's impute command for missing values in mother's and father's survey reports. The imputation model includes variables reported by mothers and fathers that are associated with either the dependent variable of interest, father involvement, or the likelihood of having missing data (Allison 2002). This includes parents' relationship status at baseline, parents' employment and educational characteristics, fathers' race, child gender, and fathers' history of drug use and incarceration.

4. In the qualitative analysis, fathers who maintained intensive regular contact with their children usually visited them several times a week or had them for weekend stays. This level of involvement was what most fathers saw as ideal. Thus, we used the standard of at least eight days per month to distinguish this group.

5. BJ's father has since died from a drug overdose.

6. Lerman and Sorensen (2000) also follow a particular nonmarital birth to chart the dynamics of father involvement over six years' time and find that the proportion of men who rarely or never visit a given nonmarital child rises sharply (from 18 to 30 percent) while the percentage of fathers visiting at least once a week drops from 28 to 20 percent.

References

Allison, Paul D. 2002. *Missing data*. Thousand Oaks, CA: Sage.

Amato, Paul, and Sandra J. Rezac. 1994. Contact with nonresident parents: Interparental conflict, and children's behavior. *Journal of Family Issues* 15:191-207.

Anderson, Elijah. 1993. Sex codes and family life among poor inner-city youths. In *Young unwed fathers: Changing roles and emerging policies*, ed. Robert I. Lerman and Theodora J. Ooms, 74-98. Philadelphia: Temple University Press.

Anderson, Elijah. 1996. The black inner city grandmother: Transition of a heroic type. In *America's working poor*, ed. Thomas R. Swartz and Kathleen Maas Weigert, 9-42. Notre Dame, IN: University of Notre Dame Press.

———. 2001. *Children's experiences of family disruption and family formation: Evidence from 16 FFS countries*. Rostock, Germany: Max Plank Institute for Demographic Research.

Argys, Laura M., and H. Elizabeth Peters. 2001. Patterns of nonresident father involvement. In *Social awakenings: Adolescent behavior as adulthood approaches*, ed. Robert T. Michael, 49-78. New York: Russell Sage Foundation.

Argys, Laura M., Elizabeth Peters, Steven Cook, Steven Garasky, Lenna Nepomnyaschy, and Elaine Sorenson. 2007. Measuring contact between children and nonresident fathers. In *Handbook of measurement issues in family research*, ed. Sandra L. Hofferth and Lynn M. Casper, 375-98. Mahwah, NJ: Erlbaum.

Bell Kaplan, Elaine. 1997. *Not our kind of girl: Unraveling the myths of teenage motherhood*. Berkeley: University of California Press.

Bennett, William. 2001. *The broken hearth*. New York: Random House.

Blankenhorn, David. 1995. *Fatherless America: Confronting our most urgent social problem*. New York: Random House.

Brown, Janet, Patricia Anderson, and Barry Chevannes. 1993. *Report on the contribution of Carribean men to the family*. Kingston, Jamaica: The Carribean Child Development Centre, University of the West Indies.

Brown, Janet, Arthur Newland, Patricia Anderson, and Barry Chevannes. 1997. Caribbean fatherhood underresearched misunderstood. In *Caribbean families: Diversity among ethnic groups*, ed. Jaipaul L. Roopnarine and Janet Brown. Westport, CT: Greenwood.

Carlson, Marcia, and Frank Furstenberg. 2006. The prevalence and correlates of multipartnered fertility among urban U.S. parents. *Journal of Marriage and Family* 68:718-32.

Center for Research on Child Wellbeing. 2000. Dispelling myths about unmarried fathers. Fragile Families Research Brief no. 1, Center for Research on Child Wellbeing, Princeton University, Princeton, NJ.

Cherlin, Andrew. 1978. Remarriage as an incomplete institution. *American Journal of Sociology* 84:634-50.

———. 2004. The deinstitutionalization of American marriage. *Journal of Marriage and the Family*. 66848-61.

Clarke, Edith. 1957. *My mother who fathered me: A study of family in three selected communities in Jamaica*. London: Allen & Uwin.

Cooksey, Elizabeth C., and Patricia H. Craig. 1998. Parenting from a distance: The effects of parental characteristics on contact between nonresidental fathers and their children. *Demography* 35:187-200.

Cooper, Carey E., Sara S. McLanahan, Sarah O. Meadows, and Jeanne Brooks-Gunn. 2007. Family structure transitions and maternal parenting stress. Working Paper no. 2007–16-FF, Center for Research on Child Wellbeing, Princeton, NJ.

Danziger, Sandra K., and Norma Radin. 1990. Absent does not equal uninvolved: Predictors of fathering in teen mother families. *Journal of Marriage and the Family* 52:636-42.

Edin, Kathryn, and Maria Kefalas. 2005. *Promises I can keep: Why poor women put motherhood before marriage*. Berkeley: University of California Press.

Fornby, Paula, and Andrew J. Cherlin. 2007. Family instability and child wellbeing. *American Sociological Review* 27:181-204.

Furstenberg, Frank F. 1995. Changing roles of fathers. In *Escape from poverty: What makes a difference for children?* ed. P. Lindsay Chase-Lansdale and Jeanne Brooks-Gunn, 189-210. Cambridge: Cambridge University Press.

Furstenberg, Frank F., and Andrew J. Cherlin. 1991. *Divided families: What happens to children when parents part*. Cambridge, MA: Harvard University Press.

Hamer, Jennifer. 1998. The definition of fatherhood: In the words of never-married mothers and the non-custodial fathers of their children. *Journal of Sociology and Social Welfare* 25:81-104.

———. 2001. *What it means to be a daddy: Fatherhood among black men living away from their children*. New York: Columbia University Press.

Hill, Heather. 2007. "Steppin' out": Sexual jealousy and infidelity among new unmarried parents. In *Unmarried couples with children*, ed. Paula England and Kathryn Edin, 104-32. New York: Russell Sage Foundation.

Hofferth, Sandra L., Joseph Pleck, Jeffrey L. Stueve, Suzanne Bianchi, and Liana Sayer. 2002. The demography of what fathers do. In *Handbook of father involvement*, ed. Catherine S. Tamis-LeMonda and Natasha Cabrera. Mahwah, NJ: Lawrence Erlbaum.

Huang, Chien-Cung. 2006). Child support enforcement and father involvement for children in never-married mother families. *Fathering* 4:97-111.

Juby, Heather, Jean-Michel Billette, Benoît Laplante, and Céline Le Bourdais. 2007. Nonresident fathers and children: Parents' new unions and frequency of contact. *Journal of Family Issues* 9 (28): 1220-45.

King, Valarie. 1994. Variation in the consequences of nonresident father involvement for children's well-being. *Journal of Marriage and the Family* 56:963-72.

King, Valarie, Kathleen Mullan Harris, and Holly E. Heard. 2004. Racial and ethnic differences in nonresident father involvement. *Journal of Marriage and the Family* 66:1–21.

Lerman, Robert I. 1993. A national profile of young unwed fathers. In *Young unwed fathers: Changing roles and emerging policies*, ed. Robert I. Lerman and Theodora J. Ooms, 27-51. Philadelphia: Temple University Press.

Lerman, Robert I., and Elaine Sorensen. 2000. Father involvement with their nonmarital children: Patterns, determinants and effects on their earnings. In *Fatherhood: Research, interventions, and policies*, ed. H. Elizabeth Peters, Gary W. Peterson, Suzanne K. Steinmetz, and Randal D. Day, 127-59. New York: Haworth.

Liebow, Elliott. 1967. *Tally's corner: A study of Negro streetcorner men*. Boston: Little, Brown.

Manning, Wendy D., and Pamela J. Smock. 1999. New families and nonresident father-child visitation. *Social Forces* 78:87-116.

———. 2000. Swapping families: Serial parenting and economic support for children. *Journal of Marriage and the Family* 62:111-22.

Manning, Wendy D., Susan D. Stewart, and Pamela J. Smock. 2003. The complexities of fathers' parenting responsibilities and involvement with nonresident children. *Journal of Family Issues* 24:645-67.

McLanahan, Sara. 2008. Fragile families and the reproduction of poverty. *The Annals of the American Academy of Political and Social Science* 621:111-131.

McLanahan, Sara, Irwin Garfinkel, Nancy Reichman, Julien Teitler, Marcia Carlson, and Christina Norland Audigier. 2003. *The Fragile Families and Child Wellbeing Study: Baseline national report.* Princeton, NJ: Center for Research on Child Wellbeing, Princeton University.

McLanahan, Sara, and Gary Sandefur. 1994. *Growing up with a single parent: What hurts and what helps.* Cambridge, MA: Harvard University Press.

Mincy, Ronald B., and Hillard Pouncy. 2007. *Baby fathers and American family formation.* Future of the Black Family Series, Center for Marriage and Families at the Institute for American Values. http://center.americanvalues.org/?p=64.

Mott, Frank L. 1990. When is a father really gone? Paternal-child contact in father-absent homes. *Demography* 27:499-517.

Moynihan, Daniel Patrick. 1965. *The Negro family: The case for national action.* Washington, DC: U.S. Department of Labor. http://www.dol.gov/oasam/programs/history/moynchapter2.htm.

Reed, Joanna. 2006. Not crossing the extra line: How cohabitors with children view their unions. *Journal of Marriage and Family* 68 (5): 1117-31.

Roopnarine, Jaipaul L., Janet Brown, Priscilla Snell-White, Nancy Beth Riegraf, Devon Crossley, Ziarat Hossain, and Wayne Webb. 1995. Father involvement in child care and household work in common-law dual-earner and single-earner Jamaican families. *Journal of Applied Developmental Psychology* 16 (1): 35-52.

Roopnarine, Jaipaul L. African American and Caribbean Father: Levels, quality and meaning of involvement. *In The Role of the Father in Child Development*, ed. Michael E. Lamb, 55-97. New York: Wiley & Sons.

Seltzer, Judith A. 1991. Relationships between fathers and children who live apart: The father's role after separation. *Journal of Marriage and the Family* 53:79-101.

———. 2000. Child support and child access: The experiences of marital and non-marital families. In *Child support: The next frontier*, ed. Thomas Oldham and Marygold Melli, 69-87. Ann Arbor: University of Michigan Press.

Seltzer, Judith A., and Suzanne M. Bianchi. 1988. Children's contact with absent parents. *Journal of Marriage and Family* 50:663-67.

Senior, Olive. 1991. Working miracles. In *Women's lives in the English-speaking Caribbean*, ed. Janet Brown, Patricia Anderson, and Barry Chevannes. Bloomington: Indiana University Press.

Sobolewski, Juliana M., and Valarie King. 2005. The importance of the coparental relationship for nonresident fathers' ties to children. *Journal of Marriage and Family* 67:1196-1212.

Stephens, L. S. 1996. Will Johnny see daddy this week? An empirical test of three theoretical perspectives of postdivorce contact. *Journal of Family Issues* 17:466-94.

Stewart, Susan D. 1999. Nonresident mothers' and fathers' social contact with children. *Journal of Marriage and the Family* 61:894-907.

Sullivan, Mercer L. 1993. Young fathers and parenting in two inner city neighborhoods. In *Young unwed fathers: Changing roles and emerging priorities*, ed. Robert I. Lerman and Theodora J. Ooms, 52-73. Philadelphia: Temple University Press.

Townsend. Nicolas W. 2004. *The package deal: Marriage, work, and fatherhood in men's lives.* Philadelphia: Temple University Press.

Waller, Maureen R. 2002. *My baby's father: Unwed parents and paternal responsibilities.* Ithaca, NY: Cornell University Press.

Waller, Maureen R., and Raymond Swisher. 2006. Fathers' risk factors in fragile families: Implications for healthy relationships and father involvement. *Social Problems* 53:392-420.

Young, Alford. 2003. *The minds of marginalized black men: Making sense of mobility, opportunity, and future life chances.* Princeton, NJ: Princeton University Press.

Welfare Reform in the Mid-2000s: How African American and Hispanic Families in Three Cities Are Faring

By
ANDREW CHERLIN,
BIANCA FROGNER,
DAVID RIBAR,
and
ROBERT MOFFITT

This article reports on a sample of 538 African American and Hispanic women who were receiving Temporary Assistance for Needy Families (TANF) in 1999, 416 of whom left the program by 2005. The Hispanic women consisted of a Mexican-origin group and a second group that was primarily Puerto Rican and Dominican. Combining the experiences of the employed and the non-employed welfare leavers, the authors find at best a modest decline in the average poverty rate among African American welfare leavers between 1999 and 2005. Hispanic leavers showed larger average declines in poverty. Among just the welfare leavers who were employed in 2005, the averages for women in all racial-ethnic groups showed increases in household income and declines in poverty. Among those who were not employed, African Americans had experienced a decline in household income and were further below the poverty line than in 1999, whereas Hispanic women had experienced modest declines or slight increases in their household incomes.

Keywords: welfare reform; poverty; families; African Americans; Mexican Americans; Puerto Ricans; Dominicans

W hen Daniel Patrick Moynihan submitted his report, *The Negro Family: The Case for National Action*, in 1965, welfare use was already a public issue. Between 1960 and 1965, the number of recipients of Aid to Families with Dependent Children (AFDC) had increased by more than 40 percent. Soon afterward, the rate of increase became even greater. Between 1965 and 1970, the number of recipients doubled, and it increased another 30 percent by 1972.[1] The backdrop to this rise included African American welfare rights activism and rioting in the African American neighborhoods of several cities. These events reinforced the image of AFDC in the public mind as a program that benefited African Americans even though, at all times, less than half of the recipients have been African American. In fact, welfare and race have been intertwined in the United States since the creation of welfare under the Social Security Act in 1935; and they remain intertwined today.

DOI: 10.1177/0002716208324851

It is not a pretty history. The 1935 act excluded many African Americans and Hispanics from social security coverage because, at the insistence of southern members of Congress, the initial legislation left out agricultural and domestic workers, two categories that included the bulk of black laborers in the South and many Hispanic laborers in the Southwest (Gordon 1994). Coverage was gradually expanded in later modifications of the law. The act also established Aid to Dependent Children (ADC), the forerunner of AFDC, to aid the widows of the largely white workforce that would be eligible for social security benefits. ADC remained popular until the 1960s, by which time the widows had been supplanted by never-married, divorced, and separated women, who were disproportionately drawn from minority groups.

In 1970, when President Nixon (upon the advice of Moynihan) proposed the Family Assistance Plan, a guaranteed income program for low-income families, it failed in part because southern congressmen worried that it would undercut the low-wage structure of the black labor force in their states. As Representative Phillip Landrum of Georgia famously said, "There's not going to be anybody left to roll these wheelbarrows and press these shirts" (Quadagno 1994, 130). Lee Rainwater

Andrew Cherlin is Benjamin H. Griswold III Professor of Sociology and Public Policy at Johns Hopkins University. He is the principal investigator of the Three-City Study. His research interests include the well-being of parents and children in low-income families and the changing nature of marriage and family life over the past century.

Bianca Frogner is a health economics doctoral candidate in the Department of Health Policy and Management at the Johns Hopkins Bloomberg School of Public Health. Her thesis work is on the determinants of health care expenditure growth in industrialized countries.

David Ribar is a professor of economics at the University of North Carolina at Greensboro, where he conducts research on disadvantaged families, assistance programs, and household time use. He has investigated family formation behavior, parents' child care decisions, youths' behaviors, public and private transfers to alleviate poverty, and participation in assistance programs. He is an associate investigator on the Three-City Study.

Robert Moffitt is Krieger-Eisenhower Professor of Economics at Johns Hopkins University. He is currently associated with the Institute for Research on Poverty, the National Poverty Center, and the National Bureau of Economic Research. He was chair of the National Academy of Sciences Panel on Data and Methods for Welfare Reform. He is chief editor of the American Economic Review.

NOTE: We gratefully acknowledge the support of the National Institute of Child Health and Human Development through grants HD36093 and HD25936 and of the Office of the Assistant Secretary for Planning and Evaluation, Administration on Developmental Disabilities, Administration for Children and Families, Social Security Administration, National Institute of Mental Health, the Boston Foundation, the Annie E. Casey Foundation, the Edna McConnell Clark Foundation, the Lloyd A. Fry Foundation, Hogg Foundation for Mental Health, the Robert Wood Johnson Foundation, the Joyce Foundation, the Henry J. Kaiser Family Foundation, W. K. Kellogg Foundation, Kronkosky Charitable Foundation, the John D. and Catherine T. MacArthur Foundation, Charles Stewart Mott Foundation, the David and Lucile Packard Foundation, and Woods Fund of Chicago.

and William L. Yancey, in their account of the Moynihan Report and the controversy it caused, wrote that the report put the "welfare establishment" in a difficult
position because "for years it has acquiesced to subtle and blatant discrimination
and inadequate labor and welfare services to Negroes" (Rainwater and Yancey
1967, 175). The establishment's strategy, they argued, had been to wish away race
as a category by emphasizing a self-consciously "colorblind" approach.

With this history as background, most liberal scholars and activists concerned
about the well-being of low-income African Americans were skeptical of the 1996
welfare reform law, the Personal Responsibility and Work Opportunity
Reconciliation Act (PRWORA). Its five-year time limit, its end to an entitlement
to welfare, its work requirements, and its other rules were harsh by twentieth-
century standards; and some opponents thought that the black poor would be
pushed further into poverty. Supporters of welfare reform sought, with considerable success, to focus the debate on dependency rather than poverty. Moynihan
himself had advocated this distinction: "The issue of welfare is the issue of dependency," he wrote in 1986. "It is different from poverty. To be poor is an objective
condition; to be dependent, a subjective one as well" (Moynihan 1986, 165).
Nevertheless, in the mid-1990s, Moynihan, by then a senator from New York,
vehemently denounced welfare reform. He predicted that it would be "the most
brutal act of social policy since Reconstruction."[2]

Some observers on the left have, in fact, concluded that PRWORA was discriminatory toward African Americans. Gooden and Douglas (2006) present data
showing that states with a higher percentage of African Americans tend to have
stricter rules, with time limits shorter than the five-year maximum, a loss of the
full family's grant rather than just the adult's portion when a recipient violates
rules, a refusal to increase a family's benefits if a mother receiving TANF
(Temporary Assistance for Needy Families) has another child, and so forth. Most
of these differences, however, pertain to states in the South with large black populations. In contrast, New York, the state with the largest black population, is not
unusually strict; nor are California or Michigan. This pattern suggests that the
issue is continuing traditional disparities in the South rather than a new, nationwide phenomenon that began with PRWORA.

Much less attention has been paid to the effects of PRWORA on Hispanic
families. When Moynihan wrote his report, only 4 to 5 percent of the United
States population was of Hispanic origin, and Moynihan said nothing about them.
Welfare in that era was viewed as a black-white issue. Now, however, Hispanics
constitute about 14 percent of the U.S. population, and they outnumber non-
Hispanic black Americans.[3] In 2005, 26 percent of the families receiving TANF
were Hispanic.[4]

The receipt of TANF within the Hispanic population varied greatly.
Undocumented immigrants are ineligible for public assistance programs such as
TANF. Legal immigrants who entered the United States after the passage of
PRWORA in 1996 are not eligible for TANF until they have been in the country
for five years. Country of origin, or island versus mainland origin in the case of

Puerto Ricans, is also important, as recent analyses of the pooled 1998 to 2002 March Current Population Surveys show. Among the major Hispanic groups, Puerto Ricans and Dominicans receive the highest proportion of their household incomes from TANF. Mexicans receive a lower proportion of household income from TANF; and Cubans, the most prosperous Hispanic group, receive the lowest (Reimers 2006). In addition, Puerto Ricans and Dominicans are much more likely to live in single-parent families than are Mexicans or Cubans: 42 percent of Dominican households and 34 percent of Puerto Rican households were headed by a woman with no partner present, compared to 18 percent of Mexican households and 16 percent of Cuban households (Landale, Oropesa, and Bradatan 2006).

Despite predictions by some opponents that PRWORA [the Personal Responsibility and Work Opportunity Reconciliation Act] would be disastrous for all racial and ethnic groups . . . [it] coincided with a huge drop in the welfare rolls without the terrible, widespread consequences that many had feared.

Due to their low incomes and high prevalence of single-parent families, Puerto Ricans and Dominicans are more similar to African Americans than are Mexicans. Thirty percent of African Americans lived in families with incomes below the poverty line in the period 1998 to 2002, a figure in between the poverty rates for Dominicans and Puerto Ricans but well above that for Mexicans (Reimers 2006). Forty-one percent of African American households were headed by a woman with no partner present—a figure virtually identical to the percentage among Dominicans and not far above the percentage among Puerto Ricans (Landale, Oropesa, and Bradatan 2006). Puerto Ricans and Dominicans are also the only Hispanic groups who do not have more earners per household than African Americans. Moreover, Dominicans who were born in the United States have rates of participation in TANF that are similar to the rates among African Americans; and Puerto Ricans, whether born on the mainland or the island, have higher rates of participation in TANF than do African Americans (Reimers 2006).

Despite predictions by some opponents that PRWORA would be disastrous for all racial and ethnic groups and predictions by other opponents that, like previous attempts at reform, it would hardly change the system, PRWORA coincided with a huge drop in the welfare rolls without the terrible, widespread consequences that many had feared. The labor force participation rate of single mothers rose sharply, and their poverty rate fell. To be sure, the welfare reformers had the good fortune of starting their program during the strong economy of the late 1990s. Yet, the consensus among economists, liberal and conservative, is that the economic boom was not the sole reason for the drop in the welfare rolls and the increase in employment among single mothers. Rather, they argue, welfare policy also played a role (Blank and Schmidt 2001; Blank 2002; Grogger and Karoly 2005). Currently, even after several years of slower economic growth, the labor force participation rate remains higher, and the poverty rate remains lower, for single mothers than in the pre-PRWORA years (Blank 2006).

Still, we know little about the long-term picture. Since economic growth has been slower in the 2000s, it is important to examine how those who left TANF have been faring in recent years. The Urban Institute's large study, the National Survey of America's Families (NSAF), ended in 2002.[5] The most recent, detailed information comes from the Women's Employment Survey (WES), which followed a sample of TANF recipients in one urban county in Michigan from 1997 to 2003. Slightly more than half of the women were African American, and the rest were non-Hispanic whites. The caseload in the county did not contain enough Hispanics to warrant studying.

Researchers from both the NSAF and the WES have published articles and reports on individuals who have left TANF but have not made the transition to paid work. These disconnected former recipients have income from neither cash assistance programs nor employment; and under some definitions they have no incomes from spouses or partners, either. Those who were chronically disconnected from TANF, supplemental security income (SSI), employment, and income from spouses or partners during the six years of the WES were more likely to be African American than white; and they were more likely to report a physical health limitation, low work skills, a learning disability, no car or driver's license, and substance abuse (Turner, Danziger, and Seefeldt 2006). Using the NSAF data, Loprest (2003) reported that disconnected adults were more likely to be in poor health and less likely to have completed high school or obtained a GED. Blank (2007) applied similar definitions of being disconnected to Current Population Survey data through 2004 and reported that the percentage of low-income single mothers who were receiving little or no income from welfare or employment had increased substantially since the start of welfare reform.

In this article, we present information on African American and Hispanic women in the Three-City Study, one of the longest panel surveys of low-income families in the post-PRWORA era (1999 to 2005). It provides the most recent data available, and it allows for a comparison of African Americans, Americans of

Mexican origin, and other Hispanics. We begin by presenting a series of charts displaying trends in household income and poverty status over the six years of the study for women who left TANF after the start. We then present the predictors of who was disconnected from welfare and work among all women who were receiving TANF at the start of the study.

Data and Methods

Sample design

The first interviews in this longitudinal study were conducted in 1999 in low- and moderate-income neighborhoods (93 percent of the selected block groups had poverty rates of 20 percent or more) in Boston, Chicago, and San Antonio. The researchers randomly selected households with incomes below 200 percent of the poverty line that included at least one child between the ages of zero to four or ten to fourteen (called the "focal child"), and they assessed or interviewed the children and also interviewed their primary caregivers, usually their mothers. (Children whose primary caregivers were male were not selected.)

In this article, we report on information obtained from the caregivers. The initial sample consisted of 2,458 families, and it included welfare and nonwelfare families. The response rate in the first wave of interviews was 74 percent.[6] A second wave of interviews was conducted from September 2000 to June 2001 (we refer to this as the 2001 wave) with the same children, their initial caregivers, and any new caregivers if the children's living arrangements changed, and a similar third wave was conducted in 2005. Retention in the second and third waves was high; 80 percent of the original families were successfully reinterviewed in 2005. There were no significant differences between the 1999 characteristics of the caregivers who were reinterviewed in 2005, on one hand, and the 1999 characteristics of those who were not reinterviewed in 2005, with respect to age, race and Hispanic ethnicity, educational attainment, welfare usage, or marital status.

For this article, we select caregivers who participated in all three waves, including some women who eventually lived apart from the focal child. Because we wish to examine employment behavior among potential welfare recipients, we restrict the sample to women who were sixty-two years old or younger and who were still living with at least one child under the age of eighteen in 2005. We also exclude observations for a few women who did not answer the questions relevant to our analysis, including the program use, income, and employment questions. These restrictions leave 538 African American and Hispanic women who were receiving support from TANF during the first survey in 1999. (The white sub-sample of 41 was too small to support the analyses in this article; moreover, the whites in our study were not representative of white low-income families nationally because white poverty, as Massey and Eggers [1990] and Krivo et al. [1998] have shown, is less concentrated in low- and moderate-income neighborhoods in central cites.)

TABLE 1
DEMOGRAPHIC CHARACTERISTICS AT WAVE 1 (1999) OF WOMEN WHO
WERE RECEIVING TEMPORARY ASSISTANCE FOR NEEDY FAMILIES (TANF)

	Wave 1 (1999)
Race-ethnicity	
Non-Hispanic, black	$n = 277$
Hispanic, Mexican	$n = 117$
Hispanic, other	$n = 144$
Age	
25 or younger	32.6%
26-35	41.4%
36 or more	26.0%
Education	
No degree	58.3%
High school/GED	31.9%
Above high school/GED	9.8%
Married	16.8%
Cohabiting	4.4%
Number in household	5.2
Children under three years of age in household	66.1%

NOTE: Means of characteristics for caregivers from Three-City Study who completed all three waves of data collection and who had children at all three waves. Estimates use sample weights

Of the 538 women who were receiving TANF in 1999, 416 were no longer participating in the program by 2005. About half of the leavers left by the time of the second wave—they reported receiving no income from TANF at the 2001 survey. The other half left by 2005—they were receiving TANF in 2001 but reporting no income from TANF at the 2005 survey. We combine the 2001 and 2005 leavers in this article.[7] Slightly less than half of the leavers and 22 percent of the women still receiving TANF reported in the 2005 interview that they had income from employment in the previous month. We refer to these particular women as "employed"; they include 45 percent of the African American women, 45 percent of women of Mexican origin, and 39 percent of other Hispanic women.

All of our statistical analyses use weights that adjust for differential sampling and response rates in the original interviews and for selection due to attrition and the exclusion criteria in our specific data set. Table 1 shows the weighted demographic characteristics of the 538 women who were receiving TANF in 1999. For the charts on trends among those who left TANF, we use the subsample of 416 women who left TANF by 2005. For the analysis of disconnection from welfare and work, we use all 538 cases.

The cities

The three cities were originally selected for the study because they were representative of large urban areas in the United States and because they were in states with markedly different welfare policies. In 1999, Massachusetts was a high-benefit state with short time limits, a family-cap policy, and moderate sanctions but many types of exemptions. Illinois was a medium-benefit state with a standard five-year time limit and a family-cap provision. Illinois allowed families to receive benefits for some time before requiring work, but it also imposed tougher sanctions than the other states. Texas was a low-benefit, work-first state with short time limits, no family-cap, and weak sanctions; it also emphasized diversion. All three states offered transitional Medicaid and child care to families that left welfare for employment.

For the most part, these descriptions still characterized the programs in 2005. Massachusetts continued to have the highest benefits with a maximum monthly payment of $618 for a family of three with no other income, while Texas had the lowest benefits with a maximum monthly payment of $223 for a family of three. Time-limit policies were also similar across years, with Massachusetts and Texas continuing to opt for short time limits and Illinois keeping the five-year federal limit. The states also continued to offer transitional assistance. Among the changes in policies, Illinois dropped its family-cap provision in 2004 and also adopted a diversion program.

Over the period covered by our study, welfare caseloads in all three states declined substantially. The steepest drop occurred in Illinois, where the average monthly TANF caseload fell by more than two-thirds from 123,000 families in 1999 to 38,000 families in 2005. In Texas, the average monthly TANF caseload fell by just under a quarter; while in Massachusetts, the caseload fell by one-tenth. Nationally, the average number of adult recipients of TANF fell by 31 percent between 1999 and 2005 (U.S. Department of Health and Human Services 2007).

Employment conditions also varied within and across areas. Boston (Suffolk County) and San Antonio (Bexar County) had the most favorable labor market conditions with unemployment rates of 3.5 and 3.3 percent in 1999, peak unemployment rates of 6.6 and 6.2 percent in 2003, and more favorable rates of 5.4 and 5.0 percent by 2005. The rates in 1999 were below the corresponding national average, while the rates in later years were generally at or above the national averages. Unemployment was higher in Chicago (Cook County), where the rates were 5.0 percent in 1999, 7.4 percent in 2003, and 6.5 percent in 2005. In terms of poverty rates, the ordering was very different with Boston (Suffolk County), San Antonio (Bexar County), and Chicago (Cook County) experiencing poverty rates of 21, 17, and 15 percent, respectively, in 2005.

TANF participation among the Three-City caregivers fell by more than two-thirds from 32 percent in 1999 to 12 percent in 2005. This drop was greater than the average leaving rates recorded for our states. The larger drop in the Three-City sample may be attributable to life-cycle changes among the cohort of respondents. As the caregivers aged and their youngest children reached school age, their assistance needs may have diminished. This seems, however, to be an incomplete explanation, as participation in other types of assistance, including food stamps, held fairly steady over the period.

Another explanation for the large drop in welfare use, at least initially, is "regression to the mean." The Three-City sample was initially selected on the basis of its income characteristics and therefore included some households whose incomes were permanently low and others whose incomes were only temporarily low. Over time, we would expect that households with temporarily low incomes would return to their long-term trends. In a general longitudinal sample, households with temporarily high and low incomes balance out; however, our initial sample excluded high-income households. As a consequence, the reversions to long-term trends overwhelmingly involved shifts up in income.

Racial and ethnic composition

The analysis sample of 538 women receiving TANF in 1999 included 261 Hispanics and 277 non-Hispanic African Americans.[8] We refer to the latter group simply as "African Americans." The number of Hispanics was large enough to disaggregate into two groups. The first group consisted of 117 women of Mexican origin. Large concentrations of them exist in both the Chicago and San Antonio samples. Chicago has a greater percentage of Mexicans who have immigrated recently, whereas San Antonio has a greater percentage of people who have been in the country for several generations. The second group comprised 144 Hispanics of non-Mexican origin. Of this second group, 58 percent were Puerto Rican and 19 percent were Dominican. The Puerto Ricans were in both the Boston and Chicago samples, while the Dominicans were largely in the Boston sample. Small numbers of Hispanics with origins in several other Central and South American countries made up the balance of the second group, which we call "other Hispanic."

Measures

Employment status is defined as receipt by the caregiver of any earnings from employment during the month preceding the 2005 interview. Household income is defined as the sum of income from all sources by all members of the household. As the reader will learn, a self-reported measure of work-related health problems emerged as a significant predictor of disconnection in one of the regression models we present later in this article. It is constructed from the answers to two questions that were asked in the 1999 survey: The first asked the caregiver, "Does an ongoing physical or mental health problem or disability prevent you from working?" If her answer was negative, she was asked a second question: "Does an ongoing physical or mental health problem or disability limit you in the kind of work or amount of work that you can do?" We consider a caregiver to have what we call a "work-limiting disability" if she answered affirmatively to either of these questions. A negative answer to both questions served as the reference category for the regression model.

Other measures in the regression model include the following:

- A general health question that is widely used in surveys: "In general, how is your health? Would you say it is excellent, very good, good, fair, or poor?" (Any of the first categories received a score of 1; a response of "fair" or "poor" received a score of 0.)
- Age, in years.
- Age of youngest child, in years.
- Educational attainment: more than a high school degree or GED; high school degree or GED; less than a high school degree or GED (reference category).
- Score on the Woodcock-Johnson Letter-Word test, a measure of cognitive ability and achievement.
- Whether from her birth to age sixteen, her family ever received "public assistance such as welfare, public aid, Food Stamps, WIC (Women, Infants and Children Nutrition program) or SSI (Supplemental Security Income)" (no is reference category).
- Whether anyone in the household owned a car or truck (no is reference category).
- Brief Symptom Inventory: an eighteen-item scale of psychological distress, reflecting symptoms of anxiety, depression, and somatization (Derogatis 2000). To address skewness, the natural logarithm of the score is used.
- Alcohol or drug use scale: how often during the past twelve months (never, once or twice, several times, or often), the woman: (1) used marijuana or hashish; (2) used hard drugs such as heroin, LSD, or cocaine; (3) sold drugs; or (4) had gotten drunk. The natural logarithm of the score is used.
- Whether in general the focal child's health was excellent, very good, or good (fair or poor is the reference category).
- Domestic abuse scale: whether the woman had experienced various kinds of physical, emotional, or sexual or abuse as an adult. The square-root of the score is used.
- Whether her race-ethnicity was African American, Mexican-origin (the reference category), other Hispanic.
- City of residence (Boston is the reference category).

Trends in Income and Poverty after Leaving TANF

In this section, we present charts showing trends from 1999 to 2005 in income and poverty for the 416 women who left TANF, by racial-ethnic group and, in the later charts, also by employment status. Figure 1 shows the total monthly household incomes of women who left TANF between 1999 and 2005 for the three racial-ethnic groups. Income amounts were adjusted by the Consumer Price Index for All Urban Consumers and expressed as constant, December 2005 dollars; and here we follow the definition of income used in calculating the official government poverty line, which excludes income from food stamps and from the Earned Income Tax Credit (EITC). (The numbers used in constructing the charts in this article are presented in Appendixes A, B, and C.)

In 1999, when everyone was receiving TANF, the mean household incomes of the three groups were similar, suggesting that all three groups started the study in similar economic circumstances. By 2005, however, when none of the women were receiving TANF, the household income of African Americans was less than that of the two Hispanic groups. African Americans had experienced, on average, a 7 percent gain in household income, well below the 48 percent increase among

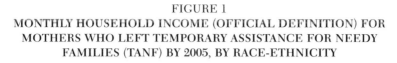

FIGURE 1
MONTHLY HOUSEHOLD INCOME (OFFICIAL DEFINITION) FOR
MOTHERS WHO LEFT TEMPORARY ASSISTANCE FOR NEEDY
FAMILIES (TANF) BY 2005, BY RACE-ETHNICITY

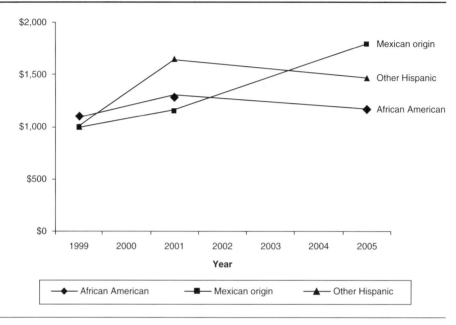

the other Hispanic group and the 79 percent increase among Hispanics of Mexican origin. This differential could reflect differences in women's earnings, in the earnings of other household members, or in the receipt of program income other than TANF.

Figure 2 shows the percentage of women in each group with incomes that fell below the federal poverty line. There was virtually no change in the official rate of poverty among African American women who left welfare: 86 percent were poor by this definition in 1999 when they were all receiving TANF, and 85 percent were poor in 2005 when none were receiving TANF. In contrast, both Hispanic groups showed declines in the percentage below the poverty line: a 16 percentage point drop for other Hispanics and a 24 percentage point drop for those of Mexican origin. So even a Hispanic group composed mainly of Puerto Ricans and Dominicans made some progress, on average, in leaving poverty after they exited welfare, but African Americans made almost none.

The federal poverty line is the most widely cited figure in discussions and debates about low incomes, poverty, and inequality, and it has the advantage of historical continuity because it has been calculated the same way since the 1960s. Many poverty analysts argue, nevertheless, that the restricted definition of what counts as income has made the official poverty line increasingly unrealistic as a

FIGURE 2
PERCENTAGE POOR (OFFICIAL DEFINITION) FOR MOTHERS
WHO LEFT TEMPORARY ASSISTANCE FOR NEEDY FAMILIES
(TANF) BY 2005, BY RACE-ETHNICITY

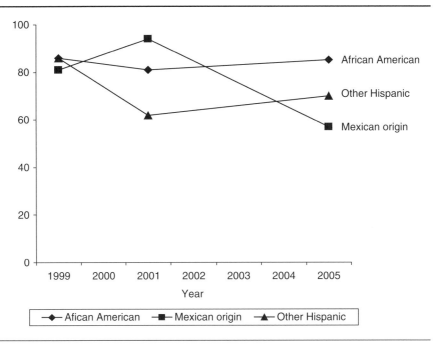

measure of household income. For instance, the expansion of the EITC program since its inception in 1975 is not reflected in the poverty line, and it now costs the federal treasury more than TANF. Nor is the value of food stamps counted. In addition, leaving welfare could have improved the economic circumstances of some poor families by raising them closer to the federal poverty line without pushing them across the line, and this kind of progress cannot be assessed in analyses that simply look at the percentage above and below the line.

Another way of measuring progress in reducing poverty is to calculate for each family the poverty gap. For a mother below the poverty line, the gap is calculated as the official poverty line for her household minus her household income. It is a measure of how far the household's income falls short of reaching the line. For households with incomes above the line, the poverty gap is zero. We calculated the monthly poverty gap for each household, defined as one-twelfth of the federal poverty line for that household minus monthly household income, including income from food stamps and potential EITC income.[9] If the result was a negative number, the gap was assigned to be zero. The results are presented in Figure 3.

The poverty gap declined for all three groups, meaning that the average amount of additional income it would take for every family in the group to be at

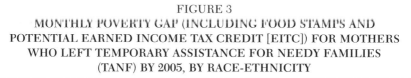

FIGURE 3
MONTHLY POVERTY GAP (INCLUDING FOOD STAMPS AND
POTENTIAL EARNED INCOME TAX CREDIT [EITC]) FOR MOTHERS
WHO LEFT TEMPORARY ASSISTANCE FOR NEEDY FAMILIES
(TANF) BY 2005, BY RACE-ETHNICITY

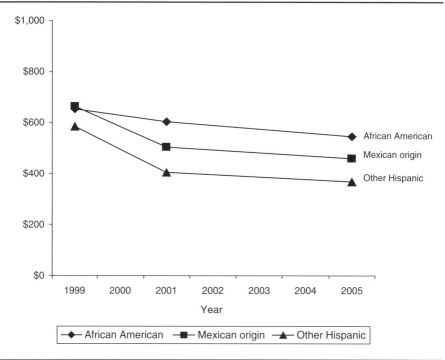

or above the poverty line declined as they left welfare from 1999 to 2005. Put another way, the average family that was still below the line in 2005 was less poor—closer to the line—in 2005 than in 1999. Once again, the improvement was smallest for African Americans, among whom the poverty gap declined by 17 percent, compared to 31 percent among Hispanics of Mexican origin and 37 percent of other Hispanics.

So far, we have presented only the average experience of all African American women, all women of Mexican origin, and all women of other Hispanic origins. But the experiences of women within each group combine those who are employed and those who are not employed. Clearly, the trajectories of the employed are likely to differ from the trajectories of the unemployed. In that sense, the "average" effect of leaving welfare is likely to be misleading since it combines the experiences of those whose economic situation may have improved and those whose situation may have deteriorated.

In Figures 4 and 5, we present two trend lines for each group, one for women who were employed at the 2005 wave and one for those who were not employed

FIGURE 4
MONTHLY HOUSEHOLD INCOME (INCLUDING FOOD STAMPS
AND POTENTIAL EARNED INCOME TAX CREDIT [EITC]) FOR MOTHERS
WHO LEFT TEMPORARY ASSISTANCE FOR NEEDY FAMILIES (TANF)
BY 2005, BY RACE-ETHNICITY AND EMPLOYMENT STATUS IN 2005

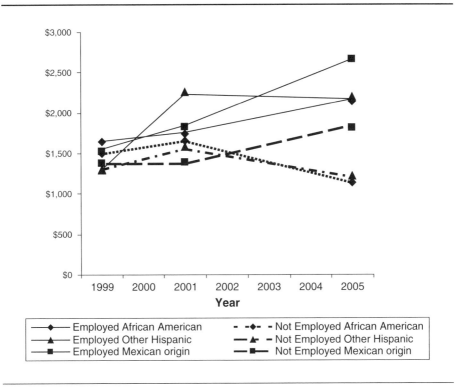

in 2005, where "employed" is defined as having income from employment in the previous month. Women in all of the groups may or may not have been employed in 1999 and 2001; our classification is based only on 2005 employment. As shown in Figure 4, which presents trends in monthly household income including Food Stamps and potential EITC, much less variation existed in 1999 than in subsequent years. Indeed, by 2005, the variation is substantial.

The average household income for Mexican-origin women who were employed in 2005 increased by 93 percent, whereas for other Hispanics who were employed, it increased by 68 percent. For African Americans who were employed, household income increased by 30 percent. For women who were not employed in 2005, however, the situation is much different. African American women who were not employed in 2005 had household incomes that had declined by 24 percent since 1999. Mexican-origin women who were unemployed nevertheless saw an increase of 18 percent in their household incomes.

FIGURE 5
MONTHLY POVERTY GAP (INCLUDING FOOD STAMPS AND POTENTIAL
EARNED INCOME TAX CREDIT [EITC]) FOR MOTHERS WHO LEFT
TEMPORARY ASSISTANCE FOR NEEDY FAMILIES (TANF) BY 2005,
BY RACE-ETHNICITY AND EMPLOYMENT STATUS IN 2005

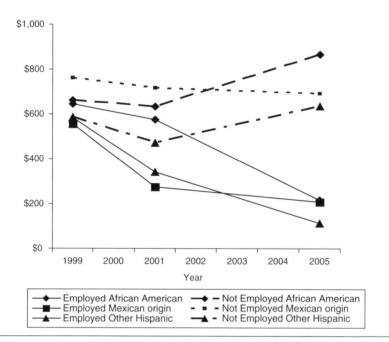

Women of other Hispanic origin who were not employed in 2005 were treading water: their incomes had decreased by 5 percent. In other words, among non-employed welfare leavers in 2005, African American and to a lesser extent other Hispanic women experienced an absolute decrease in their average household incomes, whereas Mexican-origin women who were not employed were able to increase their incomes, on average.

Figure 5 displays the poverty gap for the employed and unemployed and tells a similar story. The only group that displayed a substantially worsening trajectory was African Americans who were not employed in 2005. Their poverty gap had increased by nearly one-third, on average, from $662 to $867. Almost all of them had been below the poverty line to begin with in 1999, and they were even further below the poverty line in 2005. Hispanics of non-Mexican origin who were not employed showed a modest increase in their average poverty gap (worsening economic status), while Mexican-origin Hispanics who were not employed showed a modest decrease in their poverty gap (improving economic situation). In contrast, employed women in all three racial-ethnic groups decreased their average poverty gaps substantially. Among African Americans who were

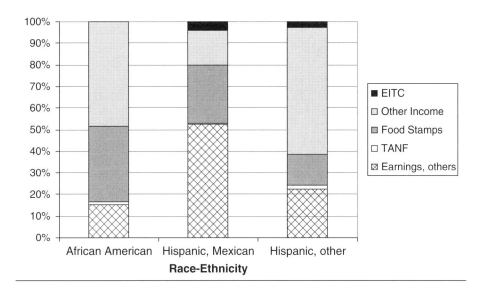

employed, for instance, the average gap fell from $645 to $216. Overall, employed
women from all three racial-ethnic groups were faring much better economically
in 2005 than in 1999, while nonemployed Hispanic women had experienced
small upward or downward changes and nonemployed African American women
had experienced a substantial worsening of their economic situation.

Why were nonemployed Mexican-origin women able to increase their household incomes and decrease their poverty gaps modestly whereas nonemployed
African Americans were not? The reason is that they were more likely to live in
households in which other members contributed earnings. Nonemployed
Hispanics of Mexican origin were able to insulate themselves from declines in
income caused by leaving TANF by adding earners to their households and
through the increased earnings of already existing household members. In contrast, African Americans, both employed and not employed, drew the least
income from additional household members. Indeed, food stamps constituted a
larger share of the household income among African Americans, and both
African Americans and non-Mexican Hispanics relied more on a broad category
we have labeled "other income," which includes SSI, social security disability
insurance, child support payments, and assistance from people outside the
household (see Figure 6).[10]

Predictors of Disconnection

What predicts being disconnected from sources of income at the end of the study? In this section, we examine the predictors of being disconnected in 2005 using three definitions similar to those used in previous studies (Loprest 2003; Turner, Danziger, and Seefeldt 2006; Blank 2007); and to be consistent with previous studies, we include all women who were receiving TANF in 1999, not just the women who had left TANF by 2005. Under the first and simplest definition, a woman is considered disconnected if at the time of the 2005 interview she was receiving income from neither TANF nor employment. The second definition adds the criterion that she also was not receiving cash assistance from SSI or Unemployment Insurance (UI) programs. The third adds the further criterion that she was not living with a spouse or partner who was employed at the 2005 interview. Thus, under the third definition, a woman was disconnected from sources of income if she had no access to income from TANF, SSI, UI, employment, or a partner. Under the first definition, 40 percent were disconnected; under the second definition, 28 percent were disconnected; and under the third and most restrictive definition, 22 percent were disconnected.

Table 2 presents the results from logistic regression models of whether a woman was disconnected, according to each of the three definitions, as a function of the predictor variables discussed earlier. Considering the first definition of disconnection, we see that just two coefficients are statistically significant at conventional levels. One of them is age of youngest child: the older that child is, the less likely the mother is to be disconnected. This result may reflect the easing of the burden of child care that occurs when one's children are older, reducing the difficulty of combining work and child care. The second is the presence of a work-limiting disability, which greatly increases the odds of being disconnected: other things being equal, a woman who reported a work-limiting disability in 1999 was 2.7 times more likely to be disconnected in 2005 than a women who did not report one. All women who said they had a work-limiting disability were also asked what the health condition was. No condition dominated. Seventeen percent said that the problem was depression, with Hispanics more likely to mention this factor than African Americans. From 1 to 10 percent named each of the following conditions: vision problems, arthritis, back or neck problems, fractures or other injuries, heart problems, hypertension, diabetes, lung or breathing problems, and weight problems.

When the second definition is used, however, disability is no longer a significant predictor of being disconnected. This definition adds the criterion that the woman is not receiving SSI or UI. In fact, the number of welfare leavers receiving SSI increased from fifty-two in 1999 to seventy-four in 2005. The rise in SSI receipt partially compensated for the decline in TANF receipt among those with a work-related disability. Educational attainment also emerges as a significant predictor in the second definition, with a lower likelihood of disconnection among women with education beyond high school.

TABLE 2
LOGISTIC REGRESSION OF DISCONNECTED STATUS IN 2005 ($N = 516$)

	Definition 1 (Odds Ratios)	Definition 2 (Odds Ratios)	Definition 3 (Odds Ratios)
Reported a work-limiting disability in 1999	2.68°°	1.45	1.29
Health was "good" or better in 1999	0.70	1.01	0.921
Age	1.04	0.99	1.01
Age of youngest child	0.87°°	0.90°	0.89°
Educational attainment (no degree is reference category)			
High school degree or GED	0.64	0.59	0.82
More than a high school degree	0.59	0.27°	0.27°
Woodcock-Johnson Letter-Word Test score	0.99	1.0	0.99
Family received welfare from birth to age sixteen	1.48	1.34	1.38
Someone in the household owns a car or truck	0.81	0.98	1.30
Brief Symptom Inventory score	1.07	1.07	1.14
Alcohol or drug use scale score	0.92	0.93	0.91
Child's Health is "good" or better	2.70	1.68	1.38
Experienced physical or sexual abuse as an adult	1.00	1.21	1.29
Race-ethnicity (Mexican is reference category)			
African American	0.66	0.51	3.62°°
Other Hispanic	0.62	0.54	2.07
City of residence (Boston is reference category)			
Chicago	1.39	2.11	2.12
San Antonio	0.90	1.23	3.07°
–2 log-likelihood	619.6	553.2	483.8

°$p < .05.$ °°$p < .01.$

Note that there are no significant differences in the likelihood of being disconnected among the three racial-ethnic groups under definitions one and two. Under definition three, however, where we add the criterion that to be disconnected a woman also has to be living in a household without a spouse or partner with earnings, African American women become 3.6 times as likely to be disconnected as Mexican-origin women. This finding is consistent with the sources of household income that were shown in Figure 6. A much lower proportion of African American mothers, 22 percent, were living with spouses or partners in 2005, compared to 56 percent of Mexican-origin women. As a result, African American women who had no income from cash assistance or employment were less able to compensate by relying on a partner's earnings. Among the largely Puerto Rican and Dominican "other Hispanic" group, 27 percent were living with a spouse or partner, which is closer to the African American figure. The coefficient for other-Hispanic group indicates a likelihood of disconnection that was between African Americans and Mexicans; it was not significantly different from either.

Conclusion

Nine years after the passage of PRWORA and six years after we began our three-city study, the economic circumstances of the women who were receiving welfare at the start of the study had diverged by their subsequent TANF receipt, employment status, and race-ethnicity. At the start of the study, when all of the women were receiving TANF, their income and poverty levels were similar. By 2005, a large majority had left TANF, and about half of the leavers were employed. African Americans who left TANF were faring substantially worse in 2005 than Hispanics of Mexican origin; and on some measures, they were faring worse than non-Mexican Hispanics (mostly Puerto Rican and Dominican), whose national levels of poverty and single-parent families are close to the national levels of African Americans.

African American welfare leavers experienced at best a modest decline in poverty, depending on the measure of poverty that is used, and a modest increase in household income. Hispanic leavers experienced larger declines in poverty and increases in income. African American welfare leavers were far more likely than Mexican leavers to be living without a spouse or partner, which increased the likelihood that they would be disconnected from welfare, work, and spouse's or partner's earnings in 2005.

Among welfare leavers who were in employed in 2005, we found a substantial gain in household incomes and a narrowing of the gap between their incomes and the poverty line among all three racial-ethnic groups. Nonemployed African American welfare leavers, however, experienced an increase of one-third in the gap between their incomes and the poverty line since 1999. They were a very impoverished group. Hispanic welfare leavers who were not employed were able to compensate better through earnings from others in their households.

Do the findings in this article help answer the common question posed by Blank (2006) and others of whether welfare reform has been a success? No social scientific analysis can provide a definitive answer because people with different moral and political views will look at the same data and arrive at different conclusions. But the results from the Three-City Study do help narrow the answer somewhat. Even if welfare reform is to be judged a success, it has been less of a success for African Americans than for Hispanics, particularly Mexican-origin Hispanics; if welfare reform is to be judged problematic, it has been more problematic for African Americans. Welfare reform appears to have helped African American families in which women were able to leave the assistance rolls and find employment. Their numbers—nearly half of the African Americans in our study—are higher than many critics of the 1996 law expected. Yet, the other half is increasingly impoverished. Welfare reform has not managed to put to rest the regrettable historical pattern of American social welfare programs, in which African Americans tend to benefit the least.

INCOME AT WAVES 1, 2, AND 3 FOR NON-HISPANIC, AFRICAN AMERICAN WELFARE LEAVERS, EMPLOYED AND NOT EMPLOYED IN WAVE 3

	All Leavers			Leaver Employed in Wave 3			Leavers Not Employed in Wave 3		
	Wave 1	Wave 2	Wave 3	Wave 1	Wave 2	Wave 3	Wave 1	Wave 2	Wave 3
N	215			106			109		
Monthly household income (official poverty rate definition)	1,100	1,280	1,172	1,149	1,294	1,612	1,052	1,266	740
Poverty rate									
Official definition (%)	86	81	85	80	75	77	92	86	94
With Earned Income Tax Credit (EITC) and food stamps (%)	74	66	64	65	60	37	83	71	89
Poverty gap									
Official definition	1,005	935	911	982	938	573	1,028	932	1,242
With EITC and food stamps	654	604	545	645	575	216	662	633	867
Monthly earnings									
Individual	362	594	541	475	767	1,094	251	425	0
Others in household	109	246	259	122	196	346	96	295	174
Temporary Assistance for Needy Families (TANF)	428	178	8	413	112	0	442	243	16
Food stamps	384	305	358	390	283	319	378	326	396
Other income	202	261	363	139	220	172	263	303	551
EITC income (potential)	84	116	101	101	170	205	68	62	2
Percentage of households with earnings from someone other than the individual	17	26	25	21	21	36	13	32	15
Percentage of households with a spouse present	11	10	14	16	14	18	7	6	10
Percentage of households with a partner present	7	7	11	7	6	9	6	9	14

NOTE: Means of characteristics for caregivers from Three-City Study who completed all three waves of data collection and who had children at all three waves. Estimates use sample weights. Income amounts adjusted by the Consumer Price Index for All Urban Consumers (CPI-U) and expressed as constant (December 2005) dollars. Other income includes supplemental security income, social security disability income, social security, other types of welfare assistance, workers compensation or disability payments, pension or retirement income, child support, and help from friends and relatives.

APPENDIX B

INCOME AT WAVES 1, 2, AND 3 FOR HISPANIC WELFARE LEAVERS OF MEXICAN ORIGIN, EMPLOYED AND NOT EMPLOYED IN WAVE 3

	All Leavers			Leavers Employed in Wave 3			Leavers Not Employed in Wave 3		
	Wave 1	Wave 2	Wave 3	Wave 1	Wave 2	Wave 3	Wave 1	Wave 2	Wave 3
N	98			45			53		
Monthly household income (official poverty rate definition)	996	1,144	1,786	981	1,364	2,364	1,010	940	1,250
Poverty rate									
Official definition (%)	81	94	57	72	92	41	88	95	72
With Earned Income Tax Credit (EITC) and food stamps (%)	67	70	53	71	61	38	64	77	67
Poverty gap									
Official	1,010	886	798	857	650	443	1,153	1,105	1,127
With EITC and food stamps	663	503	459	556	274	207	762	716	892
Monthly earnings									
Individual	65	421	638	90	488	1,327	41	360	0
From others in household	463	465	931	440	680	907	485	266	353
Temporary Assistance for Needy Families (TANF)	354	158	4	337	147	0	369	168	7
Food stamps	333	287	331	268	254	166	393	319	184
Other income	114	100	213	114	49	130	115	147	290
EITC income (potential)	125	166	100	124	204	126	126	131	77
Percentage of households with earnings from someone other than the individual	39	38	60	33	58	65	45	19	55
Percentage of households with a spouse present	43	29	48	43	44	57	42	16	40
Percentage of households with a partner present	1	6	10	1	5	5	0	7	15

NOTE: Means of characteristics for caregivers from Three-City Study who completed all three waves of data collection and who had children at all three waves. Estimates use sample weights. Income amounts adjusted by the Consumer Price Index for All Urban Consumers (CPI-U) and expressed as constant (December 2005) dollars. Other income includes supplemental security income, social security disability income, social security, other types of welfare assistance, workers compensation or disability payments, pension or retirement income, child support and help from friends and relatives.

APPENDIX C

INCOME AT WAVES 1, 2, AND 3 FOR HISPANIC WELFARE LEAVERS OF OTHER THAN MEXICAN ORIGIN, EMPLOYED AND NOT EMPLOYED IN WAVE 3

	All Leavers			Leavers Employed in Wave 3			Leavers Not Employed in Wave 3		
	Wave 1	Wave 2	Wave 3	Wave 1	Wave 2	Wave 3	Wave 1	Wave 2	Wave 3
N	103			56			47		
Monthly household income (official poverty rate definition)	994	1,648	1,467	1,009	1,959	1,893	979	1,322	1,020
Poverty rate									
Official (%)	86	62	70	86	59	51	86	64	90
With Earned Income Tax Credit (EITC) and food stamps (%)	78	57	53	77	52	22	80	63	85
Poverty gap									
Official	846	585	526	856	540	270	836	632	795
With EITC and food stamps	585	405	369	584	341	113	586	472	637
Monthly earnings									
Individual	173	720	685	243	1,109	1,340	99	313	0
Others in household	65	360	263	75	475	251	55	241	276
Temporary Assistance for Needy Families (TANF)	484	193	15	486	181	9	482	205	22
Food stamps	245	189	135	213	189	100	280	188	172
Other income	273	375	503	205	194	294	343	563	722
EITC income (potential)	61	90	119	88	110	203	32	71	32
Percentage of households with earnings from someone other than the individual	12	37	27	13	44	22	11	30	33
Percentage of households with a spouse present	11	6	12	8	10	15	14	2	10
Percentage of households with a partner present	3	19	14	4	13	14	2	24	14

NOTE: Means of characteristics for caregivers from Three-City Study who completed all three waves of data collection and who had children at all three waves. Estimates use sample weights. Income amounts adjusted by the Consumer Price Index for All Urban Consumers (CPI-U) and expressed as constant (December 2005) dollars. Other income includes supplemental security income, social security disability income, social security, other types of welfare assistance, workers compensation or disability payments, pension or retirement income, child support and help from friends and relatives.

Notes

1. U.S. Administration for Children and Families (2007).

2. Quoted in Katz (2001, 327).

3. U.S. Census Bureau (2002, 2005).

4. "Temporary Assistance for Needy Families—Active Cases," http://www.acf.hhs.gov/programs/ofa/character/FY2005/tab08.htm (accessed September 24, 2007). The figures are for October 2004 to September 2005. Thirty-seven percent of the families were African American, and 32 percent were white.

5. See http://www.urban.org/center/anf/nsaf.cfm (accessed September 4, 2007).

6. See Pamela Winston (1999).

7. Two percent of mothers received Temporary Assistance for Needy Families (TANF) in 1999, did not receive it in 2001, but received it again in 2005. We exclude these mothers from our analyses.

8. The subsample of 416 women who left TANF after 1999 included 201 Hispanics and 215 non-Hispanic African Americans.

9. Potential Earned Income Tax Credit (EITC) amounts were calculated using the TAXSIM program available at http://www.nber.org/~taxsim (Feenberg and Coutts 1993). Our calculations assume that all eligible families participate and claim the maximum possible amount based on an annualization of their monthly incomes. Recent studies suggest that at least 75 percent of families eligible for the EITC participate in the program. See Holt (2006).

10. The small amount of TANF income among Hispanic welfare leavers (no African American woman reported any) was contributed by subfamilies in the woman's household, such as a sister and her child, that were receiving TANF. Similarly, the small amount of EITC income reflects tax credits on the earnings of others in the household.

References

Blank, Rebecca M. 2002. Evaluating welfare reform in the U.S. *Journal of Economic Literature* 40:1105-66.
———. 2006. Was welfare reform successful? *Economists' Voice* 3 (4): Article 2.
———. 2007. Improving the safety net for single mothers who face serious barriers to work. *The Future of Children* 17:183-97.
Blank, Rebecca M., and Lucie Schmidt. 2001. Work, wages, and welfare. In *The new world of welfare*, ed. R. M. Blank and R. Haskins, 70–96. Washington, DC: Brookings Institution.
Derogatis, Leonard R. 2000. *Brief Symptom Inventory 18: Administration, scoring, and procedures manual.* Minneapolis, MN: National Computer Systems.
Feenberg, Daniel, and Elisabeth Coutts. 1993. An introduction to the TAXSIM model. *Journal of Policy Analysis, and Management* 12:189-94.
Gooden, Susan T., and Nakeina E. Douglas. 2006. Ever present, sometimes acknowledged, but never addressed: Racial disparities in U.S. welfare policy. In *The promise of welfare reform: Political rhetoric and the reality of poverty in the twenty-first century*, ed. K. M. Kilty and E. A. Segal, 207-22. New York: Haworth.
Gordon, Linda. 1994. *Pitied but not entitled: Single mothers and the history of welfare.* New York: Free Press.
Grogger, Jeffrey T., and Lynn A. Karoly. 2005. *Welfare reform: Effects of a decade of change.* Cambridge, MA: Harvard University Press.
Holt, Steve. 2006. *The Earned Income Tax Credit at age 30: What we know.* Washington, DC: Brookings Institution, Metropolitan Policy Program. http://www.brookings.edu/metro/pubs/20060209_Holt.htm.
Katz, Michael B. 2001. *The price of citizenship: Redefining the American welfare state.* New York: Metropolitan Books.
Krivo, Lauren J., Ruth D. Peterson, Helen Rizzo, and John R. Reynolds. 1998. Race, segregation, and the concentration of disadvantage: 1980–1990. *Social Problems* 45:61-80.
Landale, Nancy S., R. Salvador Oropesa, and Cristina Bradatan. 2006. Hispanic families in the United States: Family structure and process in an era of family change. In *Hispanics and the future of America*, ed. Marta Tienda and Faith Mitchell, 138-78. Washington, DC: National Academies Press.
Loprest, Pamela. 2003. Disconnected welfare leavers face serious risks. Washington, DC: Urban Institute. http://www.urban.org/url.cfm?ID=310839 (accessed October 25, 2007).

Massey, Douglas S., and Mitchell T. Eggers. 1990. The ecology of inequality: Minorities and the concentration of poverty, 1970-1980. *American Journal of Sociology* 95:1153-88.

Moynihan, Daniel P. 1986. *Family and nation*. San Diego, CA: Harcourt, Brace, Jovanovich.

Quadagno, Jill S. 1994. *The color of welfare: How racism undermined the war on poverty*. New York: Oxford University Press.

Rainwater, Lee, and William L. Yancey. 1967. *The Moynihan Report and the politics of controversy*. Cambridge, MA: MIT Press.

Reimers, Cordelia. 2006. Economic well-being. In *Hispanics and the future of America*, ed. M. Tienda and F. Mitchell, 291-461. Washington, DC: National Academies Press.

Turner, Leslie J., Sheldon Danziger, and Kristin S. Seefeldt. 2006. Failing the transition from welfare to work: Women chronically disconnected from employment and cash income. *Social Science Quarterly* 87:227-49.

U.S. Administration for Children and Families. 2007. Temporary Assistance for Needy Families, separate state program-maintenance of effort, Aid to Families with Dependent Children: Caseload data. http://www.acf.hhs.gov/programs/ofa/caseload/caseloadindex.htm#afdc (accessed October 11, 2007).

U.S. Census Bureau. 2002. Historical census statistics on population totals by race, 1790 to 1990, and by Hispanic origin, 1970 to 1990, for the United States, regions, divisions, and states. Working Paper Series no. 56. http://www.census.gov/population/www/documentation/twps0056.html (accessed June 27, 2007).

———. 2005. The Hispanic population in the United States: 2004. http://www.census.gov/population/www/socdemo/hispanic/cps2004.html (accessed June 27, 2007).

U.S. Department of Health and Human Services. 2007. Indicators of welfare dependence: Annual report to Congress 2007. http://aspe.hhs.gov/hsp/Indicators07/ (accessed September 6, 2007).

Winston, Pamela. 1999. Welfare, Children, and Families: A Three-City Study. Overview and design. In collaboration with Ronald J. Angel, Linda M. Burton, P. Lindsay Chase-Lansdale, Andrew J. Cherlin, Robert A. Moffitt, and William Julius Wilson. http://web.jhu.edu/threecitystudy/images/overviewanddesign.pdf.

The New U.S. Immigrants: How Do They Affect Our Understanding of the African American Experience?

By
FRANK D. BEAN,
CYNTHIA FELICIANO,
JENNIFER LEE,
and
JENNIFER VAN HOOK

Because Moynihan's 1965 report (in)famously emphasized the need to change black family culture to ameliorate black poverty, his work holds relevance for understanding factors affecting color lines. The implications of recent immigration for U.S. race relations depend on family cultural orientations among Mexican Americans, as well as on how Anglos culturally perceive this group. Mexican-origin family behaviors are often reified as either being unduly familistic or largely governed by culture of poverty tendencies. Here, we review research suggesting that neither of these is accurate, thus indicating that future Mexican-origin economic advancement is as likely to turn on the availability of structural opportunities as on cultural factors. In-depth interviews with Anglos further suggest that Mexican-origin persons are culturally viewed with less prejudice and discrimination than blacks, which implies that the integration of Mexican-origin persons into American society (unlike that of blacks) is progressing at a steady if not rapid pace.

Keywords: welfare; employment; poverty; family structure; immigration; culture; color line

Oscar Handlin (1951/1973, 1959) powerfully argued that much of U.S. history could be written in terms of immigration. To a considerable extent, this meant recognizing that the country had assertively sought settlers from northern Europe, initially to populate its rural frontiers and then subsequently to labor in its expanding urban industries (Zolberg 2006). In turn, such an "open-door" approach fostered the integration of European newcomers, many of whom faced considerable national origin discrimination but were nonetheless implicitly treated upon arrival as apprentice citizens for whom subsequent formal citizenship was taken for granted (Motomura 2006). Today, memories of the national origin diversity of historical flows and their successful absorption appear to have faded, replaced for some by sharply etched impressions that contemporary immigration is generating racial divisiveness.

DOI: 10.1177/0002716208325256

Although earlier immigration was never as easy or positive for the country as Handlin claimed (see Gerstle 1999), the meaning of contemporary flows for the country's purpose and destiny looms more controversial than ever. While worries about labor market competition almost always play a role in the emergence of immigration anxiety, much of the intensity of negative feeling about immigrants seems to derive from fears that contemporary newcomers, because they are non-European, threaten national identity more than did early-twentieth-century immigrants (Reimers 1998; Huntington 2004).

Certainly the Hart-Celler Act of 1965, passed after a four-decade hiatus in immigration, modified the social logic of immigrant admissions through its abolition of national origin quotas. It thus led to both largely non-European entrants and profound changes in the racial and ethnic mix of post-1965 immigrant flows (Bean and Stevens 2003). As a result, by 2006, 38 million foreign-born persons were living in the United States, a number that exceeded the country's 34 million native-born African Americans (U.S. Census Bureau 2006). To be sure, in census data, a few of these are students or visitors, but the vast majority consists of immigrants; if we include children of the foreign-born in the total, the figure would be over 68 million, more than twice the number of native blacks. Moreover, about two-thirds of those arriving since 1965 come from Asian, African, or Latino countries (Office of Immigration Statistics 2007). Thus, about 42 million first- or second-generation nonwhite persons are now living in the country (i.e., nonwhite,

---

Frank D. Bean is chancellor's professor in the School of Social Sciences and director of the Center for Research on Immigration, Population and Public Policy at the University of California, Irvine. Prior to joining the UCI faculty, he served as Ashbel Smith Professor of Sociology and Public Affairs, director of the Population Research Center, and chair of the Department of Sociology at the University of Texas at Austin. He was also the founding director of both the Program for Research on Immigration Policy and the Population Studies Center at the Urban Institute in Washington, D.C. He is the coauthor (with Gillian Stevens) of America's Newcomers and the Dynamics of Diversity *(Russell Sage Foundation 2003).*

Cynthia Feliciano is assistant professor of sociology and Chicano/Latino studies and a faculty research associate of the Center for Research on Immigration, Population and Public Policy at the University of California, Irvine. A specialist in immigration (especially the second generation) and race/ethnicity, she is currently conducting research on ethnic and gender differences in educational outcomes among minority children and on racial exclusion in dating as an indicator of the incorporation of new immigrant groups.

Jennifer Lee is an associate professor of sociology and a faculty research associate of the Center for Research on Immigration, Population and Public Policy at the University of California, Irvine. She is author of Civility in the City: Blacks, Jews, and Koreans in Urban America *(Harvard University Press 2002) and coeditor of* Asian American Youth: Culture, Identity, and Ethnicity *(Routledge 2004). She is currently working on a book with Frank D. Bean about the way that immigration, interracial marriage, and multiraciality is changing the meaning of race/ethnicity in the United States.*

Jennifer Van Hook is an associate professor of sociology and demography and a faculty associate of the Population Research Institute at the Pennsylvania State University. Her current research focuses on immigration and the family, immigrant children and health, and the estimation of the volume and flows of immigration to the United States.

nonblack, foreign-born persons and their children) (U.S. Census Bureau 2006). Immigration trends since 1966 have clearly resulted in a recent nonwhite minority that is larger than the native black minority.

As the country moves now nearly a decade past the millennium, what do these trends mean for racial/ethnic relations in the United States? What do they imply about the possibility of ameliorating the economic hardship faced by native blacks and outlined in the Moynihan Report?[1] At a minimum, they raise questions about whether W. E. B. Du Bois's hundred-year-old prophecy that the black-white color line would constitute *the* problem of the twentieth century still retains relevance in the twenty-first century. Given the large numbers of non-white but also nonblack immigrants who have come to the country over the past four decades, it becomes important to ask what kind of color line now exists in the United States (Lee and Bean 2007). Is it a variation of the traditional black-white divide, with a line now emerging that separates whites from nonwhites and looms ever more significant as immigration adds more nonwhites to the population? Or has the old divide largely faded away altogether as a result of Jim Crow and discriminatory federal laws having been eliminated? As Brown et al. (2003) note, such a view often seems to underlay the perspectives of those who advocate "color-blind" public social policies. Or is some entirely new structural divide emerging, one that perhaps involves multiple lines separating whites, blacks, and other nonwhites; or maybe one separating blacks from nonblacks? This article argues that yesterday's color line has been transformed into a black/nonblack demarcation that undergirds racial/ethnic divisions, not a more complex tripartite structure. In this new bipolar pattern, many if not all new nonwhite immigrants seem now to fall on the white rather than the black side of the line.

What difference do such boundaries make? How do the kinds of racial/ethnic divides currently holding sway in America and reflecting the nature and availability of economic opportunities matter for the Moynihan Report's forty-year-old analysis of the black family, a study that coincidentally was released the same year the new immigration spawned by Hart-Celler began? We argue here that they matter a great deal. The Moynihan Report brilliantly highlighted the devastating economic disadvantages faced by African American males in the United States. It also insightfully portrayed the tangle of structural inequalities contributing to the development of such outcomes (U.S. Department of Labor 1965). However, the power of its analysis was compromised by its further assertions that black matriarchal family patterns both reflected and perpetuated instability and dysfunctionality in the black family (Rainwater and Yancey 1967).

This conclusion generated a firestorm of protest from observers who feared such arguments fell perilously close to "blaming the victim" and embraced a culture-of-poverty thesis (Jencks 1965), which in fact they did. By focusing on the problems of the black family as the major factor limiting black economic integration, Moynihan's depiction of the legacy of slavery targeted only part of the cultural problem. Another important part of the cultural legacy of slavery manifested itself less in the survival strategies of blacks than in the persistence of attitudes and stereotypes held by whites about blacks, cultural orientations that countless analysts thought would fade away once legal discrimination was curtailed (Glazer 1997). While the basic motif of the Moynihan Report did not gainsay this possibility, its formula for finding a locus for change falsely attributed to the black family a causal significance that actually more nearly lay in lingering white cultural value orientations and institutions. In short, its remedy was to treat the symptom, not the disease.

Today's racial/ethnic boundaries matter because they shed light on the degree to which deeply embedded and ingrained cultural orientations operate with similar force for native blacks and new nonwhite immigrants. To the extent that racial discrimination against blacks continues today as in the past (at least in its effects if not its form), and to the degree that parallel kinds of discrimination similarly adversely affect nonwhite immigrants and their children, then the millions of additional nonwhites who have recently come to the country, by enlarging the nation's nonwhite minority group, might contribute to a worsening of racial/ethnic relations, exacerbating the harsh realities often referenced in statements that "two Americas" exist, one largely minority and poor and one more white and well-off.

Stated differently, if the recent experiences of nonwhite immigrants were found to be substantially more like those of blacks than earlier European immigrants, nonwhite immigration could be expanding the kind of social devastation and divisiveness that Moynihan so cogently chronicled more than four decades ago. What is centrally at issue for today's color lines is thus the degree to which the disadvantages faced by blacks and nonwhites derive from similar discriminatory legacies. What does the experience of the new immigrants, particularly the experience of contemporary Mexican immigrants who are especially disadvantaged in terms of education and who often enter the country with the additional handicap of unauthorized status, suggest about the degree of discrimination they face compared to blacks?

Such questions are never easy to answer. For one thing, it is difficult, indeed perhaps impossible, to disentangle cultural from structural forces, if for no other reason than change in one often leads to change in the other. That is, they are endogenous. Given this, it often seems both necessary and sensible to begin either scholarly analyses or policy interventions with a focus on only one or the other. But however necessary this may be, it carries the unfortunate consequence of promoting political debate and partisanship over the preferred starting point, with those on the left favoring beginning with structural solutions and those on the right supporting culturally oriented interventions. It thus induces analysts to overlook the inherent contingency of structural and cultural factors, which do not merely intersect in their influence, but rather *depend* on each other. This means both must occur for policy interventions to have much chance of success. Thus, generating employment opportunities is likely to be most effective when training and education programs that improve cultural "tool kits" and knowledge repertoires are also instigated; to implement either strategy without the other risks failure.

Ironically, any possibility of combining structural and cultural policy ameliorations as a result of Moynihan's analyses became lost in the report's controversial political legacy. The potential policy impact of its brilliant structural analysis, which might have constituted a basis for addressing both kinds of factors, became overwhelmed by the controversy emanating from the report's cultural conclusions about the black family. Moynihan attributed the extreme labor market disadvantages faced at the time by black males to structural deprivation deriving from persistent and long-lasting cultural prejudice among whites rooted in the historical legacy of slavery and expressed in legal strictures discriminating against blacks. His focus on the origins of the associated difficulties faced by the black family was also similarly insightful. However, the report's implicitly derisive and patronizing characterization of the black family as involving the emergence of a matriarchal cultural form not in step with majority cultural norms about family life was off-target. Not surprisingly, this conclusion was quickly and rightly attacked by many observers as insulting to blacks, as indeed it was (e.g., Carper 1966). It was especially denigrating to black women, whose strong initiatives and efforts then (and now) constitute heroic examples of compensatory actions taken to enhance family survival in the face of societally imposed black male deprivation (Riessman 1966).

Ironically, this may have had the effect of reinforcing, if not instigating, a "cultural turn" in social science and political discourse, a tendency to look only to the family as providing answers to problems of poverty and inequality. Thus, while the political left castigated Moynihan for emphasizing the liabilities of the black family, the political right welcomed his drawing attention to the importance of family responsibilities. But both the left and the right, each in its eagerness to criticize the other about how to conceptualize the family, lent implicit credence to the idea that cultural change alone, as represented in this instance by family form and functioning, was of primary importance. The report's emphasis on the black family, if not explicitly endorsing the idea that policy headway in ameliorating black disadvantage could best be achieved by focusing only on cultural factors that allegedly operate to perpetuate poverty (what is often termed a "culture-of-poverty perspective"), certainly lent impetus to that suggestion.

In the decades after the Moynihan Report was issued, a veritable flood of analysts and commentators seized upon and promulgated the idea that what was needed to address racial or ethnic disadvantage was for the poor, especially African Americans, to develop greater personal responsibility, something it was claimed could best (if not only) be inculcated by stable, conventional majority-group kinds of family relationships (Murray 1984; Sleeper 1997; Jacoby 1998; D'Souza 1995; Thernstrom and Thernstrom 1997). In such views, eliminating moral hazard and encouraging certain kinds of family forms and values was argued to matter more than changing structures or contexts to overcome social and economic inequalities.

It is against this backdrop that we seek to assess the kind and degree of racial/ethnic discrimination facing the new immigrant groups, especially Mexicans, and how it affects their own senses of racial/ethnic identity. Of all of the new nonwhite groups, Mexican immigrants and their descendants are most crucial for study, because of both increasing numbers of Mexican migrants and mounting concerns about unauthorized entrants (most of whom are Mexicans) (Bean and Lowell 2004). Mexicans, whether legal or unauthorized, are by far the largest of the recent immigrant groups. In 2005 alone, 161,445 persons from Mexico became "legal permanent residents" (14.4 percent of the total) (Office of Immigration Statistics 2005). That same year, 300,000 unauthorized Mexicans also established de facto residency, which brought the total number of unauthorized Mexicans to 6.2 million (or 56 percent of all unauthorized persons) (Passell 2006). These numbers dwarf those from any other country. The second largest number of legal entrants in 2005 came from India (84,681 persons, or 7.5 percent of all legal permanent residents), while the second largest number of unauthorized persons living in the country originated in Latin American countries other than Mexico (2.5 million, or 22 percent of the total unauthorized).

Observers at both ends of the political spectrum have often portrayed the American experiences of Mexican immigrants as closer to those of blacks than to those of earlier-arriving European immigrant groups. Some emphasize structural factors and some cultural ones. One cultural portrayal often argues that Mexicans exhibit unusually strong families because of their Mexican cultural heritage. This idea contradicts an idea other cultural observers have set forth, namely, that Mexicans share with blacks a cultural proclivity for welfare dependency. Such contradictory positions are impossible to reconcile in substantive terms, which suggests that one or both may be wrong. Whatever the case, both share a similar claim that personal responsibility and "self-help" as nurtured by strong family values are key factors in overcoming poverty. Both also imply these are lacking in the case of blacks, the former by asserting that Mexican immigrants culturally embrace stronger families, something that sets them apart from blacks, and the latter by arguing that Mexican immigrants become like African Americans in their development of cultural dependencies on welfare.

Below, we argue that each of these perspectives is inaccurate in the case of Mexican immigrants. We focus, first, on the question of the degree to which Latinos in general and Mexican Americans in particular are actually substantially more familistic in cultural orientation than other groups; second, on the degree to which Mexican immigrants come to embrace cultural leanings that incline them toward welfare dependency. Third, given the conclusions of the first two endeavors, we ask what nonwhite racial identifications, both as self- and other-perceptions, mean for emerging color lines in the United States, especially in the case of the new immigrants. Finally, we discuss what such color lines mean for African Americans.

Familistic Culture among Mexican Immigrants?

The importance of the nature and value of the family among Latinos in the United States is not a new question. Scholars and pundits have long debated whether U.S. Latinos, in general, and the Mexican-origin population, in particular, exhibit a greater emphasis on family than do other racial or ethnic groups (Lewis 1959, 1961, 1965; Valenzuela and Dornbusch 1994; Vega 1995). If, in fact, the family does carry more importance among Latinos, then further questions are raised about whether such emphasis exerts primarily salutary or debilitating influences on other aspects of Latino life. In short, are Latino families stronger and more supportive than other families, especially Anglo families?

This is not a trivial question. Latinos overall, and Mexicans in particular, continue to lag well behind the general population in education and earnings, despite indications of considerable Latino upward economic mobility over the past thirty years, especially in the case of native-born Latinos (Grogger and Trejo 2002; Bean et al. 2001). Family values receive a lot of attention in the media and from politicians. For example, in the *New York Times*, David Brooks (2004) argued that escaping poverty is more a matter of culture than economic opportunity, more a result of embracing the right values (including family values) than of government programs that provide cash or support assistance. To what degree do cultural factors in fact account for variations in family patterns between Latinos and Anglos? By cultural factors, we mean those norms, values, and expectations that are customary and taken for granted.

The literature on Latino families has focused on a long-standing debate concerning the accuracy of the traditional family-oriented Latino/a stereotype. These stereotypes are pervasive in both popular culture and social science literature (Baca Zinn 1998; Vega 1990). The Mexican American family, which dominates the literature on Latino families, has often been depicted as an especially cohesive unit, one favoring collective over individual needs (Keefe 1980; Mirande 1977). Many scholars have described this as "familism," which is thought to be a key component of traditional Mexican culture that immigrants bring with them to the United States (Baca Zinn 1982/1983; Sena-Rivera 1979).

Despite the nearly universal assumption of familism across many Latino groups, the empirical evidence supporting this view is actually quite limited. Ethnographic studies emphasizing the nature and strength of family cohesion in Mexican American families, for example, while quite rich in detail, cannot tell us whether such patterns are unique to Latinos, or whether similar findings would be found among, say, African American or non-Latino white families. Most population-based studies on extended family living arrangements, for example, merely infer the independent significance of culture in explaining family patterns, rather than provide direct evidence of it. Thus, Tienda and Angel (1982) assume the differences in extended family arrangements that remain after controlling for economic and social factors are evidence of cultural preferences. Likewise, Kamo (2000, 223) concludes that "upward extension often results from cultural prescription of familism among . . . Hispanics" and that those living in ethnic neighborhoods are more likely to live in extended family households.

Overall, however, the social science literature has recognized that family patterns must be understood as responses to economic circumstances and social structural positions that are related to racial, ethnic, class, and gender inequalities (Baca Zinn and Wells 2003). The results of recent research call into question long-standing beliefs about the cultural determinants of marriage patterns and family living arrangements. While high marriage rates among Mexican Americans are often assumed to reflect strong familistic orientations, for example, recent perspectives point out the economic and situational foundations of marriage. Thus, marrying or remaining married may not necessarily reflect the influence of family values but instead be an adaptation to difficult social and economic circumstances.

The finding that the marriages of Mexican immigrants, who are of lower socioeconomic status compared with later generations, are not only less likely to end in divorce or separation than those of later generations, but also of those Mexicans living in Mexico, supports this view (Bean, Berg, and Van Hook 1996). Thus, Bean, Berg, and Van Hook (1996, 612) conclude, "The greater marital stability often observed among Mexican Americans, rather than reflecting a general cultural value characteristic of the entire ethnic group, owes much of its existence to the social, structural, and economic situations of immigrants, especially lower-education immigrants." In other words, the fact that divorce rates among Mexican immigrants are lower than those for Mexicans in Mexico implies that exigencies associated with immigration itself rather than familistic cultural emphases explain greater marital stability among first-generation compared to later-generation Mexican-origin persons, a result also found by Van Hook and Glick (2007) in their examination of Mexican-origin household living arrangements.

The Culture of Poverty and Immigrant Welfare Receipt

What does social science research reveal about the degree to which culture-of-poverty factors cause immigrants to display different welfare patterns than natives? Many observers and policy makers, arguing that indeed the very existence of relatively universal public assistance acts as a "magnet" to draw newcomers to the country (Borjas 2003), appear in general to assume that immigrants are similar to poor natives in tendencies to exploit the availability of welfare. Thus, policies providing welfare to immigrants have been viewed not only as discouraging hard work and individual responsibility (e.g., Murray 1984), but also as encouraging the immigration of persons seeking handouts rather than employment opportunities (Borjas 2001; Brimelow 1995).

Such cultural orientations among immigrants are thought to be reinforced after immigrants arrive in the United States, particularly when they reside in areas with high concentrations of poverty (Auletta 1982). Such circumstances are seen as encouraging the learning and adoption of welfare participation as an acceptable way of life. Whether such orientations are thought to result primarily from severe long-term economic disadvantage (Auletta 1982), or from the loss of central-city jobs and lack of geographic mobility (Wilson 1987, 1996; Wilson and Neckerman 1986) associated with residence in inner-city neighborhoods, this view sees cultural orientations fostering welfare usage and dependency as acquired and reinforced by isolation from other more advantaged members of society and by the often geographic concentration of persons with such orientations in the same areas.

Hence, a culture-of-poverty theory envisions welfare as linked to learned values whose influence works all the more strongly in areas where persons with similar orientations are concentrated (Bane and Ellwood 1994). Much social science research, however, suggests an alternative to this view, often noting that the successful integration of immigrants is fostered by supportive social contexts providing opportunities for upward mobility and economic integration (Bloemraad 2006; Reitz 2003; Hechter 1971). For example, recent studies find that the probability of naturalization is higher in those states with more favorable and welcoming attitudes toward immigrants than in less receptive states, all else equal (Van Hook, Brown, and Bean 2006). Such results suggest an additional welfare dynamic beyond one involving "moral hazard" or the culture of poverty.

Among many poor immigrants, especially those whose primary reason for coming to the country is to find employment, the provision of assistance, in whatever form, may rather constitute temporary de facto settlement aid. Such assistance helps to foster immigrant economic integration, particularly in the case of the large group of poorly educated Mexican labor migrants coming to the United States over the past three decades (Bean and Stevens 2003). Notably, the United States has not traditionally provided settlement assistance to immigrants except in the case of refugees; persons who enter as refugees subsequently experience greater earnings growth than other kinds of immigrants (Cortes 2004). This suggests that forms of "backdoor" help like cash and noncash public assistance may provide "bridge" support to newcomers to facilitate their transition from time of arrival to subsequent labor market attachment, or from episodes of joblessness to periods of gainful employment, especially to the degree that immigrants differ from poor natives in fundamental orientations toward employment.

An alternative sociocultural perspective, however, emerges from the idea that immigrants arrive in the United States strongly expecting to work and thus are less welfare-prone than natives. This viewpoint draws upon social psychological expectancy theory (Atkinson 1964; Fishbein and Ajzen 1975), which suggests that orientations and expectations about success in the labor market influence welfare recipiency and the duration of welfare spells (Bane and Ellwood 1994). People who "expect" they can get and keep work because they think they can do so (for whatever reason) would be hypothesized to be less likely to participate in welfare programs. Conversely, people without the confidence that they can control work-related outcomes would be more likely to become discouraged and less likely to go off welfare.

As applied to immigrants, the idea would be that the acquisition of certain behaviors (i.e., welfare recipiency versus employment) would have less to do with learning to accept dependency than with immigrants' viewing their work prospects in the United States in positive or negative terms. When maladaptive behaviors occur, they are thought most likely to emerge among those for whom there is a lack of sufficient perceived or real economic opportunity (Fernández-Kelly and Schauffler 1996, 31). The prediction of a cultural work expectancy model is that immigrant women are less likely to receive welfare, all else equal, a view that accords more with the findings of prior research than does a culture-of-poverty hypothesis (Bean, Stevens, and Van Hook 2003).

Van Hook and Bean (2008) have carried out new analyses to evaluate these characterizations of immigrant public assistance recipiency using Survey of Income and Program Participation (SIPP) data. Their results indicate, first, no evidence in support of the culture-of-poverty perspective. Immigrant welfare recipiency, retention levels tend to be concentrated only among newly arrived immigrants, and for the 1.5 generation, they are not significantly different from those of natives. Welfare receipt thus does not appear to have become a permanent way of life for most immigrants. Second, while prior research has shown that immigrants tend to settle in higher-benefit states, thus appearing to buttress the view that welfare acts as a magnet for immigrants, Van Hook and Bean (2008) also note that Mexican immigrants are actually no more likely the receive welfare themselves than others in such states, thus calling into question the "magnet" hypothesis.

These results are thus consistent with the predictions of cultural expectancy perspective and support the ideas that an unusually strong work ethic characterizes Mexican immigrants and that Mexicans' reasons for using welfare are different and more temporary than those that typically lead natives to welfare. For example, accounts of working-poor natives characterize welfare recipients and former welfare recipients as sometimes fearful of leaving their neighborhoods to search for work or seek out new experiences. Shipler (2004, 125) writes, "They did not want to leave their compounds. The outside culture, with alien rules and fearsome challenges, seemed so daunting that residents preferred work inside the projects." Furthermore, welfare recipients and former recipients often lack the "soft skills" necessary to obtain and keep a job, such as "punctuality, diligence, and a can-do attitude." Immigrants, on the other hand, especially female labor migrants, are selected for precisely the opposite characteristics (Bean and Stevens 2003). Their reasons for seeking welfare are undoubtedly different. They may go on public assistance simply because, as newcomers, they are unfamiliar with the labor market, do not possess well-developed nonfamilial social networks, and have less control over or ability to alter their circumstances in the United States. Unlike many of the reasons natives go on welfare, such reasons may fade with time, as would such labor migrants' need for assistance.

The Transformation of America's Color Lines

The above suggests Mexican immigrants do not embrace the familistic or culture-of-poverty cultural orientations that are so often attributed to them. Rather, research on welfare receipt shows patterns that are consistent with the notion that a very strong work ethic drives much of their behavior. But this might not mean that other cultural forms of discrimination against today's Mexican immigrants are less severe than they are against blacks. As noted above, today's immigrant newcomers have transformed a largely black-white society at the end

of World War II to one now consisting of multiple racial and new nonwhite ethnic groups (Alba and Nee 2003, Bean and Stevens 2003, Sears et al. 2003).
Moreover, America's Latino and Asian populations are continuing to expand, and
according to National Research Council projections, by the year 2050, they are
likely to constitute about 25 and 8 percent of the U.S. population, respectively
(Smith and Edmonston 1997).

Other changes are also augmenting the racial/ethnic diversity of the United
States, most notably the rise in intermarriage and the growth of the multiracial
population. Intermarriage rose more than twentyfold over a forty-year period,
from 150,000 marriages in 1960 to 3.1 million in 2000 (Jacoby 2001; Lee and
Edmonston 2005). Today, about 13 percent of American married couples involve
partners of different races, a significant increase that cannot be attributed to population growth alone (Bean and Stevens 2003). The upswing in interracial
marriage is responsible in large part for a growing multiracial population, which
became highly visible when the 2000 Census allowed Americans for the first time
to mark more than one race to identify themselves. Currently, one in forty
Americans identifies himself or herself as multiracial, and by the year 2050, this
ratio could soar to one in five (Farley 2001; Smith and Edmonston 1997).

Each of these phenomena—the new nonwhite racial/ethnic diversity occurring
through immigration, the rise in intermarriage, and the growing multiracial population—suggests that the traditional black-white color line could be losing
salience and that new divides might be emerging. Lee and Bean (2008) have conducted research seeking to provide a sense of the nature of America's new color
lines through the examination of both nationally representative census data and
in-depth qualitative interviews with multiracial Americans, focusing specifically on
Asians, Mexicans, and blacks. Information on the prevalence of and feelings about
multiracial identification reflects the meaning of race in American society and perceptions about the permeability and rigidity of racial/ethnic boundaries. Such data
also signal where group boundaries are fading most rapidly and where they continue to endure. As Gans (1999a, 1999b) argues, multiracial identification reflects
the diminishing significance of the current racial scheme, which he predicts will
become increasingly less relevant in each generation until it disappears into obscu-
rity. Multiracial identification thus provides an important analytical lens through
which to gauge the strength, placement, and shifts of America's color lines.

America's multiracial population: Census data

The 2000 Census for the first time allowed Americans to mark "one or more"
races to indicate their racial identification. This is a landmark change in the way
the census measures race, first because it acknowledges the reality of racial mixing. However, it also reflects the view that race no longer requires an official
construction as an absolutely bounded, mutually exclusive set of categories—a
momentous shift considering that the United States had historically been hostile
to racial mixture as evidenced by the legal invocation of the "one-drop" rule of

hypodescent constraining the racial identity options for multiracial blacks (Dalmage 2004; Davis 1991; Farley 2002; Haney-Lopez 1996; Hirschman, Alba, and Farley 2000; Hollinger 2003; Morning 2000; Nobles 2000; Waters 1990, 2000; Williams 2006). While only about 2.4 percent of the population identified itself as multiracial, a recent National Academy of Sciences study reported that, given trends in intermarriage, the multiracial population could increase to 21 percent of the population by 2050, when as many as 35 percent of Asians and 45 percent of Hispanics might have multiracial backgrounds (Smith and Edmonston 1997).

America's multiracial population is clustered in the western region of the United States, with nearly two-thirds residing in just ten states. In California, 1.6 million people identified multiracially, accounting for 4.7 percent of its population, or one in every twenty-one Californians. To help put this figure into perspective, the number of multiracial births already exceeds the number of black and Asian births in the state (Tafoya, Johnson, and Hill 2005). A key sign of a growing multiracial population is its youthfulness. Among Americans who identified multiracially, 42 percent were under the age of eighteen, compared to 25 percent of other Americans. Thus, the multiracial population is almost twice as likely to be under the age of eighteen. In California, 7.3 percent of those under the age of eighteen identified multiracially, which translates into one in every fourteen young Californians. The greater proportion of young multiracials is, in part, a product of the increase in interracial unions, especially among the young, native-born Asians and Latinos.

Wide variations in rates of multiracial reporting also occur across groups. Twelve percent of Asians and 16 percent of Latinos identified multiracially in 2000, yet only 4 percent of the black population did.[2] The black rate of multiracial reporting was much lower compared to other groups, even after controlling for differences in age, education, nativity, gender, and region of the United States (Tafoya, Johnson, and Hill 2005). Moreover, while the Census Bureau estimates that at least three-quarters of blacks in the United States are ancestrally multiracial, just over 4 percent choose to identify as such, indicating that most black Americans do not depend strictly on their genealogy to identify themselves, but instead rely on the social construction of racial boundaries. However, that the rate of multiracial reporting is much higher among Asians and Latinos suggests that the historical absence of a constraining "one-drop" rule for these groups may provide more leeway in exercising discretion in the selection of racial/ethnic identities (Harris and Sim 2002; Xie and Goyette 1997).

Qualitative interviews with multiracial adults

Lee and Bean (2008) conducted in-depth interviews with adult multiracial respondents. The resulting qualitative data revealed that multiracial-background blacks are substantially less likely to identify themselves in multiracial terms compared with Asians and Latinos, in large part because of outsiders' ascriptions, which powerfully influence the choice of identity. Sociologists have noted that racial/ethnic identity is a dialectical process—one that involves both internal and external opinions and processes (Nagel 1994; Rodríguez and Cordero-Guzman

1992; Waters 1990, 1999). Researchers have also shown that outsiders' ascription most powerfully constrains the racial/ethnic options for blacks. While African Americans themselves make distinctions based on ethnicity, class, nativity, and skin tone, the power of race—and blackness in particular—often overrides these internal differences when interacting with the public (Kasinitz 1992; Waters 1999). Lee and Bean also asked the multiracial respondents about how they felt about their backgrounds, focusing specifically on the meaning and content that multiracial identification holds for them. They found that for most Asian-white and Latino-white multiracials, ethnic identities were more symbolic than instrumental. While none denied the racial/ethnic mixture of their background, most felt that race held little consequence in their daily lives.

[M]ultiracial-background blacks are substantially less likely to identify themselves in multiracial terms compared with Asians and Latinos, in large part because of outsiders' ascriptions, which powerfully influence the choice of identity.

For the Asian-white and Latino-white multiracial respondents, claiming a white racial identity did not preclude them from also claiming an Asian or Latino ethnicity; they thought they could be white, yet also be Asian Indian, Japanese, Hispanic, or Mexican, signifying that Asian and Latino ethnicities are adopting the symbolic character of European ethnicity prevalent among white Americans. By contrast, black multiracial respondents were unable to do the same; they could not claim a white or nonblack racial identity and see such identities as accepted by others, signaling that blackness remains a relatively fixed racialized category.

The experiences of Asian-white and Latino-white multiracials thus differ starkly from those of black multiracials. Not only were Latinos and Asians more likely to report multiracial identifications, but they were more likely to describe their Asian and Latino identities as voluntary and optional rather than ascribed and instrumental, suggesting that the Asian and Latino identities reflect the symbolic character of white ethnicity. These results suggest that group boundaries are fading more rapidly for Latinos (including Mexicans) and Asians than for blacks, signaling that today's new nonwhites are *not* strongly assimilating into U.S. society as racialized minorities who see their experiences with race as akin to those of blacks, as would be predicted by the possibility of a white-nonwhite model.

Likewise, the assimilation of America's nonwhite newcomers does not seem to be following a triracial model, in which Latinos and other new immigrants are grouped into a separate category and labeled as "racial others." Instead, the lived experiences of multiracial Latinos and Asians seem to place them closer to whites than to blacks. Racial affiliations and ethnic identities are much less matters of choice for multiracial blacks, suggesting that the designation "black" remains a significant racial category. The lower rate of black multiracial reporting and the racial constraints that many multiracial blacks experience suggest that blackness continues to constitute a fundamental racial construction in American society. Hence, it is not simply that race matters but, more specifically, that *black* race matters, a result consistent with an African American exceptionalism thesis.

Conclusion and Discussion

A black-nonblack divide appears to be taking shape in the United States, in which Asians and Latinos are closer to whites than are blacks to whites (Gans 1999a, 1999b, 2005; Glazer 1997; Lee and Bean 2007; Quillian and Campbell 2003; Sears 2003; Sears et al. 2003; Waters 1999; Yancey 2003). Hence, America's color lines are moving toward a new demarcation that places many blacks in a position of disadvantage similar to that resulting from the traditional black-white divide. In essence, rather than erasing racial boundaries, the country is simply reinventing a color line that continues to separate blacks from other racial/ethnic groups. Thus, a black-nonblack divide appears to depict the color line at the moment. It is important to recall, however, that whiteness as a category has expanded over time to incorporate new immigrant groups in the past, and it may stretch yet again to include new groups (Gallagher 2004; Gerstle 1999; Warren and Twine 1997). Based on the patterns of multiracial identification noted above, Asians and Latinos may be moving closer and closer to a "white" category, with multiracial Asian-whites and Latino-whites standing at the head of the queue. This could indicate the reemergence of a black-white color line. However, regardless of whether a divide were to fall along black-nonblack or black-white lines, the position of blacks could remain severely disadvantaged.

New nonwhite immigration could thus be causing Moynihan's warnings about black disadvantage to be overlooked once again, this time not for reasons of political controversy, but rather because of false optimism. If the new nonwhite immigrants fall along a color line that more strongly separates nonblacks from blacks than one that divides whites from nonwhites, it could invite misinterpretation about progress in black-white relations in the United States. Because boundaries are loosening for some nonwhite groups, this could lead to the erroneous conclusion that race is declining in significance for all groups, with some observers arguing that race relations are improving at the same pace for all racial/ethnic minorities.

In essence, rather than erasing racial boundaries, the country is simply reinventing a color line that continues to separate blacks from other racial/ethnic groups.

The results noted above suggest that the social construction of race continues to be more consequential for blacks than for Asians and Latinos. Not accounting for this difference could easily lead to the endorsement of a flawed logic that if race does not substantially impede the incorporation of Asians and Latinos, then perhaps it no longer matters much for blacks either. Not only is this line of reasoning incorrect, but it also risks fostering support for so-called "color-blind" policies that fail to recognize that race and the color line have different consequences for different minority groups (Brown et al. 2003; Loury 2002).

Moreover, a logic of presumed "color-blindness" fails to consider that boundary maintenance and change are two-sided processes that involve both choice and—perhaps more important—constraint (Alba 1999; Bobo 1997; Lamont 2000). This means not only that members of racial/ethnic minority groups have to pursue entry and incorporation into social contexts occupied by the majority group, but also that members of the majority group must be willing to accept their admission. Both motivation and opportunity, both culture and structure, are important in these matters.

Based on patterns of multiracial reporting, it appears that Asians and Latinos are simultaneously more actively pursuing entry into the majority group and that whites are more willing to accept their entry compared to that of blacks. At this time, the boundaries for Asians and Latinos appear more elastic than they seem for blacks, consequently reinforcing the racial stigma attached to blackness (Loury 2002). The fact that boundary dissolution is neither uniform nor unconditional indicates that the United States cannot be complacent about the degree to which opportunities are improving for all racial/ethnic groups, particularly when a deep and persistent divide continues to separate blacks from all other groups.

Notes

1. The report is printed in Rainwater and Yancey (1967) and is available online at http://www.dol.gov/oasam/programs/history/webid-meynihan.htm.

2. We should note that "Latino" or "Hispanic" was not considered a racial category in the 2000 Census. The census form mandated two distinct questions regarding a person's racial/ethnic background: one about race and a second about whether a person was "Spanish/Hispanic/Latino." Someone who self-designated as "Spanish/Hispanic/Latino" could thus report any race. In the 2000 Census, 42 percent of Latinos chose

"Other" as their racial category, and in both the 1990 and 2000 Censuses, 97 percent of those who marked "Other" as their race were Latinos (Anderson and Fienberg 1999; Grieco and Cassidy 2001; Rodríguez and Cordero-Guzman 1992; U.S. Census Bureau 2001). While the census does not treat those of "Spanish/Hispanic/Latino" as a distinct racial category, we treat them as such here for two reasons. First, many Latinos see themselves as belonging in a separate category, as indicated by the fact that so many identify as "Other" race in the census. That is, they feel that the racial categories presented do not fit them well (Rodríguez 2000). Second, Latinos have been legally treated as a separate group and often as a racial minority group that qualifies for and benefits from federal programs designed to assist disadvantaged minorities, such as affirmative action programs. Latinos have also been protected by civil rights legislation and the Voting Rights Act, both of which are aimed to help racial minorities (Glazer 1997; Skrentny 2002). Hence, not only do Latinos see themselves as belonging to a separate category, but they are also often treated if they were a distinct racial category by the U.S. government.

References

Alba, Richard. 1999. Immigration and the American realities of assimilation and multiculturalism. *Sociological Forum* 14 (1): 3-25.

Alba, Richard, and Victor Nee. 2003. *Remaking the American mainstream: Assimilation and contemporary immigration*. Cambridge, MA: Harvard University Press.

Anderson, Margo J., and S. E. Fienberg. 1999. *Who counts? The politics of census-taking in contemporary America*. New York: Russell Sage Foundation.

Atkinson, John W. 1964. *An introduction to motivation*. Princeton, NJ: D. Van Nostrand.

Auletta, K. 1982. *The underclass*. New York: Random House.

Baca Zinn, Maxine. 1982/1983. Familism among Chicanos: A theoretical review. *Humboldt Journal of Social Relations* 10:224-38.

———. 1998. Race and the family values debate. In *Challenges for work and family in the twenty-first century*, ed. D. Vannoy and P. J. Dubeck. New York: Aldine de Gruyter.

Baca Zinn, Maxine, and Barbara Wells. 2003. Diversity within Latino families: New lessons for family social science. In *Family in transition*, ed. A. S. Skolnick and J. H. Skolnick, 389-415. Boston: Pearson Education.

Bane, Mary Jo, and David T. Ellwood. 1994. *Welfare realities: From rhetoric to reform*. Cambridge, MA: Harvard University Press.

Bean, Frank D., Ruth R. Berg, and Jennifer V. W. Van Hook. 1996. Socioeconomic and cultural incorporation and marital disruption among Mexican Americans. *Social Forces* 75:593-617.

Bean, Frank D., and B. Lindsay Lowell. 2004. NAFTA and Mexican migration to the United States. In *NAFTA'S impact on North America: The first decade*, ed. S. Weintraub, 263-84. Washington, DC: Center for Strategic and international Studies.

Bean, Frank D., and Gillian Stevens, eds. 2003. *America's newcomers and the dynamics of diversity*. New York: Russell Sage Foundation.

Bean, Frank D., Gillian Stevens, and Jennifer Van Hook. 2003. Immigrant welfare receipt: Implications for policy. In *America's newcomers and the dynamics of diversity*, ed. F. D. Bean and G. Stevens, 66-93. New York: Russell Sage Foundation.

Bean, Frank D., Stephen J. Trejo, Randy Capps, and Michael Tyler. 2001. *The Latino middle class: Myth, reality and potential*. Claremont, CA: Tomas Rivera Policy Institute.

Bloemraad, Irene. 2006. *Becoming a citizen: Incorporating immigrants and refugees in the United States and Canada*. Berkeley: University of California Press.

Bobo, Lawrence. 1997. The color line, the dilemma, and the dream: Race relations in America at the close of the twentieth century. In *Civil rights and social wrongs: Black-white relations since World War II*, ed. J. Higham, 31-55. University Park: Pennsylvania State University Press.

Borjas, George. 2001. Welfare reform and immigration. In *The new world of welfare*, ed. R. Blank and R. Haskins, 369-90. Washington, DC: Brookings Institution Press.

———. 2003. Welfare reform and immigrant participation in welfare programs. In *Host societies and the reception of immigrants*, ed. J. G. Reitz, 289-325. La Jolla: Center for Comparative Immigration Studies University of California, San Diego.

Brimelow, Peter. 1995. *Alien nation: Common sense about America's immigration disaster*. New York: Random House.

Brooks, David. 2004. More than money. *New York Times*, March 2, p. 23.

Brown, Michael K., Martin Carnoy, Elliott Currie, Troy Duster, David B. Oppenheimer, Marjorie M. Shultz, and David Wellman. 2003. *Whitewashing race: The myth of a color-blind society*. Berkeley: University of California Press.

Carper, Laura. 1966. The Negro family and the Moynihan Report. *Dissent*, March-April, pp. 266-67.

Cortes, Kalena E. 2004. Are refugees different from economic immigrants? Some empirical evidence on the heterogeneity of immigrant groups in the United States. *Review of Economics and Statistics* 86:465-80.

Dalmage, Heather M. 2004. *The politics of multiracialism*. Albany: State University of New York Press.

Davis, F. James. 1991. *Who is black? One nation's definition*. University Park: Pennsylvania State University Press.

D'Souza, Dinesh. 1995. *The end of racism: Principles for a multiracial society*. New York: Free Press.

Farley, Reynolds. 2001. *Identifying with multiple races: A social movement that succeeded but failed?* Ann Arbor: Population Studies Center, University of Michigan.

———. 2002. Racial identities in 2000: The response to the multiple-race response option. In *The new race question: How the census counts multiracial individuals*, ed. J. Perlmann and M. C. Waters, 33-61. New York: Russell Sage Foundation.

Fernández-Kelly, M. Patricia, and Richard Schauffler. 1996. Divided fates: Immigrant children and the new assimilation. In *The new second generation*, ed. A. Portes, 30-53. New York: Russell Sage Foundation.

Fishbein, Martin, and I. Ajzen. 1975. *Beliefs, attitudes, intentions and behaviour*. Reading, MA: Addison-Wesley.

Gallagher, Charles A. 2004. Racial redistricting: Expanding the boundaries of whiteness. In *The politics of multiracialism: Challenging racial thinking*, ed. H. M. Dalmage, 59-76. Albany: State University of New York Press.

Gans, Herbert J. 1999a. The possibility of a new racial hierarchy in the twenty-first century United States. In *The cultural territories of race: Black and white boundaries*, ed. M. Lamont, 371-90. Chicago and New York: University of Chicago Press and Russell Sage Foundation.

———. 1999b. Toward a reconciliation of assimilation and pluralism: The interplay of acculturation and ethnic retention. In *The handbook of international migration*, ed. C. Hirschman, J. DeWind, and P. Kasinitz, 161-71. New York: Russell Sage Foundation.

———. 2005. Race as a class. *Contexts* 4 (4): 17-21.

Gerstle, Gary. 1999. Liberty, coercion, and the making of Americans. In *The handbook of international migration*, ed. C. Hirschman, J. DeWind, and P. Kasinitz, 275-93. New York: Russell Sage Foundation.

Glazer, Nathan. 1997. *We are all multiculturalists now*. Cambridge, MA: Harvard University Press.

Grieco, Elizabeth M., and Rachel C. Cassidy. 2001. *Overview of race and Hispanic origin*. Washington, DC: Government Printing Office.

Grogger, Jeffrey, and Stephen Trejo. 2002. *Falling behind or moving up? The intergenerational progress of Mexican Americans*. San Francisco: Public Policy Institute of California.

Handlin, Oscar. 1951/1973. *The uprooted: The epic story of the great migrations that made the American people*. Boston: Little, Brown.

———. 1959. *Immigration as a factor in American history*. Englewood Cliffs, NJ: Prentice Hall.

Haney-Lopez, Ian. 1996. *White by law: The legal construction of race*. New York: New York University Press.

Harris, D. R., and J. J. Sim. 2002. Who is multiracial? Assessing the complexity of lived race. *American Sociological Review* 67:614-27.

Hechter, Michael. 1971. Towards a theory of ethnic change. *Politics and Society* 2:21-45.

Hirschman, Charles, Richard Alba, and Reynolds Farley. 2000. The meaning and measurement of race in the U.S. Census: Glimpses into the future. *Demography* 37:381-93.

Hollinger, D. A. 2003. Amalgamation and hypodescent: The question of ethnoracial mixture in the history of the United States. *American Historical Review* 108:1363-90.

Huntington, Samuel P. 2004. *Who are we? The challenges to America's national identity*. New York: Simon & Schuster.

Jacoby, Tamar. 1998. *Someone else's house: America's unfinished struggle for integration*. New York: Free Press.
———. 2001. An end to counting race? *Commentary* 111 (6): 37-40.
Jencks, Christopher. 1965. The Moynihan Report. *New York Review of Books*, October, pp. 216-18.
Kamo, Yoshinori. 2000. Racial and ethnic differences in extended family households. *Sociological Perspectives* 43:211-29.
Kasinitz, Philip. 1992. *Caribbean New York*. Ithaca, NY: Cornell University Press.
Keefe, Susan E. 1980. Acculturation and the extended family among urban Mexican Americans. In *Acculturation: Theory, models and some new findings*, ed. A. M. Padilla, 85-110. Boulder, CO: Westview.
Lamont, Michèle. 2000. *The dignity of working men*. Cambridge, MA, and New York: Harvard University Press and Russell Sage Foundation.
Lee, Jennifer, and Frank D. Bean. 2007. Reinventing the color line: Immigration and race/ethnicity in the United States. *Social Forces* 86 (2): 551-686.
———. 2008. Beyond black and white: Remaking race in America. In *The contexts reader*, ed. J. Goodwin and J. M. Jasper, 286-94. New York: Norton.
Lee, Sharon M., and Barry Edmonston. 2005. New marriages, new families: U.S. racial and hispanic intermarriage. *Population Bulletin* 60 (2): 1-36.
Lewis, Oscar. 1959. *Five families: Mexican case studies in the culture of poverty*. New York: Basic Books.
———. 1961. *The children of Sanchez: Autobiography of a Mexican family*. New York: Viking.
———. 1965. *La Vida: A Puerto Rican family in the culture of poverty—San Juan and New York*. New York: Vintage.
Loury, Glenn C. 2002. *The anatomy of racial inequality*. Cambridge, MA: Harvard University Press.
Mirande, Alfredo. 1977. Chicano family—Reanalysis of conflicting views. *Journal of Marriage and the Family* 39:747-56.
Morning, Ann. 2000. Counting on the color line. Paper presented at the annual meeting of the Population Association of America, Los Angeles.
Motomura, Hiroshi. 2006. *Americans in waiting: The lost story of immigration and citizenship in the United States*. New York: Oxford University Press.
Murray, Charles. 1984. *Losing ground: American social policy, 1950-1980*. New York: Basic Books.
Nagel, Joane. 1994. Constructing ethnicity: Creating and recreating ethnic identity and culture. *Social Problems* 41 (1): 152-76.
Nobles, Melissa. 2000. *Shades of citizenship: Race and the census in modern politics*. Stanford, CA: Stanford University Press.
Office of Immigration Statistics. 2005. *Statistical yearbook of immigration*. Washington, DC: U.S. Department of Homeland Security.
———. 2007. *2006 yearbook of immigration statistics*. Washington, DC: U.S. Department of Homeland Security.
Passell, Jeffrey S. 2006. *The size and characteristics of the unauthorized migrant population in the U.S.* Washington, DC: Pew Hispanic Center.
Quillian, Lincoln, and Mary Campbell. 2003. Beyond black and white. *American Sociological Review* 68:540-66.
Rainwater, Lee, and William L. Yancey. 1967. *The Moynihan Report and the politics of controversy*. Cambridge, MA: MIT Press.
Reimers, Cordelia W. 1998. Unskilled immigration and changes in the wage distributions of black, Mexican American, and non-Hispanic white male dropouts. In *Help or hindrance? The economic implications of immigration for African Americans*, ed. D. S. Hamermesh and F. D. Bean, 107-48. New York: Russell Sage Foundation.
Reitz, Jeffrey G. 2003. *Host societies and the reception of immigrants*. La Jolla: Center for Comparative Immigration Studies, University of California, San Diego.
Riessman, Frank. 1966. In defense of the Negro family. *Dissent*, March-April, pp. 266-67.
Rodríguez, Clara E. 2000. *Changing race: Latinos, the census, and the history of ethnicity in the United States*. New York: New York University Press.
Rodríguez, Clara E., and Hector Cordero-Guzman. 1992. Placing race in context. *Ethnic and Racial Studies* 15 (4): 523-42.
Sears, David O. 2003. Black-white conflict. In *New York & Los Angeles*, ed. D. Halle, 367-89. Chicago: University of Chicago Press.

Sears, David O., Mingying Fu, P. J. Henry, and Kerra Bui. 2003. The origins and persistence of ethnic identity among the "new immigrant" groups. Social Psychology Quarterly 66 (4) 419-37.

Sena-Rivera, Jaime. 1979. Extended kinship in the United States: Competing models and the case of La Familia Chicana. Journal of Marriage and the Family 41:121-29.

Shipler, David K. 2004. The working poor: Invisible in America. New York: Knopf.

Skrentny, John D. 2002. The minority rights revolution. Cambridge, MA: Harvard University Press.

Sleeper, Jim. 1997. Liberal racism. New York: Penguin.

Smith, James P., and Barry Edmonston. 1997. The new Americans: Economic, demographic, and fiscal effects of immigration. Washington, DC: National Academy Press.

Tafoya, Sonya M., Hans Johnson, and Laura E. Hill. 2005. Who chooses to choose two? In The American people: Census 2000, ed. R. Farley and J. Haaga, 332-51. New York: Russell Sage Foundation.

Thernstrom, Stephan, and Abigail Thernstrom. 1997. America in black and white: One nation, indivisible. New York: Simon & Schuster.

Tienda, Marta, and Ronald Angel. 1982. Headship and household composition among blacks, Hispanics, and other whites. Social Forces 61:508-31.

U.S. Census Bureau. 2001. United States Census 2000. Washington, DC: Government Printing Office.

———. 2006. Current Population Survey: Annual demographic files. Washington, DC: Government Printing Office.

U.S. Department of Labor. 1965. The Negro family: The case for national action. Washington, DC: U.S. Department of Labor, Office of Policy Planning and Research.

Valenzuela, Angela, and S. M. Dornbusch. 1994. Familism and social capital in the academic-achievement of Mexican origin and Anglo adolescents. Social Science Quarterly 75:18-36.

Van Hook, Jennifer, and Frank D. Bean. 2008. Explaining the distinctiveness of Mexican-immigrant welfare behaviors: The importance of employment-related cultural repertoires. Manuscript, Center for Research on Immigration, Population and Public Policy, University of California, Irvine.

Van Hook, Jennifer, Susan K. Brown, and Frank D. Bean. 2006. For love or money? Welfare reform and immigrant naturalization. Social Forces 85:643-66.

Van Hook, Jennifer, and Jennifer E. Glick. 2007. Immigration and living arrangements: Moving beyond economic need versus acculturation. Demography 44:225-49.

Vega, William A. 1990. Hispanic families in the 1980s—A decade of research. Journal of Marriage and the Family 52:1015-24.

———. 1995. The study of Latino families: A point of departure. In Understanding Latino families: Scholarship, policy, and practice, ed. R. E. Zambrana, 3-17. Thousand Oaks, CA: Sage.

Warren, Jonathan W., and France Winddance Twine. 1997. White Americans, the new minority? Journal of Black Studies 28:200-218.

Waters, Mary C. 1990. Ethnic options: Choosing identities in America. Berkeley: University of California Press.

———. 1999. Black identities: West Indian immigrant dreams and American realities. New York and Cambridge, MA: Russell Sage Foundation and Harvard University Press.

———. 2000. Multiple ethnicities and identity in the United States. In We are a people: Narrative and multiplicity in constructing identity, ed. P. Spikard and W. J. Burroughs, 23-40. Philadelphia: Temple University Press.

Williams, Kim. 2006. Mark one or more. Ann Arbor: University of Michigan Press.

Wilson, William Julius. 1987. The truly disadvantaged: The inner city, the underclass, and public policy. Chicago: University of Chicago.

———. 1996. When work disappears: The world of the new urban poor. New York: Knopf.

Wilson, William J., and Kathryn M Neckerman. 1986. Poverty and family structure: The widening gap between evidence and public policy issues. In Fighting poverty: What works and what doesn't, ed. S. Danziger and D. Weinberg. Cambridge, MA: Harvard University Press.

Xie, Yu, and Kimberly Goyette. 1997. The racial identification of biracial children with one Asian parent: Evidence from the 1990 Census. Social Forces 76:547-70.

Yancey, George. 2003. Who is white? Boulder, CO: Lynne Rienner.

Zolberg, Aristide R. 2006. A nation by design: Immigration policy in the fashioning of America. New York and Cambridge, MA: Russell Sage Foundation and Harvard University Press.

The Black Family and Mass Incarceration

By
BRUCE WESTERN
and
CHRISTOPHER WILDEMAN

Released in 1965, the Moynihan Report traced the severe social and economic distress of poor urban African Americans to high rates of single-parenthood. Against Moynihan's calls for social investment in poor inner-city communities, politics moved in a punitive direction, driving massive growth in the prison population. The authors document the emergence of mass incarceration and describe its significance for African American family life. The era of mass incarceration can be understood as a new stage in the history of American racial inequality. Because of its recent arrival, the social impact of mass incarceration remains poorly understood. The authors conclude by posing several key research questions that can illuminate the effects of dramatic growth in the American penal system.

Keywords: mass incarceration; family; inequality; Daniel Patrick Moynihan

Today, we read Daniel Patrick Moynihan's 1965 report, *The Negro Family: The Case For National Action*, with a sense of lost opportunity. The report drew attention to the problems of chronic idleness, addiction, and serious violence in minority urban neighborhoods of concentrated poverty. Moynihan traced these problems to the breakdown of the African American family. High

Bruce Western is a professor of sociology and director of the Multidisciplinary Program in Inequality and Social Policy, John F. Kennedy School of Government at Harvard University. His research interests include the sociology of crime and punishment, social stratification, and political sociology. His recent book Punishment and Inequality in America *(Russell Sage Foundation 2006) examines the impact of the growth of the penal system and its effects on economic inequality and U.S. race relations.*

Christopher Wildeman is a Robert Wood Johnson Foundation Health & Society Scholar at the Center for Social Epidemiology and Population Health at the University of Michigan. He is also a postdoctoral affiliate in the Population Studies Center at the University of Michigan. He received his PhD in sociology and demography from Princeton University in 2008.

NOTE: This research was supported by grants from the National Science Foundation, the Russell Sage Foundation, and a Guggenheim Fellowship.

DOI: 10.1177/0002716208324850

nonmartial birth rates, divorce and separation, and single-parenthood, in Moynihan's analysis, all contributed to ghetto poverty, crime, and other dislocations. Although Moynihan did not offer a detailed policy solution, he understood that the social problems of the urban poor stood in the way of the historic promise of full African American citizenship demanded by the civil rights movements.

Sounding the alarm over ghetto poverty in 1965, Moynihan named a social problem and suggested a direction for its solution. Viewed in hindsight, the report marked a fork in the road. Many of the social problems Moynihan identified have subsequently worsened. Joblessness among young, black, noncollege men climbed through the 1960s and 1970s. Crime rates and rates of single-parenthood also escalated. While Moynihan called for increased social investment to avert the problems of crime and poverty, public policy turned instead in a punitive direction, massively expanding the role of the criminal justice system. By the early 2000s, more than a third of young black noncollege men were incarcerated. Among black men younger than forty, there were nearly twice as many prison records as bachelor's degrees. The spectacular growth of the American penal system has transformed the institutional context of urban poverty in a way that was wholly unexpected by Moynihan or other students of social policy of his time.

Although family breakdown was not the immediate cause of the American prison boom, mass incarceration has had potentially profound effects on the family life of those caught in the web of the criminal justice system.

In this article, we describe the main contours of the American prison boom and its effect on the lives and structure of poor African American families. We argue that in the wake of the Moynihan Report, economic conditions among the ghetto poor continued to deteriorate. Instead of a movement for social investment in the urban poor that Moynihan supported, politics turned to the right. Political currents flowed to law and order and away from rehabilitative criminal justice policy. Retribution and incapacitation were embraced as the main objectives of criminal punishment. As a result, the prison population ballooned through the 1980s and 1990s, producing astonishing incarceration rates among young African American men. Although family breakdown was not the immediate cause of the American prison boom, mass incarceration has had potentially profound effects on the family life of those caught in the web of the criminal justice system. Research is still in its infancy, but we conclude by describing what we see as the most important questions linking mass incarceration to the family life of America's urban poor.

Political and Economic Roots of the Prison Boom

Mass imprisonment of the late 1990s can be traced to two basic shifts in politics and economics. The growth of harsh sentencing policies and a punitive approach to drug control began with a rightward shift in American politics, first visible at the national level in the mid-1960s. Barry Goldwater's ill-fated presidential run in 1964 was pivotal (Beckett 1997; Gest 2001). Goldwater, in accepting the Republican nomination, warned that crime and disorder were threats to human freedom, and freedom must be "balanced so that liberty lacking order will not become the license of the mob and of the jungle." The Republican campaign of 1964 linked the problem of street crime to civil rights protest and the growing unease among whites about racial violence.

Although Goldwater was roundly defeated by Lyndon B. Johnson, conservatives within the Republican Party had brought to the national stage a new kind of politics. Historically, responsibilities for crime control were divided mostly between state and local agencies. The Republicans had placed the issue of crime squarely on the national agenda. What is more, by treating civil rights protest as a strain of social disorder, veiled connections were drawn between the crime problem, on one hand, and black social protest, on the other.

The social problem of crime became a reality as rates of murder and other violent crimes escalated in the decade following the 1964 election. Throughout the 1960s, urban riots in Los Angeles, New York, Newark, Detroit, and dozens of other cities provided a socially ambiguous mixture of disorder and politics. Despite Goldwater's defeat, support grew for the new law and order message, particularly among southern whites and northern working-class voters of Irish, Italian, and German descent who turned away from the Democratic Party in the 1970s (Edsall and Edsall 1991).

Elevated crime rates and the realigned race relations of the post–civil rights period provided a receptive context for the law and order themes of the Republican Party. In state politics, Republican governors and legislators increased their representation through the South and West and placed themselves in the vanguard of the movements for mandatory minimum sentences, sentence enhancements for repeat offenders, and expanded prison capacity (Western 2006; Davey 1998; Jacobs and Carmichael 2001). Quantitative analyses show that incarceration rates grew fastest under Republican governors and state legislators (Western 2006, chap. 3).

Although Republicans were quick to promote prison expansion and tough new criminal sentences, Democrats also came to support punitive criminal justice policy. Perhaps the clearest signal that Democrats too were tough on crime was sent by President Clinton's Violent Crime Control and Law Enforcement Act (1994). The Clinton crime bill earmarked $9.9 billion for prison construction and added life terms for third-time federal felons (Windelsham 1998, 104-7). By the 1990s, Democrats and Republicans had come to support the sentencing policies and capital construction campaigns that grew the penal population.

Shifts in politics and policy, however, are only half the story. The newly punitive system of criminal sentencing would have had largely symbolic significance but for the ready supply of chronically idle young men that came to swell the nation's prisons and jails. Urban deindustrialization eroded the labor market for unskilled young men while punitive politics gained momentum in the 1970s and 1980s. Wilson's (1987) study of *The Truly Disadvantaged* provides the classic analysis. The decline of manufacturing industry employment in the Midwest and the Northeast coupled with the exodus of middle class and working-class blacks from inner cities produced pockets of severe unemployment in poor urban neighborhoods.

From 1969 to 1979, central cities recorded enormous declines in manufacturing and blue collar employment. New York, for example, lost 170,000 blue-collar jobs through the 1970s, another 120,000 jobs were shed in Chicago, and blue-collar employment in Detroit fell by 90,000 jobs (Kasarda 1989, 29). For young black men in metropolitan areas, employment rates fell by 30 percent among high school dropouts and nearly 20 percent among high school graduates. Job loss was only a third as large among young noncollege whites (Bound and Holzer 1993, 390).

Variation in imprisonment is closely linked to variation in wages and employment. Weekly earnings for young low-education men declined through the 1980s and 1990s while imprisonment rates were rising. Among black men, unemployment increased steeply with declining education. One study estimates that if wages and employment had not declined among low-education men since the early 1980s, growth in prison admission rates would have been reduced by as much as 25 percent by 2001 (Western, Kleykamp, and Rosenfeld 2004).

The urban deindustrialization that produced the raw material for the prison boom was as much a failure of institutions as a failure of markets. Large job losses in the mid-1970s and early 1980s were concentrated in unionized industries (Farber and Western 2001). De-unionization thus joined manufacturing decline to drive down the incomes of unskilled inner city workers. Besides unemployment insurance, which provided only temporary assistance, few social programs were available to supplement the incomes or retrain or mobilize young able-bodied men into new jobs. The welfare system was also poorly equipped to handle the social problems linked to male unemployment. Drug addiction, petty offending, and public idleness all afflicted the neighborhoods of concentrated disadvantage.

Idle young men in poor minority neighborhoods supplied a large share of the inmates that drove the prison boom. The path from concentrated economic disadvantage to mass imprisonment runs partly through the mechanism of crime, but policy also played a vital role. At any given point in time, crime among young disadvantaged men is higher than in the rest of the population. For example, the murder rates—victimization and offending—are about twenty-five times higher for black men aged eighteen to twenty-four than for white men aged twenty-five and older (Pastore and Maguire 2006). Violent crime is also a more serious problem in poor communities than affluent ones (e.g., Sampson 1987; see also the review of Braithwaite 1979). The criminal involvement of young, economically disadvantaged men makes them more likely at a given point in time to go to prison than others who are less involved in crime.

Crime cannot explain, however, why disadvantaged young men were so much more likely to go to prison by the end of the 1990s than two decades earlier. Indeed, survey data show that poor male youth were much less involved in crime at the height of the prison boom, in 2000, than at its inception, in 1980. To explain the growing risk of imprisonment over time, the role of policy is decisive. Because the system of criminal sentencing had come to rely so heavily on incarceration, an arrest in the late 1990s was far more likely to lead to prison time than at the beginning of the prison boom in 1980 (Blumstein and Beck 1999).

The drug trade holds a special place in this story. The drug trade itself became a source of economic opportunity in the jobless ghetto. Ethnographers paint striking pictures of how the inner-city drug trade becomes a focal point for the problems of economic disadvantage, violence, and state control. Sudhir Venkatesh and Steven Levitt (2000) describe how drug trafficking thrived in the vacuum of legitimate employment in Chicago's South Side neighborhoods. Chicago youth spoke to Venkatesh and Levitt of their "gang affiliation and their drive to earn income in ways that resonated with representations of work in the mainstream corporate firm. Many approached [gang] involvement as an institutionalized path of socioeconomic mobility for down-and-out youth" (p. 447). In Elijah Anderson's (1999) account, violence follows the drug trade as crime becomes a voracious force in the poor neighborhoods of Philadelphia:

> Surrounded by violence and by indifference to the innocent victims of drug dealers and users alike, the decent people are finding it harder and harder to maintain a sense of community. Thus violence comes to regulate life in the drug-infested neighborhoods and the putative neighborhood leaders are increasingly the people who control the violence. (P. 134)

The picture drawn by the ethnographic research is of poor neighborhoods, chronically short of legitimate work and embedded in a violent and illegal market for drugs. High rates of joblessness and crime, and a flourishing street trade in illegal drugs, combined with harsher criminal penalties and intensified urban policing to produce high incarceration rates among young unskilled men in inner cities. In the twenty-five years from 1980, the incarceration rate tripled among white men in their twenties, but fewer than 2 percent were behind bars by 2004. Imprisonment rates for young black men increased less quickly, but one in seven were in custody by 2004. Incarceration rates are much higher among male high school dropouts in their twenties. Threefold growth in the imprisonment of young white male dropouts left 7 percent in prison or jail by 2004. The incarceration rate for young low-education black men rose by 22 points in the two decades after 1980. Incredibly, 34 percent of all young black male high school dropouts were in prison or jail on an average day in 2004, an incarceration rate forty times higher than the national average (Western 2006, chap. 1).

Tough sentences for drug and repeat offenders, strict policing and prosecution of drug traffic and public order offending, and unforgiving parole supervision broadened the use of imprisonment from its traditional focus on serious crime. Certainly

FIGURE 1
INCARCERATION RATES PER ONE HUNDRED THOUSAND RESIDENTS,
UNITED STATES AND WESTERN EUROPE, 2004

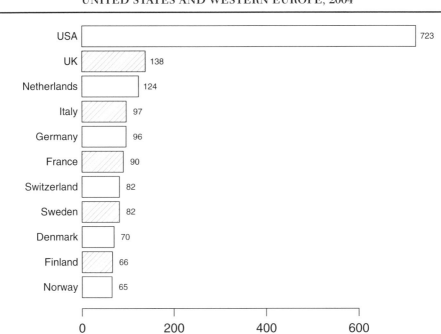

SOURCE: Aebi (2005); Harrison and Beck (2006).

sentences increased for serious crime, and this contributed to incarceration rates too. For example, time served for murderers increased from five to eleven years, from 1980 to 1996 (Blumstein and Beck 1999, 36). But growth in the share of less serious offenders in state prison increased much more rapidly (Blumstein and Beck 1999, 24, 37). Growth in the numbers of drug offenders, parole violators, and public order offenders reflects the use of penal policy as a surrogate social policy, in which a troublesome and unruly population is increasingly managed with incarceration.

Mass Incarceration

The scale of the penal system is usually measured by an incarceration rate. The incarceration rate records the number of people in prison or jail on a given day per 100,000 of the population. Figure 1 compares the United States's incarceration rate in 2004 to the incarceration rates of the long-standing democracies of

FIGURE 2
U.S. STATE AND FEDERAL IMPRISONMENT RATES, 1925-2005;
U.S. PRISON AND JAIL INCARCERATION RATES, 1983-2005

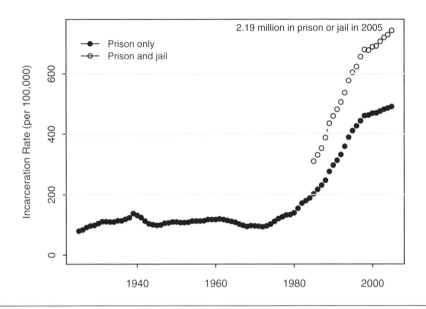

SOURCE: Maguire and Pastore (2007).

Western Europe. The penal systems of Western Europe locked up, on average, about 100 per 100,000. The United States by contrast incarcerated more than seven times the European average, with an incarceration rate of more than 700 per 100,000.

The contemporary scale of criminal punishment is also historically unusual. Although we do not have long time series of the total penal population of prison and jail inmates, data on the state and federal prison populations extend back to 1925. The time series in Figure 2 shows that between 1925 and 1973, the fraction of the U.S. population in state and federal prison varied in a narrow range of around 100 per 100,000—close to the total incarceration rates in Western Europe. Beginning in 1974, the prison population began to grow, and the incarceration rate increased continuously for the next three decades. By 2005, nearly 2.2 million people were in custody, either in prison for felony convictions or in local jails awaiting trial or serving short sentences. These figures do not fully reflect the contemporary correctional population. In 2005, another 784,000 men and women were under community supervision on parole, while 4.1 million people were on probation. The total population under correctional supervision thus includes more than 7 million people, or about 3.1 percent of all U.S. adults (Glaze and Bonczar 2006).

The broad significance of the penal system for American social inequality results from extreme social and economic disparities in incarceration. More than 90 percent of all prison and jail inmates are men. Women's incarceration rates have increased more quickly than men's since 1980, but much higher rates persist for men, leaving women to contend with raising children while their partners cycle in and out of jail. These men are young, of working age, many with small children. About two-thirds of state prisoners are over eighteen years old but under age thirty-five. With this age pattern, only a small number of people are incarcerated at any point in time, but many more pass through the penal system at some point in their lives.

Incarceration is also concentrated among the disadvantaged. High incarceration rates among low-status and minority men are unmistakable. The 1997 survey of state and federal prisoners shows that state inmates average less than eleven years of schooling. A third were not working at the time of their incarceration, and the average wage of the remainder is much lower than that of other men with the same level of education. African Americans and Hispanics also have higher incarceration rates than whites, and together the two groups account for about two-thirds of the state prison population.

The black-white difference in incarceration rates is especially striking. Black men are eight times more likely to be incarcerated than whites, and large racial disparities can be seen for all age groups and at different levels of education. The large black-white disparity in incarceration is unmatched by most other social indicators. Racial disparities in unemployment (two to one), nonmarital childbearing (three to one), infant mortality (two to one), and wealth (one to five) are all significantly lower than the eight to one black-white ratio in incarceration rates (see Western 2006). If white men were incarcerated at the same rate as blacks, there would be more than 6 million people in prison and jail, and more than 5 percent of the male working-age population would be incarcerated.

Age, race, and educational disparities concentrate imprisonment among the disadvantaged. Figure 3 shows trends in incarceration rates for young black and white men with different levels of schooling. From 1980 to 2004, the percentage of young white men in prison or jail increased from 0.6 to 1.9 percent. Among young white men with only a high school education, incarceration rates were about twice as high. At the dawn of the prison boom, in 1980, the incarceration rate for young black men, 5.7 percent, was more than twice as high as that for low-education whites. By 2004, 13.5 percent of black men in their twenties were in prison or jail. Incarceration rates were higher in the lower half of the education distribution. More than one in five young noncollege black men were behind bars on a typical day in 2004.

Incarceration rates offer a snapshot of the extent of penal confinement. Time series of incarceration rates tell us how the extent of penal confinement has shifted historically. We can also study, not the level of incarceration at a point in time, but how the risk of incarceration accumulates over an individual's life. This kind of life course analysis asks what is the likelihood an individual will go to prison by age twenty-five, thirty, or thirty-five. Instead of providing a snapshot of the risk of incarceration, this analysis describes a typical biography.

FIGURE 3
THE PERCENTAGE OF MEN, AGED TWENTY-TWO TO THIRTY,
IN PRISON OR JAIL BY RACE AND EDUCATION

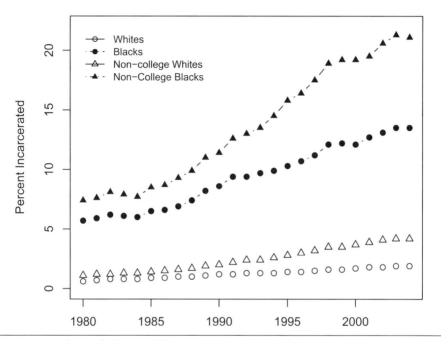

SOURCE: Authors' tabulations, following Western (2006, 17).

The life course perspective provides a compelling account of social integration. In this account, the passage to adulthood is a sequence of well-ordered stages that affect life trajectories long after the early transitions are completed. In modern times, arriving at adult status involves moving from school to work, then to marriage, to establishing a home and becoming a parent. Completing this sequence without delay promotes stable employment, marriage, and other positive life outcomes. The process of becoming an adult thus influences success in fulfilling adult roles and responsibilities.

As an account of social integration, life course analysis has attracted the interest of students of crime and deviance. Criminologists point to the normalizing effects of life course transitions. Steady jobs and good marriages build social bonds that keep would-be offenders in a daily routine. They enmesh men who are tempted by crime in a web of supportive social relationships. Strong family bonds and steady work restrict men's opportunities for antisocial behavior and offer them a stake in normal life. For persistent lawbreakers, the adult roles of spouse and worker offer a pathway out of crime (Sampson and Laub 1993; Warr 1998; Hagan 1993). Those who fail to secure the markers of adulthood are more likely to persist in criminal behavior. This idea of a normalizing, integrative life path offers a powerful alternative to claims that criminality is a stable trait possessed by some but absent in others. Above all else, the life course account of crime is dynamic, describing how people change as their social context evolves with age.

Imprisonment significantly alters the life course. Working life is disrupted as workers with prison records try to find jobs from employers who are deeply suspicious of applicants with criminal records. The stigma of a prison record also creates legal barriers to skilled and licensed occupations, rights to welfare benefits, and voting rights (Holzer 1996; Pager 2003; Uggen and Manza 2002). Ex-prisoners are also less likely to get married or cohabit with the mothers of their children (Lopoo and Western 2005). By eroding opportunities for employment and marriage, incarceration may also lead ex-inmates back to a life of crime. The volatility of adolescence may last well into midlife for men serving prison time. In short, imprisonment is a turning point in which young crime-involved men acquire a new status involving diminished life chances.

To place the risks of imprisonment in the context of the life course, we report new estimates of the cumulative risks of imprisonment by age thirty to thirty-four, for five-year birth cohorts born through the postwar period (see Table 1). Because most inmates enter prison for the first time before age thirty-five, these cumulative risks of imprisonment roughly describe lifetime risks of imprisonment. We emphasize that these lifetime risks of incarceration are for imprisonment, as opposed to jail incarceration. Imprisonment here describes a sentence of twelve months or longer for a felony conviction, now about twenty-eight months of time served, at the median.

The oldest cohort was born just after World War II, and its members reached their midthirties in 1979, just at the takeoff of the prison boom. In this group, just over 1 percent of whites and 9 percent of blacks would go to prison. As incarceration rates climbed through the 1980s, lifetime imprisonment risks also increased. The big jump in imprisonment separates men born in the 1950s and earlier from those born in the 1960s and later. The pervasive presence of the criminal justice system in the lives of African American men only emerges among those born since the mid-1960s who were reaching their midthirties from the end of the 1990s. Like the long time series of incarceration rates, these figures on postwar birth cohorts underscore the historic novelty of mass incarceration. Only through the 1990s did the penal system figure prominently in the lives of young black men.

Like incarceration rates, lifetime risks of imprisonment are also steeply stratified by education. We report cumulative risks of imprisonment for men who have had at least some college education and for all those with just a high school education. Among those with just a high school education, we separate high school dropouts and high school graduates. We report figures for all noncollege men because—particularly for African Americans—those without college education have remained an approximately constant proportion of the population. Educational attainment has increased across birth cohorts chiefly because the proportion of high school dropouts has declined.

TABLE 1
CUMULATIVE RISK OF IMPRISONMENT BY AGE THIRTY TO THIRTY-FOUR BY
RACE AND EDUCATION FOR MEN BORN 1945 THROUGH 1949 TO 1975
THROUGH 1979 (IN PERCENTAGES)

	1945-1949	1950-1954	1955-1959	1960-1964	1965-1969	1970-1974	1975-1979
White men							
High school dropouts	4.2	7.2	8.0	8.0	10.5	14.8	15.3
High school only	0.7	2.0	2.1	2.5	4.0	3.8	4.1
All noncollege	1.8	2.9	3.2	3.7	5.1	5.1	6.3
Some college	0.7	0.7	0.6	0.8	0.7	0.9	1.2
All men	1.2	1.9	2.0	2.2	2.8	2.8	3.3
Black men							
High school dropouts	14.7	19.6	27.6	41.6	57.0	62.5	69.0
High school only	10.2	11.3	9.4	12.4	16.8	20.3	18.0
All noncollege	12.1	14.1	14.7	19.9	26.7	30.9	35.7
Some college	4.9	3.5	4.3	5.5	6.8	8.5	7.6
All men	9.0	10.6	11.5	15.2	20.3	22.8	20.7

SOURCE: Data sources and methods are described in Pettit and Western (2004).
NOTE: Estimates for the cohorts born after 1969 are based on data from the 2004 Survey on Inmates of States and Federal Correctional Facilities.

Lifetime risks of imprisonment among black men with little schooling are particularly striking. For noncollege African American men, about 12 percent of those born just after the war would ultimately go to prison. For those born thirty years later, reaching their thirties in 2005, at least 36 percent would serve prison time. The latter figure is actually a slight underestimate, because those born 1975 to 1979 have not been exposed to the risk of imprisonment for as long as the older cohorts.

At the very bottom of the education distribution, among high school dropouts, prison time has become extraordinarily prevalent. For black male dropouts born since the mid-1960s, 60 to 70 percent go to prison. For this very poorly schooled segment of the population, serving time in prison has become a routine life event on the pathway through adulthood. Indeed, we need only go back several decades to find a time when incarceration was not pervasive in the lives of young black men with little schooling.

Detailed figures on the racial and educational differences in imprisonment also show another pattern. While lifetime risks of imprisonment grew threefold for men without a college education, imprisonment among the college-educated less than doubled. In short, most of the growth in imprisonment was concentrated among those with little schooling. At the same time, racial disparities in imprisonment risks, while large, did not increase significantly. The figures thus indicate that in the period of the prison boom, class inequality in incarceration clearly increased, but racial inequality did not. Because racial disparities in imprisonment were so large to begin with, however, the prison boom produced extraordinarily high rates of incarceration among young noncollege black men.

From a life course perspective, we can compare imprisonment to other significant life events that are commonly thought to mark the path through young adulthood. Life course researchers have previously studied college graduation, military service, and marriage as key milestones that move young men forward in life to establishing a household and a steady job. Comparing imprisonment to these life events suggests how the pathway through adulthood has been changed by the prison boom.

[M]ost of the growth in imprisonment was concentrated among those with little schooling.

The risks of each life event are different for blacks and whites, but racial differences in imprisonment greatly overshadow any other inequality. By their early thirties, whites are more than twice as likely to hold a bachelor's degree compared with blacks, whereas blacks are about 50 percent more likely to have served in the military. However, black men in their early thirties are about seven times more likely than whites to have a prison record. Indeed, recent birth cohorts of black men are more likely to have prison records (22.4 percent) than military records (17.4 percent) or bachelor's degrees (12.5 percent). The share of the population with prison records is particularly striking among noncollege men. Whereas few noncollege white men have prison records, nearly a third of black men with less than a college education have been to prison. Noncollege black men in their early thirties in 1999 were more than twice as likely to be ex-felons as veterans (see Table 2).

By 1999, imprisonment had become a common life event for black men that sharply distinguished their pathway through adulthood from that of white men. David Garland coined the term "mass imprisonment" to refer to the high rate of incarceration in the contemporary United States. In Garland's definition, mass imprisonment has two characteristics. First, he writes, "mass imprisonment implies a rate of imprisonment . . . that is markedly above the historical and comparative norm for societies of this type" (Garland 2001, 1). Indeed, we have seen that the rate of incarceration in the United States by the late 1990s was far higher than in Western Europe and without precedent in U.S. history. Second, Garland argues, the demographic concentration of imprisonment produces not the incarceration of individual offenders, but the "systematic imprisonment of whole groups of the population" (Garland 2001, 2).

The empirical markers of mass imprisonment are more slippery in this case. When will the incarceration rate be high enough to imprison, not the individual, but the group? The picture painted by the statistics in this article helps us answer

TABLE 2
PERCENTAGE OF NON-HISPANIC BLACK AND WHITE MEN,
BORN 1965 TO 1969, EXPERIENCING LIFE EVENTS BY 1999

Life Event	Whites	Blacks
All men		
Prison incarceration	3.2	22.4
Bachelor's degree	31.6	12.5
Military service	14.0	17.4
Marriage	72.5	59.3
Noncollege men		
Prison incarceration	6.0	31.9
High school diploma/GED	73.5	64.4
Military service	13.0	13.7
Marriage	72.8	55.9

SOURCE: Pettit and Western (2004).
NOTE: The incidence of all live events except prison incarceration were calculated from the
2000 Census. To make the incarceration risks comparable to census statistics, the estimates are
adjusted to describe the percentage of men, born 1965 to 1969, who have ever been imprisoned and survived to 1999.

this question. Not only did incarceration become common among young black
men at the end of the 1990s, but its prevalence also exceeded that of other life
events that we usually associate with passage through the life course. More than
college graduation or military service, incarceration has come to typify the
biographies of African American men born since the late 1960s.

Mass Incarceration and Family Life

As imprisonment became common for low-education black men by the end of
the 1990s, the penal system also became familiar to poor minority families. By
1999, 30 percent of noncollege black men in their midthirties had been to prison,
and through incarceration, many were separated from their wives, girlfriends,
and children. Women and children in low-income urban communities now routinely cope with absent husbands and fathers lost to incarceration and adjust to
their return after release. Poor single men detached from family life are also
affected, bearing the stigma of a prison record in the marriage markets of disadvantaged urban neighborhoods.

Discussions of the family life of criminal offenders typically focus on the
crime-suppressing effects of marriage, not the effects of incarceration on family
life. Researchers find that marriage offers a pathway out of crime for men with
histories of delinquency. Not a wedding itself, but marriage in the context of a
warm, stable, and constructive relationship, offers the antidote to crime (Sampson
and Laub 1993; Laub, Nagin, and Sampson 1998). Wives and family members in

such relationships provide the web of obligations and responsibilities that restrains young men and reduces their contact with the male friends whose recreations veer into antisocial behavior (Warr 1998).

The prison boom places the link between crime and marriage in a new light. If a good marriage is important for criminal desistance, what is the effect of incarceration on marriage? The connections between incarceration, marriage, and the family are also implicated in the larger story of rising urban inequality. In the past three decades, American family life was transformed by declining marriage rates and growth in the number of single-parent households. Marriage rates fell among women from all class backgrounds. Between 1970 and 2000, the share of white women aged twenty-five to thirty-four who were married declined from more than 80 percent to just over 60 percent. Marriage rates for African American women halved from 60 to around 30 percent. The decline in marriage propelled growth in the number of single-parent households, although this effect was confined to those with little education (Ellwood and Jencks 2004). The share of college-educated women who were single mothers remained constant at around 5 percent between 1970 and 2000, while the fraction of single mothers among low-education white women increased from 8 to 18 percent. Trends were most dramatic among black women. In 1970, about one-third of low-education black women were single parents, but the number increased to more than 50 percent in the next thirty years. By 2000, stable two-parent households became relatively rare, especially among African Americans with little schooling (Western 2006, chap. 1).

Poverty researchers closely followed the changing shape of American families. Growing numbers of female-headed families increased the risks of enduring poverty for women and children. Growing up poor also raised a child's risk of school failure, poor health, and delinquency. Writing in the mid-1980s, William Julius Wilson (1987) traced the growth in the number of female-headed black families to the shrinking number of "marriageable men" in poor urban areas. The shortage of suitable husbands in ghetto neighborhoods was driven by two processes. High rates of male incarceration and mortality tilted the gender ratio, which made it harder for poor urban women to find partners. These effects were small, however, compared to the high rate of joblessness that left few black men in inner cities able to support a family. Many studies later examined the impact of men's employment on marriage rates and found that the unemployed are less likely to be married and that joblessness can increase chances of divorce or separation (e.g., Lichter, LeClere, and McLaughlin 1991; McLanahan and Casper 1995; Blau, Kahn, and Waldfogel 2000). Studies of the effects of employment dominated research on marriage among the disadvantaged, and the idea that incarceration destabilized family life was undeveloped.

To study the family ties of prisoners, we begin by simply describing the levels of marriage and fatherhood in the penal population. Figure 3 compares rates of marriage and fatherhood in the penal population to those for men who are not incarcerated. Levels of marriage are measured for noninstitutional men and male prison and jail inmates, aged twenty-two to thirty, in 2000. Rates of fatherhood are the percentage of noninstitutional men and male state prisoners, aged thirty-three to forty, who had children by 1997 to 1998.

Marriage rates among prison and jail inmates are very low compared to those on the outside. White male inmates in their twenties are less than half as likely to be married as young white noninstitutional men of the same age. The incarceration gap in marriage is also large for black and Hispanic men. The general level of marriage is highest for Hispanics, but in this case, inmates are only half as likely to be married as their counterparts in the noninstitutional population. Although marriage rates are lowest for black men, only 11 percent of young black inmates are married, compared to a marriage rate of 25 percent among young black men outside of prison and jail. In short, marriage rates among male prisoners in their twenties are only around half as high as in the free population.

Although marriage is uncommon among prisoners, they are just as likely as other men to have children. Figure 3 shows the percentage of men who have ever had children by their late thirties. The prevalence of fatherhood among prisoners is almost identical to that on the outside. For example, 73 percent of noninstitutional black men have had children by their late thirties, compared to 70 percent of black male prisoners of the same age. Male fertility rates among prisoners and nonprisoners are also very similar for whites and Hispanics.

Just as incarceration has become a normal life event for disadvantaged young black men, parental incarceration has become commonplace for their children.

The combination of high incarceration rates with a large proportion of fathers among inmates means many children now have incarcerated fathers. Data from surveys of prison and jail inmates can be used to calculate the numbers of children with fathers in prison or jail. A time series for 1980 to 2000 shows that the total number of children with incarcerated fathers increased sixfold from about 350,000 to 2.1 million, nearly 3 percent of all children nationwide in 2000. Among whites, the fraction of children with a father in prison or jail is relatively small—about 1.2 percent in 2000. The figure is about three times higher (3.5 percent) for Hispanics. Among African Americans, more than a million, or one in eleven, black children had a father in prison or jail in 2000. The numbers are higher for younger children: by 2000, 10.4 percent of black children under age ten had a father in prison or jail. Just as incarceration has become a normal life event for disadvantaged young black men, parental incarceration has become commonplace for their children.

To better gauge the impact of mass incarceration on children, we report the cumulative risks that one of their parents will be sent to prison. We also report these risks of parental incarceration for black and white children of parents at different levels of education. Just as lifetime risks of imprisonment help describe the life course of adults, cumulative risks of parental imprisonment tell us about the early life course of children.

These figures include incarceration among mothers as well as fathers. The rapid growth in incarceration among women is reflected in these figures. Although incarceration rates among mothers are much lower than those for fathers, the effects of maternal imprisonment on parental separation from children are relatively large. Whereas just under half of fathers were living with their children at the time they were sent to prison, nearly two-thirds of mothers sent to prison were living with their children (Mumola 2000, 3).

Table 3 reports the risks of parental imprisonment by age fourteen for children born in 1978 and 1990 (see Wildeman forthcoming). Among white children born in 1978 who reached their teenage years in the early 1990s, around 2 percent experienced a parent being sent to prison. Among African American children born in the same year, around 14 percent had a parent sent to prison by age fifteen. Twelve years later, among children born in 1990, about a quarter of all black children had a parent sent to prison. Indeed, the proportion of black children who had a mother sent to prison (a relatively rare event) nearly equaled the proportion of white children who had a father sent to prison.

The children of low-education parents were far more exposed to the criminal justice system than the population in general. These estimates indicate that among children born in the late 1970s to noncollege African American parents, about one in seven had a parent sent to prison by the time they reached their teenage years. Just over a decade later, more than a quarter of the children of noncollege black parents experienced parental imprisonment. For black children whose parents dropped out of high school, around half had a parent sent to prison by the early 2000s. Just as imprisonment had become a normal life event for young black male dropouts, so had parental imprisonment become normal for their children.

The prevalence of marriage and fatherhood among prison and jail inmates tells us something about the incapacitation effect of incarceration. Men behind bars cannot fully play the role of father and husband. Single incarcerated men are unlikely to get married while they are locked up. On the outside, the incapacitation effect takes the form of lopsided gender ratios of poor communities. For example, in the high-incarceration neighborhoods of Washington, D.C., there are only sixty-two men for every one hundred women (Braman 2004, 86). Studying U.S. counties, William Sabol and James Lynch (1998) quantify the effects of the removal of men to prison. After accounting for educational attainment, welfare receipt, poverty, employment, and crime, Sabol and Lynch find that the doubling of the number of black men admitted to prison between 1980 and 1990 is associated with a 19 percent increase in the number of families headed by black women.

TABLE 3
CUMULATIVE RISKS OF PATERNAL AND MATERNAL IMPRISONMENT
FOR CHILDREN BORN IN 1978 AND 1990, BY PARENTS' RACE
AND EDUCATION (IN PERCENTAGES)

	Whites		Blacks	
	Maternal	Paternal	Maternal	Paternal
Born 1978				
All	0.2	2.1	1.4	13.4
High school dropout	0.2	4.0	1.9	21.4
High school graduate	0.2	2.0	0.9	9.9
All noncollege	0.2	2.8	1.5	15.1
Some college	0.2	1.4	1.2	7.1
Born 1990				
All	0.6	3.6	3.2	24.5
High school dropout	1.0	7.1	5.0	49.4
High school graduate	0.7	4.7	2.6	20.0
All noncollege	0.8	5.5	3.6	24.5
Some college	0.3	1.7	2.6	13.2

SOURCE: Sources, methods, and figures are reported in Wildeman (forthcoming).

The incapacitation effect captures only part of the impact of the prison boom on marriage. In Wilson's terms, incarceration also damages men's marriageability. Wilson (1987, 83-92) traced declining marriage rates among the ghetto poor to the increasing inability of young disadvantaged black men to support families. Incarceration erodes men's economic desirability even more. Incarceration reduces men's wages, slows the rate of wage growth, increases unemployment, and shortens job tenure. If a poor employment record damages the marriage prospects of single men and contributes to the risk of divorce among those who are married, the economic effects of incarceration will decrease the likelihood of marriage among men who have been to prison and jail.

Wilson (1987) measured marriageability mostly by employment, but a man's criminal record also signals his ability to care and provide for his family. While poor women care about men's economic status, they also worry about men's honesty and respectability. Edin's (2000) ethnographic interviews showed that these noneconomic concerns weighed heavily on low-income women in metropolitan Philadelphia. The women Edin interviewed were deeply distrustful of men. The respondents were often reluctant to marry or develop romantic relationships because they viewed men's marital infidelity as inevitable. Some women's trust in men was shaken by boyfriends who spent household savings on drugs or drink and neglected children in their care.

This wariness was compounded by the men's low social status. For the women in Edin's sample, marriage offered a route to respectability, but "marriage to an economically unproductive male means . . . permanently taking on his very low status" (Edin 2000, 29). Elijah Anderson (1999, 163) makes a similar point in the opposite way, by describing the dreams of teenage girls in ghetto neighborhoods, a "dream of living happily ever after with one's children in a nice house in a good neighborhood—essentially the dream of the middle-class American lifestyle." In these cases, it is the social status of jobless men, their lack of esteem, as much as their material resources, which limits their appeal as husbands.

If reliability and reputation measure the noneconomic aspects of marriageability, incarceration has likely eroded the pool of marriageable men. Just as the stigma of incarceration confers disadvantage in the labor market, it also undermines a man's prospects in the marriage market. Men in trouble with the authorities cannot offer the respectability that many poor women seek from their partners. A prison record—the official stamp of criminality—can convey trouble to mothers looking for a stable home. For example, Edin's (2000, 28) interviews described women's aversion to drug dealing, even when it provided a couple with income: "Mothers fear that if their man gets involved in drug dealing, he might stash weapons, drugs, or drug proceeds in the household, that the violence of street life might follow him into the household." Because marriage offers a way of enhancing status, the trouble foreshadowed by a prison record may be even more repellent than chronic unemployment.

The stigma of incarceration also strains existing relationships. Erving Goffman (1963, 30) describes stigma's contagious quality, suffusing personal relationships: "In general the tendency for a stigma to spread from the stigmatized individual to his close connections provides a reason why such relations tend either to be avoided or to be terminated where existing." Braman's (2004) fieldwork in Washington, D.C., provides empirical support. The high prevalence of incarceration, he finds, does little to reduce its stigmatic effect. Braman describes the experience of Louisa, whose husband Robert was arrested on an old armed robbery charge after a lengthy period out of prison and in recovery from drug addiction. The couple

> had come to think and present themselves as morally upstanding citizens and churchgoers. Because of this, Louisa felt the stigma of her husband's most recent incarceration all the more intensely. She began to avoid friends and family, not wanting to talk about Robert's incarceration and lying to them when she did. (P. 170)

Louisa came to withdraw from her extended family and grappled with depression during Robert's incarceration. Braman argues that the stigma of incarceration is even more severe for family members than the offender, because wives and children live and work outside the prison, exposed to the condemnation of neighbors and other community members.

The separation imposed by incarceration also weighs heavily on relationships. Interviews with ex-offenders suggest that the friendships underlying romantic relationships are diluted by time apart. Often women become more independent and self-sufficient while their partners are incarcerated (Nurse 2002, 109). Just as Edin's (2000) female respondents distrusted men's commitment, Ann Nurse

(2002) reports that individuals in her Californian sample of juvenile offenders were constantly suspicious of the fidelity of their wives and girlfriends. Often, these fears were well-founded, and many romantic relationships failed while men were incarcerated (see also Edin, Nelson, and Paranal 2004, 62).

Quantitative analysis of survey data is generally consistent with the field research. Black single men are especially likely to remain unmarried if they have prison records. The gap in marriage rates between black noninmates and ex-inmates is estimated to be anywhere from 20 to 200 percent. Survey data point more strongly to the destabilizing effects of incarceration on couples. Consider an analysis of the Fragile Families Survey of Child Wellbeing—a survey of poor urban couples with infant children. The survey shows that men who are living with the mothers of their newborn children are three times more likely to separate within the year if they have a history of incarceration (Western 2006, chap. 7).

Unanswered Questions

Moynihan traced the dilapidated state of the black family of the early 1960s to the burdens of slavery and a history of discrimination. In the early 2000s, however, the family life of poor African Americans in urban neighborhoods of concentrated poverty is also strained by mass incarceration. Emerging only in the closing years of the 1990s, mass incarceration has routinely drawn young noncollege black men and their families into the orbit of the penal system.

While a handful of ethnographic studies are beginning to shed light on the effects of incarceration on the family life of the urban poor, and several quantitative studies have examined the effects of incarceration on marriage and divorce, research is still in its infancy. We close our discussion by describing what we see as the central research questions and offering some hypotheses for understanding the family life of the urban poor in the era of mass incarceration.

How does incarceration affect family violence and other victimization? In many cases, violent husbands and fathers are removed from households by incarceration. Survey data indicate that men who have been incarcerated are much more likely to have violent relationships with their partners, even if they were incarcerated for nonviolent offenses. From this perspective, mass incarceration may have significantly reduced family violence and other conflict in poor households. On the other hand, removing a father from the household may also open the door to other adult males who also pose a risk to poor women and their children. If children are at greater risk of abuse, for example, when a nonbiological adult male begins living in the household, mass incarceration may contribute to victimization rather than reduce it. What is more, returning prisoners may present more of a risk of family violence as a consequence of their incarceration. Very little is known about the patterns of violence and abuse that follow the removal of a parent from a family by incarceration. In assessing the effects of incarceration on the lives of poor families, this question is perhaps paramount.

What are the financial consequences of incarceration for poor families? Research shows that incarceration is associated with reductions in employment and earnings of ex-prisoners after release (Western 2006; see the review of Western, Kling, and Weiman 2001). The annual earnings of ex-prisoners are about 40 percent lower than before imprisonment, controlling for changes in age, work experience, and schooling. The economic penalties of incarceration for ex-prisoners, however, do not necessarily translate into economic losses for their families. If men going to prison are only weakly connected to their families or make little financial contribution to their household, their earnings loss while incarcerated and poor job prospects after release may have little effect on the family economy.

A parent in prison may also impose a direct financial burden, however. The costs of visiting far-flung facilities, accepting collect calls, and retaining legal representation all add to the financial strains of poor families. The extent of these costs is largely unknown. The economic effect of mass incarceration on families is thus fundamentally an empirical question. Research on the pay and employment of ex-prisoners suggests that the economic effects of mass incarceration on families may be large, but this hinges on the strength of the connection between crime-involved men and their families before and after incarceration.

What are the effects of incarceration on the supervision and socialization of children? As with the question of economic effects, much turns here on the involvement of incarcerated fathers in their families before they were sent to prison. If fathers were not highly involved, the effects of incarceration would be quite small. Inmate surveys show that nearly half of state prisoners who are fathers were living with at least some of their children at the time of their incarceration. For those children, incarceration contributes to family breakup. Poor fathers, even if nonresident, frequently maintain some kind of supportive relationship with their partners and children. For these children, paternal incarceration likely involves the loss of an adult figure that could play some role in the supervision and socialization of children.

We have seen that rates of maternal incarceration are much lower, but incarcerated mothers are more likely to be living with their children at the time of imprisonment. Again, the effects of imprisonment depend on the quality of the relationship between parent and child, and here relatively little is known. While the loss of a parent to the criminal justice system likely affects the socialization of children, children's aspirations and sense of self-worth are likely to be affected by the stigma of imprisonment. Although Goffman (1963) writes about the contagious character of social stigma, few studies have examined how children may be affected in their peer groups or at school (though see Comfort 2002).

We have argued here that the emergence of mass imprisonment has transformed the institutional context of America's urban poor. In this sense, this new era of mass incarceration adds another chapter to Moynihan's original analysis of urban poverty and its social correlates. The data suggest that the prison boom has been massively corrosive for family structure and family life, but much work remains to be done. In the background of this research agenda is the key question of the durability of urban poverty in the era of mass incarceration. If pervasive imprisonment undermines family life and disrupts the developmental path of children into young adulthood, the inequalities produced by mass incarceration may be exceptionally enduring. If the children of the prison boom are at greater risk of poverty and violence and are more involved in crime themselves, they too will risk following their parents into prison. Under these circumstances, the inequalities of mass incarceration will be sustained not just over a lifetime, but from one generation to the next.

References

Aebi, Marcelo. 2005. *Council of Europe annual penal statistics.* Strasbourg, France: Council of Europe.

Anderson, Elijah. 1999. *Code of the street: Decency, violence, and the moral life of the inner city.* New York: Norton.

Beckett, Katherine. 1997. *Making crime pay: Law and order in contemporary American politics.* New York: Oxford University Press.

Blau, Francine D., Lawrence M. Kahn, and Jane Waldfogel. 2000. Understanding young women's marriage decisions: The role of labor and marriage market conditions. *Industrial and Labor Relations Review* 53:624-47.

Blumstein, Alfred, and Allen J. Beck. 1999. Population growth in U.S. prisons, 1980-1996. In *Crime and justice: Prisons,* vol. 26, ed. Michaelkl Tonry and Joan Petersilia, 17-62. Chicago: University of Chicago Press.

Bound, John, and Harry Holzer. 1993. Industrial shifts, skill levels, and the labor market for white and black men. *Review of Economics and Statistics* 75:387-96.

Braithwaite, John. 1979. *Inequality, crime and public policy.* London: Routledge.

Braman, Donald S. 2004. *Doing time on the outside: Incarceration family life in urban America.* Ann Arbor: University of Michigan Press.

Comfort, Megan. 2002. Papa's house: The prison as domestic and social satellite. *Ethnography* 3:467-99.

Davey, Joseph D. 1998. *The politics of prison expansion: Winning elections by waging war on crime.* Westport, CT: Praeger.

Edin, Kathy. 2000. Few good men: Why poor mothers don't marry or remarry. *American Prospect* 11:26-31.

Edin, Katherine, Timothy Nelson, and Rechelle Paranal. 2004. Fatherhood and incarceration as potential turning points in the criminal careers of unskilled men. In *Imprisoning America: The social effects of mass incarceration,* ed. Mary Patillo, David Weiman, and Bruce Western, 46-75. New York: Russell Sage Foundation.

Edsall, Thomas B., and Mary D. Edsall. 1991. *Chain reaction: The impact of race, rights, and taxes on American politics.* New York: Norton.

Ellwood, David, and Christopher Jencks. 2004. The uneven spread of single-parent families: What do we know? Where do we look for answers? In *Social inequality,* ed. Katherine Neckerman, 3-77. New York: Russell Sage Foundation.

Farber, Henry S., and Bruce Western. 2001. Accounting for the decline of unions in the private sector, 1973-1998. *Journal of Labor Research* 22:459-86.

Garland, David. 2001. Introduction: The meaning of mass imprisonment. In *Mass imprisonment: Social causes and consequences,* ed. David Barland, 1-3. Thousand Oaks, CA: Sage.

Gest, Ted. 2001. *Crime and politics: Big government's erratic campaign for law and order.* New York: Oxford University Press.

Glaze, Lauren E., and Thomas P. Bonczar. 2006. *Probation and parole in the United States, 2005.* Washington, DC: U.S. Department of Justice.

Goffman, Erving. 1963. *Stigma: Notes on the management of spoiled identity.* Englewood Cliffs, NJ: Prentice Hall.

Hagan, John. 1993. The social embeddedness of crime and unemployment. *Criminology* 31:465-91.

Harrison, Paige M., and Allen J. Beck. 2000. *Prison and jail inmates at midyear 2000.* Bureau of Justice Statistics Bulletin. NCJ 208801. Washington, DC: U.S. Department of Justice.

Holzer, Harry J. 1996. *What employers want: Job prospects for less-educated workers.* New York: Russell Sage Foundation.

Jacobs, David, and Jason T. Carmichael. 2001. The politics of punishment across time and space: A pooled time-series analysis of imprisonment rates. *Social Forces* 80:61-91.

Kasarda, Jack. 1989. Urban industrial transition and the underclass. *The Annals of the American Academy of Political and Social Sciences* 501:26-47.

Laub, John H., Daniel S. Nagin, and Robert J. Sampson. 1998. Trajectories of change in criminal offending: Good marriages and desistance processes. *American Sociological Review* 63:225-38.

Lichter, Daniel T., Felicia B. LeClere, and Diane K. McLaughlin. 1991. Local marriage markets and the marital behavior of black and white women. *American Journal of Sociology* 96:843-67.

Lopoo, Leonard M., and Bruce Western. 2005. Incarceration and the formation and stability of marital unions. *Journal of Marriage and the Family* 65:721-34.

Maguire, Kathleen, and Ann L. Pastore, eds. 2007. *Sourcebook of criminal justice statistics.* http://www.albany.edu/sourcebook/ (accessed December 2007).

McLanahan, Sara, and Lynne Casper. 1995. Growing diversity and inequality in the American family. In *State of the union, America in the 1990s: Social trends*, ed. Reynolds Farley, 1-46. New York: Russell Sage Foundation.

Mumola, Christopher. 2000. *Incarcerated parents and their children.* Washington, DC: U.S. Department of Justice.

Nurse, Ann M. 2002. *Fatherhood arrested: Parenting from within the juvenile justice system.* Nashville, TN: Vanderbilt University Press.

Pager, Devah. 2003. The mark of a criminal record. *American Journal of Sociology* 108:937-75.

Pastore, Ann L., and Kathleen Maguire, eds. 2006. *Sourcebook of criminal justice statistics.* http://www.albany.edu/sourcebook/ (accessed December 2007).

Pettit, Becky, and Bruce Western. 2004. Mass imprisonment and the life course: Race and class inequality in U.S. incarceration. *American Sociological Review* 69:151-69.

Sabol, William J., and James P. Lynch. 1998. Assessing the longer-run consequences of incarceration: Effects on families and unemployment. Paper Presented at the 20th annual conference of the Association for Public Policy and Analysis, New York.

Sampson, Robert. 1987. Urban black violence: The effect of male joblessness and family disruption. *American Journal of Sociology* 93:348-82.

Sampson, Robert J., and John H. Laub. 1993. *Crime in the making: Pathways and turning points through life.* Cambridge, MA: Harvard University Press.

Uggen, Christopher, and Jeff Manza. 2002. Democratic contraction? Political consequences of felon disenfranchisement in the United States. *American Sociological Review* 67:777-803.

Venkatesh, Sudhir A., and Steven D. Levitt. 2000. Are we a family or a business? History and disjuncture in the urban American street gang. *Theory and Society* 29:427-62.

Warr, Mark. 1998. Life-course transitions and desistance from crime. *Criminology* 36:183-216.

Western, Bruce. 2006. *Punishment and inequality in America.* New York: Russell Sage Foundation.

Western, Bruce, Meredith Kleykamp, and Jake Rosenfeld. 2004. Crime, punishment, and American inequality. In *Social inequality*, ed. Katherine Neckerman, 771-96. New York: Russell Sage Foundation.

Western, Bruce, Jeffrey R. Kling, and David F. Weiman. 2001. The labor market consequences of incarceration. *Crime and Delinquency* 47:410-27.

Wildeman, Christopher. Forthcoming. Parental imprisonment, the prison boom, and the concentration of childhood disadvantage. *Demography.*

Wilson, William Julius. 1987. *The truly disadvantaged: The inner city, the underclass and public policy.* Chicago: University of Chicago Press.

Windelsham, Lord. 1998. *Politics, punishment and populism.* New York: Oxford University Press.

Race in the American Mind: From the Moynihan Report to the Obama Candidacy

By
LAWRENCE D. BOBO
and
CAMILLE Z. CHARLES

In 1965 Daniel Patrick Moynihan observed that the "racist virus in the American blood stream still afflicts us." The authors assess the tenor of racial attitudes in white and black America across the ensuing four decades. Their core conclusion is paradoxical. On one hand, a massive positive change in social norms regarding race has taken place that dislodged Jim Crow ideology and now calls for integration and equality as the rules that should guide black-white interaction. On the other hand, negative stereotypes of African Americans, cultural (not structural or discrimination-based) accounts of black disadvantage, and deep polarization over the appropriate social policy response to racial inequality yield an ongoing legacy of tension and division. The authors link these trends in attitudes to broader changes in society (i.e., racial segregation, job discrimination, rates of intermarriage), patterns of intergroup and interpersonal behavior, and national political dynamics.

Keywords: Daniel Patrick Moynihan; racial attitudes; stereotypes; segregation; discrimination; inequality; Barack Obama; Colin Powell

The Moynihan Report was written at a time of enormous social tumult around race. The civil rights movement was approaching its zenith. Black activists had already pushed successfully for the passage of the Civil Rights Act of 1964. Demonstrations, marches, and protests were the stuff of regular news coverage. Most Americans ranked civil rights as one of the most important problems facing the nation. As fraught as the issue of race was in early 1965, it is worth recalling that the Moynihan Report precedes by many months the Selma, Alabama, protests that would help propel passage of the Voting Rights Act later that year, as well as the explosive Watts riots of 1965 and the rise to great prominence of the "black power" slogan and so-called "black militants" in 1966 and thereafter.

The report itself became embroiled in bitter and intense controversy. Its attempt to bring careful social science thinking and evidence to bear on public policy and to focus our attention

DOI: 10.1177/0002716208324759

on how to improve the material living circumstances of African Americans became lost in acrimonious challenges to its depiction of the state and internal dynamics of many black families. As the report acknowledged, the issues were changing from a core concern with basic civil rights protections to a new focus on equal opportunities and life chances. It likewise noted that black America's demand for full inclusion was not going to be silenced or curbed. And yet, the report became a lightning rod for contention.

It is not our purpose here to rehearse or parse these well-worn debates. However, Moynihan himself was well aware of the issue that hews close to our current preoccupations. As he wrote in the first page of the report as to why further progress for blacks would be difficult: "The racist virus in the American blood stream still afflicts us: Negroes will encounter serious personal prejudice for at least another generation."

Our purpose is to analyze, if you will, this virus. We seek not to provide an assessment of those times, the report itself, or its legacy. We focus instead on one critical aspect of the fundamental social context in which the report was written and in which its legacy has played out: namely, how Americans—especially but not exclusively white and black Americans—think and feel about the matter of race. Our main argument here will be twofold.

First and most centrally, we offer a story of complexity. Despite the tendency in lay discourse and much social science work to rely on simple phrases or sweeping characterizations, "racist America" versus "the end of racism," we believe attitudes and beliefs about race have long been internally complex and have only become more so since the time of the Moynihan Report. It is in some respects misleading to ask whether people are more or less prejudiced than in the past, since the answer often depends on the domain of life, the specific social context, as well as other individual factors at play, not to mention the exact standard for assessing "prejudice" one chooses to impose. Second, and without apology or excuse, we are comfortable asserting that dynamics, conditions, and patterns of belief and behavior remain that should trouble us as a nation and that continue to make the terms *prejudice* and *racism* important and deeply meaningful facets of the American social, cultural, and political landscape.

Lawrence D. Bobo is the W. E. B. Du Bois Professor of the Social Sciences at Harvard University. He is coauthor of the award-winning book Racial Attitudes in America: Trends and Interpretations *(Harvard University Press 1997); senior editor for* Prismatic Metropolis: Inequality in Los Angeles *(Russell Sage Foundation 2000); and coeditor of* Racialized Politics: The Debate on Racism in America *(University of Chicago Press 2000). His most recent book is titled* Prejudice in Politics: Public Opinion, Group Position, and the Wisconsin Treaty Rights Dispute *(Harvard University Press 2006).*

Camille Z. Charles is the Edmund J. and Louise W. Kahn Term Professor in the Social Sciences and director of the Center for Africana Studies at the University of Pennsylvania. She is author of Won't You Be My Neighbor: Race, Class and Residence in Los Angeles *(Russell Sage Foundation 2006), which examines cross-cutting, individual-level factors thought to influence aggregate housing patterns; and coauthor of* The Source of the River: The Social Origins of Freshmen at America's Selective Colleges and Universities *(Princeton University Press 2003). Her research interests are in the areas of racial inequality, racial attitudes and intergroup relations, racial residential segregation, and minorities in higher education.*

In a way, the tone we wish to set is that of a recent editorial by economist and *New York Times* columnist Paul Krugman. In referring to the 2007 events in Jena, Louisiana, and subsequent protests he wrote, "The reality is that things haven't changed nearly as much as people think. Racial tension, especially in the South, has never gone away, and has never stopped being important. And race remains one of the defining factors in American politics" (Krugman 2007). And yet, just a few paragraphs later, Krugman declared, "It would be wrong to suggest that the nation has made no progress. Racism, though not gone, is greatly diminished: both opinion polls and daily experience suggests that we are becoming a more tolerant, open society" (Krugman 2007). Both statements are true. We hope to flesh out a way to understand these contradictory claims.

Racial Attitudes in America: Progress and Stagnation

The second half of the twentieth century was a period of "steady and sweeping movement toward general endorsement of the principles of racial equality and integration" (Bobo 2001, 294, 269). By principles of racial equality and integration, we are referring to those questions in surveys that ask Americans about the basic rules that should govern black-white interactions (Schuman et al. 1997): in essence, such questions as whether we as a society should segregate or integrate on the basis of race, and whether we should actively discriminate or treat all without regard to racial background. While blacks have a long tradition of endorsing principles of racial egalitarianism and integration, this has not been the case for a substantial segment of the white population. By the early 1970s, however, the vast majority of whites endorsed equal access to employment and the integration of public transportation. The positive shift in white attitudes toward public school integration took longer, but by the mid-1990s, whites showed near-universal endorsement of this principle as well. Despite these positive changes, whites continued to show less support for equality of access to housing and remained particularly opposed to interracial marriage. Together, these trends suggest that the greatest shifts in whites' racial attitudes occurred with respect to the most public, impersonal domains of society (Bobo 2001; Schuman et al. 1997).

Overall, however, these improvements in whites' racial attitudes are sweeping and robust, illustrating a favorable shift "in fundamental norms with regard to race" (Bobo 2001, 273). Despite frequent forecasts of an impending "white backlash," the available national sample survey data for the post–World War II period yield no real evidence of a turn backward at the level of racial principles. Faced with broad evidence of such a steady and socially pervasive change—across regions of the country, age groups, and educational levels—Schuman and colleagues (1997) concluded that

> what has changed over the past half century is the normative definition of appropriate relations between blacks and whites. Whereas discrimination against, and enforced segregation of, black Americans were taken for granted by most white Americans as recently as the World War II years, today the norm holds that black Americans deserve

the same treatment as whites, and in addition, that racial integration in all public spheres of life is a desirable goal. (Pp. 911-12)

Unfortunately, this real racial progress is juxtaposed with clear and convincing evidence of persisting racial tensions: a substantial portion of the white population still holds negative stereotypes of blacks and other minorities, and whites and minority groups have decidedly different views about the persistence of racial discrimination as well as the causes of racial inequality in American society. These trends no doubt contribute to the persistence of feelings of social distance between whites and racial minority groups, in addition to feelings of alienation among blacks, Latinos, and Asians (Bobo and Hutchings 1996; Bobo and Zubrinsky 1996; Hutchings et al. 2006).

[W]hites and minority groups have decidedly different views about the persistence of racial discrimination as well as the causes of racial inequality in American society.

Negative racial stereotypes and beliefs about racial inequality

Although the proportion of whites who negatively stereotype blacks and other minorities has declined significantly, negative racial stereotypes remain the norm in white America. Between half and three-quarters of whites in the United States still express some degree of negative stereotyping of blacks and Latinos. A smaller share of whites expresses negative stereotypes of Asians (between one-tenth and two-fifths). An important change in modern racial stereotyping is the way that many whites express their views. In previous eras, many whites categorically asserted that blacks and other minorities were biologically inferior; it was socially acceptable to say so. Now, however, racial and ethnic stereotypes are typically expressed more in terms of degrees of difference, rather than as categorical group distinctions. Critically, these perceptions rest upon more cultural and volitional explanations of minority group inferiority. For example, rather than viewing blacks as less intelligent, one might assert that they tend to be lazy and lack motivation, or that their group subculture is deficient. Yet, even perception of small, qualified differences between groups can become the basis for consequential patterns of discrimination and the maintenance of group social distance (Jackman 1994). Further complicating the issue, whites are not alone in their proclivity for negative racial stereotyping—racial minority groups also hold negative stereotypes, both of whites and of each other (Bobo 2001; Bobo and Massagli 2002; Charles 2006).

Another area of concern is a persisting racial divide in beliefs about both the prevalence of racial discrimination and the causes of racial inequality. On one side of the perceptual divide are whites, who are increasingly less inclined to believe that blacks and other minorities face structural barriers to upward mobility. Rather, if blacks cannot get ahead, whites increasingly blame blacks themselves for a lack of effort, motivation, or will (Bobo 2001; Hunt 2007; Kluegel 1990). Between 1977 and 2004, the proportion of whites fully embracing this perspective increased from 21 to 27 percent; alternatively, the share of whites asserting that persisting racial discrimination is the main cause of inequality remained constant at 20 percent during this period; 12.6 percent of whites said access to a good education is the primary barrier to blacks' upward mobility in 2004, nearly double the figure in 1977 (Hunt 2007, 401). Similarly, between one-fifth and one-quarter of whites believe that blacks and Latinos face "a lot" of discrimination in the labor market; even fewer (less than 10 percent) believe that labor market discrimination is a problem for Asians (Bobo 2001, 281-82).

On the other side of this perceptual divide are blacks—as well as Latinos and, to a lesser degree, Asians—who tend to view racial discrimination as systemic, pervasive, and therefore deeply implicated in minority disadvantage. Upwards of two-thirds of blacks as well as 60 percent of Latinos believe that structural barriers inhibit their groups' upward mobility, compared to only 10 percent of Asians (Bobo 2001; Bobo and Suh 2000; Zubrinsky and Bobo 1996). Adding complexity to these trends, however, is evidence of increasing conservatism among blacks: between 1977 and 2004, the share of blacks asserting purely motivation-based explanations for their group's inequality nearly doubled, from 6 to 11 percent. During this same period, those asserting purely structural explanations for black disadvantage declined by roughly a third, to 41 percent (Hunt 2007, 401).[1] Furthermore, research by Hunt (2007) reveals a clear tendency among Latinos to "occupy a distinct middle ground," falling between whites and blacks in their support for the individual and structural explanations for minority disadvantage (see also Bobo 2001).

The implementation gap

The persistence of antiminority stereotypes combined with these clear-cut differences in opinions about racial discrimination and inequality affect political attitudes in meaningful ways. This is especially true regarding support for progressive social policies. Specifically, Kluegel and Smith (1982) find that the more one's beliefs about the fundamental causes of racial inequality are rooted in cultural or volitional deficiencies (and less in structural barriers), the less likely one is to support government intervention aimed at eradicating racial disparities.

Support for progressive social policies also varies by the type of integration involved: following trends in the liberalization of whites' racial attitudes detailed at the outset, whites' support for intervention tends to be highest when targeting the most public and impersonal domains of societal life (e.g., access to public transportation). Alternatively, efforts to integrate more personal spaces like neighborhoods and schools are more likely to face resistance from whites. Thus, in the early 1970s, the vast majority of whites favored integrating public transportation and believed that blacks should have equal opportunities in employment. As recently as 1988, however, only half of whites expressed support for a law barring racial discrimination in the sale or rental of housing (Bobo 2001; Schuman et al. 1997).[2]

Similar patterns emerge regarding affirmative action. While a majority of whites in the twenty-first century embrace racial equality in principle and believe in increasing the human capital characteristics of disadvantaged groups, their increasing inclination to blame blacks themselves (or Latinos) for their disadvantaged status results in what we call an *implementation gap*: whites are increasingly unwilling to support public policies such as affirmative action that they believe offer unfair advantages to a group of people they believe are unwilling to help themselves (Bobo 2001; Schuman et al. 1997). Blacks, in contrast, tend to express support for a broader range of affirmative action policies. This is in part because these policies are viewed as compensation for past discrimination, but also because such initiatives are perceived to represent important strategies for combating ongoing discrimination (Schuman et al. 1997). Nonetheless, both whites and blacks shy away from policies involving quotas (Bobo and Kluegel 1993; Kluegel and Smith 1982; Steeh and Krysan 1996).

Ethno-racial alienation

An important though troubling consequence of racial group differences in beliefs about discrimination and the sources of inequality is that these perceptual differences also contribute to feelings of social distance and alienation between various racial/ethnic groups (Bobo 2001; Bobo and Hutchings 1996; Bobo and Zubrinsky 1996; Charles 2006). One understudied dimension has been characterized as racial or ethnic alienation. Interest in the sense of racial alienation grew out of the wave of research following the "race riots" of the late 1960s when there was a more intensive focus on the thinking and feelings of African Americans (Schuman and Hatchett 1974). Little in the way of national reliable trend data is available. Previous research has pointed to several potentially important patterns. Substantial fractions of the African American population affirm the idea that blacks as a group simply have not been treated fairly in American society. Some evidence suggests that dimensions of this alienation may have risen during the course of the 1990s (see Bobo 2001).

Moreover, racial/ethnic alienation falls into a clear rank order, with African Americans most likely to express such views, followed by Hispanics, and next Asians; least likely are non-Hispanic whites (see Bobo 2001, 286). Fuller multivariate examination of such sentiments suggests that these views are not much affected by socioeconomic status indicators such as education or income, but instead seem to capture collective sentiments rooted in distinctive racial-ethnic historical and social experiences (Bobo and Hutchings 1996; Hutchings et al. 2006).

Racial Attitudes in Core Domains of Life

To this point we have mainly emphasized trends and patterns in popular racial attitudes. To be sure, this is an important matter, but how might these attitudes influence group relations in specific domains of social life and in terms of more concrete social behaviors? There is a long history of debate over the link between attitudes and behavior. We do not attempt a full examination of that debate here, but we do examine how racial attitudes affect such critical domains of life as access to housing and to jobs? How might these attitudes affect close interpersonal relations? What role do they may play in our political lives?

Housing and segregation

We are not as segregated as we were in the late 1960s. Toward the close of that decade, the average level of racial residential segregation was 85. This means that 85 percent of the black (or white) population would have had to move to achieve a completely even, integrated mixture of the population in the United States (Massey and Denton 1993). During this period, more than half of whites in national surveys (56 percent) agreed with the statement that "white people have a right to keep Negroes out of their neighborhoods if they want to, and Negroes should respect that right." The most recent national data show the average level of residential segregation to be about 62, a 23-point decline.[3] Similarly, the number of whites who agree with the attitude statement about keeping blacks out of their neighborhoods fell below 20 percent in the mid-1990s and continues to edge downward.

Forty years later, however, blacks in twenty-nine U.S. metropolitan areas—home to 40 percent of the total black population—experience "extreme, multidimensional, and cumulative residential segregation" (Denton 1994, 49). Equally troubling is that this is nearly double the number of hypersegregated cities on record in 1980.[4] Throughout the twentieth century, blacks were unique in this experience, which contrasts sharply with the more moderate (and temporary) segregation experienced by other groups (Denton 1994; Massey and Denton 1993). According to new analysis by Iceland and Wilkes (2004), Latinos in both Los Angeles and New York are also experiencing hypersegregation from whites. In general, though, both Latinos and Asians are less segregated from whites than blacks are, although both groups have become more segregated since 1980 as immigration from Asia and Latin America skyrocketed (Charles 2006). There is good reason to suspect that the racial attitudes detailed above play an important role in maintaining residentially segregated neighborhoods.

The institutional practices that created racially segregated neighborhoods—redlining, restrictive covenants, blockbusting—were outlawed by the Fair Housing Act in 1968. Yet a growing body of research finds the persistence of more subtle forms of racial discrimination in the housing market (Bobo 1989; Charles 2006; Cutler, Glaeser, and Vigdor 1999; Yinger 1995). Since the mid-1950s, audit studies have been extremely valuable in detecting these more subtle forms of housing market discrimination.[5] Both national- and local-level studies suggest that racial discrimination continued to be a dominant feature of the housing market during the 1980s (Galster 1990). In a review of fifty local studies, Galster (1992) concluded that blacks and Latinos suffered discriminatory treatment in half of their interactions with real estate agents and landlords. This finding was confirmed by evidence from the 1989 HUD-sponsored Housing Discrimination Study (HDS). Discriminatory treatment took many forms, including differential access to information about housing units, special rental incentives, and outright denial (being told the unit is no longer available). Geographic steering was also quite common: for every four visits to a real estate agent, black and Latino home-seekers were steered away from predominantly white areas 40 and 28 percent of the time, respectively. Whites, on the other hand, were often steered away from racially mixed communities. Both types of steering are prohibited by law (Yinger 1995).

Ten years later, results from the 2000 HDS send mixed signals regarding the persistence of discrimination in the housing market. Both blacks and Latinos received less unfavorable treatment than in the previous study; however, steering of black home-seekers away from predominantly white neighborhoods increased (there was no significant change in steering for Latinos) (Turner et al. 2002). Racial attitudes are in play here to the extent that individual agents and/or landlords act on their own negative racial attitudes or the perceived attitudes of the communities they serve.

At the individual level, members of racial/ethnic groups differ significantly with regard to both the meaning and preferred levels of racial integration. Whites, blacks, Latinos, and Asians all exhibit preferences for both meaningful integration and a substantial coethnic presence; however, preferences for same-race neighbors are not uniform across groups. Interestingly, whites exhibit the strongest preference for same-race neighbors, blacks the weakest. At the extreme are preferences for entirely same-race neighborhoods. This option is chosen by roughly 12 percent of whites and 3 to 4 percent of blacks and native-born Latinos; less than 1 percent of native-born Asians prefer entirely same-race neighborhoods.[6] The average white person prefers a neighborhood that is just over half white; this represents what whites mean by "integrated." For blacks and native-born Latinos, an integrated neighborhood is roughly two-fifths same-race; native-born Asians prefer a neighborhood that is about one-third same-race. Equally important, preferences vary by the race of potential neighbors and highlight a commonly understood rank-ordering of out-groups. Whites are always the most desirable out-group and blacks are always the least desirable. Thus, 20 percent of whites exclude blacks entirely from their neighborhoods, as do 15 percent of native-born Asians and 19 percent of native-born Latinos (Charles 2006).[7]

Active racial prejudice—negative racial stereotypes, feelings of social distance, and perceptions of racial group competition—is the primary factor driving preferences for neighborhood racial integration, and prejudice is therefore implicated in the persistence of racially segregated communities. The relationship between racial attitudes and preferences for neighborhood racial integration is strongest among whites, but it is also a key component of minority-group preferences. Minority groups' concerns about white hostility are also influential in understanding their preferences for white neighbors—above and beyond traditional measures of prejudice. Moreover, neighborhood racial composition preferences are not at all tied to perceptions of racial/ethnic groups as economically disadvantaged or to neutral ethnocentrism as has been claimed (Bobo and Zubrinsky 1996; Charles 2003, 2006; Emerson, Chai, and Yancey 2001; Krysan 2002). Indeed, new research by Krysan and Bader (2007) shows that these clearly racial concerns are influential independent of any efforts to avoid economically disadvantaged neighborhoods. Finally, credible evidence indicates that our preferences regarding the racial composition of our neighborhoods are associated with the racial composition of our actual neighborhoods (Charles 2006; Ilandfeldt and Scafidi 2002a, 2002b).

The labor market

The facts of racial inequality in the labor market are well known. On average, African Americans continue to earn lower wages and have higher rates of unemployment than whites, even after accounting for objective differences in human capital characteristics and other important factors. In 1950, the average black male earned 52 cents for every dollar earned by a comparable white male; by 1975, black male earnings increased to 76 percent of whites', and this 24-cent gap in wages persists into the present (Holzer 2001; Massey 2007). Similarly, Western (2006) estimates that the jobless rate for black men between twenty-two and thirty years of age has remained constant at about 23 percent since 1980.[8] Differences in the human capital characteristics of whites and blacks (e.g., educational attainment, years of experience) explain part of these disparate outcomes; ample evidence, however, shows persisting racial discrimination in U.S. labor markets. Labor market discrimination takes two forms: *direct* discrimination occurs when employers simply refuse to hire workers from a particular racial/ethnic group; when employers screen and then exclude applicants on the basis of characteristics highly correlated with race (e.g., place of residence or surname), it is *indirect* or statistical discrimination (Massey 2007).

In a now-famous study of Chicago-area employers, Kirschenman and Neckerman (1991) found ample evidence that employers (1) adhered to negative stereotypes of blacks (and to a lesser extent Latinos) as employees and (2) used applicants' race and residential locations as a basis for hiring decisions. Applicants from poor neighborhoods and those living in public housing were perceived as undesirable; the extreme levels of residential segregation in the city all but guaranteed that these applicants were nonwhite. Although the employers interviewed for this study did openly engage in negative stereotyping of blacks and Latinos as workers, they made their hiring decisions without explicit mention of race.

A more recent survey of employers in Atlanta, Boston, Detroit, and Los Angeles also found meaningful evidence of indirect or statistical discrimination against African Americans (Moss and Tilly 2001). While employers did not make blanket statements about different racial groups being better suited to particular jobs, roughly one in five employers surveyed believed that inner-city residents are "poor performers" and said that their customers were biased (Moss and Tilly 2001, 152-53). Nearly half of the employers found fault with African Americans as employees—often citing a lack of motivation or problems associated with single parenting, welfare dependence, or the inner-city environment (Moss and Tilly 2001, 153).

Two recent, innovative studies provide insights about whether the actual decisions of employers are racially biased. In the first, researchers mailed out resumes applying for more than one thousand jobs advertised in Boston- and Chicago-area newspapers. Two resumes were sent for each job they responded to—one from an applicant with a white-sounding name (e.g., Chad), the other from an applicant with a black-sounding name (e.g., Jamal). Every effort was made to ensure that this was the only difference between "applicants," including the random assignment of residential location to avoid the use of street address as a proxy for race (Bertrand and Mullainathan 2004). The results are telling. "Black" applicants were half as likely as "white" applicants to get a callback overall. Moreover, whites saw greater returns to their human capital than blacks did: whites applying for high-skilled jobs had a 14 percent callback rate, but the rate was only 10 percent for low-skilled jobs. For black applicants, skill made almost no difference (each had a callback rate of about 7 percent). A low-skilled white applicant was more sought after than a high-skilled black applicant (Bertrand and Mullainathan 2004).

In another study, Pager (2003) conducted an audit study of the labor market in Milwaukee, Wisconsin, which focused on jobs requiring little skill, and found that an applicant's race was more important than having been convicted of a crime. Just more than one-third of whites with no criminal record were called back, as were 17 percent of whites convicted of a nonviolent drug offense. Astonishingly, only 14 percent of blacks with no criminal record received callbacks—a rate lower than for white "criminals." As expected, very few blacks with criminal histories (5 percent) received callbacks. Pager's study included telephone surveys of these same employers regarding their hiring practices that revealed a substantial difference in words and actions: nearly two-thirds of the employers indicated a willingness to hire someone with a criminal record irrespective of the applicant's race (Pager and Quillian 2005). These assertions are clearly not supported by their actions—far fewer employers actually take a chance with a convicted criminal, and the applicant's race clearly influences their willingness to do so.[9]

Together, these results from studies using various methodological techniques in several locations offer compelling evidence of persisting racial discrimination in the labor market. Moreover, results from studies of employers' actual attitudes and behaviors are consistent with African Americans' reports of experiences with discrimination (e.g., Feagin and Sikes 1994).[10]

Close interpersonal relationships

Forty years ago, more than half of whites (56 percent) nationally supported laws against interracial marriage (a much higher percentage of southern whites compared to whites in the North). This was the sentiment of the "typical white person" a full year after the Supreme Court overturned bans on interracial marriage in the seventeen states where they remained in place. According to data from the 2004-2005 National Politics Study (NPS), 19 percent of whites continue to express opposition to interracial marriage. This trend toward more favorable attitudes is consistent with actual social trends in interracial marriage. In 1960, about one-third of the 150,000 interracial marriages in the United States were black-white. By 2000, the number of black-white interracial couples had grown to 363,000—a sevenfold increase—but this coupling represented only about one-quarter of all interracial unions (1.46 million) (Joint Center for Political and Economic Studies 2001).

Politics and political behavior

Numerous studies examine the impact of race and racial attitudes on voting behavior, basic partisan identifications, and public opinion on an array of public policy questions (Krysan 2000; Hutchings and Valentino 2004; Lee 2008). Several conclusions seem warranted on the basis of this literature. First, racial considerations have played an important role in the shifting partisan alignments in the United States, particularly in the shift of southern white voters from primarily Democratic Party identification to increasingly Republican Party identification and of African Americans to overwhelming Democratic Party identification nationwide (Hutchings and Valentino 2004). Second, candidate race and the degree of a candidate's perceived affinity for the interests and agendas of African Americans can affect who supports a candidate and the level of that support in important ways.

Third, some prominent political issues, of course, have an explicit race-related component, such as race-targeted affirmative action in employment or access to higher education, and raise the likelihood of racial polarization and of prejudice-based effects on relevant policy views. A strong body of research indicates that a variety of antiblack attitudes substantially affect the way many white Americans respond to explicit racial policy questions (Bobo and Kluegel 1993; Kinder and Sanders 1996; Sears et al. 1997). To say that "race matters" is not, however, to say nothing else is relevant. Evidence also shows that conventional nonracial considerations, such as political ideology (conservative versus liberal) and beliefs about the appropriate role of government, also shape views even on explicitly race-related public policy questions (Sniderman and Carmines 1997).

Fourth, much of the way that race matters in politics occurs via a process of "racial coding." Accordingly, certain issues become understood as linked to the interests or demands of African Americans. When a candidate or ballot proposition is linked to black demands, then racial considerations, or underlying racial schema, are likely to figure into voter behavior. For example, strong evidence indicates that the issues of "welfare" (Gilens 1999; Fox 2004) and of "crime" (Entman and Rojecki 2000; Bobo and Johnson 2004) are now strongly linked in the mind of many white Americans to blacks. Political sociologist Martin Gilens (1999) has shown that large fractions of the white public overestimate the level of black dependency on welfare and, in particular, perceive blacks as particularly undeserving recipients (consistent with the earlier stereotyping trends we discussed) of government assistance. Political communication researchers have found that merely mentioning these issues in the course of a political campaign or advertisement, depending upon how it is done, can cue underlying negative racial attitudes and thereby lend such tendencies greater political consequence in how voters think and react in particular contests (Mendelberg 2001; Valentino, Hutchings, and White 2002).

Conclusion

Does "the racist virus in the American blood stream" still afflict us, as Moynihan put it so poignantly back in 1965? In many ways, the answer depends on what standard of evaluation, which indicator, and which trend or outcome one wishes to emphasize. The most positive aspect of the literature and research we have reviewed concerns the fundamental principles or norms that Americans expect to guide black-white relations. Here, the change is enormous, clear-cut, consistent, and we believe profoundly consequential. Most white Americans not only no longer endorse segregation, white privilege, and antiblack discrimination as rules that should guide black-white relations, but in fact endorse broad goals of integration, equality, and equal treatment without regard to race. We are convinced that this shift cuts much deeper for most people than mere lip-service adherence to what "one is supposed to say." Rather, consistent with the view espoused by social psychologist Gaertner and Dovidio (1986), a nondiscriminatory or colorblind identity is, in fact, important to most white Americans.

Yet, this facet of our culture and of individual psychological makeup is compromised or checked (or undermined) by a series of other cultural and individual psychological conditions (both of which have larger structural underpinnings; see Bobo, Kluegel, and Smith [1997] for a fuller elaboration). Public policy issues raise questions of government authority, access to material and symbolic resource distribution, and group rights and entitlements, the full sum of which greatly tests the readiness of many whites to incur potential costs or burdens of social change consistent with these new norms. Moreover, negative racial stereotypes did not vanish; they merely became less categorical and less firmly rooted in ascription to natural or biological (as opposed to cultural and volitional) differences between the races. What is more, perceptions of fundamental structural and race-discrimination-based barriers to black advancement, while common among African Americans, were never embraced by large fractions of the white public.

The full array of patterns in racial attitudes and beliefs, we believe, are borne out in parallel social conditions and trends. Whether the domain is the housing market, the labor market, the marriage market, or the world of politics, one can identify huge positive change consistent with the normative transformation we review, as well as patterns of ongoing black inequality and disadvantage traceable to lingering negative racial stereotypes, doubts about the modern relevance of race discrimination, and differences in basic perspective that derive from the historic and contemporary social locations of black and white Americans.

Nothing brings home the complexity of the current moment more than the nomination of Barack Obama for the Democratic nomination for president of the United States. Consistent with that great transformation in norms, Obama has waged a successful effort to become the first African American to secure the presidential nomination of one of the major political parties. Yet, two patterns raise concerns about even the very popular and charismatic Obama's ability to transcend the racial divide.

First, as became a matter of concern in the New Hampshire primary and several subsequent contests, some white voters appear to tell pollsters one thing but do another once in the voting booth. Some polls suggested Obama was comfortably ahead of Hillary Clinton in New Hampshire even though he narrowly lost when the final votes were in. This sort of discrepancy had been seen before, of course, when L. Douglas Wilder ran for governor in Virginia, when David Dinkins ran for mayor of New York, and when Thomas Bradley ran for governor in California (see Hutchings and Valentino 2004).

Second, throughout the primary season, especially in its later stages in such states as Ohio, Pennsylvania, Kentucky, and West Virginia, it is clear that a nontrivial number of white voters openly rejected Obama largely on the basis of race. Some estimates suggest that as many as one in five voters in Kentucky, for example, preferred Hillary Clinton over Obama largely on the basis of racial considerations. Such racial considerations seem to have greatest currency among older, less well-educated, white males (exactly as the survey-based literature would indicate; see Schuman et al. 1997).

Is it possible to transcend race? We do have a telling if largely hypothetical case. At the start of the 1996 presidential campaign, there was a buzz that then–former chair of the Joint Chiefs of Staff, General Colin Powell, would run for the Republican presidential nomination. Polling results indicated that after the successful Gulf War, he was actually perceived as favorably as Dwight Eisenhower had been at the end of World War II. Moreover, his popularity was so great that it transcended both the party and racial divides, as very careful analyses by political scientists Donald Kinder and Corrinne McConnaughy show (2006, esp. 147). Of course, Powell did not run, so the case remains a hypothetical. And the full analysis suggests that a Powell candidacy did not in any way represent the end of race and racial prejudice as political influences: he was more the exception that proved the rule. Powell, the authors argue, effectively became an exception to prevailing racial stereotypes and expectations, or "racial prototypes," as they put it. Achieving that exceptional status is what made Powell so seemingly viable. As Kinder and McConnaughy explained,

> Powell is an anomaly, and for a bundle of reasons. He is of Jamaican heritage. He is light-skinned. He keeps company with white people. He is a Republican. He speaks, Powell says himself, "like a white person." And perhaps not least, he is a victorious general. Powell is immune to racial stereotyping and racial identification, we suggest, because he deviates so markedly from the prototype. (P. 163)

Obama shares some of these features: namely, he is light-skinned, of mixed racial and immigrant background, speaks "like a white person," and has come to prominence without dependence on the usual black institutions or sponsors. However, he is a Democrat, he has clear roots in the black community, and his primary season success was heavily dependent on mobilizing black voters. And of course, a variety of implicit and explicit strategies were deployed to cast him as "the black candidate." It is thus little surprise that in this real contest involving an actual candidate, race and racial prejudice rise more directly to prominence, though these factors in no way decide the outcome of this contest.

This exact complex, murky situation is, we believe, where the matter of race now stands in the minds of Americans. The metaphor of the "virus" remains apt. While the virus is not yet defeated or fully eradicated from the body politic, we can find a number of encouraging indicators, including the Obama candidacy, that can be thought of as part of an effort to push the healing process to its next stage.

Notes

1. Only about 5 percent of these cite lack of access to education as the primary cause of inequality; for the rest, persisting discrimination is the culprit.

2. We should also note that antiminority animus is not the only source of opposition to government involvement in effecting positive racial change.

3. This decline in black-white segregation is due overwhelmingly to increasing residential contact between blacks and Latinos. Between 1980 and 2000, while black-white dissimilarity declined, blacks' exposure to whites was stagnant (Charles 2006).

4. Studies of residential segregation generally rely on one or more of six measures, each of which captures a different dimension of the spatial distribution of groups. *Evenness*, measured as the index of dissimilarity (D), describes the degree to which a group is evenly distributed across neighborhoods or tracts. A score of 60 is interpreted as extreme segregation between two groups, indicating the percentage of either group that would have to move to another tract to achieve within-tract population distributions that mirror those of the metro area. *Isolation*, measured as (P°xx), is interpreted as the percentage of the same race in the average group member's neighborhood or tract; scores of 70 and over, indicating that the average person lives in an area that is 70 percent same-race, are considered extreme. The inverse of isolation is *exposure* (P°xy), interpreted as the average probability of contact with a person of another race comparison group (usually whites). These are the most commonly reported measures. On three other measures—*concentration* (a group's degree of density), *clustering* (proximity to the central business district), and *centralization* (the contiguity of their neighborhoods)—scores greater than 60 are considered extreme. A group is hypersegregated if it scores in the extreme range on at least four of these measures (Denton 1994; Massey and Denton 1989, 1993).

5. In an audit study, pairs of trained testers with similar economic and family characteristics (one white and the other either black or Latino) successively inquire about housing. After a visit, each auditor completes a detailed report of his or her experiences with the real estate agent or landlord; discrimination is defined as systematically less favorable treatment of the nonwhite tester and is documented by direct observation during the interaction (Ondrich, Stricker, and Yinger 1998). Housing units are selected randomly from metro-area newspapers. Examples of the experience that are detailed by auditors range from aspects of seemingly race-neutral interactions (e.g., how promptly phone calls are returned or whether both members of an audit pair are shown additional units) to the obviously racially motivated act of steering minority auditors toward mixed or segregated areas (or whites to predominantly white areas).

6. The foreign-born Latino and Asian populations are considered separately as their immigrant status plays an important role in their preferences for same-race neighbors. Still, only about 8 percent of each of these groups states a preference for entirely same-race neighborhoods. The average Latino and

Asian immigrant wants a neighborhood that is nearly half same-race. Immigrant Latinos and Asians are even more likely than whites to exclude blacks entirely from their neighborhoods (38 and 44 percent, respectively; Charles 2006, 127).

7. For a detailed discussion of this research, see Charles (2003, 2006).

8. In fact, when the significant increase in incarceration among black men in this age group is taken into account, the joblessness rate has increased to nearly 33 percent—the stability in rates of black male joblessness is simply an artifact of rising rates of black male incarceration (Massey 2007; Western 2006).

9. Pager and Western (2006) replicated the Milwaukee study in New York City and report similar findings.

10. Self-reports of this type run the risk of either underestimating or overestimating the prevalence of discrimination. In the case of the former, the target does not know the reason for the negative outcome; in the case of the latter, a negative outcome could be wrongly attributed to discrimination (Quillian 2006).

References

Bertrand, Marianne, and Sendhil Mullainathan. 2004. Are Emily and Greg more employable than Lakisha and Jamal? A field experiment on labor market discrimination. *American Economic Review* 94 (4): 991-1013.

Bobo, Lawrence D. 1989. Keeping the linchpin in place: Testing the multiple sources of opposition to residential integration. *International Review of Social Psychology* 2:305-23.

———. 2001. Racial attitudes and relations at the close of the twentieth century. In *America becoming: Racial trends and their consequences*, vol. 1, ed. N. J. Smelser, W. J. Wilson, and F. Mitchell, 264-301. Washington, DC: National Academy Press.

Bobo, Lawrence, and Vincent L. Hutchings. 1996. Perceptions of racial group competition: Extending Blumer's theory of group position to a multiracial social context. *American Sociological Review* 61:951-72.

Bobo, Lawrence, and Devon Johnson. 2004. A taste for punishment: Black and white Americans' views on the death penalty and the war on drugs. *Du Bois Review* 1 (1): 151-80.

Bobo, Lawrence D., and James R. Kluegel. 1993. Opposition to race-targeting: Self-interest, stratification ideology, or racial attitudes? *American Sociological Review* 58:443-64.

Bobo, Lawrence D., James R. Kluegel, and Ryan A. Smith. 1997. Laissez faire racism: The transformation of racial attitudes. In *Racial attitudes in the 1990s: Continuities and change*, ed. S. Tuch and J. K. Martin, 15-42. Westport, CT: Praeger.

Bobo, Lawrence D., and Michael P. Massagli. 2001. Stereotyping and urban inequality. In *Urban inequality: Evidence from four cities*, ed. A. O'Connor, C. Tilly, and L. D. Bobo, 89-162. New York: Russell Sage Foundation.

Bobo, Lawrence D., and Susan Suh. 2000. Surveying racial discrimination: Analyses from a multiethnic labor market. In *Prismatic metropolis: Inequality in Los Angeles*, ed. L. D. Bobo, M. L. Oliver, J. H. Johnson, and A. Valenzuela, 527–64. New York: Russell Sage Foundation.

Bobo, Lawrence, and Camille L. Zubrinsky. 1996. Attitudes on residential integration: Perceived status differences, mere in-group preferences, or racial prejudice? *Social Forces* 74:883-909.

Charles, Camille Z. 2003. The dynamics of racial residential segregation. *Annual Review of Sociology* 29:167–207.

———. 2006. *Won't you be my neighbor?: Race, class, and segregation in Los Angeles*. New York: Russell Sage Foundation.

Cutler, David M., Edward L. Glaeser, and Jacob L. Vigdor. 1999. The rise and decline of the American ghetto. *Journal of Political Economy* 107 (3): 455–506.

Denton, Nancy A. 1994. Are African Americans still hypersegregated? In *Residential apartheid: The American legacy*, ed. Robert Bullard, Charles Lee, and J. Eugene Grigsby. Los Angeles: UCLA Center for African American Studies.

Emerson, Michael O., Karen J. Chai, and George Yancey. 2001. Does race matter in explaining residential segregation? Exploring the preferences of white Americans. *American Sociological Review* 66 (6): 922-35.

Entman, Robert M., and Andrew Rojecki. 2000. *The black image in the white mind: Media and race in America*. Chicago: University of Chicago Press.

Feagin, Joe R., and Melvin Sikes. 1994. *Living with racism: The black middle class experience*. Boston: Beacon.

Fox, Cybelle. 2004. The changing color of welfare? How whites' attitudes toward Latinos influence support for welfare. *American Journal of Sociology* 110 (3): 580-625.

Gaertner, Samuel L., and John F. Dovidio. 1986. The aversive form of racism. In *Prejudice, discrimination, and racism*, ed. J. F. Dovidio and S. L. Gaertner, 61-89. San Diego, CA: Academic Press.

Galster, George. 1990. Racial steering in housing markets during the 1980s: A review of the audit evidence. *Journal of Planning and Education Research* 9:165-75.

———. 1992. Research on discrimination in housing and mortgage markets: Assessment and future directions. *Housing Policy Debate* 3 (2): 639-83.

Gilens, Martin. 1999. Correlational framing: Media portrayals of race and poverty. Political Psychology Newsletter, Political Psychology Section of the American Political Science Association, Washington, DC.

Holzer, Harry J. 2001. Racial differences in labor market outcomes among men. In *American becoming: Racial trends and their consequences*, vol. 2, ed. Neil Smelser, William Julius Wilson, and Faith Mitchell. Washington, DC: National Academies Press.

Hunt, Matthew O. 2007. African American, Hispanic, and white beliefs about black/white inequality, 1977–2004. *American Sociological Review* 72 (3): 390-415.

Hutchings, Vincent L., and Nicholas Valentino. 2004. The centrality of race in American politics. *Annual Review of Political Science* 7:383-408.

Hutchings, Vincent, Cara Wong, James Jackson, and Ronald Brown. 2006. Whose side are you on? Explaining perceptions of competittive threat in a multi-racial context. Presented at the annual meeting of the American Political Science Association, August 31-September 3, Philadelphia.

Iceland, John, and Rima Wilkes. 2004. Does socioeconomic status matter? Race, class, and residential segregation. *Social Problems* 53:248-73.

Ilandfeldt, Keith R., and Benjamin Scafidi. 2002a. Black self-segregation as a cause of neighborhood racial segregation: Evidence from the multi-city study of urban inequality. *Journal of Urban Economics* 31:366-90.

———. 2002b. The neighborhood contact hypothesis: Evidence from the multi-city study of urban inequality. *Urban Studies* 39:619-41.

Jackman, Mary R. 1994. *The velvet glove: Paternalism and conflict in gender, class, and race relations*. Berkeley: University of California Press.

Joint Center for Political and Economic Studies. 2001. Marriage and African Americans. http://www.jointcenter.org/DB/printer/marital.htm (accessed March 27, 2008).

Kinder, Donald R., and Corrine M. McConnaughy. 2006. Military triumph, racial transcendence, and Colin Powell. *Public Opinion Quarterly* 70:139-65.

Kinder, Donald R., and Lynn M. Sanders. 1996. *Divided by color: Racial politics and democratic ideals*. Chicago: University of Chicago Press.

Kirschenman, Joleen, and Kathryn M. Neckerman. 1991. "We'd love to hire them, but . . . ": The meaning of race for employers. In *The urban underclass*, ed. Christopher Jencks and Paul E. Peterson. Washington, DC: Brookings Institution Press.

Kluegel, James R. 1990. Trends in whites' explanations of the gap in black-white socioeconomic status, 1977–1989. *American Sociological Review* 55:512-25.

Kluegel, James R., and Eliot R. Smith. 1982. Whites' beliefs about blacks' opportunity. *American Sociological Review* 47:518-32.

Krugman, Paul. 2007. Politics in black and white. *New York Times*, September 24.

Krysan, Maria. 2000. Prejudice, politics, and public opinion: Understanding the sources of racial policy attitudes. *Annual Review of Sociology* 26:135-68.

———. 2002. Whites who say they'd flee: Who are they, and why would they leave? *Demography* 39 (4): 675-96.

Krysan, Maria, and Michael Bader. 2007. Perceiving the metropolis: Seeing the city through a prism of race. *Social Forces* 86 (2): 701-33.

Lee, Taeku. 2008. Race, immigration and the identity-to-politics link. *Annual Review of Political Science* 11:457-78.

Massey, Douglas S. 2007. *Categorically unequal: The American stratification system*. New York: Russell Sage Foundation.

Massey, Douglas S., and Nancy A. Denton. 1989. Hypersegregation in US metropolitan areas: Black and Hispanic segregation along 5 dimensions. *Demography* 26:373-91.

———. 1993. *American apartheid: Segregation and the making of the underclass.* Cambridge, MA: Harvard University Press.

Mendelberg, Tali. 2001. *The race card: Campaign strategy, implicit messages, and the norm of equality.* Princeton, NJ: Princeton University Press.

Moss, Philip, and Chris Tilly. 2001. *Stories employers tell: Race, skill, and hiring in America.* New York: Russell Sage Foundation.

Ondrich, Jan, Alex Stricker, and John Yinger. 1998. Do real estate brokers choose to discriminate? Evidence from the 1989 Housing Discrimination Study. *Southern Economic Journal* 64:880-902.

Pager, Devah. 2003. The mark of a criminal record. *American Journal of Sociology* 108 (5): 937-75.

Pager, Devah, and Lincoln Quillian. 2005. Walking the talk: What employers say versus what they do. *American Sociological Review* 70 (3): 355-80.

Pager, Devah, and Bruce Western. 2006. Race at work: Realities of race and criminal record in the New York City job market. http://www.princeton.edu/%7Epager/race_at_work.pdf.

Quillian, Lincoln. 2006. New approaches to understanding racial prejudice and discrimination. *Annual Review of Sociology* 32:299-328.

Schuman, Howard, and Shirley Hatchett. 1974. *Black racial attitudes: Trends and complexities.* Ann Arbor: Institute for Social Research, University of Michigan.

Schuman, Howard, Charlotte Steeh, Lawrence Bobo, and Maria Krysan. 1997. *Racial attitudes in America: Trends and interpretations.* Rev. ed. Cambridge, MA: Harvard University Press.

Sears, David O., Collete van Laar, M. Carrillo, and Rick Kosterman. 1997. Is it really racism? The origins of white American opposition to race-targeted policies. *Public Opinion Quarterly* 61:16-53.

Sniderman, Paul M., and Edward Carmines. 1997. *Reaching beyond race.* Cambridge, MA: Harvard University Press.

Steeh, Charlotte G., and Maria Krysan. 1996. The polls-trends: Affirmative action and the public. *Public Opinion Quarterly* 60:128-58.

Turner, Margery Austin, Stephen L. Ross, George C. Galster, and John Yinger. 2002. *Discrimination in metropolitan housing markets: National results from Phase I HDS 2000.* Washington, DC: U.S. Department of Housing and Urban Development.

Valentino, Nicholas A., Vincent L. Hutchings, and Ismail K. White. 2002. Cues that matter: How political ads prime racial attitudes during campaigns. *American Political Science Review* 96:75-90.

Western, Bruce. 2006. *Punishment and inequality in America.* New York: Russell Sage Foundation.

Yinger, John. 1995. *Closed doors, opportunities lost: The continuing costs of housing discrimination.* New York: Russell Sage Foundation.

Zubrinsky, Camille L., and Lawrence Bobo. 1996. Prismatic metropolis: Race and residential segregation in the City of the Angels. *Social Science Research* 25:335-74.

Racial Stratification and the Durable Tangle of Neighborhood Inequality

By

ROBERT J. SAMPSON

This article revisits neglected arguments of the Moynihan Report to yield insights for a contemporary understanding of racial inequality in American cities. The author argues that the logic of Moynihan's reasoning implies three interlinked hypotheses: (1) the tangle of "pathology," or what today we call social dislocations, has a deep neighborhood structure, as does socioeconomic disadvantage; (2) the tangle of neighborhood inequality is durable and generates self-reinforcing properties that, because of racial segregation, are most pronounced in the black community; and (3) neighborhood "poverty traps" can ultimately only be broken with government structural interventions and macro-level policies. Examining longitudinal neighborhood-level data from Chicago and the United States as a whole, the author finds overall support for these hypotheses. Despite urban social transformations in the post-Moynihan era, neighborhoods remained remarkably stable in their relative economic standing. Poverty is also stubbornly persistent in its ecological concentration with other social disadvantages, especially in the black community.

Keywords: Daniel Patrick Moynihan; The Negro Family; Chicago; neighborhoods; durable inequality; "poverty traps"; racial stratification

Social scientists are commonly criticized for their poor predictions and tendency to focus on minutiae. We are so often reminded—albeit after the fact—that we fail to anticipate crucial events and miss the proverbial big picture. A revisit to the Moynihan Report shows us how a different kind of social science got many important things right—*prospectively*, not looking backward. With a no-holds-barred, unflinching eye, Daniel Patrick Moynihan forecast key social trends and identified fundamental social problems confronting the urban United States (Moynihan 1965), perhaps none more salient than the so-called "tangle of pathology" in the black ghetto (see also Clark 1965). The language was unusually blunt, which ignited a firestorm

NOTE: I thank Steve Raudenbush for comments on the article and conversations over the years on racial inequality.

DOI: 10.1177/0002716208324803

of protest that was not soon forgotten. To this day, the term *pathology* is avoided like the plague among social scientists.

Yet, many of the underlying facts Moynihan confronted remain stubbornly alike to this day, compelling us to address the world as it is, not only as we wish it to be. In this spirit my goal is to dig a bit deeper, getting beyond the timeworn "pathology" debate and focusing instead on the larger notion of what I think Moynihan was trying to achieve. My take, like that of Kenneth B. Clark's similarly unflinching portrait at the same time (1965), is that Moynihan wanted social policy to focus primarily on the "tangle"—the knot of inequality in U.S. cities that resides at the structural and social-ecological level, not just the individual or family level.[1] My specific thesis is that Moynihan identified a *neighborhood* tangle of inequality—one inextricably tied to race—and that he emphasized its *durability of influence* absent *government intervention*. Furthermore, the neighborhood tangle of inequality implied the disproportionate or unique causal exposure in the lives of black children to a bundle of spatially defined disadvantages. I believe Moynihan was right to warn about the differential exposure to risk imposed by racial stratification.

Consider first the very idea of the tangle. Many view the Moynihan Report as an indictment of joblessness as the primary driver of social problems. Although joblessness was always high on the agenda, the facts provoked Moynihan to emphasize *interconnections*, not single variables. Throughout the report he noted how family instability, joblessness, poor health, substance abuse, poverty, welfare dependency, and crime were intertwined. In chapter 3, "The Roots of the Problem," Moynihan cited ecological analyses in Washington, D.C., on what we might today call "concentration effects." For example, he described in some detail the correlation of illegitimacy rates in census tracts with male unemployment and poverty rates. He also noted Franklin Frazier and the work of other social scientists on social disadvantages in the city. Although not cited in the original report, this genre is perhaps best exemplified in the classic *Black Metropolis*, originally published in 1945 (Drake and Cayton 1945/1993), and later in Clark's *Dark Ghetto* (1965). As shown in the original publication *Black Metropolis*, from "disease and death" (p. 205) to "poverty and social disorganization" (p. 203), the city of Chicago in the mid-twentieth century was highly stratified by an ecological structure of disadvantage and risk.

Robert J. Sampson is the Henry Ford II Professor of the Social Sciences and chairman of the Department of Sociology at Harvard University. For the past twelve years, he has served as scientific director of the Project on Human Development in Chicago Neighborhoods (PHDCN), which has been the source for much of his research on neighborhood effects, crime, inequality, and the social structure of the contemporary city. He is the author of many journal articles and several books, including The Explanation of Crime: Context, Mechanisms, and Development *(Cambridge University Press 2006);* The Social Ecology of Crime *(Springer-Verlag 1996); and the award-winning* Crime in the Making: Pathways and Turning Points through Life *(Harvard University Press 1993) and* Shared Beginnings, Divergent Lives: Delinquent Boys to Age 70 *(Harvard University Press 2003).*

Unfortunately, not much has changed. More than seventy years later, specific neighborhoods may have shifted or traded places, with poverty tending to move outward from the inner city, but the pattern of ecological concentration and racial stratification remains (Sampson and Morenoff 2006). Akin to Drake and Cayton's (1945/1993) maps, for example, I have shown that the ecological distribution of homicides matches the distribution of low-birth-weight babies (Sampson 2003, 54). There is nary a difference in the ecological pattern despite the seemingly distinct etiological origins of these two phenomena. Dozens of other maps could make the same point about concentrated health risks.

In short, evidence indicates that "things go together" still—that not much has changed since Moynihan's day in terms of the general mechanisms of uneven spatial concentration. A host of social problems and dislocations (pathologies?)—call them what you will—are undeniably clustered for many in society who lack the resources to escape communities of disadvantage. Although often overlooked, Moynihan was insistent on this point, so much so that in what is arguably the most important chapter of his report, "The Case for National Action," he argues against the singular "variable" approach (Abbott 1997) and for a holistic approach that turns on the tangle, or knot of connections. To quote directly,

> It is our view that the problem is so inter-related, one thing with another, that any list of program proposals would necessarily be incomplete, and would distract attention from the main point of *inter-relatedness* [emphasis added]. We have shown a clear relation between male employment, for example, and the number of welfare dependent children. Employment in turn reflects educational achievement, which depends in large part on family stability, which reflects employment. Where we should break into this cycle, and how, are the most difficult domestic questions facing the United States. (Moynihan 1965, chap. 3, p. 1)

Furthermore, Moynihan coupled interconnectedness with durability and posited the idea of reinforcing cycles or what today might be called "poverty traps" (Bowles, Durlauf, and Hoff 2006). He noted at the beginning of his report that "so long as this situation persists, the cycle of poverty and disadvantage will continue to repeat itself." And in the final policy chapter, he warned that "three centuries of injustice have brought about deep-seated structural distortions in the life of the Negro American" and that the "present tangle of pathology is capable of perpetuating itself without assistance from the white world. The cycle can be broken only if these distortions are set right" (Moynihan 1965, chap. 5, p. 1). In other words, he argued that once set in motion, racially linked poverty is a trap that reinforces itself and that requires structural interventions to break.

Rereading the document in light of current knowledge, I would argue that Moynihan's logic implies three broad ideas or theses that are themselves interlinked:

1. The tangle of pathology (what today we call social dislocations or social problems) has a deep neighborhood or ecological structure, as does socioeconomic disadvantage.
2. The tangle of neighborhood inequality is durable and generates self-reinforcing properties that, because of racial segregation, are most pronounced in the black community. I would add to that a related implication or subthesis: black children are uniquely exposed

to the cumulative effects of concentrated structural disadvantage in ways that reinforce the cycle.

3. The "poverty trap" cycle can ultimately only be broken with structural interventions of the sort that government and other macro-level policies are best equipped to induce.

In this article, I present a sequence of empirical evidence in support of the first two of these ideas. I believe the jury is still out on the third thesis and will be for some time. I nonetheless present suggestive evidence in support of the "no change absent structural intervention" thesis and suggest avenues for further assessment. Overall, the data I shall present are descriptive, but I do not apologize for that—I believe modern social science has denigrated descriptive and synthetic work that is every bit as important as seemingly more advanced causal models. After all, pattern recognition is a fundamental goal of science. My work is based mainly (but not exclusively) on the social laboratory of Chicago because I have spent well over a decade studying this quintessentially American city, the site of much seminal work on urban poverty. My hope is that the current analysis will spur new insights and the motivation to study the fundamentals of stability and change in racial inequality in multiple places and time periods.

Thesis 1: Things Go Together

As Shaw and McKay (1942) showed us in the Chicago of the 1920s and 1930s, Drake and Cayton (1945/1993) in the mid-twentieth century, and Wilson (1987) and Massey and Denton (1993) near century's end, all manner of social problems, typically considered "outcomes," cluster together spatially. Whether low birth weight or murder, compromised well-being remains concentrated in early-twenty-first-century Chicago. This pattern suggests a deep continuity to the urban concentration of well-being. But what about what are often considered the structural *sources* of well-being, such as unemployment, segregation, poverty, or family structure—the staples of Moynihan's reasoning? There are theoretical reasons to expect that socioeconomic and family factors cluster together in certain communities as well and that this process may be implicated in the long-standing association of social disadvantage with health, crime, and other quality-of-life indicators (Massey, Condran, and Denton 1987; Massey and Shibuya 1995).

In particular, Wilson (1987) famously argued that the social transformation of inner-city areas in the decades of the 1970s and 1980s resulted in an increased concentration of the most disadvantaged segments of the urban black population—especially poor, female-headed families. The consequences of these differential ecological distributions are profound because they mean that relationships between race and individual outcomes are systematically confounded with important differences in community contexts. The concentration of poverty and also joblessness (Wilson 1996) has been argued to result from macrostructural economic changes related to the de-industrialization of central cities where low-income minorities are disproportionately located. These changes include a shift

from goods-producing to service-producing industries, the increasing polarization of the labor market into low wage and high wage sectors, and the relocation
of manufacturing out of the inner city. According to Wilson, the related exodus
of middle- and upper-income black families from the inner-city also removed an
important social buffer that could potentially deflect the full impact of prolonged
joblessness and industrial transformation (Wilson 1987, 56). The social milieu of
increasing stratification among blacks differs significantly from the environment
that existed in inner-city neighborhoods in previous decades. Wilson (1996)
argues, in other words, that income mixing within communities was more characteristic of ghetto neighborhoods during previous decades, whereas inequality
among communities today has become more pronounced as a result of the
increasing spatial separation of middle- and upper-income blacks from lower-
income blacks (see also Jargowsky 1997).

Focusing instead on racial segregation, Massey and Denton (1993) describe
how increasing social differentiation caused by economic dislocation interacts
with the spatial concentration of a minority group to create a set of structural circumstances that reinforce the effects of social and economic deprivation. They
show that, in a segregated environment, exogenous economic shocks that cause a
downward shift in the distribution of minority income not only bring about an
increase in the poverty rate for the group as a whole but also cause an increase in
the geographic concentration of poverty. This geographic intensification of
poverty occurs because the additional poverty created by macroeconomic conditions is spread unevenly over the metropolitan area (Morenoff and Sampson
1997). That is, as segregation increases, a smaller number of neighborhoods
absorb the shock, resulting in a more severe concentration of poverty (Massey
and Denton 1993; Massey and Eggers 1990). Recent work by Quillian (1999)
shows that the distinct mechanisms hypothesized by Wilson and Massey are both
operative and combine to produce the high levels of racially stratified urban
poverty that we see in the United States.

Concentrated disadvantage and racial stratification

Taken as a whole, empirical research on social-ecological differentiation lines
up well with the central assertion in the Moynihan Report and expectations from
the Wilson-Massey debate that (1) considerable social inequality exists between
neighborhoods in terms of socioeconomic and racial/ethnic segregation,[2] and
(2) these factors are connected in that concentrated poverty and other correlates
of disadvantage coincide with the geographic isolation of racial minority and
immigrant groups (Sampson, Morenoff, and Gannon-Rowley 2002). Moreover,
these patterns are not unique to any one city and extend across multiple ecological units of analysis ranging from census tracts to metropolitan areas and even
states (Land, McCall, and Cohen 1990).

I extend the debate by considering here new evidence on empirical patterns
for a core set of socioeconomic indicators for Chicago and the United States. My
colleagues and I (Sampson, Sharkey, and Raudenbush 2008) recently investigated

the notion that disadvantage is not encompassed in a single characteristic but rather is a synergistic composite of social factors that mark the qualitative aspects of growing up in truly disadvantaged neighborhoods (Wilson 1987). We focused on six characteristics of census tracts nationwide, taken from the 1990 and 2000 Census, to create a measure of concentrated disadvantage: welfare receipt, poverty, unemployment, female-headed households, racial composition (percentage black), and density of children. These indicators formed a single principal component of "concentrated disadvantage" across both decades in both Chicago and the rest of the United States, the latter representing some sixty-five thousand census tracts (Sampson, Sharkey, and Raudenbush 2008, table 1, p. 848). The main difference of note between the United States as a whole and Chicago neighborhoods is that the exposure of children under 18 years of age to concentrated economic disadvantage and racial segregation is more pronounced in Chicago.

There are important implications of this synergistic clustering for studying any race-specific outcome. When we defined concentrated disadvantage as falling within the most disadvantaged quartile of Chicago census tracts, for example, the result was that *no* white families and only a few Hispanic families in a representative sample of children from Chicago lived in disadvantage. This result is not simply attributable to percentage black being included in the scale of concentrated disadvantage. When we re-created the scale of concentrated disadvantage with no measure of neighborhood racial composition, the resulting scale correlated at .99 with the initial scale that includes percentage black.

The stratification of Chicago's urban landscape by race precludes the estimation of a single causal effect of disadvantage for all racial groups, as commonly attempted in the literature. Thus, our initial attempts to estimate causal models using pooled samples consisting of all racial and ethnic groups failed precisely because of the lack of "common support" in the exposure variable—only by defining poverty very broadly, and by ignoring segregation, can we include whites and even most Hispanics, but at that point virtually all blacks are at risk of exposure to the treatment because of concentrated racial inequality (Sampson, Sharkey, and Raudenbush 2008, 849). As Massey and Denton (1993) argue more generally, race and the multiple dimensions of disadvantage are ecologically intertwined and thus confounded at the neighborhood level in most large U.S. cities.

To grasp this point visually, Figure 1 presents the simple per capita income distribution in 2000 in black and white neighborhoods in Chicago (defined here as census tracts with 75 percent or more of each group). The left panel indicates the location of the median for per capita income in neighborhoods that are predominantly black. The right panel shows the distribution of income in white neighborhoods, with an arrow denoting the location of the black median. The bottom-line result is that residents in not one white community experience what is most typical for those residing in segregated black areas with respect to the basics of income—the entire distribution for white communities sits to the right of the mean of black communities. Trying to estimate the effect of concentrated disadvantage on whites is thus tantamount to estimating a phantom reality.

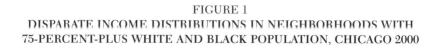

FIGURE 1
DISPARATE INCOME DISTRIBUTIONS IN NEIGHBORHOODS WITH
75-PERCENT-PLUS WHITE AND BLACK POPULATION, CHICAGO 2000

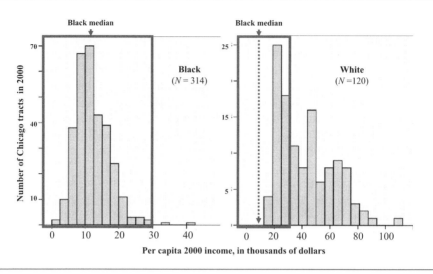

NOTE: Black mean = $12,276 ($2,465-$42,011); White mean = $42,508 ($15,040-$107,023).

I argued above that Moynihan's tangle of pathology thesis implied that the knot of inequality was also tighter in the black community than the white community. In some sense, Figure 1 already confirms this point, but another way to examine this thesis more directly is to examine how the relationship between the unemployment rate and poverty varies by the racial status of the neighborhood. Unemployment in the black community was seen by Moynihan as one of the central drivers of poverty, a relationship that he felt was intensified over time by discrimination and segregation. The implication is that resources available in white communities would be able to offset, to some extent, the deleterious connection of unemployment with poverty.

Although indirectly, I assess this prediction by dividing Chicago neighborhoods into four race/ethnic strata. Specifically, I define areas where whites, Latinos, and blacks are 75 percent or more of the population, with mixed areas (where no one group dominates) making up the fourth type. Figure 2 is consistent with the general argument that minority and heterogeneous communities bear a greater burden when unemployment reigns. For example, although the N is small, across predominantly white communities there is essentially no relationship between unemployment and poverty rates, whereas across Latino, mixed, and especially black areas the relationship is much stronger ($R = .78$ for variability across segregated black neighborhoods). This finding suggests that the much tighter connection among economic-related indicators in black or minority

FIGURE 2
CONNECTION OF JOBLESSNESS WITH CONCENTRATED
POVERTY INTERACTS WITH RACE: CHICAGO 2000

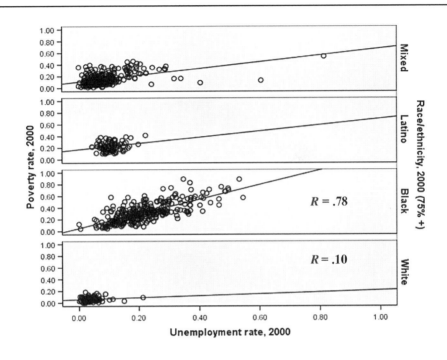

areas compared to white areas is part of what helps create the synergistic intersection of racial segregation with concentrated racial resource disadvantage.

Thesis 2: Durability and Poverty Traps

Perhaps the most provocative component of Moynihan's thesis concerns the durability of racial inequality, a long-standing concern of sociologists most recently developed in the work of the late Charles Tilly (1998). At the neighborhood level, Sampson and Morenoff (2006) presented data from Chicago showing the persistence of poverty during the 1970s through the 1990s, a time of great changes in U.S. cities (Wilson 1987). They reported a very high correlation ($r = .87$) between neighborhood poverty rates in 1970 and 1990 such that neighborhoods that were poor in 1970 generally continued to be poor in 1990. Most of the variance in poverty (67 percent) was also due to differences *between* neighborhoods rather than differences over time *within* neighborhoods, implying that between-neighborhood differences in poverty were quite stable over time. Yet, there was

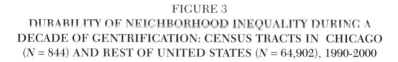

FIGURE 3
DURABILITY OF NEIGHBORHOOD INEQUALITY DURING A
DECADE OF GENTRIFICATION: CENSUS TRACTS IN CHICAGO
($N = 844$) AND REST OF UNITED STATES ($N = 64,902$), 1990-2000

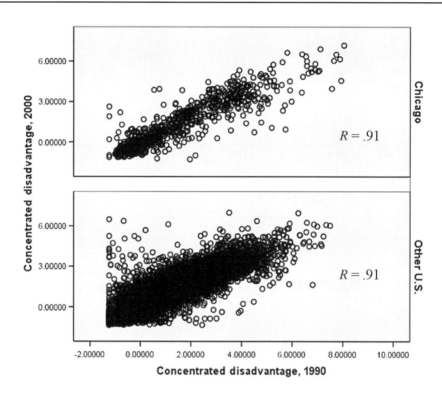

significant secular change, as the poverty rate for the average neighborhood increased from 11 percent in 1970 to 20 percent in 1990. This change was even more pronounced at the upper tail of the neighborhood poverty distribution. The 75th percentile of the distribution corresponded to a poverty rate of only 14 percent in 1970, but by 1990, it had more than doubled, increasing to 30 percent. In short, there was a dramatic growth in neighborhood poverty between 1970 and 1990, but despite this change, there was stability in the relative rank order of neighborhoods vis-à-vis poverty. Neighborhood poverty was thus both a persistent and increasingly prevalent condition.

I turn now to the most recent decade, one considered by many students of the city to be characterized by gentrification. Does stability still hold? Figure 3 provides a clear answer, and not just for Chicago. Using a principal-component, regression-weighted scale of the concentrated disadvantage indicators introduced above,[3] I plot the relationship predicting disadvantage in 2000 from 1990

FIGURE 4
STABLE ASYMMETRY OF RACIAL CHANGE OVER THREE
DECADES IN CHICAGO: 1970-2000

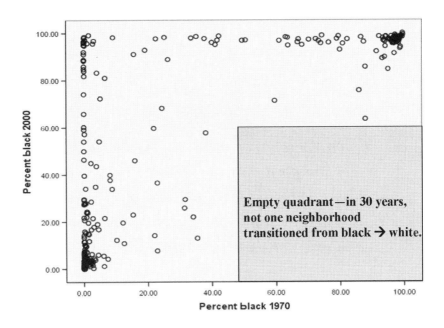

disadvantage. Whether for the city of Chicago or for the sixty-four thousand census tracts across the rest of the United States, overall disadvantage demonstrates strong inertial tendencies at the ecological level. Note that the correlation is greater than .9 at both the local and national level with an identical pattern.

To further elaborate the persistence of racial segregation, I extend the analysis of Sampson and Morenoff (2006) by examining *changes* in racial composition across a period of three decades. Figure 4 plots the percentage of a neighborhood's population that was black in 2000 against percentage black in 1970, just before the major urban transformations Wilson (1987) wrote about. This graph shows that where racial change is abundant it is structured in an asymmetric way, yielding three types of neighborhoods. The first two reflect durable segregation—those that are stably black (upper right) and those that are stably white (lower left). The third type reflects transitional neighborhoods that went either from all white to black or partially black to segregated black (up the left side and across top)—"white flight." That much is not a surprise.

What is startling is the missing fourth type—in the third largest city in America, *not one neighborhood transitioned from black to white*. The lack of observations in the lower-right quadrant of the graph indicates that none of the areas that had large percentages of black population in 1970 lost significant shares over time. In fact, there appears to be a threshold effect of around 40 percent black, above which all neighborhoods either maintained or increased their share of black population. Figure 4 thus tells a story of change within a stable ecological system: there were great shifts in neighborhood racial composition from 1970 to 1990, but neighborhoods that were initially black stayed that way over time, while at the same time, many areas of the city remained off-limits to blacks. In light of this pattern, Chicago has the distinction of being not just one of the most racially segregated cities in America (Massey and Denton 1993) but one that is durably so.

[T]here were great shifts in neighborhood racial composition from 1970 to 1990, but neighborhoods that were initially black stayed that way over time, while at the same time, many areas of the city remained off-limits to blacks.

    Another implication of Moynihan's reasoning, as explicated above, is that the grip of neighborhood inequality—the tangle—is exacerbated in the black community and is therefore more durable. The empirical expectation is that we should see more persistence in disadvantage in minority or black communities than white ones. Chicago, with its segregated urban structure, affords an opportunity to assess this notion within relatively homogeneous subgroups. Similar to Figure 2, I again disaggregate the city into four race/ethnic strata—predominantly white, black, Latino, and other (mixed). Figure 5 presents the persistence over the decade of the 1990s of concentrated disadvantage by race/ethnicity. In minority areas, the continuity is much higher, but the pattern is especially striking when comparing segregated black neighborhoods, where the correlation is .83, to white neighborhoods, where the stability is much less (.24).
    This divergent pattern is even more evident for the durability of unemployment that Moynihan emphasized. For simplicity, Figure 6 presents the prediction of neighborhood unemployment rates in 2000 from unemployment rates in 1990 for predominantly black compared to predominantly white neighborhoods. The pattern is rather unambiguous. In Chicago at least, the correlation of unemployment over time is high (.64) in the black community but nonexistent in the white community. Note, too, that the distributions are for all intents and purposes incomparable, explaining the differential correlations. Most white neighborhoods

FIGURE 5
DURABILITY OF CONCENTRATED DISADVANTAGE INTERACTS WITH
RACIAL STRATIFICATION, CHICAGO 1990-2000

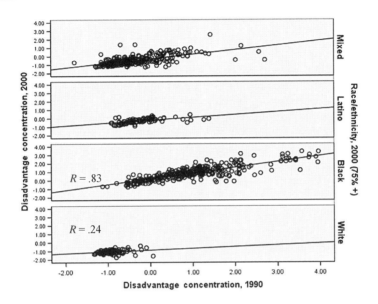

FIGURE 6
DURABILITY OF NEIGHBORHOOD JOBLESSNESS INTERACTS
WITH RACE, CHICAGO 1990-2000

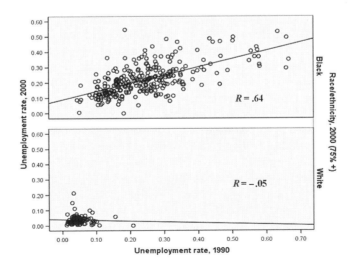

sit to the left of where the black distribution even starts. Once again, the data reveal that blacks and whites in segregated communities live in different social worlds. Much in the way that Moynihan worried about in 1965, unemployment appears to recycle itself in the black community.

The role of disorder and violence

Beginning about 1965, which Robert Putnam (2000) argues is the point of decline of American civic life, crime rates began to explode in American cities. They rose to unprecedented heights and fluctuated at high levels in the 1970s and 1980s, a period of intensifying concentration of poverty. I believe that crime, disorder, and violence have been overlooked in the feedback processes that help perpetuate poverty traps, especially in precipitating selective out-migration from central cities burdened with high rates of victimization. For example, there is evidence that fear of violence leads to a "hunkering down" and shunning of neighbors and local institutions that otherwise might support local social control (Skogan 1990). In this way, crime is both influenced by and reciprocally influences the informal control structures and mobilization capacity of communities. Violence and robbery may also prompt the withdrawal of businesses and middle-class families from inner-city areas, which may fuel more crime and a further deepening of poverty. Moreover, in areas of segregated poverty, violence may beget violence by way of predatory forms of adaptation (Massey 1995), again potentially feeding into a vicious cycle.

Neighborhoods with high crime and "signs of disorder" are especially prone to developing reputations as "bad" and thus to be avoided. Stigmatization sets in, and when linked to the historical legacy in U.S. cities whereby racial segregation and poverty are bound up with structural patterns of disinvestment (Massey and Denton 1993), a form of self-fulfilling prophecy can take place (Loury 2002). Residents acting on their perceptions of disorder will undertake actions that have the effect of increasing that very disorder (Sampson and Raudenbush 2004).

Although the number of empirical studies is small, empirical evidence indicates that crime does undermine the social and economic fabric of urban areas. Bursik (1986) found that delinquency rates are not only one of the outcomes of urban change but also an important part of the process of urban change. Studying Chicago neighborhoods, Bursik found that "although changes in racial composition cause increases in the delinquency rate, this effect is not nearly as great as the effect that increases in the delinquency rate have in minority groups being stranded in the community" (p. 73). In a study of forty neighborhoods in eight cities, Skogan (1990) found that high rates of crime and disorder were associated with higher rates of fear, neighborhood dissatisfaction, and intentions to move out. Morenoff and Sampson (1997) showed that increases in violent crime along with proximity to violence contributed to the population loss and decline of neighborhoods in Chicago. The effect of crime on population loss is also observed at the city level. More than twenty years ago, I showed in a study that

FIGURE 7
PERCEIVED DISORDER PREDICTS LATER POVERTY:
CHICAGO NEIGHBORHOODS 1995 TO 2000

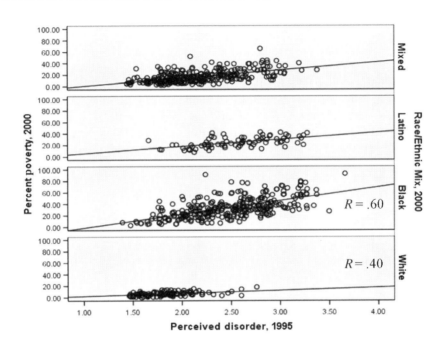

increases in homicide were strongly associated with population decline and increases in the poverty of the black population in a sample of major U.S. cities, independent of the usual demographic predictors of urban change (Sampson 1986). Liska and Bellair (1995) similarly found that robbery rates played a significant role in white flight from central cities, therefore exacerbating racially segregated urban poverty.

I extend this line of inquiry here by considering the role of perceived disorder as conceptualized by Sampson and Raudenbush (2004). Using the same 1995 community survey, I examine a scale that taps neighborhood-level differences in the perception of both physical aspects of disorder (e.g., graffiti) and social aspects of disorder (e.g., public drinking). I specifically consider the simple prediction of *future* poverty from prior states of subjectively perceived disorder. Figure 7 demonstrates a positive prediction in a pattern that is becoming repetitive, with black neighborhoods again bearing the brunt of the underlying dynamics. Note that in predominantly black areas, perceptions of disorder foretell where a neighborhood will end up in the stratification hierarchy. The prediction line is flatter and the correlation smaller for white areas. Is this just due to past poverty?

The answer is no, at least in minority areas, for when I control for poverty in 1990, disorder still significantly predicts poverty in 2000 in mixed, Latino, and black neighborhoods ($p < .01$). Only in white neighborhoods is the disorder-poverty prediction attenuated ($p > .05$), which suggests that stigmatization by disorder carries a strong racial undertone when it comes to understanding population dynamics of the city (Quillian and Pager 2001).

In short, many cities and neighborhoods, especially in the North and Midwest, not only have lost population but also have become poorer and more racially isolated in recent decades (Wilson 1987; Massey and Denton 1993). An important part of this racially selective decline in population and economic status may stem from increases in violent crime (Morenoff and Sampson 1997) and stigmatizing perceptions of disorder (Sampson and Raudenbush 2004), suggesting that research on poverty traps needs to expand its theoretical framework on urban change.

Thesis 3: Structural Interventions: Breaking the Trap?

How can the durable inequality I have documented be changed? This question is the hardest of all, and as Moynihan seemed to intuit, there are no easy answers. This is especially true in a culture where freedom of choice, and hence resident movement, is highly valued.

Recent work in Chicago has therefore attempted to increase our knowledge of processes of inequality by taking seriously individual selection decisions and neighborhood choice. It turns out that even when we consider a host of individual characteristics of movers and stayers alike, concentrated racial inequality is reproduced, suggesting in a different way that powerful social forces undergird a stable equilibrium of ecologically based racial stratification (Sampson and Sharkey 2008). In particular, the lion's share of racial and ethnic inequality in neighborhood attainment cannot be explained by changing economic circumstances, life cycle stage, or other major characteristics of families or individuals that might influence residential decisions. After accounting for these and other factors typically not considered in the mobility literature, we found that whites attain neighborhoods that are substantially more affluent than do nonwhites (see also Massey, Condran, and Denton 1987; Massey and Fong 1990).

Furthermore, consistent with the logic of Moynihan's overarching thesis, race interacts with changes in the racial composition of the origin neighborhood to influence the likelihood that an individual will move and thereby exacerbate patterns of segregation. Specifically, whites *and* Latinos living in Chicago neighborhoods with growing populations of nonwhites are more likely to exit the city, providing evidence that realized mobility arises, at least in part, as a response to changes in the racial mix of the origin neighborhood (Sampson and Sharkey 2008, 20). The same, however, is not true of black families—it is not African Americans' preference for same-race neighbors that seems to matter as much as whites' and

FIGURE 8
NO CHANGE ABSENT INTERVENTION? CONCENTRATED
POVERTY IN CHICAGO COMMUNITY AREAS, 1990-2000

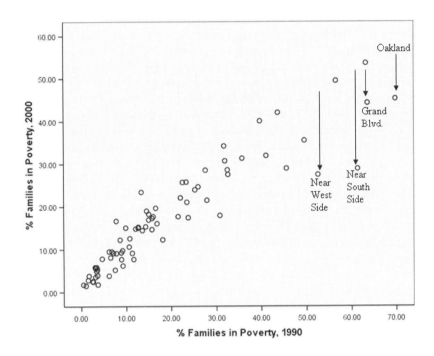

Latinos' eagerness to exit neighborhoods with growing populations of blacks (Charles 2000, 2001, 2003). Neighborhood conditions appear to matter a great deal for influencing neighborhood selection decisions, suggesting a different kind of neighborhood effect—*sorting as a social process* in the reproduction of urban inequality.

Additional research is necessary to clarify how discrimination and revealed preferences for "in-group" and "out-group" neighbors interact to produce what appears to be a stratified pattern of neighborhood poverty traps (Sampson and Morenoff 2006). It is likely that some of the inequality reproduction is "chosen," not in the sense of an intended consequence but because African Americans trade off more affluent white neighborhoods for ones perceived to be more hospitable and racially diverse, not unreasonably given the grim history of U.S. race relations. There is also evidence that members of minority groups make residential sorting decisions based on their perceptions of a racialized hierarchy of places, even if felt to be unjust, and net of legal or outright institutional discrimination (Bobo and Zubrinsky 1996; Wilson and Taub 2006).

In short, the data suggest that the residential racial stratification visible in Chicago and beyond is reproduced by movers and stayers of every race/ethnic group (Sampson and Sharkey 2008, 26). This perspective views individuals as making heterogeneous choices and revealing their preferences about where to reside, with the parameters of choice tightly bounded by the stratified landscape in which choices are made. Preferences and structural constraints thus simultaneously and dynamically work together to yield a self-reinforcing cycle of inequality (Loury 2002), or what Tilly (1998) referred to as "durable inequality" and Moynihan earlier referred to as the cycle of poverty. It follows logically that poverty traps are difficult to escape and likely to continue absent state-led interventions (e.g., de-concentration of public housing; community policing) or cultural changes that yield visions of social life where ethnic and class diversity is seen as an urban amenity rather than a stigma (Sampson and Sharkey 2008, 27).

This hypothesis leads to my final example. Figure 8 reconsiders the continuity of concentrated disadvantage during the decade of the 1990s, this time for larger community areas in Chicago that are still widely recognized by administrative agencies, local institutions concerned with service delivery, and residents. These communities have distinct names and reputations that are widely known (e.g., Hyde Park, Grand Boulevard, South Shore, and Lincoln Park) and that serve as markers of difference and symbolic value (Hunter 1974; Wilson and Taub 2006). Community areas also have political force that continues (Suttles 1990), and Wilson's (1987) thesis of concentration effects was developed based on data from community areas in Chicago.

It is likely that some of the inequality reproduction is "chosen" . . . because African Americans trade off more affluent white neighborhoods for ones perceived to be more hospitable and racially diverse.

By putting names to communities, the pattern of change in Figure 8 becomes apparent. The communities that are significantly below the regression line of continuity share a similar profile. Grand Boulevard, Oakland, and the Near South Side were mainly poor black communities that witnessed major interventions, including the dismantling of segregated high-rise public housing and considerable investment by the city and local institutions, such as the University of Chicago, in both the physical infrastructure and educational system (e.g., charter schools). The Near West Side also saw considerable investment by the city and economic developers.

Although not sufficient evidence to support a causal claim, it is notable that each community undergoing large "interventions" saw significant unexpected declines in the rate of concentrated poverty as predicted from 1990 levels alone. Stability is not inevitable, then—reversal of fortune is possible. But in the case of Chicago at least, and I suspect other cities, structural levers are needed to spur change in deeply distressed minority communities. Examples of other interventions are mixed-income housing developments, industrial zones, and community policing. The larger point is that in an ongoing process with durable or self-reinforcing properties, macro interventions of the sort government is uniquely suited to mount, or support through zoning changes, need to be at the top of our policy considerations and evaluation efforts.

The mid- to late 1990s was an especially propitious time for structural interventions because an important natural change was taking place across much of the country—crime and violence rates were falling sharply. I have noted the centrality of crime and violence in earlier eras in driving down central-city populations and in contributing to the widespread sense of urban decline. The time was thus ripe to take advantage of a renewed appreciation for the viability of cities, reclaiming them from the grip of violence. Indeed, it appears that in places like Chicago, renewal is being witnessed in the heart of what were previously high-crime, very poor, and in many respects devastated areas. No one factor can be credited, but together it appears that smart local decisions, which capitalize on secular changes that are benefiting cities, are possible.

Conclusion

If there is one message of this article, it is that poverty and its correlates are stubbornly persistent in terms of neighborhood concentration, especially for black areas. Despite urban social transformation in the post-Moynihan era (Wilson 1987), neighborhoods remained remarkably stable in their relative economic standing despite the in-flow and out-flow of individual residents. It follows that an enduring poverty vulnerability of neighborhoods is not simply a matter of the current income of residents. Neighborhoods possess reputations both positive and negative, which, when coupled with the residential mobility decisions of residents of all race and income groups, tend to reproduce existing patterns of inequality (Sampson and Sharkey 2008).

What change does occur reveals strong patterns of asymmetry by race and class, which suggests that once a neighborhood is beyond a certain threshold or "tipping point" of either percentage black or percentage poor—but especially the former—further change is invariably in the direction of greater racial homogeneity and more poverty. It is worth repeating that not one neighborhood in Chicago more than 40 percent black in 1970 became predominantly white by 2000, fully thirty years later (see Figure 4). By contrast, a large number of white neighborhoods turned black even as the polar extremes (all-black and all-white neighborhoods) remained the dominant pattern. Neighborhoods also tended either to stay in the same poverty category or move to a higher poverty category over time—upgrading (e.g., gentrification) was quite rare even in the 1990 to 2000 period when we consider concentrated disadvantage whether in Chicago or the United States as a whole.

Although beyond the scope of this article, the consequences of durable and increasing poverty appear to be long-lasting, at least with respect to predicting key social processes. Controlling for the sociodemographic location of individual respondents, for example, Sampson and Morenoff (2006) found that both persistent poverty and increases in poverty from 1970 to 1990 predicted lower collective efficacy and the moral cynicism of neighborhood residents in 1995—a span of some twenty-five years. When adjusting for recent compositional changes (Sampson and Graif forthcoming), trust in 1995 is also lower in neighborhoods that, decades earlier, were characterized by pronounced concentrated poverty. These findings are consistent with the scenario that certain urban neighborhoods get locked into structural dynamics that generate systematic social dynamics, such as mistrust and cynicism, that in turn may contribute to their further stigmatization, disorder, out-migration, crime, withdrawal of civic involvement, and eventually the deepening of poverty.

Overall these findings resonate with the concerns of Moynihan (1965) and those reflected in other works at the time such as Clark (1965). The findings may not be palatable, but they signal a distressing reality of urban America that demands serious policy attention. It is perhaps sobering that forty-plus years after the Moynihan Report, the same questions must be raised again. The language may be different, but many of the issues remain the same. Moynihan did hypothesize a partial solution, however, in the form of structural government interventions. The jury is still out, but the preliminary data presented here suggest a glimmer of hope that cycles of poverty can be broken providing examples of poor communities that are radically repositioning themselves to an upward trajectory. How pervasive the phenomenon is remains to be seen; research so far has not tracked the consequences of change in one community on changes for other, perhaps even distant communities that may be receiving new burdens. In the case of Chicago, for example, the tens of thousands of poor residents uprooted from the Robert Taylor Homes on the south side went *somewhere*. If most moved to other, poorer communities further south, as evidence indicates, then it may well be that the burdens of poverty are simply being redistributed, not solved. Either way, questions of stability and change in concentrated poverty should remain at the top of our agenda.

Notes

1. Criticisms of the social science use of terms like "pathology" and "disorganization" are well known and need not be rehearsed (Sampson 2002). I would add here only that the usage by Moynihan was not, in my view, essentialist in its connotations or somehow limited to the black community. The manifestations of pathology were instead thought to vary by location in the social structure. Indeed, Kenneth Clark, Moynihan's contemporary and apparent originator of the "tangle of pathology" concept, wrote of the pervasive unhappiness and emptiness that he argued characterized white suburbs at the time. Although not violent, white pathology was suffocating nonetheless and was no less despairing, which led Clark to ask, "Why, then, would members of the city's ghettos seek to embrace a pathology of the suburb in exchange for their own?" (Clark 1965, 108). The terminology of pathology is certainly problematic for social phenomena, but we should not lose sight of the social structural logic that framed the larger argument.

2. Although not reviewed here, the social-ecological literature has considered aspects of neighborhood differentiation related to life-cycle status, residential stability, home ownership, density, land use, and ethnic heterogeneity. The evidence linking these factors to health and other outcomes is mixed, especially for population density and ethnic heterogeneity (Brooks-Gunn, Duncan, and Aber 1997; Morenoff, Sampson, and Raudenbush 2001).

3. Poverty, female-headed families, welfare assistance, unemployment, and percentage black all formed one principal component that accounted for approximately 70 percent of the common variance nationally *and* in Chicago. Based on results in Sampson, Sharkey, and Raudenbush (2008), I exclude density of children from further consideration in the new analyses presented here. I use census tracts as the operational definition of neighborhood. In the city of Chicago, additional ecological units are available for study, such as neighborhood clusters and community areas. As noted further below, results across levels of aggregation in Chicago are very similar (see also Land, McCall, and Cohen 1990).

References

Abbott, Andrew. 1997. Of time and space: The contemporary relevance of the Chicago School. *Social Forces* 75:1149-82.

Bobo, Lawrence D., and Camille L. Zubrinsky. 1996. Attitudes on residential integration: Perceived status differences, mere in-group preference, or racial prejudice? *Social Forces* 74:883-909.

Bowles, Samuel, Steve Durlauf, and Karla Hoff, eds. 2006. *Poverty traps*. Princeton, NJ: Princeton University Press.

Brooks-Gunn, Jeanne, Greg Duncan, and Lawrence Aber, eds. 1997. *Neighborhood poverty: Policy implications in studying neighborhoods*. New York: Russell Sage Foundation.

Bursik, Robert J. 1986. Delinquency rates as sources of ecological change. In *The social ecology of crime*, ed. James M. Byrne and Robert J. Sampson, 63-76. New York: Springer-Verlag.

Charles, Camille Zubrinsky. 2000. Neighborhood racial-composition preferences: Evidence from a multi-ethnic metropolis. *Social Problems* 47:379-407.

———. 2001. Processes of residential segregation. In *Urban inequality: Evidence from four cities*, ed. Alice O'Connor, Chris Tilly, and Lawrence Bobo, 217-71. New York: Russell Sage Foundation.

———. 2003. The dynamics of racial residential segregation. *Annual Review of Sociology* 29:167-207.

Clark, Kenneth B. 1965. *Dark ghetto: Dilemmas of social power*. New York: Harper & Row.

Drake, St. Clair, and Horace R. Cayton. 1945/1993. *Black metropolis: A study of Negro life in a northern city*. Chicago: University of Chicago Press.

Hunter, Albert. 1974. *Symbolic communities: The persistence and change of Chicago's local communities*. Chicago: University of Chicago Press.

Jargowsky, Paul. 1997. *Poverty and place: Ghettos, barrios, and the American city*. New York: Russell Sage Foundation.

Land, Kenneth, Patricia McCall, and Lawrence E. Cohen. 1990. Structural covariates of homicide rates: Are there any invariances across time and space? *American Journal of Sociology* 95:922-63.

Liska, Allen E., and Paul E. Bellair. 1995. Violent-crime rates and racial composition: Convergence over time. *American Journal of Sociology* 101:578-610.

Loury, Glenn C. 2002. *The anatomy of racial inequality*. Cambridge, MA: Harvard University Press.

Massey, Douglas S. 1995. Getting away with murder: Segregation and violent crime in urban America. *University of Pennsylvania Law Review* 143:1203-32.

Massey, Douglas, Gretchen Condran, and Nancy A. Denton. 1987. The effect of residential segregation on black social and economic well-being. *Social Forces* 66:29-56.

Massey, Douglas S., and Nancy Denton. 1993. *American apartheid: Segregation and the making of the underclass*. Cambridge, MA: Harvard University Press.

Massey, Douglas S., and Mitchell L. Eggers. 1990. The ecology of inequality: Minorities and the concentration of poverty, 1970–1980. *American Journal of Sociology* 95:1153-88.

Massey, Douglas, and Eric Fong. 1990. Segregation and neighborhood quality: Blacks, Hispanics, and Asians in the San Francisco metropolitan area. *Social Forces* 69:15-32.

Massey, Douglas, and Kumiko Shibuya. 1995. Unraveling the tangle of pathology: The effect of spatially concentrated joblessness on the well-being of African Americans. *Social Science Research* 24:352-66.

Morenoff, Jeffrey, and Robert J. Sampson. 1997. Violent crime and the spatial dynamics of neighborhood transition. Chicago, 1970-1990. Social Forces 76:31-64.

Morenoff, Jeffrey D., Robert J. Sampson, and Stephen Raudenbush. 2001. Neighborhood inequality, collective efficacy, and the spatial dynamics of urban violence. Criminology 39:517-60.

Moynihan, Daniel P. 1965. The Negro family: The case for national action. Washington, DC: Office of Policy Planning and Research, U.S. Department of Labor.

Putnam, Robert. 2000. Bowling alone: The collapse and renewal of American community. New York: Simon & Schuster.

Quillian, Lincoln. 1999. Migration patterns and the growth of high-poverty neighborhoods, 1970–1990. American Journal of Sociology 105:1-37.

Quillian, Lincoln, and Devah Pager. 2001. Black neighbors, higher crime? The role of racial stereotypes in evaluations of neighborhood crime. American Journal of Sociology 107:717-67.

Sampson, Robert J. 1986. The contribution of homicide to the decline of American cities. Bulletin of the New York Academy of Medicine 62:562-69.

———. 2002. Organized for what? Recasting theories of social (dis)organization. In Crime and social organization: Advances in criminological theory, ed. Elin Waring and David Weisburd, 95-110. New Brunswick, NJ: Transaction.

———. 2003. The neighborhood context of well being. Perspectives in Biology and Medicine 46:S53-S73.

Sampson, Robert J., and Corina Graif. Forthcoming. Structural and temporal contexts of trust: Durable social processes in Chicago neighborhoods. In Trust, ed. Karen Cook, Russell Hardin, and Margaret Levi. New York: Russell Sage Foundation.

Sampson, Robert J., and Jeffrey D. Morenoff. 2006. Durable inequality: Spatial dynamics, social processes and the persistence of poverty in Chicago neighborhoods. In Poverty traps, ed. Samuel Bowles, Steve Durlauf, and Karla Hoff, 176-203. Princeton, NJ: Princeton University Press.

Sampson, Robert J., Jeffrey D. Morenoff, and Thomas Gannon-Rowley. 2002. Assessing "neighborhood effects": Social processes and new directions in research. Annual Review of Sociology 28:443-78.

Sampson, Robert J., and Stephen W. Raudenbush. 2004. Seeing disorder: Neighborhood stigma and the social construction of broken windows. Social Psychology Quarterly 67:319-42.

Sampson, Robert J., and Patrick Sharkey. 2008. Neighborhood selection and the social reproduction of concentrated racial inequality. Demography 45:1-29.

Sampson, Robert J., Patrick Sharkey, and Stephen Raudenbush. 2008. Durable effects of concentrated disadvantage on verbal ability among African-American children. Proceedings of the National Academy of Sciences 105:845-52.

Shaw, Clifford R., and Henry D. McKay. 1942. Juvenile delinquency and urban areas. Chicago: University of Chicago Press.

Skogan, Wesley. 1990. Disorder and decline: Crime and the spiral of decay in American cities. Berkeley: University of California Press.

Suttles, Gerald D. 1990. The man-made city: The land-use confidence game in Chicago. Chicago: University of Chicago Press.

Tilly, Charles. 1998. Durable inequality. Berkeley: University of California Press.

Wilson, William Julius. 1987. The truly disadvantaged: The inner city, the underclass, and public policy. Chicago: University of Chicago Press.

———. 1996. When work disappears: The world of the new urban poor. New York: Knopf.

Wilson, William Julius, and Richard Taub. 2006. There goes the neighborhood: Racial, ethnic, and class tensions in four Chicago neighborhoods and their meaning for America. New York: Knopf.

Moynihan Was Right: Now What?

By
RON HASKINS

In 1965, Daniel Patrick Moynihan predicted that the exposure of so many black children, especially males, to fatherless families would prevent many from seizing new opportunities through the civil rights revolution. Although Moynihan was excoriated in the academic world and beyond, subsequent events have proven him correct. Today, in part because of the continuing demise of married-couple families, the average black is far behind the average white in educational achievement, employment rates, and earnings; blacks also have much higher crime and incarceration rates. These outcomes have led to growing recognition that the promise of the civil rights revolution will not be achieved until the black family is repaired. This article proposes a series of policies intended to increase and reward work, reduce nonmarital births and increase marriage rates, expand preschool education, and reduce incarceration rates and integrate former prisoners back into society—all designed to reduce lone parenting or deal with its effects.

Keywords: Daniel Patrick Moynihan; *The Negro Family;* family structure; employment opportunities; preschool education; incarceration

In 1965, Daniel Patrick Moynihan wrote that black Americans would not be able to fully capitalize on the civil rights revolution then in full swing because of weakness in the black family that resulted in the inadequate development of children, especially males. He was apocalyptic about black males, and argued that because such a large percentage were being reared in female-headed families without male influence, many would grow up to reject the normal values of community life, such as work,

Ron Haskins is a senior fellow in the Economic Studies Program and codirector of the Center on Children and Families at the Brookings Institution and senior consultant at the Annie E. Casey Foundation. He is the author of Work over Welfare: The Inside Story of the 1996 Welfare Reform Law *(Brookings Institution 2006) and a senior editor of* The Future of Children, *a journal on policy issues that affect children and families. In 2002 he was the senior advisor to the president for welfare policy.*

DOI: 10.1177/0002716208324793

marriage, fatherhood, and abiding by the law. Years later, in one of the most chilling passages in the history of social science, Moynihan wrote in the Catholic journal *America* that

> [F]rom the wild Irish slums of the 19th century Eastern seaboard, to the riot-torn suburbs of Los Angeles, there is one unmistakable lesson in American history: a community that allows a large number of young men to grow up in broken families, dominated by women, never acquiring any stable relationship to male authority, never acquiring any set of rational expectation about the future—that community asks for and gets chaos. Crime, violence, unrest, disorder—most particularly the furious, unrestrained lashing out at the whole social structure—that is not only to be expected; it is very near to inevitable. And it is richly deserved. (Moynihan 1986, 227)

For the original 1965 report, he was excoriated and vilified (Rainwater and Yancey 1967), and the topic of black families was largely removed from the agenda of scholars and public intellectuals for more than two decades. During this time, the problems that so worried Moynihan grew rapidly, festered, and proved his concerns and predictions to be correct. However, only a few brave souls spoke up to call attention to the continuing demise of the black family and to the seeming split of the black community into a thriving and advancing middle class prepared to take advantage of the new opportunities and a floundering lower class in constant turmoil (Auletta 1982; Murray 1984).

It was inevitable that the facts would overcome the political correctness of ignoring the family's role in the growth of the black underclass. If we are to fix a date when the thaw became obvious, a good bet would be the publication of William Julius Wilson's *The Truly Disadvantaged* in 1987. Wilson's brave and adventurous book offered two big ideas (Blankenhorn n.d.). First, he argued that those who tended to minimize the problems imposed on black society and the nation by the pathology of the black family were misguided. Second, he continued his argument, first developed in the *Declining Significance of Race* in 1978, that employment problems are the single most important cause of the problems experienced by black families and, in turn, the entire self-perpetuating pathology of the black ghetto.

Books and articles with frank and often dramatic assessments of the plight of the black family and community followed. By 2007, comedian Bill Cosby and Harvard psychiatrist Alvin Poussaint could write in *Come On People* (2007) about black males "selling drugs, stealing, or shooting their buddies over trivia," (p. 9); about the "estrangement of fathers and their children"; and about black males "inflicting the most damage" on the black community (p. 16). A growing list of reputable scholars, journalists, and other public figures, many of them black, joined the prescient Professor Moynihan in agreeing that something was wrong in the black family and community—not least that its leadership was too focused on rights and not focused enough on personal responsibilities (Williams 2007; Patterson 1998; Steele 2006; McWhorter 2000).

Today, we still lack an analysis of what holds back so many blacks in America. Why have so many, especially males, turned their backs on routine achievement, separated from their children and their children's mothers, and joined a criminal subculture? The following sections will attempt to provide that analysis through an examination of family dissolution, educational failure, labor force declines, and incarceration.

Moynihan Revisited: Four Continuing Problems

Family dissolution

When Moynihan wrote his report in 1965, about 25 percent of black children were born outside marriage, up from less than 10 percent in 1950. Nonmarital births continued to increase relentlessly until the mid-1990s. By 1995, seven in ten black babies were born outside marriage. One reason for the high nonmarital birth rate was that marriage rates for blacks declined from more than 66 percent in 1960 to 56 percent in 2006 (U.S. Census Bureau 2007), resulting in an increase in the number of years the average woman is at risk for a nonmarital pregnancy. With declining marriage rates, to avoid pregnancy outside marriage, black couples must remain abstinent longer (a solution to pregnancy not overly prized by either adolescents or those in their twenties, black or white) or have great vigilance in use of birth control to avoid pregnancy.

Against all odds, abstinence actually increased among teenage blacks in the late 1990s, but little is known about the sexual behavior of black couples in their twenties and early thirties when a majority of nonmarital births occur. There has been some control in fertility because overall birthrates among blacks have declined from 91 per 1,000 females over age fifteen in 1989 to around 68 per 1,000 in 2005 (Hamilton, Martin, and Ventura 2007). But this decline in overall birthrates was not enough to compensate for the fall in the marriage rate and the consequent rise of years at risk for a nonmarital birth. The net result was that nonmarital births among blacks increased until the mid-1990s and then fluctuated around the extraordinary rate of 70 percent for the next decade.

The increase in nonmarital births was accompanied by a high rate of divorce among black couples. Betsey Stevenson and Justin Wolfers (2007) of the National Bureau of Economic Research analyzed longitudinal data from the Survey of Income and Program Participation and found that of black couples born between 1940 and 1955, about 43 percent of first marriages had ended in divorce by age forty-five. The upshot of these dramatic trends in marriage rates, divorce rates, and nonmarital birth rates is an increase in the share of black children in single-parent families.

As shown in Figure 1, the share of both black and white children in single-parent families has increased sharply since the late 1960s. Although the black rate has been more or less stable at a little above 55 percent since the early 1990s, while the rate for white children continues to increase slowly, nonetheless, the black rate is still well over twice the white rate. Even these figures, however, are somewhat misleading because they tell us the percentage of children in a single-parent family only at one point in time. Over the entire period of childhood, something like 80 percent of black children experience life in a single-parent family.[1]

FIGURE 1
PERCENTAGE OF BLACK AND WHITE CHILDREN
LIVING IN SINGLE-PARENT FAMILIES, 1968-2006

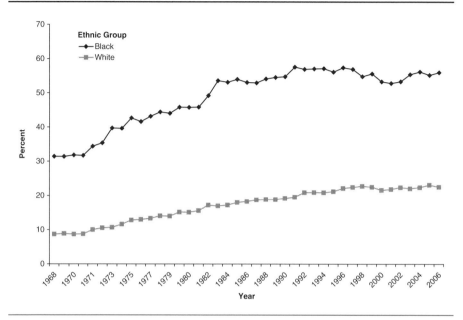

Of all the consequences of family dissolution that are harmful to blacks, none is more important than the effect of lone parenting on the development of black children. The poverty rate of children in female-headed families is five or six times as high as that of children in married-parent families.[2] An analysis by Adam Thomas and Isabel Sawhill of Brookings Institution estimated that if the United States had had the marriage rate in 2002 that it had in 1970, poverty would have been lower than it was by almost 30 percent (Thomas and Sawhill 2002). Equally important, researchers now widely agree that the best rearing environment for children is the one provided by their married parents (McLanahan, Donahue, and Haskins 2005).

It is not necessary to demean the efforts of single mothers to observe that their children would be better off on average if the mother and father were married and provided a low-conflict environment for their children (Terry-Humen, Manlove, and Moore 2005). Table 1, based on the work of Paul Amato of Pennsylvania State University, provides an idea of the consequences for children of being reared in single-parent families. It is based on the difference in rates of various afflictions experienced by teens in single-parent families as compared with teens living with continuously married parents in the National Study of Adolescent Health. Amato projected how many fewer teens would experience each of the problems if the marriage rate were the same as in 1980 instead of what it actually was in 2002. According to Amato's estimates, higher marriage rates would have meant nearly 300,000 fewer children repeating a grade, 211,000 fewer being involved in violent acts, 240,000 fewer smokers, and nearly 29,000 fewer suicide attempts (Amato 2005, 86).[3]

TABLE 1
**WELL-BEING OF ADOLESCENTS IF MORE LIVED
WITH THEIR MARRIED PARENTS**

Behavioral Problem	Actual (2002)	Projected
Repeated grade	6,948,530	−299,968
Suspended from school	8,570,096	−485,165
Delinquency	11,632,086	−216,498
Violence	11,490,072	−211,282
Therapy	3,412,678	−247,799
Smoked in the last month	5,083,513	−239,974
Thought of suicide	3,692,358	−83,469
Attempted suicide	636,164	−28,693

SOURCE: Paul Amato (2005, 89).
NOTE: Based on comparison of rates of behavioral problems in married-couple families and single-parent families from the National Longitudinal Study of Adolescent Health, 2002. The "Projected" column extrapolates the incidence of each behavioral problem if the same percentages of adolescents had lived in married-couple families as in 1980.

*Of all the consequences of family dissolution
that are harmful to blacks, none is more
important than the effect of lone parenting
on the development of black children.*

Similar findings are reported in this volume by Harry Holzer, based on analysis of data from the National Longitudinal Survey of Youth. Even after controlling for household income, Holzer finds that children from never-married families are more likely to drop out of high school, less likely to enroll in and graduate from college, and more likely to be incarcerated. In addition, children from never-married families had lower high school grades and lower scores on an intelligence test. On all these measures, black males are behind every other demographic group in American society.

An even worse outcome is the number of children removed from their biological families and placed in foster care. The most recent statistics show that about 1.6 percent of black children, as compared with 0.3 percent of white children, had families so troubled that government child protection agencies found it necessary to remove the children and place them in foster care over the course of a recent year.[4]

Children who enter foster care are much more troubled than children in the general population and show higher incidences of school failure, teen pregnancy, mental health problems, and physical health problems—and the longer they are in foster care (especially when they are subjected to serial placements), the more likely they are to have these problems (Rubin et al. 2007). The intervention of the child protection system in lives of families is probably necessary in most of these cases, and even rescues some children from injury or worse. Nonetheless, the high level of intervention by child protection agencies in the lives of black families is yet another sign of the problems associated with the extraordinary high levels of single-parenting among blacks.

Educational failure

A second set of causal factors relates to educational achievement—or more accurately the gaps in both educational achievement and performance on standardized tests between black and white children. The gaps set in early and last a lifetime. By age three, as Christopher Jencks of Harvard and Meredith Phillips of the University of California, Los Angeles, show based on representative samples from the National Longitudinal Survey of Youth, the gap between black and white preschoolers is already substantial (Jencks and Phillips 1998). Although genes and early environment are both implicated in accounting for this gap, no one has shown genetic differences in intelligence or achievement between blacks and whites. There is no reason to think the gap cannot be closed or reduced (Fischer and Hout 2006).

The nation has been trying and has achieved some important successes. Figures 2 and 3, based on the work of Claude Fischer and Michael Hout of Berkeley (2006), show changes in the percentage of blacks, whites, Hispanics, and Asians who graduated from high school and four-year colleges during the course of the twentieth century. The dramatic increase in levels of education by all ethnic groups is striking, but almost as striking is the separation between blacks and Hispanics, on one hand, from whites and Asians, on the other. Early in the century, only 5 percent of blacks who turned twenty-one in 1901 had finished high school by the age of thirty, compared with around 20 percent of whites. Over the next century, the graduation rate rose for both groups, but the black rate of 81 percent for those who turned 21 in 1991 was still behind the white rate of 91 percent and the Asian rate of 94 percent.

In terms of college graduation, the patterns are similar though the rates are naturally lower. As shown in Figure 3, whereas the percentage of college graduates among whites grew from 4 percent in 1901 to 30 percent in 1991, and for Asians went from 3 to 47 percent, the percentage for blacks went only from 1 to 14 percent, yielding a 16 point gap from whites and a 33 point gap from Asians. Furthermore, as is the case with so many demographic variables, black males seem not only to have reached a plateau but also to have fallen slightly.

FIGURE 2
HIGH SCHOOL GRADUATION RATES BY ETHNIC GROUP, 1900-2000

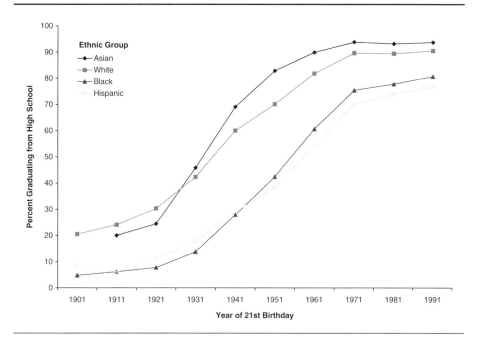

FIGURE 3
COLLEGE GRADUATION RATES BY ETHNIC GROUP, 1900-2000

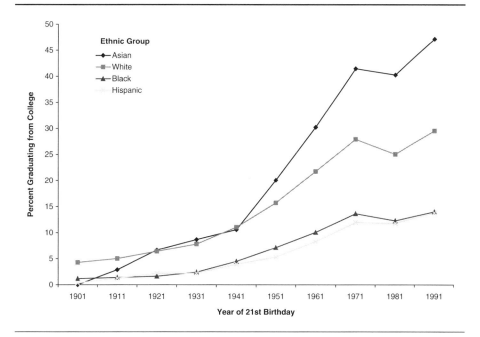

Standardized measures of learning also show that many black children perform poorly whereas few perform well. The National Assessment of Educational Progress (NAEP 2007), probably the best standard measure of school performance for the nation as a whole and for subgroups of students, shows large gaps between black and white children. More specifically, black children are more likely to perform below the "basic" level (meaning that they demonstrate only "partial mastery" of knowledge and skills "fundamental for proficient work") and are less likely to perform at the advanced level (defined as "superior" performance).

As shown in Figure 4, both black and white children have made some progress in the past fifteen years, and blacks have even slightly reduced the gaps at both the bottom and the top of the distribution. Even so, blacks were still almost two and half times more likely to perform below the basic level and less than a fifth as likely to perform at the advanced level or above as compared with white students. The simple fact that more than half of all blacks are failing to learn at even a basic level whereas only about 2 percent perform at the advanced level suggests that we have a long way to go as a nation.

We might conclude from these data that public schools are failing black children, and certainly the schools must accept major responsibility for their low levels of learning; but it must be recalled that decades of educational research have confirmed the fact that the single factor most closely associated with school performance is family background (Coleman 1966; Jencks 1972). Again echoing Moynihan, the fragmentation of the black family is deeply implicated in one of the most important measures of children's preparation for life in the twenty-first century.

Falling labor force participation

Without discussing whether employment of males is the central factor in the tangle of black pathology, as argued by William Julius Wilson (1987), Moynihan, and many others, I simply assume that any reasonable public policy to address the problems of black families, black poverty, and black crime would focus on the employment of black males as a central concern. The problem of nonwork by black males is deep and perplexing, however.

The Holzer article in this volume presents a thorough analysis of employment trends for young black males. Figure 5 shows the work effort expended by black males and females between ages sixteen and twenty-four in years since the Moynihan report was produced in 1965. At that time, the employment to population ratio for sixteen- to twenty-four-year-old males was 53, compared with 30 for females. Thus, the work effort of young black males was about 75 percent greater than that of young black females. Over the ensuing years, however, the work effort of black males fell while that of black females rose, and by 2000, the ratio for black females had reached 45 whereas that for black males had dropped to 43.

Over the same period, immigration to the United States exploded, which indicates that job availability was not the issue. Similarly, when never-married mothers were required to work by welfare reform in 1996, their work rates increased dramatically at a time when the work rates of young black males were stable, again

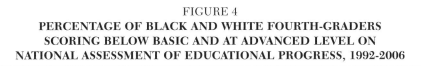

FIGURE 4
**PERCENTAGE OF BLACK AND WHITE FOURTH-GRADERS
SCORING BELOW BASIC AND AT ADVANCED LEVEL ON
NATIONAL ASSESSMENT OF EDUCATIONAL PROGRESS, 1992-2006**

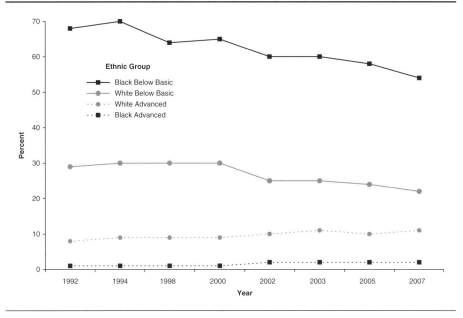

indicating that job availability did not explain the poor work record of black males. Moreover, as Holzer (this volume 2008) shows, work by young blacks has declined by some 15 percentage points since the late 1970s and now stands at only two-thirds the average level observed for Hispanics and whites.

These employment trends actually understate the true level of work decline by black males because unprecedented numbers of young blacks have been confined in jails and prisons in recent years, and the incarcerated are omitted from the calculations (see the article by Western and Wildeman in this volume). Thus, the problem of nonwork by black males—which Moynihan saw as the key to understanding ghetto pathology—is now undeniably worse than it was in 1965.

Exploding rates of incarceration

Moynihan mentions crime and incarceration at several points in his report, but neither Moynihan nor anyone else could possibly have imagined that incarceration rates for black males would soon explode to an unprecedented level, much greater even than the rate in the South during the height of Jim Crow. Based on census data and survey data of prison populations, Becky Pettit of the University of Washington and Bruce Western of Harvard (2004) estimate that for males born between 1965, the year of the Moynihan report, and 1969, 3 percent of

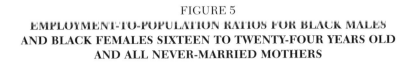

FIGURE 5
EMPLOYMENT-TO-POPULATION RATIOS FOR BLACK MALES
AND BLACK FEMALES SIXTEEN TO TWENTY-FOUR YEARS OLD
AND ALL NEVER-MARRIED MOTHERS

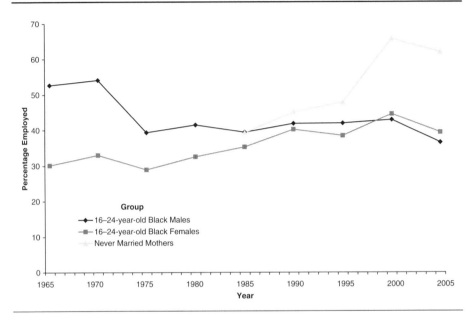

whites and 20 percent of blacks had been in prison by the time they reached their early thirties. This rate of incarceration for blacks was nearly double the rate for blacks born in the late 1940s and about seven times the rate for whites in the same age cohort. More amazing still, 60 percent of black high school dropouts in the 1960s birth cohort spent time in prison. This rate is all the more shocking given the high rates of school dropout among black males.

These spectacular trends reflect at least two underlying sets of causes. The first is the unfair and unwise set of laws and institutions that are the immediate cause of high incarceration rates. Prompted by the crack cocaine epidemic that was causing such high rates of addiction and stimulating such high rates of violence in most large American cities during the 1980s, lawmakers at the federal and state level enacted draconian laws on dealing drugs that featured long, mandatory sentences, which contravened the judicial tradition of leaving sentencing discretion to judges. In addition, federal antidrug laws passed in the 1980s imposed especially tough sentences on the sale of crack cocaine. First-time offenders were to receive a mandatory minimum sentence of five years for selling just five grams of crack; selling more resulted in longer mandatory minimum sentences. These long sentences were especially likely to ensnare blacks because they were disproportionately likely to sell and use crack cocaine whereas whites were more likely to sell and use powdered cocaine. Stuart Taylor, the moderate editorial writer for *National Journal* who enjoys a solid reputation on both sides of the aisle in Washington, has called such mandatory sentences for crack cocaine "grossly excessive" and "savagely severe" (2007, 17).

The second probable cause of high black incarceration rates is the high level of criminal behavior by young blacks. Based on both arrest records and convictions, it is clear that blacks commit significantly more crimes than whites. Consider homicide rates. The 2005 rate of 3.5 per 100,000 for whites as compared with 26.5 for blacks gives an idea of the dramatic differences in crime rates between the two groups (Bureau of Justice Statistics 2007b, 2007c). Some degree of caution is required here because in all likelihood both the police and the courts have a degree of bias against black males—as do many blacks themselves, who often view young black males as threatening.[5] Furthermore, evidence indicates that blacks are more likely than whites to sell drugs on the streets rather than in an enclosed space and to sell to strangers rather than people they know, both of which increase the chances of arrest and conviction (Ramchand, Pacula, and Iguchi 2006).

Why do young black males commit more crimes than whites? As Orlando Patterson, a black sociologist at Harvard, wrote in 2006, the propensity to commit crimes by black youth is due in part to the "catastrophic state of black family life."[6] Undoubtedly, other factors, including discrimination, limited economic opportunities, and problems in gender relations are involved, but the lack of male influence in the home contributes to all of these as well as directly to crime and once again demonstrates the power of Moynihan's argument about black families. Without increasing the number of black children, especially males, reared in married-couple families, all the other interventions will at best be only partially successful in reducing incarceration rates among blacks.

In place of a strong home life featuring limits enforced by fathers, Patterson (2006) holds that young black men have created what he calls the "cool pose culture" that functions "almost like a drug" in compelling young black men to hang out on the street; dress sharply; make sexual conquests; use drugs; and listen to hip-hop music with lyrics glorifying violence, misogyny, drugs, and sex. How to break the hold of this culture, which Patterson thinks now has about one-fifth of young black males in its grip, is one of the top issues for both the black community and for policy makers at all levels of government.

What to Do: Four Strategies

It is something of an understatement to observe that Moynihan was right about the breakdown of the black family and the consequences for child rearing, socialization, school performance, nonmarital births, employment, and crime. One suspects, however, that rather than take much satisfaction from outlasting his critics, he would—as he did up until the end of his life[7]—search for public policies to reduce the problem or minimize its consequences. We can do no less.

But we need to start by dismissing the sense of hopelessness that often pervades discussions about equalizing opportunity and by recognizing that blacks have made enormous progress in America, breaking virtually every racist and ability-determined ceiling that existed before the civil rights revolution began. There is now a large black middle class, black education levels improved remarkably during the course of the twentieth century, American attitudes on race have changed dramatically (Gallup 2007), and there is even modest progress in closing the educational achievement gap.

Moreover, we need to correct the mistaken impression that the United States has had a stingy social policy and that social programs have been cut in recent years. Figure 6, based on data from the nonpartisan Congressional Research Service (2006), shows that spending on programs that help low-income families has increased almost every year since the late 1960s.[8] During the four decades since the Moynihan Report, federal and state governments have not only increased spending on these programs from $88 billion to well over $500 billion in constant dollars[9] but have also developed important new programs such as the Earned Income Tax Credit (EITC), child care, food stamps, child support enforcement, and child protection.

One advantage policy makers have today that they did not have when Moynihan wrote his report is a robust set of high-quality demonstrations and studies showing which programs do and do not produce reliable results. In 1965, there was little evidence that any of the programs implemented in President Johnson's War on Poverty would actually work. Head Start, Job Corps, and Community Action were all developed through the use of logic, guess work, and anecdote, but by almost no systematic data (Gillette 1996).

In contrast, for virtually every social policy idea in circulation today, evidence, often from random-assignment experiments, can confirm whether the program will actually produce its intended impacts. As shown in Table 2, high-quality studies show that many interventions pertinent to the problems raised by the Moynihan Report are capable of producing significant impacts. Equally important, American social science has developed research and demonstration methods and statistical techniques that will provide accurate answers about whether any new idea works as intended and under what circumstances (Orr 1999; Rossi, Lipsey, and Freeman 2004). These considerations provide a surprising level of confidence that new public policies, aggressively implemented and subjected to modifications based on evaluation of outcomes, could lead to progress in reversing the problems that are now holding back so many young blacks. We turn now to proposing a set of strategies that might produce good results.

Strategy 1: Increasing and rewarding work

Upon winning control of Congress after the 1994 congressional elections, Republicans—eventually joined by President Bill Clinton and half the Democrats in Congress—were intent on shifting social policy to conform to their vision of strong families based on work and marriage. Three major goals of their reforms, most of which were enacted in the welfare reform law of 1996, were to

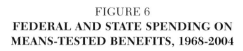

FIGURE 6
**FEDERAL AND STATE SPENDING ON
MEANS-TESTED BENEFITS, 1968-2004**

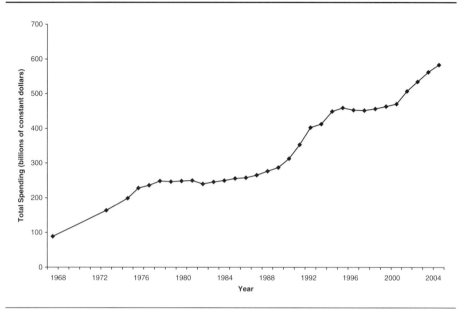

reduce federal and increase state control of social programs, to reduce cash welfare and increase work effort by mothers on welfare, and to promote marriage
while reducing nonmarital births (Haskins 2006).

The New Deal program Aid to Families with Dependent Children (AFDC)
was repealed and replaced by a block grant that gave states flexibility in deciding
how to achieve the goals of welfare reform. Although states were free to develop
their own programs, they were required to place at least half their cash welfare
caseload in a work program and were hit with financial penalties if they failed.
The law also required individuals receiving assistance to meet state work requirements or have their benefits reduced or ended. The new program was called
Temporary Assistance for Needy Families (TANF), with the emphasis on "temporary," as demonstrated by the federal requirement that no state could use federal dollars to give cash welfare to a given family for longer than five years (with
a few exceptions). In short, the new program replaced welfare, in which millions
of poor mothers were entitled to cash benefits, with a program in which cash
benefits were contingent on work (Haskins 2006, 206).

Implementation of the new law occurred under optimum circumstances.
First, the U.S. economy was on fire, generating a net increase of more than
19 million jobs between 1991 and 2000 (12 million in the years following welfare
reform and the turn of the century; U.S. Census Bureau 2006, 373). Second, for
the first time in two decades, wages at the bottom of the distribution rose during

TABLE 2
EXAMPLES OF SCIENTIFICALLY EVALUATED INTERVENTION
PROGRAMS FOR DISADVANTAGED YOUTH AND ADULTS

Study	Target Group	Program Model	Summary of Results
National Supported Work Demonstration	Seventeen- to twenty-year-old high school dropouts and other disadvantaged groups	Paid work experience, with graduated stress	No lasting impacts for youth target group; some employment impacts for other groups
New Chance	Sixteen- to twenty-two-year-old teenage mothers who were high school dropouts	Wide range of education, employment, and family services	Increases in GED receipt; no impacts on labor market outcomes
American Conservation and Youth Service Corps	Mostly eighteen- to twenty-five-year-old out-of-school youth	Paid work experience in community service projects; encouragement of education (e.g., getting a GED)	Increases in employment outcomes and decreases in arrests, particularly for African American males
National Guard Youth Challenge Evaluation	Sixteen- to eighteen-year-old high school dropouts	Education, service to community, and other components in a quasi-military residential setting; twelve-month postresidential mentoring program	Very early results show large increases in diploma/GED receipt, self-efficacy, and other outcomes
Career Academies	Students entering ninth grade	Schools-within-schools featuring small learning communities, work internships	Substantial, long-term (up to eight years) increases in earnings for males; increases in marriage rate; no impact on educational outcomes
Big Brothers/ Big Sisters	Ten- to sixteen-year-olds	Community-based mentoring	Decreases in drug use; improvements in some academic outcomes

(continued)

TABLE 2 (CONTINUED)

Study	Target Group	Program Model	Summary of Results
Nurse-Family Partnership	Pregnant low-income women	Home visits by specially trained nurses during pregnancy and infancy; women given advice about nutrition, child rearing, employment, smoking, and other factors	Substantial, long-term improvements in child rearing, mothers' employment, child outcomes, and other outcomes
Carrera Adolescent Pregnancy Prevention Program	Economically disadvantaged teens	Comprehensive youth development program	Reduction in teen pregnancy and births; increases in high school graduation and college enrollment
Riverside Greater Avenues for Independence (GAIN) Program	Welfare recipients	Help for welfare recipients in preparing for, finding, and applying for employment	Increases in employment and earnings; reduction in welfare dependency; savings to government
Canadian Self-Sufficiency Project	Long-term welfare recipients	Increased work incentive for full-time work through large wage subsidy	Increases in employment, earnings, and family income; improvements in school performance by children
Minnesota Family Investment Program	Welfare recipients who cannot find work	Help with finding jobs and sizeable earnings supplement	Increases in employment and earnings, reduction in poverty rates for single parents and long-term recipients

the 1990s. Third, at least forty states had been experimenting with welfare reform and already had experience with many of the provisions of the new federal work requirements, thereby ensuring that states not only agreed with the federal requirements but were already in the process of training staff, opening offices, and developing their own policies and procedures to do exactly what the federal law required (Nathan and Gais 1999).

Owing to this constellation of factors, and at least one other to be described below, former welfare recipients left welfare for work in droves. Between 1962 and 1994, the welfare rolls virtually never declined—in bad economies and good, the welfare rolls grew.[10] Moreover, in the very hot economy of the 1960s, the rolls more than doubled; similarly, in the strong economy of the late 1980s, following an earlier (1988) version of welfare reform that did not require work (U.S. Congress 1989), the welfare rolls expanded sharply despite a strong economy. And yet, following welfare reform of 1996, the welfare rolls fell by half in four years (U.S. Congress 2004, 7-31).

Meanwhile, poor and uneducated mothers not only joined the labor force but raised their earnings (primarily by working more hours) as never before and pulled themselves and their children out of poverty. Child poverty enjoyed its most consistent decline since the early 1970s, falling nearly 30 percent between 1993 and 2000. Black child poverty reached its lowest level ever; by 2000, it had fallen by one-third. Census data on income among female-headed families during these years show that it was mothers' earnings and not welfare payments that made the difference in reducing child poverty. Indeed, welfare income actually fell during these years (Haskins 2006, chap. 15).

The most innovative and arguably draconian feature of welfare reform was the willingness on the part of Republicans to subject welfare mothers to more economic risk by making the cash income strand of the safety net (AFDC) dependent on work and by imposing a time limit on cash benefits to send a clear signal that cash welfare was temporary and mothers were expected to work.

But there also was bipartisan agreement—and had been since at least the 1980s—that government should provide carrots to lure people into work and then make work more financially rewarding than the low wages for which most welfare mothers were qualified. Over a period of two decades or more, Congress and a series of presidents had constructed what we might call a work support system consisting of cash wage subsidies, child care assistance, food subsidies, and medical coverage (Haskins 2006, 340-42; L. Wilson and Stoker 2006). As part of the 1996 reforms, Congress also provided more funds for child care and strengthened the child support enforcement program, hoping to increase the probability that more poor mothers would receive a stream of steady income from nonresident fathers—and a source of income that would not fall, as government means-tested benefits inevitably do, as earnings rise.

Figure 7 provides a graphic idea of the seriousness with which federal policy makers developed the work support system. Based on a study by the nonpartisan Congressional Budget Office, the two bar graphs present estimates of how much working families would receive from programs in the work support system as they existed in 1984 and in 1999. If the law on child care, medical assistance, the child tax credit, and the EITC had not changed after 1984, in 1999, working families would have received a mere $5.6 billion in benefits, but because Congress expanded or created all these work support programs after 1984, by 1999,

FIGURE 7
SUPPORT FOR WORKING FAMILIES, 1984 AND 1999

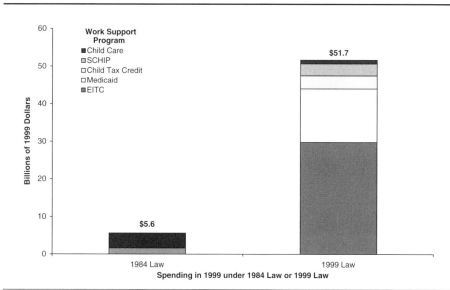

NOTE: SCHIP = State Children's Health Insurance Program; EITC = Earned Income Tax Credit.

working families qualified for $51.7 billion in benefits. A more recent estimate of benefits for working families by Sheila Zedlewski of the Urban Institute shows that between 1996 and 2002, work support benefits grew by 27 percent in real dollars (Zedlewski et al. 2006).

Although this inherently bipartisan approach of using sticks and carrots to encourage work has produced good (but not perfect; Haskins 2006, 342-54) results with poor mothers, stimulating a great increase in their work effort and major reductions in child poverty, it is far less effective with poor males and fathers. Federal and state policy currently has mostly sticks for fathers in the form of prison and strict child support enforcement.

The biggest carrot offered by the work support system is the EITC. But singles without children and parents who do not have custody of children are eligible for only a small EITC of around $400, while custodial parents, usually mothers, are eligible for up to $4,500. Gordon Berlin (2007), the president of MDRC in New York, has recently recommended that the EITC for noncustodial workers be dramatically expanded and has provided a detailed proposal for doing so. Briefly, his proposal is to provide noncustodial workers age twenty-one or older with an EITC of up to nearly $2,000 per year for full-time work (thirty hours per week or more).

Berlin (2007) holds that because his proposal is contingent on full-time work, goes to individuals regardless of family status, and treats the EITC as individual income rather than joint family income for income tax purposes, his proposal hits a policy trifecta by increasing work incentive (even for low-wage jobs) for young males, advancing equity in tax policy between men and women, and maintaining or perhaps even increasing marriage incentives. Equally important, this wage supplement could serve the important purpose of increasing the opportunity cost of criminal activity by raising the relative income of legitimate work. As shown by Berlin, most of these claims about the benefits of cash wage subsidies for low-wage workers are supported by data from high-quality demonstrations.

When fully implemented, Berlin (2007) estimates that the new EITC would cost around $30 billion per year. This cost renders the expanded EITC unlikely in the immediate future. However, it is more likely that Congress would appropriate, say, $3 billion a year for ten years to implement the Berlin EITC expansion in two or three states and carefully study its implementation and impacts. Finding effective policies to expand work by black males is important in its own right but is also a key to success of other policies to be discussed below.

A second stick-and-carrot approach to helping fathers, a variant of which has been proposed recently by Lawrence Mead (2007) of New York University, would be to figure out ways to make work by fathers mandatory and then reward their work. Welfare reform resulted in greatly increased work effort by mothers in part because a stick—the threatened removal of all or part of their cash benefit—was available, when necessary, to push mothers into the labor market. But young males are eligible for few welfare benefits to use as sticks.[11]

Even so, two groups of fathers, both disproportionately black and young, could possibly be pushed and pulled into the labor force by using sticks and carrots. The first group is prisoners. Men in local jails and state or federal prison who have committed nonviolent crimes or are nearing the end of their sentences could be offered reduced sentences in exchange for participation in a mandatory work program that would first try to help them find work and, that failing, place them in a community service job at minimum wage.

The second group includes men who are behind in making child support payments, many of whom are subject to incarceration under current law. The child support program, although fully justified as a way to force men to meet their financial obligation to their children, needs some modification if mandatory work programs for young males are to be successful. Without changing the underlying statutes, poor fathers who do not meet their child support obligation could be offered a deal: temporary forgiveness of their child support debt in exchange for either finding a job and working or participating in a mandatory work program. In either case, fathers would be required to pay a reasonable amount of child support on a regular schedule in the future.

States and localities should be free to operate these programs as they see fit, but some of the programs should be operated by child support agencies because they are already familiar with the child support program and many of them are already operating beyond the traditional approach of relentlessly pursuing fathers for child support. These new programs, albeit still rare, are trying to help fathers by offering job search and other support services (Miller and Knox 2001). Under current law, states have the authority to suspend the part of the child support owed to the state; modest changes in federal law could give states the authority to suspend the federal part of the payment as well if the father is working.

Although the mother also owns a portion of the child support indebtedness, most women would be willing to suspend overdue support if they can be guaranteed current and future payments on a timely basis. Research shows that child support indebtedness is one of the factors that drives poor fathers into underground and illegal employment because the child support system is akin to the IRS in its ability to locate and seize legitimate income (Holzer, Offner, and Sorensen 2005). Reforms of the child support system, such as the temporary forgiveness of child support debt, are an essential part of any overall attempt to lure young males into the labor market. These reforms can be accomplished without compromising—and may even enhance—the child support program's major goal of collecting child support payments.

Beyond an expansion of the EITC and reforms of child support, a host of tested interventions help adolescents make the transition from school to work, including those who have dropped out of school. These are reviewed in the article by Harry Holzer (this volume 2008); I find his recommendations sensible and worthy of public investments. But I would propose another idea, which is based on solid empirical evidence, for helping poor young workers find jobs, increase their earnings, and take full advantage of the work support system. This proposal, similar to one recently spelled out in a Brookings paper by Hans Bos and his colleagues (2007), is based on the remarkable New Hope program in Milwaukee. Organized by community activists and business leaders in the mid-1990s, the program was evaluated by random-assignment design and shown to produce impacts on employment, family income, poverty, and even the school achievement and behavior of children (Duncan, Huston, and Weisner 2007).

The essence of the New Hope program is a bargain: if an adult will work full-time, New Hope guarantees him or her a wage supplement, health insurance, and a child care subsidy. If these adults look for but cannot find a job, they are given minimum-wage community service jobs plus all the other elements of the bargain. Other than the guaranteed job, all or parts of the New Hope bargain are already in place as national policy. In bringing the nation's work support system up to the standard of New Hope, the required upgrades include extending Medicaid health insurance to adults and ensuring that enough funds are available to provide the child care subsidy.[12] Thus, with modest investments, it would be possible to create a work support system that equals or exceeds the New Hope guarantee.

An important element of complex programs like New Hope is the creation of an effective agency to run the program.[13] Under current law, local welfare departments and the One-Stop Career Centers, mostly operated by state departments of labor, already conduct programs that are similar to the New Hope guarantee. Indeed, the U.S. Department of Labor has funded a large-scale study, called the Work Advancement and Support Center Demonstration, in four sites around the country to test whether job coaches can help low-wage workers improve their earnings and navigate the complexities of the work support system (Tessler and Seith 2007). These centers could be encouraged to focus on young males, as some already do.

A similar demonstration program that would offer the New Hope guarantee—including assistance with finding a job or a better job, the type of child support reforms outlined above, and a focus on young males—should be funded by the federal government, with implementation carried out by five or so states or local government agencies. The federal government should make funds available as part of the demonstration to pay for child care and for health insurance for those not already covered. At least one of the demonstrations should include men being released from prison—or even who are released from prison early in accord with the program outlined above. The federal government should also pay the cost, perhaps in collaboration with foundations, of a high-quality evaluation.

Strategy 2: Reducing nonmarital births and increasing marriage

If, as Moynihan claimed, living with both parents is a crucial condition for optimum child development, and if the share of children—especially black children—living with their married parents has declined precipitously since Moynihan's report, it is regrettable that scholars and program innovators have produced so little information about how to restore marriage rates. The lack of tested approaches to increasing the share of children living in married-couple families is surprising because there is much greater agreement today than in 1965 that living with both parents is the optimum condition for child rearing (McLanahan and Sandefur 1994; McLanahan, Donahue, and Haskins 2005). To expand our knowledge base in this area and then support what seems to work, several propositions seem reasonable.

The first is that we should do more to reduce nonmarital births. Along with the entry of women into the paid labor force, the revival of immigration, and the aging of the population, the rise of nonmarital births is perhaps the most important demographic event of our times (Murray 1984). Moynihan may have been among the first to recognize the threat imposed on children by nonmarital births, but many others have followed his lead in the case of births to teens. In sharp contrast with the modest concern over nonmarital births among older women and over declining marriage rates, the scholarly and policy worlds have long tried to figure out why so many teens give birth outside marriage and how to do something about it. The consequences of teen births have been shown to be serious for the teen mother herself and for her baby (Furstenberg, Brooks-Gunn, and Morgan 1987; Terry-Humen, Manlove, and Moore 2005). Not the least of these consequences is that having a baby outside marriage reduces the mother's chances of eventually marrying.

Until recently, the nation enjoyed great success in reducing teen births. After a period of steep increases, the rate declined every year between 1991 and 2005 before rising slightly in 2006. Over the period, the teen birth rate fell by nearly 35 percent (Hamilton, Martin, and Ventura 2007). Two direct ways to reduce birthrates are to increase abstinence and to increase more frequent and effective use of birth control. It would appear from survey data that both an increase in abstinence and use of birth control by teens contributed to the fall of teen birthrates after 1991, although the use of birth control appears to be more important (Santelli et al. 2007).

Thus, it is unfortunate that the adults who have influence over sex education in the public schools have fallen into ideological debate about whether sex education should teach abstinence only or both abstinence and methods of birth control. Without rehashing the arguments here, it seems reasonable to conclude that, since both abstinence and birth control have contributed to reducing teen births, a strategy employing both approaches is appropriate. Those who advocate abstinence argue that teaching both methods is hypocritical and ineffective (Martin, Rector, and Pardue 2004). In an area with little good evidence and mountains of ideological rhetoric, it is hard to know whether the abstinence claims are correct. In the meantime, adolescents should receive a consistent message through their public school classes, churches, and families that abstinence is the only certain way to avoid pregnancy and sexually transmitted diseases. However, they should also be well schooled in the use of birth control.

Good evidence shows that several types of programs that engage teens can reduce both pregnancy rates and nonmarital births without increasing abortion rates. These programs are reviewed in great detail by Douglas Kirby (2007) for the National Campaign to Prevent Teen and Unplanned Pregnancy. The programs that have proved most effective in reducing both pregnancy rates and sexually transmitted diseases among teens are based on tested curriculums that emphasize, among other factors,

- focusing on specific goals and working to change behaviors in such a way as to approach these goals (especially increasing abstinence and use of condoms);
- changing factors that affect sexual behavior such as knowledge of perceived risks, attitudes, perceived norms about abstinence, and self-efficacy;
- involving youth in constructive activities with adults such as mentoring and community service; and
- securing support from schools, departments of health, and community-based organizations.

Many communities already have programs under way—mostly in the public schools—but many are based on curriculums and activities that have little or no evidence of success. Congress should provide the U.S. Department of Health and Human Services (HHS) with up to $1 billion a year for five years to provide money to states and local school districts and other community-based organizations to implement tested programs that have been shown to reduce sexual activity and teen pregnancy rates. All funded programs should emphasize either abstinence or abstinence and condom use and must agree to collect a standard set of data on outcomes. HHS should give priority to jurisdictions that have high poverty rates and should select several exemplary programs for careful evaluation by third parties, with results reported periodically to the public.

Second, both the federal and state governments should experiment with ways to increase marriage rates among couples who want to marry, especially low-income couples. If the goals of the TANF program can be accepted as statements of national policy, increasing marriage rates and the share of children in married-couple families is already an official goal of federal policy.[14] Research conducted on representative samples of couples who have had a baby outside marriage—a group that is disproportionately poor and minority—show that half of them live together, a total of 60 percent say they are in love, and 90 percent of those who live together say their chances of marriage are "fifty-fifty or better" (McLanahan 2008 [this volume]). If couples say they want to marry, why not fund community-based agencies to help them move toward marriage and to acquire the relationship skills that research shows can increase marital satisfaction and reduce divorce rates (Markman et al. 1993)?

Two actions that have already been taken to promote healthy marriage deserve public scrutiny. The first is the Bush administration's use of discretionary funds to establish high-quality demonstration programs designed to build and strengthen marriage (Meckler 2006). Some of the programs are designed for young unmarried couples who have had a baby together (and often cohabit; Dion 2005); some for young couples who are already married (Knox 2007); and some to promote community-wide programs, such as use of the media to point out the advantages of marriage for children, adults, and communities and the use of churches and other nonprofit organizations to promote and strengthen marriage (Lerman 2007).

A useful early outcome of the administration's promarriage agenda has been the creation of a simple model of building healthy couple relationships that could lead to marriage or reduce the chances of divorce. The model, first proposed by Mathematica Policy Research, is based on the assumption that marriage can be promoted by offering marriage education, a family coordinator, and various services to young couples (Dion et al. 2008). This approach is now being evaluated by the administration's random-assignment demonstrations, both with young couples who have had a baby together outside marriage and with young couples who are already married.

Marriage education typically is conducted in a setting with four or five couples and involves instruction and discussion of topics shown by research to be key issues in most marriages, including communication, money management, dispute settlement, child rearing, trust, family violence, and sexual fidelity. The sessions often follow clearly specified lessons and activities from curriculums developed for young couples, including those developed specifically for low-income black and Hispanic couples. Many of the programs employ a program coordinator to maintain at least weekly contact with the couples, helping them arrange needed services (including employment and mental health services) and often becoming a trusted advisor and mentor to the young family.

A host of random-assignment studies are now being conducted around the nation to determine whether this kind of program can increase marriage rates or reduce divorce rates. The studies are also collecting information on child outcomes, including performance on standardized tests and school performance, to determine whether children benefit if their parents participate in marriage education programs. The federal government should continue these demonstration programs for at least another five years to determine whether carefully implemented marriage education that includes family coordinators and services can improve relationship satisfaction, increase marriage rates or reduce divorce rates, or improve child development.

The Bush administration also sponsored legislation that now provides $100 million a year for five years to support about 150 programs throughout the nation that aim to support healthy marriage (Administration for Children and Families 2007). Most of the programs are sponsored by community-based organizations like churches and programs that provide services to poor and low-income families. At the moment, none of these programs are being evaluated by well-designed studies. Someone with political sensibilities might notice that these programs might have the effect of creating a network of local organizations and individuals who are advocates for the program and who could play a role when the question of reauthorizing the $100 million program comes up in the Congress four or five years from now.

The administration's demonstration programs well illustrate the new tools at the disposal of policy makers and scholars who are serious about discovering whether their ideas work. Within a few years, all of the random-assignment projects will produce estimates of program impacts on the couples' relationship quality, on the duration of the relationship or marriage, on possible increases in marriage rates, and on impacts on children. More than likely, some of the programs will produce significant impacts while others will not. At that point, it would be wise policy to fund expansion of the programs that work.

Yet, another way to increase the incentives for marriage is to reduce financial penalties in both the tax code and in transfer programs for couples who marry (Carasso and Steuerle 2005). Congress has already taken several actions to reduce tax penalties for married couples and has even modified the EITC so that married couples get to keep more of their EITC as their earnings rise. Careful research on a representative national sample by Gregory Acs and Elaine Maag (2005) of the Urban Institute shows that for most cohabiting couples under 200 percent of poverty, the major penalties of marriage come from loss of benefits in transfer programs rather than the EITC. Based on this research, the federal or state governments should authorize demonstrations that study the effects of allowing couples who marry to retain their welfare benefits, especially TANF and food stamps, for a year or two after marriage.

Finally, it may be that real change requires a cultural shift, such as occurred with attitudes toward welfare reform. It is true that a large number of federal and state statutory provisions were changed to produce both sticks, as represented by work requirements and time limits, and carrots, as represented by child care, health insurance, and wage subsidies for those who work. Many of these reforms were supported by scientific demonstrations showing that they would increase work and even save government money.

However, having visited many of the programs, both before and after welfare reform, and having discussed the reforms with welfare recipients, welfare administrators, politicians from both sides of the aisle at the federal and state level, and many scholars who study poverty and welfare, I would make the subjective claim that during the 1990s something very near to a consensus was developed on the need to increase personal responsibility and reduce welfare dependency among the poor. When public figures—and in this regard President Clinton and the National Governors Association deserve great credit—are singing a common tune of personal responsibility and work, and when this music is consistent with sharp changes in programs throughout the nation that are willingly and skillfully implemented by agents of government, something that might be called cultural change is afoot. The welfare reform movement changed the way many politicians, welfare administrators, and welfare recipients themselves viewed both welfare and work. Without similar broad changes in society about the importance of marriage to adults and children, Moynihan's predictions about the life course of young men will continue to be fulfilled.

Strategy 3: Expand preschool education

Strong evidence indicates that preschool education can produce a wide range of long-term impacts on children's development, but so far these effects have mostly been confined to small, model programs. It is reasonable for scholars and policy makers to be skeptical supporters of preschool programs—supporters because there is evidence from superb studies that they can produce lasting effects, skeptical because these few model programs have been oversold by too many for too long. The two most remarkable studies are the Abecedarian preschool program conducted at the University of North Carolina (Ramey and Campbell 1984) and the Perry preschool program conducted in Ypsilanti, Michigan (Schweinhart, Barnes, and Weikart 1993). Both studies randomly assigned children to experimental and control groups, collected extensive data on the children and their families, and followed the children until they reached at least their midtwenties.

There were other similarities as well. Both involved a preschool program featuring a carefully designed and administered curriculum that was implemented by experienced teachers. Both involved parents, but the Abecedarian program did not begin systematic parent involvement until children reached school age; parents were an integral part of the Perry preschool program from age three. Abecedarian children began the program by roughly three months of age and attended the program full-time, five days per week, for forty-nine weeks per year until they entered the public schools at about age five. By contrast, the Perry program started when children were either three or four years of age (some children attended the preschool for two years).

A major limitation of these studies is that they were both small-scale, involving fewer than 125 children, raising the issue of whether a national program for a few million children could produce the same results. Another limitation is that the programs were both of very high quality, again raising the question of whether a large-scale program could achieve and then maintain such a high level of quality.

A third exemplary program, the Chicago Parent-Child Centers, involved more than fifteen hundred children and operated in twenty schools (with five control schools) in Chicago, thereby reducing concerns inevitably associated with small-scale programs operated under ideal circumstances like Abecedarian and Perry (Reynolds 2000; Reynolds et al. 2001). The program consisted of half-day classes delivered at ages three and four during the school year, used a formal curriculum that emphasized speaking and listening skills, required parental

TABLE 3
EFFECTS OF SELECTED EARLY CHILDHOOD PROGRAMS
ON ADOLESCENT AND ADULT BEHAVIORS

Intervention and Outcomes	Control or Comparison Group	Group Receiving Preschool Program
Teenage parenting rates		
Abecedarian	45	26
Perry Preschool	37	26
Chicago Child-Parent Centers	27	20
Well-being		
Health problem (Perry Preschool)	29	20
Drug user (Abecedarian)	39	18
Needed treatment for addition (Perry Preschool)	34	22
Abortion (Perry Preschool)	38	16
Abuse/neglect by age seventeen (Chicago Child-Parent Centers)	9	6
Criminal activity		
Number of felony violent assaults (Perry Preschool)	0.37	0.17
Juvenile court petitions (Chicago Child-Parent Centers)	25	16
Booked or charged with a crime (Head Start)		12 percentage points lower
Net earnings gain from participating in early Childhood programs		
Abecedarian	$35,531	
Perry Preschool	$38,892	
Chicago Child-Parent Centers	$30,638	
Head Start	No effect	

SOURCE: W. Steven Barnett and Clive Belfield (2006, 85).
NOTE: Table entries are percentages unless otherwise noted.

involvement on a weekly basis, included small classes and individualized assessment as children transitioned to the early elementary grades, and provided a comprehensive set of health and social services. Evaluations showed that the program produced impacts on math and reading abilities, as measured by standardized tests, and also reduced retention in grade, reduced placement in special education, improved rates of high school graduation, and reduced arrests. The design was not based on random-assignment, which caused some critics to argue that the results are subject to doubt (Besharov, Germanis, and Higney 2006).

All three of these model programs produced a range of impacts on tests of school achievement in math and reading, grade retention, placement in special education, high school graduation, or college attendance, which are summarized in Table 3. Equally impressive, at least one of the programs, and often more, reduced teen parenting, delinquency or crime, abuse or neglect, abortion, or drug addiction; and all three significantly increased lifetime earnings. These results are exactly the types of effects that are needed with black children, and virtually all the children in these three studies were black or Hispanic. If impacts like these could be achieved on a broad scale, a huge investment of $30 billion or more would be justified.

But there's the rub. Although the results for the Chicago program are notable because it was implemented on a fairly large scale, that scale is still modest compared with a national program. The only national preschool program is Head Start. Despite disputes about the strength of evidence from Head Start (Nathan 2007), there is some evidence of lasting impacts of the program from long-term follow-ups based on national data sets (e.g., Currie and Thomas 1995), although none of these are from random-assignment experiments. Furthermore, the results of the first random-assignment national evaluation of Head Start found only modest impacts by the time children left the program (HHS 2005). Although this evaluation will eventually produce long-term information, it is difficult to expect long-term impacts when the impacts at the end of the program are modest and, on many important measures, not statistically significant.

Even so, given the strength of evidence from the model programs, plus encouraging evidence from a new wave of state-sponsored preschool programs (Barnett, Lamy, and Jung 2005), additional public investments are justified. As this volume shows, problems with the development of black children are so serious that even risky investments are justified. However, rather than recommend a huge new public program, or even worse a simple expansion of Head Start, I recommend a series of large-scale demonstrations whose goal would be to simultaneously expand coverage of low-income children and to maintain high quality. Congress should appropriate something on the order of $3 billion a year for five years to conduct the demonstration, and then determine whether additional investments are justified at the end of that period. States that agree to meet a set of requirements would be invited to submit proposals to HHS and the best proposals would be funded on a competitive basis. The conditions would include,

- a single intervention program for all children below, say, 150 percent of poverty in the state, combining all existing funds from federal and state child care programs, state preschool funds, Title I, and Head Start supplemented by additional funds from both the federal level and the state;
- a promise to increase state spending by, say, 5 percent a year for five years;
- a plan for how the state would increase quality that would include the type of teacher training and mentoring shown in two recent demonstrations to produce major impacts on the learning of poor children (Layzer et al. 2007; Ramey and Ramey 2004);
- strong provisions for parent involvement and parent choice;
- a plan for continuous evaluation of student performance in every preschool facility and for procedures to make the results public on an annual basis; and
- a willingness to cooperate in a third-party evaluation.

The federal government would also fund a third-party evaluation to follow children for at least five years after the end of the preschool program.

Strategy 4: Reduce incarceration and help ex-felons reintegrate

As a policy analyst who has worked extensively with Republicans and has a generally conservative perspective on policy issues, I supported the tough federal laws enacted in the 1980s to reduce cocaine distribution and sales. Even when the prison population grew beyond all expectations, I was reluctant to change my views on the effectiveness of incarceration because crime rates were also falling. Then, in 2004, I encountered the estimate that six hundred thousand males, disproportionately black, would leave prison that year and return to their communities, and I read Devah Pager's (2003) work on the high levels of discrimination by employers against blacks, especially black ex-prisoners (see Pager and Karafin's article in this volume).

As I began to rebalance my thinking about the benefits and costs of high incarceration rates, more particularly by focusing attention on the cost side of the equation, I began to read Bruce Western's work proposing that for poor black males, incarceration rates were so high that prison was becoming one of the normal stages of development for black males (see Western and Wildeman's article in this volume). And as we have seen, 60 percent of black school dropouts spend time in prison. Taken together, these three considerations caused me to reverse my original thinking on the wisdom of long prison sentences for at least first-time and nonviolent offenders.

Proponents argue that incarceration produces several benefits that include taking criminals off the streets (contributing to the reduction in crime[15]), teaching at least some prisoners that crime does not pay and causing them to turn away from crime upon release, and making the public feel better in the knowledge that many criminals are off the streets. Offsetting these benefits is a set of heavy costs. Recidivism rates are high (Kurlychek, Brame, and Bushway 2006), the financial costs of incarceration to society are enormous and rising,[16] families are divided,[17] integration back into family and community life is difficult, and the costs to those imprisoned are almost beyond calculation.

In addition to exposing young men to the worst possible selection of new friends and a kind of graduate school of crime, incarceration also threatens them with physical violence including rape and murder. Moreover, as Pager (2007) has shown, their prospects of employment upon returning to society are minimal. Especially in the case of young men who have been convicted of drug offenses only, their "developmental" experiences in prison are almost guaranteed to make them less likely to be productive members of society. Ironically, the attempt to reduce crime and violence by taking young criminals off the street could well result in more and more serious crime later. Certainly, there is no need to speculate about rates of recidivism (Kurlychik, Brame, and Bushway 2006).

Reform could reduce the explosion in spending on the nation's criminal justice systems at the local, state, and federal level. In dollars adjusted for inflation, spending on the police, courts, and jails and prisons increased from $72.5 billion in 1982 to well over $204 billion in 2005. Spending on jails, prisons, and parole alone has increased from $18.3 billion to $65.1 billion, an increase of more than

250 percent in less than twenty-five years (Bureau of Justice Statistics 2007a). Sending fewer men to jail would reduce prison costs. If the high rates of recidivism could be reduced, still more savings would be produced. Although calculations are speculative until we have better evidence, it is reasonable to expect that quality programs to reduce crime, avoid incarceration, reduce the length of sentences, or reduce recidivism could pay for themselves, at least partially.

Three actions should be taken to address the extreme level of incarceration among young black men. First, the policies proposed above to reduce nonmarital births and promote marriage, if successful, would almost certainly reduce the number of young men who commit crimes. Similarly, good evidence indicates that quality preschool reduces delinquency and crime (Schweinhart, Barnes, and Weikart 1993).

The second action is to learn more about and make greater investments in prison release programs. One large-scale, random-assignment study now being conducted is of a well-known program conducted by the Center for Employment Opportunities (CEO) in New York City, an organization leading the nation in helping ex-felons find employment. Early results of the evaluation suggest that men who join the program soon after they are released were "less likely to have their parole revoked, to be convicted of a felony, and to be re-incarcerated" (Bloom et al. 2007, 2). Both states and the federal Department of Justice should ensure that such programs continue to grow and conform to the results of the numerous ongoing evaluations.

The final action and the most difficult for lawmakers will be to revise at least some of the laws that impose mandatory sentences on nonviolent criminals, including first-time offenders. The law enforcement system should concentrate on keeping young men out of prison if at all possible. The first step is to repeal the laws that provide for harsh mandatory sentences on those who sell crack cocaine and to reduce the penalties for selling crack to the same level as the penalties for selling powdered cocaine. In addition, the discretion of judges in imposing prison sentences should be restored.

The Supreme Court has recently taken significant steps in this direction. On December 10, 2007, the Court issued two 7–2 decisions (*Gall v. United States* 2007; *Kimbrough v. United States* 2007) that provided some relief from the harsh federal sentencing guidelines enacted in 1986. In *Gall*, the Supreme Court reversed an appeals court ruling that had struck down a district judge's decision to give a lighter sentence than recommended by the sentencing guidelines. Writing for the majority, Justice John Paul Stevens said the "guidelines should be the starting point and the initial benchmark," but district court judges have a right to depart from the guidelines in making an "individualized assessment."

In *Kimbrough*, the Supreme Court chided the appeals court for overruling a district court judge's "reasoned and reasonable decision" to impose a sentence lower than recommended by the guidelines (Greenhouse 2007; Editorial Board 2007). Both of these cases are consistent with urgent recommendations that have been made for several years by the United States Sentencing Commission calling for serious reductions in penalties for sale of crack cocaine. In its most recent report issued in May 2007, the Sentencing Commission emphasized its "strong desire for prompt legislative actions" to reduce the mandatory crack sentences.

Conclusion

We students of black families and black males are all descendents of Daniel Patrick Moynihan. After an unfortunate delay, the Moynihan Report has provoked scholars to study the forces causing the disintegration of the black family and to test policies, programs, and actions by government, community organizations, and individuals that could reverse those forces or ameliorate their effects. Nonetheless, since the Moynihan Report, family dissolution has greatly increased among blacks and has spread to all demographic groups in the nation. However, none has as many babies born outside marriage or as great a share of children spending a significant portion of their childhood in single-parent families as do black Americans.

Moynihan's solution was primarily economic. He called for major increases in employment programs. Ironically, employment by black mothers has increased dramatically since the Moynihan report, while the employment of black males—Moynihan's major concern—has actually declined. The employment problem is still central, and government should do more both to compel work and to make sure it is well rewarded.

But I find it impossible to believe that employment, earnings, and overall economic well-being will be greatly improved unless more black children are reared in married-couple families and more black children finish high school and achieve educational certificates or degrees beyond high school. These three problems—family composition, education, and employment—are completely intertwined, thereby virtually requiring us to initiate programs on all three fronts simultaneously. There is now a further complication. Because incarceration of black men has increased to such an astounding degree since Moynihan's assessment of the problem, the nation must also take enlightened actions to reduce the number of men going to jail, shorten the sentences of those who do go, and improve the prospects of ex-prisoners upon release. The incarceration disaster interacts with the problems of family composition and educational achievement. Improvement on each front will result in improvements on the others. Progress is possible but not inevitable.

Notes

1. If around 70 percent of black children are born outside marriage and about half of the remainder experience a divorce, it would at first seem to follow that about 85 percent of black children spend some time in a single-parent family. However, around half of the children born outside marriage are born to couples that cohabit, and some of these couples stay together and eventually marry. The best estimate is that approximately 80 percent of black children spending some time in a single-parent family.

2. According to Census Bureau data, the poverty rate for children in female-headed families in 2006 was 36.5 percent, 5.7 times the rate of 6.4 percent for children in married-couple families.

3. What researchers call "selection effects" are always an issue in correlational studies like Amato's (2005). The issue is that the factors that produce single-parent families might also be responsible for children from these families having the problems illustrated in Table 1. Thus, it might not be single-parenting itself that produced the problems shown in Table 1; rather, it is the factors that caused single-parenting that caused the problems.

4. Author's calculations.

5. In 1993, Jesse Jackson said, "There is nothing more painful to me at this stage in my life than to walk down the street and hear footsteps and start to think about robbery and then look around and see somebody white and feel relieved." In 1999, Steven Homes, a black reporter for the *New York Times*, who drove a taxi in New York City to put himself through college, said that "my sense of tolerance and racial solidarity was tested every time a casually dressed young black man, especially one in sneakers, tried to hail my cab. Most times, I drove right by" (Goldberg 1999).

6. Patterson (2006) also attributed high rates of incarceration to the "crisis in relations between [black] men and women of all classes."

7. One of Moynihan's last professional actions was participation in a scholarly conference on the future of the family for which he gave the keynote address (Moynihan, Smeeding, and Rainwater 2004).

8. The Congressional Research Service (2006) study examines the spending history at the federal and state level (if state spending is involved) of eighty-six means-tested programs in eight categories that include cash, medical, nutrition, social services, housing, education, jobs and training, and energy assistance.

9. Since 1968, federal spending on means-tested programs has increased from 6 percent to nearly 19 percent of total federal outlays and from less than 1.2 percent to nearly 3.6 percent of GDP; author's calculations.

10. In the thirty-two years between 1962 and 1994, the welfare rolls increased in all but five years (1978, 1979, 1982, 1985, and 1988).

11. Food stamps are available to everyone including fathers. The 1996 welfare reform law strengthened the food stamps work program, but the work requirements in food stamps are still too weak. They should be greatly strengthened so that all recipients who are not disabled or elderly must work at least twenty hours a week or engage in job search or training or lose their benefit.

12. Of the programs usually included in the work support system, food stamps, Medicaid, and the Earned Income Tax Credit are entitlements, meaning that all qualified individuals must be given the benefit. But child care is not guaranteed. Every year Congress and state legislatures appropriate a fixed sum of money for child care. When that money runs out, even qualified families are denied the benefit.

13. Although some scholars and editorial writers emphasize the inefficiency of government, Lawrence Mead (2004) presents abundant evidence to show how the welfare bureaucracy in Wisconsin was efficient and effective in implementing several waves of welfare reform in the 1980s and 1990s. Visits to many states and reviews of state data convince me that many states took effective action based on bureaucratic competence in implementing welfare reform.

14. Two of the four goals of Temporary Assistance for Needy Families (TANF) contain explicit statements about marriage. Goal 2 is to "end the dependence of needy parents on government benefits by promoting job preparation, work, and marriage; goal 4 is to "encourage the formation and maintenance of two-parent families." See U.S. Congress (1996, 9) (also see Title IV, Part A, Section 401 of the Social Security Act).

15. Western (2006, chap. 7) deals with this issue in great detail, concluding that imprisonment probably accounts for about 10 percent in the reduction of crime during roughly the last three decades of the twentieth century. Others have estimated that imprisonment could account for up to 40 percent in the reduction of crime rates.

16. According to the Bureau of Justice Statistics (2007a), total spending on criminal justice including police, the courts, and jails and prisons was more than $204 billion in 2005.

17. Western (2006, 136–39) uses data from the Surveys of Inmates of State and Federal Correctional Facilities and the Surveys of Inmates of Local Jails to show that between 1980 and 2000, the number of children with fathers in prison increased from about 350,000 to 2.1 million. About one of every eleven black children had a father in prison or jail in 2000.

References

Acs, Gregory, and Elaine Maag. 2005. The conflict between marriage promotion initiatives for cohabiting couples with children and marriage penalties in the tax and transfer programs. No. B-66, Series on New Federalism: National Survey of America's Families. Washington, DC: Urban Institute.

Administration for Children and Families. 2007. Healthy Marriage Initiative. www.acf.hhs.gov/healthy-marriage/about/mission.html (accessed January 2, 2008).

Amato, Paul R. 2005. The impact of family formation change on the cognitive, social, and emotional well-being of the next generation. *The Future of Children* 15 (2): 75-96.

Auletta, Ken. 1982. *The underclass*. New York: Random House.

Barnett, W. Steven, and Clive Belfield. 2006. Early childhood development and social mobility. *The Future of Children* 16 (2): 73-98.

Barnett, W. Steven, C. Lamy, and K. Jung. 2005. *The effects of state pre-kindergarten programs on young children's school readiness in five states*. New Brunswick, NJ: National Institute of Early Education.

Berlin, Gordon. 2007. Rewarding the work of individuals: A counterintuitive approach. *The Future of Children* 17 (2): 17-42.

Besharov, Douglas J., Peter Germanis, and Caeli Higney. 2006. *Summaries of twenty early childhood evaluations*. College Park, MD: Welfare Reform Academy.

Blankenhorn, David. N.d. For a new revisionism: Scholarship on black families since the Moynihan Report. Manuscript, Institute for American Values, New York.

Bloom, Dan. 2001. How welfare and work policies affect employment and income: A synthesis of research. Next Generation Project, May. New York: MDRC. http://www.mdrc.org/publications/99/full.pdf.

Bloom, Dan, Cindy Redcross, Janine Zweig, and Gilda Azurdia. 2007. *Transitional jobs for ex-prisoners*. New York: MDRC. www.mdrc.org/publications/468/overview.html (accessed December 10, 2007).

Bos, Hans, Greg J. Duncan, Lisa A. Gennetian, and Heather D. Hill. 2007. *New hope: Fulfilling America's promise to "make work pay."* Washington, DC: Hamilton Project, Brookings Institution.

Bureau of Justice Statistics. 2007a. Direct expenditure by level of government, 1982-2005. www.ojp.usdoj.gove/bjs/eande.htm (accessed December 20, 2007).

———. 2007b. FBI, Supplementary Homicide Reports, 1976-2005. Homicide trends in the U.S.: Homicide offenders by rates. www.ojp.usdoj.gov/bjs/homicide/tables/oracetab.htm (accessed December 10, 2007).

———. 2007c. FBI, Supplementary Homicide Reports, 1976-2005. Homicide trends in the U.S.: Homicide victims by rates. www.ojp.usdoj.gov/bjs/homicide/tables/vracetabl.htm.

Carasso, Adam, and C. Eugene Steuerle. 2005. The hefty penalty on marriage facing many households with children. *The Future of Children* 15:157-75.

Coleman, James. 1966. *Equality of educational opportunity*. Washington, DC: Government Printing Office.

Congressional Research Service. 2006. Cash and noncash benefits for persons with limited income: Eligibility rules, recipient and expenditure data, FY2002–2004 (RL33340). Washington, DC: Congressional Research Service.

Cosby, Bill, and Alvin F. Poussaint. 2007. *Come on people: On the path from victims to victors*. Nashville, TN: Thomas Nelson.

Currie, Janet, and Duncan Thomas. 1995. Does Head Start make a difference? *American Economic Review* 85:341-64.

Dion, M. Robin. 2005. Healthy marriage programs: Learning what works. *The Future of Children* 15:139-56.

Dion, M. Robin, Alan Hershey, Heather Zaveri, Sarah Avellar, Debra Strong, and Timothy Silman. 2008. *Implementation of the Building Strong Families Program*. Washington, DC: Mathematica Policy Research.

Duncan, Greg J., Aletha Huston, and Thomas S. Weisner. 2007. *Higher ground: New hope for the working poor and their children*. New York: Russell Sage Foundation.

Editorial Board. 2007. Justice in sentencing. *New York Times*, September 12. http://www.nytimes.com/2007/12/12/opinion/12wed1.html (accessed July 5, 2008).

Fischer, Claude S., and Michael Hout. 2006. *Century of difference: How America changed in the last one hundred years*. New York: Russell Sage Foundation.

Furstenberg, Frank F., J. Brooks-Gunn, and S. Philip Morgan. 1987. *Adolescent mothers in later life: Human development in cultural and historical context.* New York: Cambridge

Gall v. The United States. 2007. U.S. Supreme Court, 06–7949. Washington, DC: U.S. Supreme Court.

Gallup Poll. 2007. Gallup Poll: Race relations. http://www.gallup.com/poll/1687/Race-Relations.aspx?version=print (accessed December 26, 2007).

Gillette, Michael L. 1996. *Launching the War on Poverty.* New York: Twayne.

Jeffrey Goldberg, "The Color of Suspicion," *New York Times*, June 20, 1999.

Greenhouse, Linda. 2007. Court restores sentencing powers of federal judges. *New York Times*, December 10, p. A1.

Hamilton, Brady E., Joyce A. Martin, and Stephanie J. Ventura. 2007. Births: Preliminary data for 2006. *National Vital Statistics Reports* 56 (7). http://www.cdc.gov/nchs/data/nvsr56/nvsr56_07.pdf (accessed July 5, 2008).

Haskins, Ron. 2006. *Work over welfare: The inside story of the 1996 welfare reform law.* Washington, DC: Brookings Institution.

Holzer, Harry J. 2008. The labor market and young black men: Updating Moynihan's perspective. *The Annals of the American Academy of Political and Social Science* 621:47-69.

Holzer, Harry, Paul Offner, and Elaine Sorensen. 2005. Declining employment among young black less-educated men: The role of incarceration and child support. *Journal of Policy Analysis and Management* 24:329-50.

Jencks, Christopher. 1972. *Inequality: A reassessment of the effect of family and schooling in America.* New York: Basic Books.

Jencks, Christopher, and Meredith Phillips, eds. 1998. *The black-white test score gap.* Washington, DC: Brookings Institution.

Kimbrough v. The United States. 2007. U.S. Supreme Court, 06–6330. Washington, DC: U.S. Supreme Court.

Kirby, Douglas. 2007. *Emerging answers 2007: Research findings on programs to reduce teen pregnancy and sexually transmitted diseases.* Washington, DC: National Campaign to Prevent Teen and Unintended Pregnancy.

Knox, Virginia. 2007. *Supporting healthy marriage: Designing a marriage education demonstration and evaluation for low-income married couples.* New York: MDRC.

Kurlychek, Megan C., Robert Brame, and Shawn D. Bushway. 2006. Scarlet letters and recidivism: Does an old criminal record predict future offending? *Crime and Public Policy* 5:483-504.

Layzer, Jean I., Carolyn J. Layzer, Barbara D. Goodson, and Cristofer Price. 2007. *Evaluation of child care subsidy strategies: Findings from project upgrade in Miami-Dade County.* Cambridge, MA: Abt Associates.

Lerman, Robert. 2007. *An economic framework and selected proposals for demonstrations aimed at strengthening marriage, employment, and family functioning outcomes.* Washington, DC: Urban Institute, Center on Labor, Human Services, and Population. http://www.acf.hhs.gov/programs/opre/strengthen/marr_employ/reports/economic_frmwk/economic_framework.pdf (accessed July 5, 2008).

Markman, Howard J., Mari Jo Renick, Frank J. Floyd, Scott M. Stanley, and Mari Clements. 1993. Preventing marital distress through communication and conflict management training. *Journal of Clinical Psychology* 61:70-77.

Martin, Shannan, Robert Rector, and Melissa G. Pardue. 2004. *Comprehensive sex education vs. authentic abstinence: A study of competing curricula.* Washington, DC: Heritage Foundation.

McLanahan, Sara. 2008. Fragile families and the reproduction of poverty. *The Annals of the American Academy of Political and Social Science* 621:XX-XX

McLanahan, Sara, Elisabeth Donahue, and Ron Haskins. 2005. Introducing the issue. *The Future of Children* 15:3-12.

McLanahan, Sara, and Gary Sandefur. 1994. *Growing up with a single parent: What hurts, what helps.* Cambridge, MA: Harvard University Press.

McWhorter, John. 2000. *Losing the race: Self-sabotage in black America.* New York: Free Press.

Mead, Lawrence M. 2004. *Government matters: Welfare reform in Wisconsin.* Princeton, NJ: Princeton University Press.

———. 2007. Toward a mandatory work policy for men. *The Future of Children* 17:43-72.

Meckler, Laura. 2006. Poverty: The new search for solutions. *Wall Street Journal*, November 20, p. 1.

Miller, Cynthia, and Virginia Knox. 2001. *The challenge of helping low-income fathers support their children.* New York: Manpower Demonstration Research Corporation.

Moynihan, Daniel P. 1965. *The Negro family: The case for national action.* Washington, DC: U.S. Department of Labor. http://www.dol.gov/oasam/programs/history/webid-meynihan.htm (accessed July 5, 2007).

———. 1986. A family policy for the nation. *America,* March 22, pp. 224-27.

Moynihan, Daniel P., Timothy M. Smeeding, and Lee Rainwater, eds. 2004. *The future of the family.* New York: Russell Sage Foundation.

Murray, Charles. 1984. *Losing ground: American social policy, 1950-1980.* New York: Basic Books.

Nathan, Richard P. 2007. How should we read the evidence about Head Start? Three views. *Journal of Policy Analysis and Management* 26:673-89.

Nathan, Richard P., and Thomas L. Gais. 1999. *Implementing the Personal Responsibility Act of 1996: A first look.* Albany, NY: Rockefeller Institute of Government.

National Assessment of Educational Progress. 2007. The nation's report card. http://nces.ed.gov/nationsreportcard/ (accessed July 5, 2008).

Orr, Larry L. 1999. *Social experiments: Evaluating public programs with experimental designs.* Thousand Oaks, CA: Sage.

Pager, Devah. 2003. The mark of a criminal record. *American Journal of Sociology* 108:937-75.

———. 2007. *Marked: Race, crime, and finding work in an era of mass incarceration.* Chicago: University of Chicago Press.

Pager, Devah, and Diana Karafin. 2008. Bayesian bigot? Statistical discrimination, stereotypes, and employer decision making. *The Annals of the American Academy of Political and Social Science* 621:70-93.

Patterson, Orlando. 1998. *Rituals of blood: Consequences of slavery in two American centuries.* New York: Civitas.

———. 2006. A poverty of mind. *New York Times,* March 26. www.nytimes.com/2006/03/26/opinion/26patterson.html (accessed July 5, 2008).

Pettit, Becky, and Bruce Western. 2004. Mass imprisonment and the life course: Race and class inequality in U.S. incarceration. *American Sociological Review* 69:151-69.

Rainwater, Lee, and William L. Yancey. 1967. *The Moynihan Report and the politics of controversy.* Cambridge, MA: MIT Press.

Ramchand, Rajeev, Rosalie Liccardo Pacula, and Martin Y. Iguchi. 2006. Racial differences in marijuana-users' risk of arrest in the United States. *Drug and Alcohol Dependence* 84:264-72.

Ramey, Craig T., and Frances A. Campbell. 1984. Preventative education for high-risk children. *American Journal of Mental Deficiency* 88 (5): 512-23.

Ramey, Craig T., and Sharon L. Ramey. 2004. Early learning and school readiness: Can early intervention make a difference? *Merrill-Palmer Quarterly* 50:471-521.

Reynolds, Arthur. 2000. *Success in early intervention: The Chicago child-parent centers.* Lincoln: University of Nebraska Press.

Reynolds, Arthur, Judy A. Temple, Dylan L. Robertson, and Emily A. Mann. 2001. Long-term effects of an early childhood intervention on educational achievement and juvenile arrests: A 15-year follow-up of low-income children in the public schools. *Journal of the American Medical Association* 285 (18): 2339-46.

Rossi, Peter H., Mark W. Lipsey, and Howard E. Freeman. 2004. *Evaluation: A systematic approach.* New York: Russell Sage Foundation.

Rubin, David M., Amanda L. R. O'Reilly, Lauren Hafner, Xianqun Luan, and A. Russell Localio. 2007. Placement stability and early behavioral outcomes among children in out-of-home care. In *Child protection: Using research to improve policy and practice,* ed. Ron Haskins, Fred Wulczyn, and Mary Bruce Webb, 171–86. Washington, DC: Brookings Institution.

Santelli, John S., Laura Duberstein Lindberg, Lawrence B. Finer, and Susheela Singh. 2007. Explaining recent declines in adolescent pregnancy in the United States: The contribution of abstinence and improved contraceptive use. *American Journal of Public Health* 97:150-56.

Schweinhart, Lawrence J., Helen V. Barnes, and David P. Weikart. 1993. *Significant benefits: The High/Scope Perry Preschool Study through age 27.* Ypsilanti, MI: High Scope.

Steele, Shelby. 2006. *White guilt: How blacks and white together destroyed the promise of the civil rights era.* New York: HarperCollins.

Stevenson, Betsy, and Justin Wolfers. 2007. Marriage and divorce: Changes and their driving forces. Working Paper 12944, National Bureau of Economic Research, Cambridge, MA. www.nber.org/papers/w12944 (accessed July 5, 2008).

Taylor, Stuart, Jr. 2007. Criminal injustice and race. *National Journal*, October 6, pp. 17-18.

Terry-Humen, Elizabeth, Jennifer Manlove, and Kristin A. Moore. 2005. *Playing catch-up: How children born to teen mothers fare*. Washington, DC: Child Trends.

Tessler, Betsy L., and David Seith. 2007. *From getting by to getting ahead: Navigating career advancement for low-wage workers*. New York: Manpower Development Research Corporation.

Thomas, Adam, and Isabel Sawhill. 2002. For richer or for poorer: Marriage as an anti-poverty policy. *Journal of Policy Analysis and Management* 21:587-99.

United States Sentencing Commission. 2007. *Cocaine and federal sentencing policy: Report to Congress*. Washington, DC: U.S. Sentencing Commission.

U.S. Census Bureau. 2006. *Statistical abstract of the United States: 2007*. Washington, DC: Government Printing Office.

———. 2007. Marital status of the population 15 years and over, by sex and race: 1950 to present. www.census.gov/population/socdemo/hh-fam/ms1.xls (accessed December 17, 2007).

U.S. Congress. House. 1996. *Personal Responsibility and Work Opportunity Reconciliation Act of 1996, Conference Report 104-725*. Washington, DC: Government Printing Office.

U.S. Congress. House. Committee on Ways and Means. 1989. *General explanation of the Family Support Act of 1988* (WMCP: 1010-3). Washington, DC: Government Printing Office.

———. 2004. *Green book* (Committee Print 108-6). Washington, DC: Government Printing Office.

U.S. Department of Health and Human Services. 2005. *Head Start impact study: First year findings*. Washington, DC: U.S. Department of Health and Human Services.

Western, Bruce. 2006. *Punishment and inequality in America*. New York: Russell Sage.

Western, Bruce, and Christopher Wildeman. 2008. The black family and mass incarceration. *The Annals of the American Academy of Political and Social Science* 621:221-242.

Williams, Juan. 2007. *Enough: The phony leaders, dead-end movements, and culture of failure that are undermining black America—and what we can do about it*. New York: Three Rivers.

Wilson, Laura A., and Robert P. Stoker. 2006. *When work is not enough: State and federal policies to support needy workers*. Washington, DC: Brookings Institution.

Wilson, William Julius. 1978. *The declining significance of race: Blacks and changing American institutions*. Chicago: University of Chicago.

———. 1987. *The truly disadvantaged: The inner city, the underclass, and public policy*. Chicago: University of Chicago.

Zedlewski, Sheila R., Gina Adams. Lisa Dubay, and Genevieve M. Kenney. 2006. Is there a system supporting low-income working families? Low-Income Working Families Paper 4, Urban Institute, Washington, DC.

QUICK READ SYNOPSIS

The Moynihan Report Revisited: Lessons and Reflections after Four Decades

Special Editors: DOUGLAS S. MASSEY
Princeton Unviersity
and
ROBERT J. SAMPSON
Harvard University

Volume 621, January 2009

Prepared by Herb Fayer, Jerry Lee Foundation

DOI: 10.1177/0002716208328645

The Labor Market and Young Black Men: Updating Moynihan's Perspective

Harry J. Holzer, Georgetown University

Background

In 1965, Daniel Patrick Moynihan referred to the employment situation of young black men as an "unconcealable crisis."
- He identified this as a primary cause of the instability of black families and as a priority in seeking to stabilize black families.
- Moynihan's views in 1965 were very prescient, as the employment situation of young black men has steadily deteriorated since then.
- Moynihan noted the effects of employer characteristics and behavior in the broader labor market as well as those of the young men themselves in accounting for employment trends over time.

NOTE: A range of additional behaviors seem to characterize these young men as they withdraw—such as a growing participation in illegal activities, a declining tendency to marry, and even a tendency to "disconnect" from school and other mainstream behaviors at a relatively early age.

Employers and Young Black Men

Moynihan understood that observed employment outcomes of young blacks represent a range of factors and trends on the demand side of the labor market, those involving employers and their hiring patterns. They also reflect the skills and behaviors of the young men themselves and how they responded to these demand trends.
- He correctly noted the effects of growing employer skill needs (and continuing racial gaps in skills), persisting discrimination, urban segregation, and informal networks on black male employment.

- He correctly foresaw growing participation in crime and noncustodial fatherhood in this population, as well as a tendency for young black men to withdraw from the labor market altogether.
- On the other hand, no one of that time could foresee the extent to which legitimate labor markets would deteriorate for all less-educated young men, and especially black men, in the 1970s and beyond.
- He also did not foresee the booming of illegal activities, especially the crack cocaine trade, in the 1980s and the enormous growth of the offender population it would generate.

New Policies   What is needed is a more comprehensive set of policies to counter the negative trends in labor force opportunities and behaviors.
- These policies should enhance both the perceptions and the reality of greater opportunity for young people, especially through a range of improvements in education and training/labor market options for young people.
- In addition, the kinds of efforts needed to help ex-offenders and noncustodial fathers include policy changes to reduce the labor market barriers they face and greater funding for programs that seek to overcome these barriers, such as "prisoner reentry" and "fatherhood" programs.
- Improving the incentives of less educated men to stay in the labor force, through extensions of the Earned Income Tax Credit to this population, is also important.

Bayesian Bigot? Statistical Discrimination, Stereotypes, and Employer Decision Making

Devah Pager, Princeton University; and Diana Karafin, Ohio State University

Background   In this study, the authors examine the nature of employer attitudes about black and white workers and the extent to which these views are calibrated against their direct experiences with workers from each group.
- Interviews with employers reveal the persistence of strong negative associations with minority workers, with particularly negative characteristics attributed to African American men.
- Studies of hiring likewise suggest that employers strongly prefer white (and Latino) workers to otherwise similar African Americans.

NOTE: Have employers had negative experiences with African American employees in the past that have led them to shy away from hiring blacks? Or do other factors shape employer decision making?

Race as a Proxy   Employers are clearly using race as a proxy for employment-relevant characteristics, but the degree to which the use of this proxy is informed by empirical realities remains uncertain.
- Moss and Tilly (2001) found that employers readily refer to negative characteristics among African American workers, with pervasive concerns about dependability, motivation, attitude, and skill.

- Some of these employers cite concrete experiences with their own black employees as the basis of their attitudes, though a "silent majority" claim not to notice racial differences among their employees.

Findings   The findings of this research suggest that, while most employers expressed strong views about the negative characteristics of African American men, fewer than half of these employers reported observations of their own applicants or employees that were consistent with these general perceptions.
- While employers may update their expectations regarding individual workers, these experiences do not seem to have noticeable effects on their attitudes about the group as a whole.
- Rather, employer attitudes suggest a process of subtyping, whereby individuals who do not conform to a stereotype are viewed as exceptions whose characteristics have little bearing on the larger group.
- Employers surely receive relevant information about various groups from sources other than direct workplace experience.
- At the same time, it is surprising that the experiences employers report from their own direct observations do not carry greater weight in their general attitude formation.

NOTE: The results of this analysis have potentially troubling implications for hiring behavior. The majority of employers who report positive experiences with black workers (or no differences between black and white workers) nevertheless maintain strong negative attitudes about black men generally.

Q
R
S
.

If Moynihan Had Only Known: Race, Class, and Family Change in the Late Twentieth Century

Frank F. Furstenberg, University of Pennsylvania

Background   Had Moynihan been more attentive to research that focused simultaneously on social class and race, his report might have had far different political and social consequences, leading to alternative policy directions.
- By updating some of the trends, it is clear that many of the pressures on marriage and family formation that seemed uniquely relevant to blacks have been felt by low-income populations more generally.
- Moynihan was greatly influenced by the then cultural template in his analysis of the breakdown of the black family.
- Moynihan noted how matriarchal practices fostered by slavery, economic exclusion, and racial discrimination were weakening the position of men and boys in black families.
- Moynihan concluded that economic pressures and racial segregation in the postwar period were creating undue stresses on the black family.

Conclusion   Even conceding that the family circumstances of blacks and whites looked very different when Moynihan published his report, he might have been able to do a better job of unpacking the racial differences that he observed in the

family had he paid closer attention to the qualitative research produced by
social scientists in the decades leading up to his report.

- As more and more lower-income whites have faced the same set of precarious economic conditions, they have begun to exhibit the same patterns
of family formation behavior as African Americans.
- The advantages that marriage ostensibly confers become more apparent
than real in an era of great inequality, when fewer are willing to commit
or able to maintain stable unions whether they take the form of marriage
or de facto marriage.
- As a result, efforts to promote marriage without changing the economic and
social conditions that foster stable unions are destined to be ineffective.
- There is growing evidence that the Latino population is also experiencing
a change from a marriage-oriented population among the foreign-born to
an American pattern of family formation among the second generation
and among those born abroad but reared in the United States.

NOTE: The patterns suggest that it is insufficient to have strong cultural values about marriage if the economic and social conditions that foster marriage
are not maintained. To be sure, the story of change over the past forty years is
not strictly an economic one. Gender relationships, premarital sexual practices,
and social and cultural influences have all played a part in reshaping the family.

Fragile Families and the Reproduction of Poverty

Sara McLanahan, Princeton University

Background

In 1965, Moynihan argued that a self-reinforcing "tangle of pathology," consisting of nonmarital childbearing, high male unemployment, and welfare
dependence, was undermining the progress of African Americans and contributing to the perpetuation of poverty.

- Since the publication of the Moynihan Report, the proportion of African
American children born outside marriage has grown dramatically, from 24
percent in 1965 to 69 percent in 2000.
- After four decades, analysts continue to debate whether nonmarital childbearing is a consequence or a cause of poverty.

Family Study

The author uses data from the Fragile Families and Child Wellbeing Study
to address the following questions:

- To what extent does poverty and economic disadvantage increase the
chances of nonmarital childbearing?
- To what extent does nonmarital childbearing contribute to the perpetuation of poverty and economic disadvantage?

Conclusion

The study indicates that nonmarital childbearing is both a consequence and
a cause of poverty. It also indicates that to break the intergenerational cycle
of poverty, we need to find a way to persuade young women from disadvantaged backgrounds that delaying fertility while they search for a suitable
partner will have a payoff that is large enough to offset the loss of time spent
as a mother or the possibility of forgoing motherhood entirely.

Romantic Unions in an Era of Uncertainty: A Post-Moynihan Perspective on African American Women and Marriage

Linda M. Burton, Duke University; and M. Belinda Tucker,
University of California, Los Angeles

Q
R
S

Background   This article provides a brief overview of how African American women are situated in and around the thesis of the Moynihan Report.

- It discusses uncertainty in the temporal organization of poor women's lives and in the new terrains of gender relationships and how these both influence African American women's thoughts and behaviors.

- The authors argue that much is to be learned from focusing the lens in this way, as it allows us to view African American women's romantic and marital behavior in the context of broader societal trends.

- An unmarried woman's uncertainty is closely tied to her life course experiences with poverty but also is rooted in broader societal transformations that have reconfigured the temporal dimensions of everyday life and gender relations for all individuals.

- Temporal uncertainty involves women's presumed infractions against socially prescribed moral codes of time use, their beliefs and behaviors around life expectancy, and how they synchronize the daily rhythms of their family's needs with institutional timetables.

- Although the restructuring of gender relationships in society more broadly has created uncertainty about what constitutes appropriate behavior, there is even greater ambiguity surrounding African American family roles, as structural forces and sociocultural tendencies have driven new attitudinal and behavioral patterns.

NOTE: Moynihan argued that female economic dominance in and of itself was not necessarily problematic, but since the male breadwinner model was the prevailing paradigm, any marriage pattern that deviated from that model was troublesome for families and society.

Conclusion   The authors have attempted to provide an alternate lens through which to view past and current patterns of intimate union formation and maintenance by African American women.

- Uncertainty frames perceptions, attitudes, assessments, decision making, and behaviors about marriage and intimate unions for African Americans and frames how it renders contextually relevant interpretations that were sorely missing from the Moynihan discourse.

- The tasks for reducing poverty, reconciling time binds, and recalibrating gender-linked behavioral expectations is an urgent challenge for many groups and nations.

NOTE: At the height of the controversy surrounding the Moynihan Report, Eleanor Holmes Norton observed that without children as the prime reason for marriage, the institution would now have to stand on its own "inherent qualities." It may be that marriage as we have known it in contemporary times will not survive "on its own terms," but as the need for human companionship and love remains intrinsic to the human condition, serious community-wide conversations to address the current dilemma are essential.

Claiming Fatherhood: Race and the Dynamics of Paternal Involvement among Unmarried Men

Kathryn Edin and Laura Tach, Harvard University;
and Ronald Mincy, Columbia University

Background

Moynihan claimed that owing to increasing out-of-wedlock childbearing—a condition affecting only a small fraction of white children but one in five African Americans at the time—the black family was nearing what he called "complete breakdown," particularly in America's inner cities.

- Studies offered much about the lives of unmarried mothers and their progeny, yet they told us next to nothing about the fathers of these children.
- Unwed fathers' often tenuous connections to households made them hard to find, and many refused to admit they had fathered children.
- Unwed fatherhood, seen as a hit-and-run encounter, plays a dominant role in the public discourse about poverty, family structure, and race—yet these encounters are much rarer than the public assumes.

Fatherhood Involvement

More than half of nonmarital children reside with their father at the time of their first birthday, but this figure declines to 35 percent by their fifth.

- Father involvement drops dramatically after a "breakup" and after parents enter into new relationships and parenting roles.
- There is a willingness on the part of the father to remain involved regardless of his other familial commitments but less willingness by the mother to facilitate that involvement once she establishes a new family.
- All fathers, but particularly African American fathers, typically reject the "package deal" notion—that a father's parental relationship is contingent upon his relationship with the mother—although many end up living by it nonetheless.

Conclusion

Among U.S. couples, cohabiting unions among parents with children are extraordinarily fragile—far more fragile than marital unions and far more fragile than unmarried parental unions in other industrialized countries.

- While the conventional wisdom might assume that unmarried fathers are uninvolved because they are eager to evade responsibility for their progeny, the authors' results suggest a different story.
- As both the mother and the father of a child born outside of marriage move further from their failed partnership and enter new partnerships, the qualitative data show that new normative expectations are often set into motion that are in sharp competition with the old.

- Especially for mothers, new partnerships seem to provide a strong motivation to give the new partner the role of father, particularly once the mother has a child with that partner.
- In addition, African American fathers are more likely to remain in regular contact with their children even after entering into relationships with new partners and having children with them.

NOTE: As stability is critical for child well-being, the shifting cast of fathers and father figures in children's lives likely detracts from, not adds to, their well-being.

Welfare Reform in the Mid-2000s: How African American and Hispanic Families in Three Cities Are Faring

Andrew Cherlin and Bianca Frogner, Johns Hopkins University;
David Ribar, University of North Carolina at Greensboro;
and Robert Moffitt, Johns Hopkins University

Background   The authors find at best a modest decline in the average poverty rate among African American welfare leavers between 1999 and 2005.
- Hispanic leavers showed larger average declines in poverty.
- Employed leavers in 2005 showed increases in household income and declines in poverty.
- Among nonemployed leavers, African Americans had experienced a decline in household income and were further below the poverty line than in 1999, whereas Hispanic women had experienced modest declines or slight increases in their household incomes.

Outcomes   Despite predictions that PRWORA (Personal Responsibility and Work Opportunity Reconciliation Act) would be disastrous, the labor force participation rate of single mothers rose sharply, and their poverty rate fell.
- The authors present information on African American and Hispanic women in the Three-City Study, one of the longest panel surveys of low-income families in the post-PRWORA era (1999-2005).
- By 2005, when none of the women were receiving TANF (Temporary Assistance to Needy Families), the household income of African Americans in the study was less than that of the two Hispanic groups.

Conclusion   Nine years after the passage of PRWORA and six years after the study began, the economic circumstances of the women who were receiving welfare at the start of the study had diverged by their subsequent TANF receipt, employment status, and race-ethnicity.

The New U.S. Immigrants: How Do They Affect Our Understanding of the African American Experience?

Frank D. Bean, Cynthia Feliciano, and Jennifer Lee, University of California, Irvine; and Jennifer Van Hook, Pennsylvania State University

Q
R
S

Background

Today the intensity of negative feeling about immigration seems to derive from fears that contemporary newcomers, because they are non-European, threaten national identity more than did early-twentieth-century immigrants.

- About two-thirds of those arriving since 1965 come from Asian, African, or Latino countries.
- Immigration trends since 1965 have clearly resulted in a recent nonwhite minority that is larger than the native black minority.

NOTE: This article argues that yesterday's color line has been transformed into a black/nonblack demarcation that undergirds racial/ethnic divisions, not a more complex tripartite structure.

A Racial Divide

A black-nonblack divide appears to be taking shape in the United States, in which Asians and Latinos are closer to whites than are blacks to whites.

- America's color lines are moving toward a new demarcation that places many blacks in a position of disadvantage similar to that resulting from the traditional black-white divide.
- The country is simply reinventing a color line that continues to separate blacks from other racial/ethnic groups.
- Asians and Latinos may be moving closer and closer to a "white" category, with multiracial Asian-whites and Latino-whites standing at the head of the queue. This could indicate the reemergence of a black-white color line.
- Regardless of whether a divide were to fall along black-nonblack or black-white lines, the position of blacks could remain severely disadvantaged.
- Because boundaries are loosening for *some* nonwhite groups, this could lead to the erroneous conclusion that race is declining in significance for all groups.
- It appears that Asians and Latinos are simultaneously more actively pursuing entry into the majority group and that whites are more willing to accept their entry compared to blacks.

NOTE: The fact that boundary dissolution is neither uniform nor unconditional indicates that the United States cannot be complacent about the degree to which opportunities are improving for all racial/ethnic groups, particularly when a deep and persistent divide continues to separate blacks from all other groups.

The Black Family and Mass Incarceration

Bruce Western, Harvard University; and Christopher Wildeman,
University of Michigan

Q
R
S

Background	This article documents the emergence of mass incarceration and describes its significance for African American family life.
• The era of mass incarceration can be understood as a new stage in the history of American racial inequality.
• Because of its recent arrival, the social impact of mass incarceration remains poorly understood.
• Emerging only in the closing years of the 1990s, mass incarceration has routinely drawn young noncollege black men and their families into the orbit of the penal system.
Worsening Situation	Many of the social problems Moynihan identified have subsequently worsened.
• Joblessness among young, black, noncollege men climbed through the 1960s and 1970s.
• Crime rates and rates of single-parenthood also escalated.
• Public policy turned in a punitive direction, massively expanding the role of the criminal justice system.
• Now, more than a third of young black noncollege men are incarcerated.

NOTE: The mass imprisonment of the late 1990s can be traced to two basic shifts in politics and economics—the growth of harsh sentencing policies and a punitive approach to drug control. The urban deindustrialization that produced the raw material for the prison boom was as much a failure of institutions as a failure of markets. |
| *Unanswered Questions* | There are several unanswered questions needing research.
• How does incarceration affect family violence and other victimization?
• What are the financial consequences of incarceration for poor families?
• What are the effects of incarceration on the supervision and socialization of children?

NOTE: Under current circumstances, the inequalities of mass incarceration will be sustained not just over a lifetime, but from one generation to the next. |

Race in the American Mind: From the Moynihan Report to the Obama Candidacy

Lawrence D. Bobo, Harvard University; and
Camille Z. Charles, University of Pennsylvania

Background	This article assesses the tenor of racial attitudes in white and black America since 1965.

Q
R
S

- On one hand, a massive positive change in social norms regarding race calls for integration and equality as the rules that should guide black-white interaction.
- On the other hand, there is an ongoing legacy of tension and division.
- The authors link these trends in attitudes to broader changes in society (i.e., racial segregation, job discrimination, rates of intermarriage), patterns of intergroup and interpersonal behavior, and national political dynamics.
  - Moynihan wrote, "The racist virus in the American blood stream still afflicts us: Negroes will encounter serious personal prejudice for at least another generation."

NOTE: The authors assert that dynamics, conditions, and patterns of belief and behavior remain that should trouble us as a nation and that continue to make the terms *prejudice* and *racism* important and deeply meaningful facets of the American social, cultural, and political landscape.

Black-White Relations

What fundamental principles do Americans expect will guide black-white relations?

- Most white Americans not only no longer endorse segregation, white privilege, and antiblack discrimination as rules that should guide black-white relations, but in fact endorse broad goals of integration, equality, and equal treatment without regard to race.
- The authors are convinced that this shift cuts much deeper for most people than mere lip service about what "one is supposed to say."
- Public policy greatly tests the readiness of many whites to incur potential costs or burdens of social change consistent with new norms.

Barack Obama Example

Nothing brings home the complexity of the current moment more than the candidacy of Barack Obama for president of the United States.

- First, some white voters appear to tell pollsters one thing but do another once in the voting booth.
- Second, it is clear that a nontrivial number of white voters openly rejected Obama largely on the basis of race.

NOTE: While the racial virus is not yet defeated or fully eradicated from the body politic, the authors can find a number of encouraging indicators, including the Obama candidacy, which can be thought of as part of an effort to push the healing process to its next stage.

Racial Stratification and the Durable Tangle of Neighborhood Inequality

Robert J. Sampson, Harvard University

Background

Many of the underlying facts Moynihan confronted remain stubbornly alike to this day, which compels us to address the world as it is, not as we wish it to be.

- Moynihan wanted social policy to focus primarily on the "tangle"—the knot of inequality in the American city that resides at the structural and social-ecological level, not just the individual or family.
- The author's thesis is that Moynihan identified a "neighborhood" tangle of inequality—one inextricably tied to race—and that he emphasized its *durability of influence* absent *government intervention*.
- Moynihan was right to warn about the differential exposure to risk imposed by racial stratification.
- Although joblessness was always high on the agenda, Moynihan emphasized interconnections, not single variables.
- He noted how family stability, joblessness, poor health, substance abuse, poverty, welfare dependency, and crime were intertwined.

NOTE: More than forty years later, the pattern of ecological concentration and racial stratification remains.

Moynihan's Theses

Moynihan's logic implies three broad ideas or theses that are themselves interlinked.
- The "tangle of pathology" has a deep neighborhood or ecological structure, as does socioeconomic disadvantage.
- The tangle of neighborhood inequality is durable and generates self-reinforcing properties.
- The "poverty trap" cycle can ultimately only be broken with structural interventions.

Conclusion

The message of the article is that poverty and its correlates are stubbornly persistent in terms of neighborhood concentration, especially for black areas.
- There is an enduring poverty vulnerability of neighborhoods that is not simply a matter of the current income of residents.
- Neighborhoods' reputations, both positive and negative, when coupled with the residential mobility decisions of residents of all race and income groups, tend to reproduce existing patterns of inequality.
- The consequences of durable and increasing poverty appear to be long-lasting, at least with respect to predicting key social processes.

NOTE: There is hope that cycles of poverty can be broken, shown in the examples of poor communities that are radically repositioning themselves to an upward trajectory. Questions of stability and change in concentrated poverty should remain at the top of our agenda.

Moynihan Was Right: Now What?

Ron Haskins, Brookings Institution

Background

Since 1965, the problems that so worried Moynihan grew rapidly, festered, and proved his concerns and predictions to be correct.

- Employment problems are the single most important cause of both the problems experienced by black families and, in turn, the entire self-perpetuating pathology of the black ghetto.
- We need to analyze what holds so many back and why so many, especially males, have fulfilled the Moynihan prediction and turned their back on routine achievement, separated from their children and their children's mothers, and joined a criminal subculture.
- There are four continuing problems: family dissolution, educational failure, falling labor force participation, and high rates of incarceration.

Strategies   The author presents four problem-solving strategies:

- increasing and rewarding work,
- reducing nonmarital births and increasing marriage rates,
- expanding preschool education, and
- reducing incarceration and helping to reintegrate ex-felons.

NOTE: Family composition, education, and employment are intertwined, virtually requiring us to initiate programs on all three fronts simultaneously.

Classic Titles in /// *Research Methods!*

///

Bestseller!

Evaluation
A Systematic Approach
SEVENTH EDITION

Peter H. Rossi
University of Massachusetts

Mark W. Lipsey
Vanderbilt University

Howard E. Freeman

Hardcover: $74.95, ISBN: 0-7619-0894-3
2004, 480 pages

Bestseller!

Statistics For People Who *(Think They)* Hate Statistics
SECOND EDITION

Neil J. Salkind
University of Kansas

Paperback: $39.95, ISBN: 0-7619-2776-X
Hardcover: $79.95, ISBN: 0-7619-2788-3
2003, 424 pages

Bestseller!

Qualitative Research & Evaluation Methods
THIRD EDITION

Michael Quinn Patton
The Union Institute

Hardcover: $79.95, ISBN: 0-7619-1971-6
2001, 688 pages

Bestseller!

Handbook of Qualitative Research
SECOND EDITION

Edited by
Norman K. Denzin
University of Illinois at Urbana-Champaign

Yvonna S. Lincoln
Texas A&M University

Hardcover: $160.00, ISBN: 0-7619-1512-5
2000, 1143 pages

Bestseller!

Research Design
Qualitative, Quantitative, and Mixed Methods Approaches
SECOND EDITION

John W. Creswell
University of Nebraska, Lincoln

Paperbac $36.95, ISBN: 0-7619-2442-6
Hardcover: $76.95, ISBN: 0-7619-2441-8
2002, 246 pages

■■■ ▬▬▬▬▬▬▬▬▬▬▬▬▬▬▬

⑤SAGE Publications
THE ACADEMIC AND PROFESSIONAL PUBLISHER OF CHOICE
2455 Teller Road, Thousand Oaks, CA 91320 U.S.A.
Phone: 800-818-7243 (U.S.) • 805-499-9774 (Outside U.S.)
Fax: 800-583-2665 (U.S.) • 805-499-0871 (Outside U.S.)
Email: orders@sagepub.com • Web site: www.sagepub.com

HJ050321

The Content You Want, the Convenience You Need.

SAGE Journals Online
Online Journal Delivery Platform

SAGE Journals Online hosts SAGE's prestigious and highly cited journals and represents one of the largest lists in the social sciences as well as an extensive STM offering. The platform allows subscribing institutions to access individual SAGE journal titles and provides users with dramatically enhanced features and functionality, including flexible searching and browsing capabilities, customizable alerting services, and advanced, toll-free inter-journal reference linking.

Librarian-friendly features include
- Familiar HighWire subscription and administration tools
- Perpetual access to purchased content
- Temporary backfile access to 1999 (where available)
- Enhanced subscription options for most titles
- COUNTER-compliant reports
- User-friendly usage statistics
- Open-URL compliant
- Pay-per-view options

SAGE Publications
www.sagepublications.com

SAGE JOURNALS
Online